READINGS FROM
FRIEDRICH VON HÜGEL

BARON FRIEDRICH VON HÜGEL

READINGS FROM
FRIEDRICH VON HÜGEL

SELECTED BY
ALGAR THOROLD

WITH AN
INTRODUCTORY ESSAY
ON HIS
PHILOSOPHY OF RELIGION

1928
LONDON & TORONTO
J. M. DENT & SONS LTD.
NEW YORK: E. P. DUTTON & CO. INC.

PRINTED IN GREAT BRITAIN

I was as a beast before Thee.
Nevertheless I am continually with Thee:
Thou holdest me fast by my right hand.
Whom have I in heaven but Thee?
And beside Thee I desire naught upon earth.
Though my flesh and my heart fail:
Thou, God, abidest my rock and my portion for ever.

Ps. lxxiii. 22, 23, 25, 26.

Herein is love, not that we loved God, but that He loved us. We love, because He first loved us.—1 JOHN iv. 10, 19.

Thou hast created us unto Thyself, O Lord; and our heart finds no rest until it rests in Thee.—ST. AUGUSTINE, *Confessions*, i. i. 1.

CONTENTS

The Mystical Element of Religion. 2 vols. Dent. 1923. (*M. E.*). *Eternal Life.*
T. and T. Clark. 2nd edition, 1923. (*E. L.*). *Essays and Addresses on the
Philosophy of Religion.* 2 vols. Dent. (*E.*).

BOOK I

THE APPROACH TO RELIGION

BOOK II

THE SOUL OF A SAINT

vii

BOOK III

THE PHILOSOPHY OF RELIGION

CONTENTS

* NOTE: *These two extracts are reprinted by kind permission of
Messrs. T. and T. Clark.*

INTRODUCTION

Let us start from certain facts of experience which appear to me unavoidable. Our most fundamental, most irreducibly human characteristic consists far more in an indefinite capacity of reception and development than in an achievement and a definite perfection. Anyone who has truly become conscious of himself must recognise this truth. Two things are equally impossible to us. On the one hand, we should seek in vain to free ourselves from the desire which lies at the greatest depth of our soul, and which in our good moments transforms itself into effort—or, at least, into velleity of effort: desire and effort which tend to unify our interior life, to enrich it, to purify it, to fix it, and to render it productive. On the other hand, we can never exhaust these exigencies and bring to a standstill our perfection by completing it, each accomplished progress discovering to us new perspectives, higher peaks.

I THINK that these words, which I quote from an article in *La Quinzaine* of 1 June, 1904, by Baron von Hügel, furnish us with the key to much which is at first sight puzzling in his teaching. Bearing them in mind we shall be saved from the misunderstanding into which *The Times* reviewer of his first Series of Essays fell when he described the Baron as "the greatest living apologist for the Roman Church." (It will be remembered that in the following issue the Baron quaintly and delightfully retorted that, having hoped to do well in the dog class, he was hugely disconcerted by being given a first prize among cats.) His adherence to the Roman Church, his Catholicism in the only sense borne by that word outside this island, was indeed both convinced and enthusiastic, but his faith was rather his point of departure than the goal of his philosophy. His was emphatically a *Fides quærens intellectum*. And religion was to him, as we shall see, no mere matter of assent and conformity; it was a glorious, an entrancing adventure; in his vision it may truly be said that the "heavenly chariot flies thundering through the ages, the dull heresies sprawling and prostrate, the wild truth reeling but erect."

Philosophies of religion are usually either mere apologetics in disguise or else equally one-sided attempts to reduce religion to a department of anthropology or metaphysics. If we read Von Hügel from either of these points of view, we shall be disappointed. Never was a great philosopher less of a doctrinaire. There is an instructive passage in a letter of the Baron to the late Mr. Wilfrid Ward, published in Mr. Ward's Life of his father. The Baron, after drawing some contrasts tending to illustrate the precise *nuance* of W. G. Ward's mentality, proceeds:

But the difference on these points is but a consequence; I should like to try and get at the cause. Is it not this, that minds belong, roughly speaking, to two classes, which may be called the mystical and positive, and the scholastic and theoretical? The first of these would see all truth as a centre of intense light losing itself gradually in utter darkness; this centre would gradually extend, but the borders would ever remain fringe, they could never become clear-cut lines. Such a mind when weary of border-work would sink back upon its centre, its home of peace and light, and thence it would gain fresh conviction and courage to again face the twilight and the dark. Force it to commit itself absolutely to any border distinction, or force it to shift its home or to restrain its roamings, and you have done your best to endanger its faith and to ruin its happiness.

There is no doubt that in his description of the "mystical and positive" type of intellect the Baron believed himself to be describing his own mental processes. It would therefore be a waste of time to attempt to deduce from his writings anything like a complete or systematic philosophy of religion. Such philosophies are the product of what may be called, in contradistinction to his own mentality, geometrical minds. The "Encyclopædic" Croce is perhaps the best living specimen of such. These minds, instead of perceiving truth as a luminous point shading off into darkness, perceive a whole way of looking at everything in the form of a luminous outline. Within that flaming rampart lies truth; outside it, error. Such minds as these are unhesitatingly dogmatic, they are strong in refutation, they attract disciples and found schools. But these undeniable qualities have their defect. The system stands or falls as a whole and is no stronger than its weakest part.

Von Hügel's thought may perhaps be best conceived as a mine, access to which may be obtained by sinking at various points independent shafts. The stratifications of these various sinkings will be found to be identical—the stuff is there all right, richly and widely distributed; but we must not be disappointed if we find it extraordinarily difficult—perhaps even impossible — to establish underground connections. Perhaps we cannot sink a shaft deep enough for that. Anyhow, let us begin by sinking as deep a shaft as we can, and endeavouring to ascertain what are Von Hügel's most fundamental and abiding perceptions as to the nature of reality and the conditions of any successful apprehension thereof on our part. He published in the *Dublin Review* for April 1906 an article, "Experience and Transcendence," in which we shall find much that is significant for our purpose. The article opens by drawing attention to one of the principal causes of "the intellectual discomfort and unrest so unmistakably prevalent in the educated religious world of to-day." The contemporary mind seeks to apprehend reality as concrete and organic, and bases its apprehension on experience, resting ultimately on intuition, whereas the traditional method of theology inherited from the discursive Græco-Roman races remains predominantly deductive. The spiritual content of the Christian and Catholic inheritance has indeed always been intuitively apprehended in the writings of the Mystics, but the temper and method of the official analysis and presentation of this spiritual content has been, and still is, such as to create grave difficulties in the adjustment of conflicting claims for those whose mentality demands both the intuitive method as ultimately covering all accessible experience including religion, and also the unification of their intellectual and spiritual activities. To such as these the "watertight-compartment" theory of those activities is no more credible than that old "faculty psychology" with which indeed it had no uncertain connection. The point at which this conflict becomes keenest is naturally "the question as to the possibility and nature of our knowledge or experience of God." Here, if anywhere, the inductive method must prove its efficacy, or frankly admit that religion is beyond its scope.

Yet the question is very difficult. It seems to imply a sort of logical impossibility. "How can man, the finite and contingent, solidly experience the Abiding and Infinite?" And, if such an experience is possible, what will be its characteristic proofs and safeguards, what its possible perversions and degeneracies? In answer to these queries the Baron shows how the modern conception of experience tends in the direction of such a possibility, for we experience far more than we are aware of at the time, and far more than we can systematise in our subsequent reflex knowledge. Our experience is rich and dim, affecting us simultaneously in various ways; our reflex knowledge is clear-cut and consistent and, except in so far as it reawakens memories of the original impact of the experience from which it arises, abstract. This distinction between experience and reflex knowledge was first recognised by Leibniz in his *Nouveaux Essais sur l'Entendement*, published in 1765. Thus he says of sense impressions:

The perception of light and colour which holds our attention is composed of a quantity of small perceptions to which we do not attend; and a sound which we perceive obscurely, but to which we do not attend, becomes attended to by a small augmentation of sound. For if what had proceeded had made no impression upon the soul, this little addition would still produce no effect; indeed, the whole would leave us unaffected.

Leibniz extends the same criticism to our general ideas and principles:

Ideas and truths are innate within us, as inclinations, dispositions, habits, natural virtualities, and not as full actuations: and yet these virtualities are ever accompanied by some action, though this is often not clearly perceived by the agent.

Kant in his *Anthropologie* (1798) explicitly recognises the same truth, though he often forgot it:

> To have presentations and yet to be unconscious of them seems self-contradictory: for how can we know that we have them if we are not conscious of them? Answer: we can be mediately conscious of having a presentation of which we have no immediate consciousness.

In his *Varieties of Religious Experience* (1902) William James points to—

> The discovery, first made in 1886, that, in certain subjects at least, there is not only the consciousness of the ordinary field, with its usual centre and margin, but an addition thereto in the shape of a set of memories, thoughts and feelings which are extra-marginal and outside of the primary consciousness altogether, but which must be classed as conscious facts of some sort, able to reveal their presence by unmistakable signs.

Now, while it is evident that only contingent objects within the range of sense impressions or other psychic mechanisms have here been dealt with, the point which has been reached is fatal to the simple alternative between the reflex conscious knowledge of a presentation and the non-existence of such a presentation. We certainly are and contain far more than we can deliberately become aware of at any given moment. Is it possible that among these presentations which we cannot recapture in reflex knowledge there are flashes of the infinite? That we cannot recapture them does not prove that they have not come to us. On the other hand, they can hardly come without leaving some traces behind. Other presentations will have been affected; something deeper than the activity of reflex knowledge will have been modified in such a way as to qualify the whole content of reflex knowledge; if there has been, indeed, a divine touch our sinew will have shrunk. Now, this is precisely what Von Hügel thinks has happened. The point is so important for the understanding of his whole religious philosophy, that I may be pardoned for a somewhat long quotation:

> And if we consider the evidences for mankind possessing, in some such dim, though powerful way—and this also not separately, but

B

occasioned by and in turn giving a special character to the apprehension of the various kinds of the finite—a sense of the infinite; or rather for the infinite itself somehow pressing in upon and influencing all men in indefinitely various degrees and ways, yet ever really: I think we cannot but find these evidences impressively profound. For note how the most universal and specific of human characteristics is a keen sense of our relativity, of our little anthropomorphisms and provincialisms in face of Objective Reality. "Man never knows how anthropomorphic he is," says Goethe. True; yet it is a man, Goethe, and at bottom all men, in proportion as they are truly such, who have somehow discovered this truth, and who suffer from it as spontaneously as from toothache or from sleepless nights. Nor is it as though we had not now grasped the nettle of the difficulties and uncertainties of history. Indeed, an astonishingly augmented and perfected knowledge of an endless mass of apparently mere relativities of all sorts; a keen consciousness of the merely approximate and largely reversible character of this knowledge and of the contingent character of its subject-matter; and yet, for all that, an ineradicable, indeed heightened, sense of and longing for the infinite and the abiding, somehow within as well as without these merely contingent-seeming facts and apprehensions, are with us now more than ever. And the man of physico-mathematical science does not escape from, or even find a working substitute for, this sense, as soon as ever he seriously examines how he comes to know, as more than his own merely subjective impressions, the things which, alone or above all other things, seemed to him beyond question; and why loyalty, often at a painful cost to truthfulness in such matters, should be accounted as binding upon the consciences of men. Creative Art again, as distinguished from merely technical quasi-artistic reproduction; original philosophic thought, as other than a dilettante eclecticism; fruitfully inventive philanthropy and nobly daring constructive statesmanship; all and every attempted revelation in human thinking, feeling, doing, quasi-creative production or being, of the hidden meaning and reality of things, ever presents the same general characteristics. There is an opening wide and energising of the whole human being in an aspiration and effort after the infinite and abiding; a pathetic half-belief of having at last fully reached it—with, however, even then and there a strongly operative sense that, after all, the reality aimed at remains indefinitely greater and nobler than this attempt, or than the sum-total of all human attempts, to adequate or exhaust it; and then a more or less early discovery, on the part of this very labourer or of others, that his work was largely limited and permeated by ignorances as to its subject-matter and passing modes of thought and feeling as to its appropriate categories; and hence, that to remain operative at all, it has to be sifted out, re-interpreted, transformed and incorporated by other minds and generations, who in their turn again on the eternal quest, are as certainly doomed to a similar noble disappointment and unrest. . . . Now what is it that can have so immense and all-penetrative a force on human life as this? Man is, to all appearance, a creature compact of sense - impressions, an exceedingly indolent, short-sighted, cowardly, easily self-contented, utterly provincial being. Whence, then, shut up apparently within the mere contingencies of his life, this painful sense of the utter inadequacy of all mere contingency and pure subjectivity; this practical inability to acquiesce in these as the sum-total of his capacities and end? I take it that the one unforced explanation of this universal, utterly ineradicable, boundlessly powerful movement throughout human life, is that we never do have, and never could have, this clinging, penetrating, stinging sense of the relative and finite, of the merely human, except because we are all the while, in some manner and degree, experiencing not only this relative series but a contrasting other. For the sense of the contrast is too keen and unavoidable, above all too universal and operative, for its two terms not to fall, both of them, somehow within and not without our consciousness.

It is true that that other gains and maintains such clearness as it has for us, only in connection with the concomitant, contrasting and "relative" series: and that if we *will* keep the otherness too long apart, and treat our at first vivid experience and apprehension of it as an articulated "distinct" comprehension and as a starting-point and object of strict ordinary science of the mathematico-deductive type, it will rapidly lose its life and reality for us, and our deductions concerning it will quickly lead us into various antinomies and vicious circles of thought and reasoning. And then it will seem plausible to attribute so unworkable an experience to a simply subjective impression of our own. Yet such explanations explain, I think, only what, in that experience, on the assumption of its being what I am claiming for it, needs no explanation; and leave unexplained or explain away precisely its very centre. For if it be, however true, yet still a human apprehension of the infinite, it will necessarily be varying and in itself obscure. How for man, with all his present physical and psychical limitations and distractions, could it be static and clear? But how, if it be simply subjective, it ever got into a being who is in any case largely contingent and whom the sceptic claims as contingent altogether, and how it can continue to be the all-inspiring and all-dwarfing force and check of all his life—this does require explanation and this does not get explained.[1]

We have thus reached what the Baron calls a "confusedly concrete sense of the infinite," which must be carefully distinguished from the abstract philosophical idea of the infinite. This latter appeals solely to the intellect, and is reached by a process of reflex thought; the former, if the experience has been correctly analysed, is a fact. And it is a fact with this peculiarity, that it conditions every other fact of which we are conscious; it is present on introspection in all our experience. Like a ciphering note on the organ it is audible through any symphony which life may play to us.

This impression of the infinite, if indeed it be truly such, is, of course, far from determining any state of mind that can be called explicitly religious. Indeed, its effects are only mediately perceptible in the modification of the immediately perceived presentations of the mind. These effects are, if the long analysis quoted be anything like correct, very fundamental and far-reaching. They are two-fold. First an inspiration that leads us to press to the uttermost our finite presentations and the activities implied in and resulting from them, and then sooner or later a numbing chill, which creeps through our life and tends to freeze its heart. There is the classical case of the younger Mill, who, when he asked himself whether the accomplishment of all the reforms into which he had poured his energy would give him real and complete satisfaction, was obliged to answer "No." But it is not necessary to quote examples of this curious fact of the tragedy of achievement, as it may be called. No one who has lived for fifty years on this peculiar planet is without his own experiences on this subject.

Yet, although these impressions and their results are not in themselves religious, they undoubtedly form the ground of the religious sense. If, indeed, the Infinite has by this all-penetrating power over our life proved its reality, it has also proved something more. It has proved the existence of a

[1] "Experience and Transcendence." Reprinted from the *Dublin Review*, pp. 4–7.

certain affinity and likeness between itself and that finite
spirit which it touches to such momentous issues. For "nothing
that was less than spirit could so profoundly move spirit."
That spirit may be, nay, must be, infinitely nobler and
greater than we; but it must at least be spirit. The great
revelational religious systems come as the ever more or less
necessary, more or less full stimulation, response and transformation to this potential "religiosity," as it may be called,
of the human soul. It is an obscurantism of the worst kind
to confine this stimulation to Christianity. "Gautama taught
India much that cannot but be dear to God; and if Christ
Himself be 'the true Light that enlighteneth every man that
cometh into the world,' He cannot be this Light solely by
means of men's historic knowledge of the historic Christ,
since even now the large majority of men have no such
knowledge of Him." Christian testimonies to this universal
though dim experience of the divine are abundant. They
expand by fulfilment its potential religious content. St. Paul,
preaching at Athens, says that God has made men in order
"that they should seek the Lord, if haply they might feel
after him and find him, though he be not far from every
one of us: for in him we live and move and have our being"
(Acts xvii. 27). St. Augustine's teaching is the same. "Behold
Thou wast within me and I was without seeking Thee outside
me, Thou wast with me, but I was not with Thee . . . unless
the soul in some way knew the Unchangeable itself, it could
not with such certainty prefer this Unchangeable to the
mutable" (*Confessions*, Book X.). When we reach St. Thomas
we find that, in spite of the tendency to ignore these deeper
conceptions involved in his predominantly Aristotelian
methods, he clearly admits the necessity of some immediate
experience or "confused knowledge" of God by the soul.
In his *Exposition of the Book of Boëthius on the Trinity* he says:
"With regard to God, we could not know whether he exists,
unless we somehow knew what He is, even though in a
confused manner."

Von Hügel lays stress on the fact that the conception thus
reached as to the nature of God and the nature of man

is one "which is largely Platonic and, I think, alone fully Christian, but for which, in strict Aristotelianism, there is no logical place." He sums up the whole of this metaphysical ground of religion in the following truly inspired paragraph:

We have found that experience, at all the levels of our life, exceeds our powers of direct demonstration or clear analysis, and yet can be traced as operative by certain indirect indications and methods; that, in this latter way, we can show mankind to possess a direct experience of the infinite, which however springs up only on occasion of our sensible and contingent apprehensions and which, to become characteristically religious, requires to meet and accept fuller, more articulate manifestations of the presence and grace of God in other human lives; that this double spiritual experience, the general and inevitable, and the characteristic and free—each requiring the other, as the ear and a sense of music, stimulated only by the sounds of nature, require the organised tones of music to actually reveal the full soul of music to them—have left numberless records in the history of mankind and especially of its saints, and have been most delicately described by the Mystics and by the more Platonic element in the Scholastics; and that this whole position involves a conception of God as profoundly prevenient, self-manifesting, immanental as well as transcendental, a conception which alone is fully, specifically Christian.[1]

Von Hügel warns us against three possible delusions, or, as he calls them, "plausible excesses" in our manner of approaching this experienced reality. There is the ultra-ascetical excess of an extreme dualism which leads to a completely transcendental view of God. This excess is well represented by the Danish Pascal, Soren Kierkegaard, who was the original of Ibsen's Brand. In Kierkegaard's view God was so absolutely different to man that to live in communion with Him involved the acutest suffering. "A finite being is to live in the infinite: yet he is a fish upon dry land." This position is profoundly paradoxical, for it is impossible to show how, in this case, the soul becomes aware of this absolute difference. If God were absolutely different to the soul, He would be absolutely unknowable by it. This position is closely akin to Kant's profession of total ignorance as to the thing

[1] Op. cit., p. 16.

in itself combined with complete certainty as to its unlikeness to our impressions; for the epistemological distinction between thought and reality, a real metaphysical contradiction is unconsciously substituted, as Professor Volkelt has shown. We find in the counter-extreme the ultra-unitive excess. Here the better self simply *is* God. The Mystics have undoubtedly said such things. But at all events, in cases where the Mystic belongs to a Theistic religion like Christianity or Islam, such phrases should be held to exhaust their significance as expressions of a hyperbolically-worded Panentheism, an intense "consciousness of the prevenient, all-penetrative presence of God" and, in so far, to be entirely right. This excess has also arisen from "a false conception of simplicity, as a sheer numerical or material oneness, and not as a perfectly harmonised organisation, simple in proportion to the variety successfully penetrated and unified."

The third, apparently intermediate, error is ultimately agnostic and abstract. Here the sense of the infinity and incomprehensibility of God is pushed so far as to abolish all superiority of one experience or conception of God over another. That fifth-century writer in whose works the Christian world thought they recognised Denys the Areopagite, St. Paul's convert, maintains largely this view, although his writings are not devoid of a strain of positive assertion. "Is He not more nearly life and goodness than He is air or stone? And is He not further removed from debauch and wrath than he is from unspeakableness and inconceivability?"[1]

Three further points must be noted about the view that I have thus imperfectly outlined. It in no way implies that the soul possesses any single faculty of mystical apprehension of God. All the faculties of the soul are elements in—and in a sense, co-factors of—that apprehension. More than this, the human individual by himself must not be considered adequate to a rich or vivid apprehension of reality, and the deepest reality, God. It is in and through the society of his fellows, past and present, that he receives the materials and stimulations which in recollection and solitude will be elaborated

[1] *Mystical Theology*, Parker, iii. pp. 135–6.

into his full spiritual manhood, his full personality. There is, secondly, no attempt here to formulate any Ontologism. No direct clearness, not distinctness even, is predicated of this primary confused experience of God; still less is any argument for its reality based on such clearness. "Our proof lies not in simple intellection of any kind, but in the persistent pressure and fruitfulness of a strongly contrasting sense of non-contingency, of the more than merely anthropomorphic, ever awakened by all specifically human acts and impressions." And, once more, the view here proposed does not lead to Pure Mysticism, which at bottom is Pantheism. Regularly recurrent and docile contact with various contingencies, each welcomed at its characteristic level of experience, is necessary both for the apprehension and articulation of God. "Only in the shock between simply finite-seeming mind and simply finite-seeming fact, like cold steel striking against cold flint, does the latent fire, the affinity to the infinite of all true life, spring forth for a moment." Pure Mysticism would be further rejected as claiming "to hold God at any one moment in absolute purity, or to base the proof for any or all contact with God upon the moment and experience of the contact alone . . . the test as to the reality of the Divine contact will become ever less restricted to the moment or even to the individual life, as the soul, dying to all solipsism, grows in true spirituality."

In two important papers reprinted in his first volume of *Essays*, Von Hügel deals with the nature and value of religion, as it is discovered at work in human history. In the first paper, "Religion and Illusion," he discusses the solution brought by Feuerbach to the problem in his *Das Wesen des Christenthums* (1841). This work, though to a great extent dominated by doctrinaire, left-Hegelian positions in pure thought, which are no longer accepted by anyone and were indeed left behind by Feuerbach himself, who died a complete materialist (1871), "remains to this hour the most probing and thorough account of the certain, or even the simply arguable contributions made by man to religion." Nor has there been since his time any mind equal to his own that has argued so strongly "for the sheer illusion and mischievousness of all religion." Now, according to Feuerbach, man's essential nature by which he is distinguished from the animal is not only the ground of religion—which all would admit—but also its sole object. It follows that that consciousness of the infinite which is the deepest and broadest content of religion is not consciousness of an infinite over against other than man, but consciousness of his own infinite nature. "The consciousness of the infinite is nothing else than the consciousness of the infinity of the consciousness." [1] Apart from the complete gratuitousness of this statement, which claims to define the specific constitution of human consciousness in terms which precisely invert its primary data, it should be noted that this interpretation has only been reached by a few, "tens of thousands of years after millions of men have experienced this specifically human consciousness." Moreover, Feuerbach's view implies that there is only one possible object from first to last of human experience—the subject itself. Philosophy is thus starting from incomplete data, from man considered merely as abstractive, discursive mind. Yet man is very certainly more than this. He is also "sense, imagination, feeling and will," and mind itself is not solely discursive, it is also intuitive. Considerations of space will not permit me to quote at length Von Hügel's refutation of Feuerbach in detail. I will give the climax of his argument:

There then remains no way out of scepticism, where scepticism is least tolerable and where it is most ruinous, than to carry right up into religion what we believe and practise in our practical life and in our science. Just as we simply admit the existence of countless realities, more or less different from, though only lower than or equal to ourselves and our real knowledge of them, since such influence and knowledge are prior to, and are the material of, our discursive reasoning about them: so let us simply admit the existence of a perfect Reality, sufficiently like us to be able to penetrate and to move us through and through, the which, by so doing, is the original and persistent cause of this our noblest dissatisfaction with anything and all things merely human. Certainly no other explanation has ever been given which does not sooner or later mis-state

---

[1] *Das Wesen des Christenthums*, English translation, p. 4.

or explain away the very data, and the immense dynamic forces of the data, to be explained. But this, the only adequate explanation, moves us on at once, from the quicksands of religion as illusion, to the rock of religion as the witness and vehicle of reality.[1]

In his second paper, "Religion and Reality," the Baron concentrates his attention on the "Evidential Revelational quality of Religion," and the intimation which it ever bears of superhuman reality. This intimation is twofold: "*The more than human reality of the object of its experience . . . and the abiding difference between even this its present experience and the great reality thus experienced and revealed*" (Von Hügel's italics). In this double consciousness religion resembles every other living apprehension at work in our human experience. The feeling that some trans-subjective, other than merely human reality, law or energy, is somehow giving itself in his experiences, *and* that these experiences and still more such analysis and systematisation of them as he may be able to make, are quite inadequate to those realities as they are in themselves, is common to every scientist, artist and philosopher. Religion reduced to its essence is merely the mode of apprehension proper to certain ultimate realities; though specialised in its object that apprehension has the specifically human characterisation common to all our methods of taking hold of reality.

In Catholicism, as it occurs in human history, Von Hügel sees not indeed a perfect religion—such a gift as that is not for imperfect men—but the only existing system in which all the essential demands of religion are met, and all the true and characteristic activities of religion are working. I cannot do better here than refer to a paper contributed by the Baron to the *Review of the Student Christian Movement*, under the heading "The Catholic Contribution to Religion": "Catholicism, as such, always aims at, and always more or less achieves, a recognition, utilisation and harmony of *all* the great insights and forces of religion." The failure in achievement comes from nothing in the idea or

---

[1] *Essays*, pp. 30–1.

formative principles of the religion, but from the "limitations, faults and sins of its human teachers or learners or critics —usually of all three."

The Baron notes seven chief requirements of the religious instinct and their satisfaction in the Catholic system. First, spirit is primarily awakened on occasion of sense, a psychological fact and requirement which is alone fully met by the consistent and deliberate sacramental outlook of the Church. Secondly, spirit is stimulated by spirit, "one human spirit by other human spirits." Catholicism in its traditional system alone remains ceaselessly aware of this sacred torch race across the ages. Thirdly, this awakening of spirit needs for its fullest fruitfulness to take place within a social spiritual organism. The strictly institutional outlook of the Church stands for this deep fact of the personalist organism. Fourthly, man is an "amphibious" creature: he belongs to the visible world and to the invisible, i.e. to two sets of duties and satisfactions. Both these worlds, indeed, come from the one God, and will be eventually harmonised. The inter-relation of these two worlds, the world of nature and the world of grace, with their special frictions, tensions and mutual stimulations, is an essential principle of Catholicism. There is, fifthly, the problem of "the duality of suffering and renunciation, and of possession and joy, and the fruitful integration of both within a larger whole." Catholicism solves this antinomy in her comprehensive system of asceticism, so broad in range and so elastic in interpretation, which includes the body and "discriminates the one call of all men to holiness into various forms of married or celibate devotedness." Sixthly, the social organism which we have already seen to be necessary for the most fruitful awakening of spirit must be characterised by truly organic unity, no mere resultant or super-added quality, but one which from the first penetrates all its parts and elements. Such is the unity of the Church which, like other personalist organisms — the family, the guild, the state—possesses visibility with a visible head, who is the incorporation and instrument of the Church as a whole, the Pope, the "servant of the servants of God."

Finally, religion in proportion to its intensity is always and everywhere evidential, it affirms real contacts with a reality "which both occasions and transcends—which exists independently of—all these contacts." Now, Catholicism is specially concentrated, a hostile critic might say over-concentrated, on this aspect of religion. "The doctrine of, and the devotion to, Jesus Christ, truly present God and Man, body and soul, in the Holy Eucharist, thus forms, most characteristically, the very heart of the Catholic worship."

On this expression of his personal faith, I will take leave of Friedrich von Hügel. I find it hard to do so. There is so much more that might, that should be said. I have tried to indicate in these few and inadequate lines one method of approach to the rich treasure of the thought of this best of friends and kindest of masters.

I did not always understand him, and sometimes when I seemed to myself to understand, I did not agree. He was much too great to mind. On one such occasion, I remember his replying: "Well, we must, each of us, get what we can in our own way." That was certainly his method. Every thought was "got in his own way"; yet never was there a thinker of his calibre so docile to facts, so willing to learn from others and at the same time so spontaneously original.[1]

ALGAR THOROLD.

[1] Part of the above appeared in the *Edinburgh Review* for April 1922. My thanks are due to Messrs. Longmans for permission to reprint it.

BOOK I
THE APPROACH TO RELIGION

BOOK I

THE APPROACH TO RELIGION

1. AN ABIDING ENIGMA OF LIFE

AMONGST the apparent enigmas of life, amongst the seemingly most radical and abiding of interior antinomies and conflicts experienced by the human race and by individuals, there is one which everything tends to make us feel and see with an ever-increasing keenness and clearness. More and more we want a strong and interior, a lasting yet voluntary bond of union between our own successive states of mind, and between what is abiding in ourselves and what is permanent within our fellow-men; and more and more we seem to see that mere Reasoning, Logic, Abstraction,—all that appears as the necessary instrument and expression of the Universal and Abiding,—does not move or win the will, either in ourselves or in others; and that what does thus move and win it, is Instinct, Intuition, Feeling, the Concrete and Contingent, all that seems to be of its very nature individual and evanescent. Reasoning appears but capable, at best, of co-ordinating, unifying, explaining the material furnished to it by experience of all kinds; at worst, of explaining it away; at best, of stimulating the purveyance of a fresh supply of such experience; at worst, of stopping such purveyance as much as may be. And yet the Reasoning would appear to be the transferable part in the process, but not to move us; and the experience alone to have the moving power, but not to be transmissible.

Experience indeed and its resultant feeling are always, in the first instance, coloured and conditioned by every kind of individual many-sided circumstances of time and place, of race and age and sex, of education and temperament, of

3

antecedent and environment. And it is this very particular combination, just this one, so conditioned and combined, coming
upon me just at this moment and on this spot, just at this
stage of my reach or growth, at this turning of my way, that
carries with it this particular power to touch or startle, to
stimulate or convince. It is just precisely through the but
imperfectly analysable, indeed but dimly perceived, individual connotation of general terms; it is by the fringe of
feeling, woven out of the past doings and impressions, work-
ings and circumstances, physical, mental, moral, of my
race and family and of my own individual life; it is by the
apparently slight, apparently far away, accompaniment of
a perfectly individual music to the spoken or sung text of
the common speech of man, that I am, it would seem, really
moved and won.

And this fringe of feeling, this impression, is, strictly
speaking, not merely untransferable, but also unrepeatable;
it is unique even for the same mind: it never was before, it
never will be again. Heraclitus, if we understand that old
Physicist in our own modern, deeply subjective, largely
sentimental way, would appear to be exactly right: you
cannot twice step into the same stream, since never for two
moments do the waters remain identical; you yourself cannot
twice step the same man into the same river, for you have
meanwhile changed as truly as itself has done. Πάντα ῥεῖ:
all things and states, outward and inward, appear indeed
in flux: only each moment seems to bring, to each individual,
for that one moment, his power to move and to convince.

And if we transmit this emotion or conviction to another
mind, or if we seem to be able to trace such transmission
when it has been actually effected in ourselves or in others,
we shall find that, in proportion as one mind feeds, not
forces, another, the particular bond and organisation of the
mental and emotional picture which cost us so much, moved
us so much, has, in each case, been snapped and broken
up; the whole has been again resolved into its constituent
elements, and only some of these elements have been taken
up into the already existing organisation of the other mind,

or have joined together in that mind, to form there a combination which is really new. Even a simple scent or sound or sight comes charged to each of us with many but most differing connotations, arousing or modifying or supplanting old or new ideas and impressions in the most subtle, complex and individual manner. Insist upon another mind taking over the whole of this impression, and you will have rightly and necessarily aroused an immediate or remote hostility or revolt against the whole of what you bring. Hence here too we are again perplexed by the initial enigma: the apparently insurmountable individuality of all that affects us, and the equally insurmountable non-affectingness of all that is clearly and certainly transmissible from any one man to another.

And if we seem boxed up thus, each one away from our fellow, in all our really moving and determining inclinations and impressions, judgments and affections, with regard to matters on which we feel we can afford to differ deeply and to be much alone we appear to be more and not less so, in exact proportion as the importance of the subject-matter increases. In moral and spiritual, in religious and fundamental matters, we thirst more, not less, for identity of conviction and of feeling; and we are, or seem to be, more, not less, profoundly and hopelessly at variance with each other than anywhere else.

And more than this: the apparent reason of this isolation seems but to aggravate the case, because here more than anywhere else imagination, feeling, intuition seem indeed to play a predominant, determining part; and yet here more than anywhere else we feel such a predominance to be fraught with every kind of danger. Thus here especially we feel as incapable of suppressing, indeed of doing without these forces, as of frankly accepting, studying and cultivating them. Now and then we take alarm and are in a panic at any indication that these springs and concomitants of life are at work within us; yet we persist in doing little or nothing to find sufficient and appropriate food and scope and exercise for the right development, and hence the real purification of these elemental forces, forces which we can stunt but cannot kill. Nothing, we most rightly feel, can be in greater or more subtle and dangerous opposition to manly morality or enlightened religion than the seeking after or revelling in emotion; nothing, we most correctly surmise, can equal the power of strong feeling or heated imagination to give a hiding-place to superstition, sensuality, dreamy self-complacent indolence, arrogant revolt and fanaticism; nothing, even where such things seem innocent, appears less apt than do these fierce and fitful, these wayward and fleeting feelings, these sublimities and exquisitenesses, to help on that sober and stable, consistent and persistent, laborious upbuilding of moral and religious character, work and evidence which alone are wanted more and more. Indeed, what would seem better calculated than such emotion to strain the nerves, to inflame the imagination, to blunt common sense and that salt of the earth, the saving sense of the ridiculous, to deaden the springs of research and critical observation, to bring us, under the incalculably sapping influences of physical abnormalities, close up to where sanity shades off into madness, and ethical elevation breaks down into morbidness and depravity?

And the secular experience of the race would seem fully to bear out such suspicions. For have we not there a double series of personalities, events and movements far too long and widespread not to be conclusive? On the one hand, there are those that seem to spring from dimly lit or dark feeling, to arise,—as it were, hydra-like, to sting and madden, or, mist-like, to benumb all life, and turn it into mere drift and dreaming,—from out of the obscure, undrained, swampy places of human ignorance and passion. On the other hand, there are those that are formed and fashioned by clear, transparent thought; and these flourish in the cultivated, well-drained plains of human science and strict demonstration.

Among the first series, you have the Pantheistic schools and personalities of the decaying Roman Empire, Plotinus the Ecstatic, and Jamblichus, and such other dreamers, straining up into the blue; the somewhat similar, largely subterranean, Jewish and Christian sects and tendencies of the Middle Ages; the Anabaptist and other like groups, individualistic, fantastic, in considerable part anomistic and revolutionary, of the Reformation period; and such phenomena as the Eternal-Gospel troubles and the Quietistic controversy in the Roman Church. And above all, in the East, we have, from time immemorial, whole races (in the midst of a world crying aloud for help and re-fashioning, but which is left to stagnate and decay), still dreaming away their lives in Buddhistic abstraction and indifference.

Among the second, the light, clear series, you have whole races, the luminous, plastic, immensely active Greek, the strong-willed, practical, organising Roman, and the Anglo-Saxon determined "to stand no nonsense"; you have an Aristotle, sober, systematic; one side at least of the great Mediaeval Scholastic movement, culminating in St. Thomas, so orderly and transparent; above all, modern Physical Science, first subjecting all phenomena to rigorous quantitative and mathematical analysis and equation, and then reacting upon philosophy as well, and insisting, there and everywhere, upon clearness, direct comparableness, ready transferableness of ideas and their formulæ, as the sole tests of truth. Descartes; Kepler, Galileo; Hobbes, Spinoza are, in increasing degrees, still perhaps the most perfect types of this clear and cool, this ultimately mathematical and Monistic tendency and position.

And further, the personalities and schools of the interiorly experimental, emotional kind seem to appear upon the scene but as stop-gaps or compensations for the other series, in periods of transition or reaction, of uncertainty or decay. So at the break-up of the Roman Empire (Neo-Platonism); so at the end of the Patristic period and just before the official acceptance of Scholasticism (St. Bernard); so doing the foundering of the mediaeval fabric of life and thought in the Renaissance of the fifteenth and sixteenth centuries (Pico, Paracelsus); so in the German Romanticism of sixty years ago, as a reaction against the survivals of the eighteenth-century Rationalism; so now again in our own day, more slightly, but not less really, in a revival of spiritual philosophy. It looks then as though the experimental-emotional strain could only thrive fitfully, on the momentary check or ruin of the clear and "scientific" school; as though it were a perhaps inevitable disease breaking in occasionally upon the normal health of the human mind. For the eventual result of the world's whole movement surely seems to be the reclamation of ever-increasing stretches of knowledge and theory from the dominion of vague, irresponsible, untestable feeling, and their incorporation in the domain of that unbroken, universal determinism, of those clear and simple, readily analysable, verifiable, communicable and applicable laws which, more and more, are found to rule phenomena wheresoever we may look.

And if the prima facie trend of centuries of thought and conflict appears to rule out of court even such a fringe of individual experience and emotion as ever accompanies and stimulates all religion, the verdict of history, indeed of any survey of contemporary life, if only this be sufficiently large, would seem fatal to any type of religion in which this individual experience and emotion would form religion's core and centre, as in the case of the specifically experimental-emotional school generally, and of the Mystics in particular.

To take some such survey, let us look, to begin with, outside of where Catholic discipline and unity somewhat obscure, at first sight, even the legitimate and indeed the really existing diversities of school and tendency. In the Church's organism each divergence has ever been more largely tempered and supplemented by the others; and since the Reformation, indeed in part even more recently, owing to an entirely intelligible, and in part inevitable, reaction, even most legitimate and persistent divergencies, which flourished in rich and enriching variety throughout the Middle Ages, have largely ceased to appear in any obvious and distinct embodiments. Let us look then first to where such diversities grow unchecked, and indeed generally tend to excess and caricature. Let us take contemporary English Protestantism, and then Foreign Protestantism in the large lines of its history. In both cases the experimental-emotional strain and group will seem to compare unfavourably with its competitors.

For if we look about us in England, we seem to have little difficulty in classing the tendencies within the Established Church under the headings of High, Broad and Low; indeed we can readily extend this treble classification to all the various schools and bodies of English Protestantism. We can easily conceive of the greater portion of English Non-conformity as but a prolongation and accentuation of the Evangelical school in the Established Church: the readiness and ease with which the former at certain moments unite and coalesce with the latter, show quite conclusively how close is the affinity between them. We almost as readily think of the Unitarian and Theistic bodies as prolongations and further sublimations of the Anglican Broad Church view, though here, no doubt, the degrees and kinds of difference are more numerous and important. And if it would be hard to find an extension, still more an accentuation, of the Anglican High Church party amongst the English Nonconformists, a strain largely identical with the sacerdotal current elsewhere has always existed in the Presbyterian churches. Nor must we forget the powerful and constant, both repellent and attractive, influence exercised by Rome upon even those outside of her obedience. To be quite philosophical, the survey ought to include all types of English Christianity; and, in that case, the High Church position would rank rather as a dilution, as a variety, incomplete and inconsistent though it be, of the type represented most strikingly and emphatically by Rome, than as a variant of the types having their centres at Wittenberg and Geneva.

And if we next turn to German Protestantism, especially to the simultaneous variations of its short-lived, fluid, forma-tive period, we shall there too find this treble tendency. The Evangelical strain will be represented here by the numerous Illuminist and Anabaptist personalities, groups and movements to which Luther himself had given occasion, which but emphasised or caricatured his own earlier Mysticism;

but which, when they threatened, by their revolutionary, communistic fanaticism and violence, completely to discredit and ruin his own movement, he suppressed with such ruthless and illogical severity. And the Broad Church strain will here be found emphasised and caricatured in Socinianism, and in such milder forms of Rationalism as prepared the way for it or followed in its wake. And finally, the High Church strain is not so hard to discover in much of the doctrine and in some of the forms and externals of Orthodox, official Lutheranism. Indeed in foreign Protestantism generally,— in Zwinglianism, in Calvinism, and in its other bodies and sects, we can trace various forms of, and degrees of approximation to, one or other of these three types, the Historical, the Experimental, the Rational.

Now looking at the scene of battle, for the moment quite generally, it would seem as though, of these three types and tendencies, the Emotional and Experimental had proved itself decidedly the weakest for good, the strongest for evil of the three, and this both in the past and in the present, both in England and abroad. We have here in England, in the past, the Puritan excesses in Ireland, Scotland and England itself; and later on and down to the present, the largely dreary and unlovely, narrow and unjust monotony of Evangelicalism. We have there abroad, in the past, the Peasants' War and the Anabaptist Saturnalia at Münster; and later on and down to the present, that Pietism which has so often barred the way to a just appreciation of Historical Christianity and to a candid acceptance of rational methods and results, and this without its being able to find any constructive or analytic working principle of its own. Both in England and in Germany, indeed throughout the cultivated West, only the Historical, Traditional school on the one hand, and the Rationalistic, Scientific school on the other hand, seem to count at all: it is they which alone seem to gain ground, or at least to hold it, at the Universities and amongst the thinking, ruling classes generally.

And yet this first aspect of things will, I think, turn out to be largely deceptive, to be but one side and one teaching of that noble inheritance, that great output of life and experience, past and present, which is ready to our hand for ever-renewed study and assimilation in human history and society, and which, taken as it really is,—as the indefinite prolongation of our own little individual direct experiences— can alone help us to give to these latter experiences a full, life-regulating value.

2. HELLENISM, CHRISTIANITY AND SCIENCE, ALL THREE NECESSARY TO MAN

WE have seen that humanity has, so far, found and worked out three forces and conceptions of life, forces which are still variously operative in each of us, but which find their harmonious interaction in but few men, their full theoretical systematisation in none.

There is the ancient, Greek contribution, chiefly intellectual and æsthetic, mostly cold and clear, quick and conclusive, with, upon the whole, but a slight apprehension of personality and freedom, of conscience and of sin, and little or no sense of the difference and antagonism between these realities and simply Mathematical, Mechanical laws and concepts. It is a view profoundly abstract, and, at bottom, determinist: the will follows the intellect necessarily, in exact proportion to the clearness of information of the former. And the strength of this view, which was possible even to that gifted race just because of the restrictedness of its knowledge concerning the length and breadth of nature and of history, and still more with regard to the depths of the human character and conscience, consists in its freshness, completeness and unity. And this ideal of an ultimate harmonisation of our entire life and of its theory we must never lose, more and more difficult though its even approximate realisation has of necessity become.

There is next the middle, Christian contribution, directly moral and religious, deep and dim and tender, slow and far-

reaching, immensely costly, infinitely strong; with its discovery and exemplification of the mysterious depth and range
and complexity of human personality and freedom, of
conscience and of sin: a view profoundly concrete and at
bottom libertarian. The good will here first precedes, and
then outstrips, and determines the information supplied by
the intellect: "Blessed are the clean of heart, for they shall
see God." And the strength of this position consists in its
being primarily not a view, but a life, a spiritual, religious
life, requiring, implying, indeed proclaiming, definite doctrines concerning God and man, and their relations to each
other, but never exhausted by these doctrines even in their
collectivity, inexhaustible though these in their turn are by
their union with the life of the spirit, their origin and end.

There is finally the modern, Scientific contribution, intensely
impersonal and determinist, directly neither metaphysical
nor religious, but more abstract even than the Greek view,
in the mathematical constituent of its method, and more
concrete in a sense than Christianity itself, in the other, the
sensible-experiment constituent of its method. The most
undeniable of abstractions, those of mathematics (undeniable
just because of their enunciation of nothing but certain
simplest relations between objects, supposing those objects
to exist), are here applied to the most undeniable of con-
cretions, the direct experiences of the senses. And this mysterious union which, on the surface, is so utterly heterogeneous,
is itself at all explicable only on mental, metaphysical assumptions and on the admission of the reality and priority of
Mind. It is a union that has turned out as unassailable in
its own province, as it is incapable of suppressing or replacing
the wider and deeper truths and lives discovered for us respectively by Hellenism and Christianity.

Only in the case that man could but reckon mathematically
and observe with his senses, or in the case that man were
indeed provided with other faculties, but that he found
Reality outside him and within him to be properly appre-
hensible by the mathematico-experimental process alone,
could there be any serious question of such a final suppression

of by far the greater and deeper portion of himself. Instead
of any such deadlock the facts of these last four centuries
bear out the contention that neither can the religious life
suppress or do without the philosophical and the scientific,
nor can either of these other two lives suppress or permanently
do without its fellow or without religion.

3. THE THREE MEANS OF RELIGIOUS APPREHENSION

IN the doubtless overwhelming majority of cases, there came
first, as far as we can reconstruct the history of our consciousness, the appeal to our infant senses of some external religious
symbol or place, some picture or statue, some cross or book,
some movement of some attendant's hands and eyes. And
this appeal would generally have been externally interpreted
to us by some particular men or women, a Mother, Nurse,
Father, Teacher, Cleric, who themselves would generally
have belonged to some more or less well-defined traditional,
institutional religion. And their appeal would be through my
senses to my imaginative faculty first, and then to my memory
of that first appeal, and would represent the principle of
authority in its simplest form.

All here as yet works quasi-automatically. The little child
gets these impressions long before itself can choose between,
or even is distinctly conscious of them; it believes whatever
it sees and is told, equally, as so much fact, as something to
build on. If you will, it believes these things to be true, but
not in the sense of contrasting them with error; the very
possibility of the latter has not yet come into sight. And at
this stage the External, Authoritative, Historical, Traditional,
Institutional side and function of Religion are everywhere
evident. Cases like that of John Stuart Mill, of being left
outside of all religious tradition, we may safely say, will ever
remain exceptions to help prove the rule. The five senses
then, perhaps that of touch first, and certainly that of sight

most; the picturing and associative powers of the imagination; and the retentiveness of the memory, are the side of human nature specially called forth. And the external, sensible, readily picturable facts and the picturing functions of religion correspond to and feed this side, as readily as does the mother's milk correspond to and feed that same mother's infant. Religion is here, above all, a Fact and Thing.

But soon there wakes up another activity and requirement of human nature, and another side of religion comes forth to meet it. Direct experience, for one thing, brings home to the child that these sense-informations are not always trustworthy, or identical in its own case and in that of others. And, again, the very impressiveness of this external religion stimulates indeed the sense of awe and of wonder, but it awakens curiosity as well. The time of trustful questioning, but still of questioning, first others, then oneself, has come. The old impressions get now more and more consciously sought out, and selected from among other conflicting ones; the facts seem to clamour for reasons to back them, against the other hostile facts and appearances, or at least against those men in books, if not in life, who dare to question or reject them. Affirmation is beginning to be consciously exclusive of its contrary: I begin to feel that *I* hold *this*, and that *you* hold *that*; and that I cannot do both; and that I do the former, and exclude and refuse the latter.

Here it is the reasoning, argumentative, abstractive side of human nature that begins to come into play. Facts have now in my mind to be related, to be bound to other facts, and men to men; the facts themselves begin to stand for ideas or to have the latter in them or behind them. The measuring-rod seems to be over all things. And religion answers this demand by clear and systematic arguments and concatenations: this and this is now connected with that and that; this is true or this need not be false, because of that and that. Religion here becomes Thought, System, a Philosophy.

But yet a final activity of human nature has to come to its fullest, and to meet its response in a third side of Religion. For if in Physiology and Psychology all action whatsoever is found to begin with a sense-impression, to move through the central process of reflection, and to end in the final discharge of will and of action, the same final stage can be found in the religious life. Certain interior experiences, certain deep-seated spiritual pleasures and pains, weaknesses and powers, helps and hindrances, are increasingly known and felt in and through interior and exterior action, and interior suffering, effort and growth. For man is necessarily a creature of action, even more than of sensation and of reflection; and in this action of part of himself against other parts, of himself with or against other men, with or against this or that external fact or condition, he grows and gradually comes to his real self, and gains certain experiences as to the existence and nature and growth of this his own deeper personality.

Man's emotional and volitional, his ethical and spiritual powers, are now in ever fuller motion, and they are met and fed by the third side of religion, the Experimental and Mystical. Here religion is rather felt than seen or reasoned about, is loved and lived rather than analysed, is action and power, rather than either external fact or intellectual verification.

4. THE DIFFICULTIES OF TRANSITION

Now these three sides of the human character, and corresponding three elements of Religion, are never, any one of them, without a trace or rudiment of the other two; and this joint presence of three such disparate elements ever involves tension, of a fruitful or dangerous kind.

In the living human being indeed there never exists a mere apprehension of something external and sensible, without any interior elaboration, any interpretation by the head and heart. We can hardly allow, we can certainly in nowise picture to ourselves, even an infant of a few hours old as working, and being worked upon, by nothing beyond these sense-perceptions alone. Already some mental, abstractive, emotional-volitional reaction and interpretation is presumably at work; and not many weeks or months pass before this is quite obviously the case. And although, on the other hand, the impressions of the senses, of the imagination and the memory are, normally, more numerous, fresh and lasting in early than in later years, yet up to the end they continue to take in some new impressions, and keep up their most necessary functions of supplying materials, stimulants, and tests to the other powers of the soul.

Thus, too, Religion is at all times more or less both traditional and individual; both external and internal; both institutional, rational and volitional. It always answers more or less to the needs of authority and society; of reason and proof; of interior sustenance and purification. I believe because I am told, because it is true, because it answers to my deepest interior experiences and needs. And, everything else being equal, my faith will be at its richest and deepest and strongest, in so far as all these three motives are most fully and characteristically operative within me, at one and the same time, and towards one and the same ultimate result and end.

Now all this is no fancy scheme, no petty or pretty artificial arrangement: the danger and yet necessity of the presence of these three forces, the conflicts and crises within and between them all, in each human soul, and between various men and races that typify or espouse one or the other force to the more or less complete exclusion of the other, help to form the deepest history, the truest tragedy or triumph of the secret life of every one of us.

The transition from the child's religion, so simply naïve and unselfconscious, so tied to time and place and particular persons and things, so predominantly traditional and historical, institutional and external, to the right and normal type of a young man's religion, is as necessary as it is perilous. The transition is necessary. For all the rest of him is growing, —body and soul are growing in clamorous complexity in every direction: how then can the deepest part of his nature, his religion, not require to grow and develop also? And how can it permeate and purify all the rest, how can it remain and increasingly become "the secret source of all his seeing," of his productiveness and courage and unification, unless it continually equals and exceeds all other interests within the living man, by its own persistent vitality, its rich and infinite variety, its subtle, ever-fresh attraction and inexhaustible resourcefulness and power? But the crisis is perilous. For he will be greatly tempted either to cling exclusively to his existing, all but simply institutional, external position, and to fight or elude all approaches to its reasoned, intellectual apprehension and systematisation; and in this case his religion will tend to contract and shrivel up, and to become a something simply alongside of other things in his life. Or he will feel strongly pressed to let the individually intellectual simply supplant the institutional, in which case his religion will grow hard and shallow, and will tend to disappear altogether. In the former case he will, at best, assimilate his religion to external law and order, to Economics and Politics; in the latter case he will, at best, assimilate it to Science and Philosophy. In the first case, he will tend to superstition; in the second, to rationalism and indifference.

But even if he passes well through this first crisis, and has thus achieved the collaboration of these two religious forces, the external and the intellectual, his religion will still be incomplete and semi-operative, because still not reaching to what is deepest and nearest to his will. A final transition, the addition of the third force, that of the emotional-experimental life, must yet be safely achieved. And this again is perilous: for the two other forces will, even if single, still more if combined, tend to resist this third force's full share of influence to the uttermost. To the external force this emotional power will tend to appear as akin to revolution; to the intellectual side it will readily seem mere subjectivity and sentimentality ever verging on delusion. And the emotional-experimental force will, in its turn, be tempted to sweep aside both the external, as so much oppressive ballast; and the intellectual, as so much hair-splitting or rationalism. And

D

if it succeeds, a shifting subjectivity, and all but incurable tyranny of mood and fancy, will result,—fanaticism is in full sight.

5. THE THREE CONSTITUENTS OF KNOWLEDGE

If we would find, applied to other matters, the actual operation and co-operation, at the earliest stage of man's life, of the identical powers under discussion, we can find them, by a careful analysis of our means and processes of knowledge, or of the stages of all reflex action.

Even the most elementary acquisition, indeed the very possibility, of any and all certitude and knowledge, is dependent for us upon the due collaboration of the three elements or forces of our nature, the sensational, the rational, the ethico-mystical.

There is, first, in the order of our consciousness and in the degree of its undeniableness, the element of our actual impressions, the flux of our consciousness as it apprehends particular sights and sounds, smells and tastes and touches; particular sensations of rest and movement, pleasure and pain, memory, judgment and volition, a flux, "changeless in its ceaseless change." We have so far found neither a true object for thought, nor a subject which can think. And yet this element, and this alone, is the simply, passively received, the absolutely undeniable part of our experience,—we cannot deny it if we would. And again, it is the absolutely necessary prerequisite for our exercise or acquisition, indeed for our very consciousness, of the other two means or elements, without which there can be no real knowledge.

For there is, next in the logical order of the analysis of our consciousness and in the degree of its undeniableness, the element of the various forms of necessary thought, in as much as these are experienced by us as necessary. We can, with Aristotle, simply call them the ten categories; or we can, with greater precision and extension, group them, so far with Kant, under the two main heads of the two pure "æsthetic" Perceptions of time and space, on the one hand; and of the various "analytic" Forms of judgment and of the Categories of Unity, Reality, Substance, Possibility, etc., on the other hand. Now it can be shown that it is only by means of this whole second element, only through the co-operation of these "perceptions" and forms of thought, that any kind even of dim feeling of ordered succession or of system, of unity or meaning, is found by our mind in that first element. Only these two elements, found and taken together, present us, in their interaction, with even the impression and possibility of something to reason *about*, and something *wherewith* to reason.

The second element then differs from the first in this, that whereas the first presents its contents simply as actual and undeniable, yet without so far any necessity or significance: the second presents its contents as both actual and necessary. By means of the first element I see a red rose, but without any feeling of more than the fact that a rose, or at least this one, *is* red; it might quite as well be yellow or blue. By means of the second element, I think of a body of any kind, not only as actually occupying some particular space and time, but as *necessarily* doing so: I feel that I *must* so think of it.

And yet there is a third and last element necessary to give real value to the two previous ones. For only on the condition that I am willing to trust these intimations of necessity, to believe that these necessities of my subjective thought are objective as well, and correspond to the necessities of Being, can I reach the trans-subjective, can I have any real knowledge and experience of anything whatsoever, either within me or without. The most elementary experience, the humblest something to be granted as really existing and as to be reasoned from, is thus invariably and inevitably composed for me of three elements, of which only the first two are directly experienced by me at all. And the third element, the ethico-mystical, has to be there, I have to trust and endorse the intimations of necessity furnished by the second element, if anything is to come of the whole movement.

Thus, here also, at the very source of all our certainty, of

the worth attributable to the least or greatest of our thoughts
and feelings and acts, we already find the three elements:
indubitable sensation, clear thought, warm faith in and
through action. And thus life here already consists of multiplicity in unity; and what in it is absolutely indubitable, is
of value only because it constitutes the indispensable starting-
point and stimulation for the apprehension and affirmation
of realities not directly experienced, not absolutely undeniable,
but which alone bear with them all the meaning, all the
richness, all the reality and worth of life.

We can also find this same triad, perhaps more simply, if
we look to Psychology, and that most assured and most far-
reaching of all its results, the fact and analysis of Reflex
Action. For we find here that all the activities of specifically
human life begin with a sense-impression, as the first, the one
simply *given* element; that they move into and through a
central process of mental abstraction and reflection, as the
second element, contributed by the mind itself; and that
they end, as the third element, in the discharge of will and
of action, in an act of free affirmation, expansion and love.

In this endless chain composed of these groups of three
links each, the first link and the last link are obscure and
mysterious; the first, as coming from without us, and as still
below our own thought; the third, as going out from us, and
seen by us only in its external results, never in its actual
operation, nor in its effect upon our own central selves. Only
the middle link is clear to us. And yet the most mysterious
part of the whole process, the effect of it all upon the central
self, is also the most certain and the most important result of
the whole movement, a movement which ever culminates in
a modification of the personality and which prepares this
personality for the next round of sense-perception, intellectual
abstraction, ethical affirmation and volitional self-determination,—acts in which light and love, fixed and free, hard and
cold and warm, are so mysteriously, so universally, and yet
so variously linked.

6. THE THREE ELEMENTS IN THE GREAT RELIGIONS

EVEN the Greek religion, so largely naturalistic up to the very end, appears, in the centuries of its relative interiorisation, as a triad composed of a most ancient traditional cultus, a philosophy of religion, and an experimental-ethical life; the latter element being readily exemplified by the Daemon of Socrates, and by the Eleusinian and Orphic Mysteries.

In India and Tibet, again, Brahminism and Buddhism may be said to have divided these three elements between them, the former representing as great an excess of the external as Buddhism does of abstruse reasoning and pessimistic emotion. Mahometanism, while combining, in very imperfect proportions, all three elements within itself, lays special stress upon the first, the external element; and though harbouring, for centuries now and more or less everywhere, the third, the mystical element, looks, in its strictly orthodox representatives, with suspicion upon this mysticism.

Judaism was slow in developing the second, the intellectual element; and the third, the mystical, is all but wholly absent till the Exilic period, and does not become a marked feature till still later on, and in writers under Hellenistic influence. It is in the Book of Wisdom, still more in Philo, that we find all three sides almost equally developed. And from the Hasmonean period onwards till the destruction of Jerusalem by Titus, we find a severe and ardent external, traditional, authoritative school in the Pharisees; an accommodating and rationalising school in the Sadducees; and, apart from both, more a sect than a school, the experimental, ascetical and mystical body of the Essenes.

But it is in Christianity, and throughout its various vicissitudes and schools, that we can most fully observe the presence, characteristics, and interaction of these three modalities. We have already seen how the New Testament writings can be grouped, with little or no violence, according to the predominance of one of these three moods, under the heads of the traditional, historic, external, the Petrine school; the reasoning, speculative-internal, the Pauline; and the experimental, mystical-internal, the Johannine school. And in the East, up to Clement of Alexandria, in the West up to St. Augustine, we find the prevalence of the first type. And next, in the East, in Clement and Origen, in St. Gregory of Nyssa, in the Alexandrian and the Antiochene school generally, and in the West, in St. Augustine, we find predominantly a combination of the second and third types. The Areopagitic writings of the end of the fifth century still further emphasise and systematise this Neo-Platonic form of mystical speculation, and become indeed the great treasure-house from which above all the Mystics, but also largely the Scholastics, throughout the Middle Ages, drew much of their literary material.

And those six or seven centuries of the Middle Ages are full of the contrasts and conflicts between varying forms of Institutionalism, Intellectualism and Mysticism. Especially clearly marked is the parallelism, interaction and apparent indestructibleness of the Scholastic and Mystical currents. Abelard and St. Bernard, St. Thomas of Aquino and the great Franciscan Doctors, above all the often largely latent, yet really ceaseless conflict between Realism and Nominalism, all can be rightly taken as caused by various combinations and degrees, insufficiencies or abnormalities in the action of the three great powers of the human soul, and of the three corresponding root-forms and functions of religion. And whereas, during the prevalence of Realism, affective, mystical religion is the concomitant and double of intellectual religion; during the later prevalence of Nominalism, Mysticism becomes the ever-increasing supplement, and at last, ever more largely, the substitute, for the methods of reasoning. "Do penance and believe in the Gospel" becomes now the favourite text, even in the mouth of Gerson (who died in 1429), the great Nominalist Doctor, the Chancellor of the then greatest intellectual centre upon earth, the University of Paris. A constant depreciation of all dialectics, indeed largely of human knowledge generally, appears even more markedly in the pages of the gentle and otherwise moderate Thomas of Kempen (who died in 1471).

Although the Humanist Renaissance was not long in carrying away many minds and hearts from all deeper consciousness and effort of a moral and religious sort, yet in so far as men retained and but further deepened and enriched their religious outlook and life, the three old forms and modalities reappear, during the earlier stages of the movement, in fresh forms and combinations. Perhaps the most truly comprehensive and Christian representative of the new at its best, is Cardinal Nicolas of Coes, the precursor of modern philosophy. For he combines the fullest adhesion to, and life-long labour for, External Institutional authority, with the keenest Intellectual, Speculative life, and with the constant temper and practice of experimental and Mystical piety. And a similar combination we find in Blessed Sir Thomas More in England, who lays down his life in defence of Institutional Religion and of the authority of the visible Church and its earthly head; who is a devoted lover of the New Learning, both Critical and Philosophical; and who continuously cultivates the Interior Life. A little later on, we find the same combination in Cardinal Ximenes in Spain.

But it is under the stress and strain of the Reformation and Counter-Reformation movements that the depth and vitality of the three currents get specially revealed. For in Germany, and in Continental Protestantism generally, we see (immediately after the very short first "fluid" stage of Luther's and Zwingli's attitude consequent upon their breach with Rome) the three currents in a largely separate condition, and hence with startling distinctness. Luther, Calvin, Zwingli, different as are their temperaments and both their earlier and their later Protestant attitudes and doctrines, all three soon fall back upon some form and fragmentary continuation, or even in its way intensification, of Institutional Religion,— driven to such conservatism by the iron necessity of real life and the irrepressible requirements of human nature. They thus formed that heavy untransparent thing, orthodox Continental Protestantism. Laelius and Faustus Socinus attempt the construction of a purely Rationalistic Religion, and capture and intensify the current of a clear, cold Deism, in which the critical mind is to be supreme. And the Anabaptist and other scattered sects and individuals (the latter represented at their best by Sebastian Franck) attempt, in their turn, to hold and develop a purely interior, experimental, emotional-intuitive, ecstatic Religion, which is warm, indeed feverish and impulsive, and distrusts both the visible and institutional, and the rational and critical.

In England the same phenomenon recurs in a modified form. For in Anglicanism, the most characteristic of its parties, the High Church school, represents predominantly the Historical, Institutional principle. The Latitudinarian school fights for the Rational, Critical and Speculative element. The Evangelical school stands in close spiritual affinity to all but the Unitarian Nonconformists in England, and represents the Experimental, Mystical element. We readily think of Laud and Andrewes, Pusey and Keble as representatives of the first class; of Arnold, Stanley and Jowett as figures of the second class; of Thomas Scott, John Newton and Charles Simeon as types of the third class. The *Tracts for the Times, Essays and Reviews*, and (farther back) Bunyan's Works, would roughly correspond to them in literature.

And this trinity of tendency can also be traced in Catholicism. Whole Religious Orders and Congregations can be seen or felt to tend, upon the whole, to one or the other type. The Jesuits can be taken as predominantly making for the first type, for fact, authority, submission, obedience; the Dominicans for the second type, for thought, a philosophico-speculative, intellectual religion; the Benedictines, in their noble Congregation of St. Maur, for a historico-critical intellectual type; the French Oratory, for a combination of both the speculative (Malebranche) and the critical (Simon, Thomassin); and the Franciscans, for the third, for action and experimental, affective spirituality.

And yet none of these Orders but has had its individuals, and even whole secondary periods, schools and traditions, markedly typical of some current other than that specially characteristic of the Order as a whole. There are the great Critics and Historians of the Jesuit Order: the Spanish Maldonatus, the New Testament Scholar, admirable for his time, and helpful and unexhausted still; the French Denys Petau, the great historian of Christian Doctrine and of its development; the Flemish Bollandists, with their unbroken tradition of thorough critical method and incorruptible accuracy and impartiality. There are the great Jesuit Mystics: the Spanish Venerable Balthazar Alvarez, declared by St. Teresa to be the holiest mystical soul she had ever known; and the Frenchmen, Louis Lallemant and Jean Joseph Surin. There are those most attractive figures, combining the Scholar and the Mystic: Blessed Edmund Campion, the Oxford Scholar and Elizabethan Martyr; and Jean Nicolas Grou, the French translator of Plato, who died in exile in England in 1800. The Dominicans have, from the first, been really representative of external authority as well as of the speculative rational bent; and the mystical side has never been wanting to them, so amongst the early German Dominicans, Tauler and Suso, and many a Dominican female Saint. The Benedictines from the first produced great rulers; such striking types of external authority as the Pope-Saints, Gregory the Great and Gregory VII. (Hildebrand), and the great Benedictine Abbots and Bishops throughout the Middle Ages are rightly felt to represent one whole side of this great Order. And again such great mystical figures as St. Hildegard of Bingen and the two Saints Gertrude are fully at home in that hospitable Family. And the Franciscans have, in the Conventuals, developed representatives of the external authority type; and in such great philosopher-theologians as Duns Scotus and Occam, a combination which has more of the intellectual, both speculative and critical, than of the simply ascetical or even mystical type.

And if we look for individual contrasts, we can often find them in close temporal and local juxtaposition, as in France, in the time of Louis XIV., in the persons of Bossuet, Richard Simon, and Fénelon, so strikingly typical of the special

strengths and limitations of the institutional, rational, experimental types respectively. And yet the most largely varied
influence will necessarily proceed from characters which
combine not only two of the types, as in our times Frederick
Faber combined the external and experimental; but which
hold them all three, as with John Henry Newman in England
or Antonio Rosmini in Italy.

7. THE RELIGIOUS TEMPER LONGS FOR SIMPLIFICATION

How obvious and irresistible seems always, to the specifically
religious temper, the appeal to boundless simplification.
"Can there be anything more sublimely, utterly simple than
religion?" we all say and feel. In these regions, if anywhere,
we long and thirst to see and feel all things in one, to become
ourselves one, to find the One Thing necessary, the One
God, and to be one with Him for ever. Where is there room
here, we feel even angrily, for all these distinctions, all this
balancing of divers faculties and parts? Is not all this but
so much Æstheticism, some kind of subtle Naturalism, a
presumptuous attempting to build up bit by bit in practice,
and to analyse part from part in theory, what can only come
straight from God Himself, and, coming from Him the
One, cannot but bear the impress of His own indistinguishable
Unity? And can there be anything more unforcedly, unanalys-
ably simple than all actual religion,—and this in exact
proportion to its greatness? Look at St. Francis of Assisi, or
St. John Baptist; look above all at the Christ, supremely,
uniquely great, just because of His sublime simplicity! Look
at, feel, the presence and character of those countless souls
that bear, unknown even to themselves, some portion of this
His impress within themselves, forming thus a kind of indefinitely rich extension of His reign, of the kingdom of His
childlikeness. Away then with everything that at all threatens
to break up a corresponding simplicity in ourselves! Poverty

of spirit, emptiness of heart, a constant turning away from all distraction, from all multiplicity both of thought and of feeling, of action and of being; this, surely, is the one and only necessity for the soul, at least in proportion to the height of her spiritual call.

Now in all this there is a most subtle mixture of truth and of error. It is profoundly true that all that *is* at all, still more all personality, and hence above all God, the Spirit of spirits, is, just in that proportion, profoundly mysteriously One, with a Unity which all our best thinking can only distantly and analogously represent. And all religion will ever, in proportion as it is vigorous and pure, thirst after an ever-increasing Unification, will long to be one and to give itself to the One,—to follow naked the naked Jesus. Yet all the history of human thought and all the actual experience of each one of us prove that this Unity can be apprehended and developed, by and within our poor human selves, only in proportion as we carefully persist in stopping at the point where it can most thoroughly organise and harmonise the largest possible multiplicity of various facts and forces.

No doubt the living soul is not a whole made up of separate parts; still less is God made up of parts. Yet we cannot apprehend this Unity of God except in multiplicity of some sort; nor can we ourselves become rightly one, except through being in a true sense many, and very many, as well. Indeed the Christian Faith insists that there is something most real actually corresponding to this our conception of multiplicity even and especially in God Himself. For it as emphatically bids us think of Him as in one sense a Trinity as in another a Unity. And it is one of the oldest and most universal of Christian approaches to this mystery, to conceive it under the analogy of the three powers of the soul. God the Father and Creator is conceived as corresponding to the sense-perception and Imagination, to Memory-power; God the Son and Redeemer, as the Logos, to our reason; and God the Holy Spirit, as corresponding to the effective-volitional force within us; and then we are bidden to remember that, as in ourselves these three powers are all united in One personality, so in

God the Three Persons are united in One substance and
nature. Even the supremely and ineffably simple Godhead
is not, then, a mere, undifferentiated One.

And if we take the case of our Lord, even when He is
apprehended in the most abstract of orthodox ways: we get
either the duality of natures, God and Man; or a trinity of
offices, the Kingly, the Prophetic, and the Priestly,—these
latter again corresponding roughly to the External, the
Intellectual, and the Mystical element of the human soul.
And even if we restrict ourselves to His Humanity, and as
pictured in any one Gospel, nay in the earliest, simplest and
shortest, St. Mark, we shall still come continually upon a rich
multiplicity, variety, and play of different exterior and
interior apprehensions and activities, emotions and sufferings,
all profoundly permeated by one great end and aim, yet each
differing from the other, and contributing a different share
to the one great result. The astonishment at the disciples'
slowness of comprehension, the flash of anger at Peter, the
sad reproachfulness towards Judas, the love of the children,
the sympathy with women, the pity towards the fallen, the
indignation against the Pharisees, the rejoicing in the Father's
revelation, the agony in the Garden, the desolation on the
Cross, are all *different* emotions. The perception of the beauty
of the flowers of the field, of the habits of plants and of birds,
of the varieties of the day's early and late cloud and sunshine,
of the effects of storm and rain; and again of the psychology
of various classes of character, age, temperament and avo-
cation; and indeed of so much more, are all *different* obser-
vations. The lonely recollection in the desert, the nights
spent in prayer upon the mountains, the preaching from
boats and on the lake-side, the long foot-journeyings, the
many flights, the reading and expounding in the Synagogues,
the curing the sick and restoring them to their right mind,
the driving the sellers from the Temple-court, and so much
else, are all *different* activities.

And if we take what is or should be simplest in the spiritual
life of the Christian, his intention and motive; and if we
conceive this according to the evidence of the practice of

such Saints as have themselves revealed to us the actual working of their souls, and of the long and most valuable series of controversies and ecclesiastical decisions in this delicate matter, we shall again find the greatest possible Multiplicity in the deepest possible Unity. For even in such a Saint as St. John of the Cross, whose own analysis and theory of the interior life would often seem all but directly and completely to exclude the element of multiplicity, it is necessary ever to interpret and supplement one part of his teaching by another, and to understand the whole in the light of his actual, deliberate, habitual practice. This latter will necessarily ever exceed his explicit teaching, both in its completeness and in its authority. Now if in his formal teaching he never wearies of insisting upon detachment from all things, and upon the utmost simplification of the intentions of the soul, yet he occasionally fully states what is ever completing this doctrine in his own mind,—that this applies only to the means and not to the end, and to false and not to true multiplicity. "The spiritual man," he writes in one place, "has greater joy and comfort in creatures, if he detaches himself from them; and he can have no joy in them, if he considers them as his own." "He," as distinct from the unspiritual man, "rejoices in their truth," "in their best conditions," "in their substantial worth." He "has joy in all things." A real multiplicity then exists in things, and in our most purified apprehension of them; varied, rich joys related to this multiplicity are facts in the life of the Saints; and these varied joys may legitimately be dwelt on as incentives to holiness for oneself and others. "All that is wanting now," he writes to Donna Juana de Pedraça, his penitent, "is that I should forget you. But consider how that is to be forgotten which is ever present to the soul." An affection then, as pure as it was particular, was ever in his heart, and fully accepted and willed and acknowledged to its immediate object, as entirely conformable to his own teaching. St. Teresa, on the other hand, is a character of much greater natural variety, and yet it is she who has left us that most instructive record of her temporary erroneous ideal of a false simplicity, in

turning away, for a number of years, from the consideration
of the Humanity of Christ. And a constant, keen interest in
the actual larger happenings of her time, in the vicissitudes
of the Church in her day, was stamped upon all her teaching,
and remained with her up to the very end.

Perhaps the most classic expression of the true Unity is
that implied by St. Ignatius of Loyola, when he tells us that
"Peace is the simplicity of order." For order as necessarily
implies a multiplicity of things ordered as the unity of the
supreme ordering principle. Fénelon, doubtless, at times,
especially in parts of his condemned *Explication des Maximes
des Saints*, too much excludes, or seems to exclude, the element
of multiplicity in the soul's intention. Yet, both before and
after this book, some of the clearest and completest statements
in existence, as to the true unity and diversity to be found
in the most perfect life, are to be found among his writings.
In his Latin Epistle to Pope Clement XI. he insists upon the
irreducible element of multiplicity in the motives of the
very highest sanctity.

For he maintains first that, though "in the specific act of
Love, the chief of the theological virtues, it is possible to love
the absolute perfection of God considered in Himself, without
the addition of any motive of the promised beatitude," yet
that "this specific act of love, of its own nature, never excludes,
and indeed most frequently includes, this same motive of
beatitude." He asserts next that though, "in the highest
grade of perfection amongst souls here below, deliberate
acts of simply natural love of ourselves, and even supernatural acts of hope which are not commanded by love,
mostly cease," yet that in this "habitual state of any and
every most perfect soul upon earth, the promised beatitude is
desired, and there is no diminution of the exercise of the
virtue of hope, indeed day by day there is an increase in this
desire, from the specific motive of hope of this great good,
which God Himself bids us all, without exception, to hope
for." And he declares finally that "there is no state of perfection in which souls enjoy an uninterrupted contemplation,
or in which the powers of the soul are bound by an absolute

incapacity for eliciting the discursive acts of Christian piety; nor is there a state in which they are exempted from following the laws of the Church, and executing all the orders of superiors."

All the variety, then, of the interested and of the disinterested; of hope and fear and sorrow; of gratitude and adoration and love; of the Intuitive and Discursive; of Recollection and external Action, is to be found, in a deeper, richer, more multiple and varied and at the same time a more unified unity, in the most perfect life; and all this in proportion to its approach to its own ideal and normality.

Indeed the same multiplicity in unity is finely traced by St. Bernard, the great contemplative, in every human act that partakes of grace at all. "That which was begun by Grace, gets accomplished alike by both Grace and Free Will, so that they operate mixedly not separately, simultaneously not successively, in each and all of their processes. The acts are not in part Grace, in part Free Will; but the whole of each act is effected by both in an undivided operation."

8. SCIENCE: BRUTE FACT AND IRON LAW

BUT now, athwart both the Hellenic and the Christian factors of our lives, the first apparently so clear and complete and beautiful, the latter, if largely dark and fragmentary, so deep and operative, comes and cuts a third and last factor, that of Science, apparently more peremptory and irresistible than either of its predecessors. For both the former factors would appear to melt into mid-air before this last one. *They* evidently cannot ignore *it*; *it* apparently can ignore *them*. If Metaphysics and Religion seem involved in a perpetual round of interminable questions, solved, at most and at best, for but this man and for that, and with an evidence for their truth which can be and is gainsaid by many, but cannot be demonstrated with a peremptory clearness to any one: Science, on the other hand, would appear to give us just this *terra firma* of an easy, immediate, undeniable, continually growing, patently fruitful body of evidence and of fact.

And not only can Metaphysics and Religion not ignore Science, in the sense of denying or even overlooking its existence; they cannot apparently, either of them, even begin or proceed or end without constant reference, here frank and open, there tacit but none the less potent, to the enterprises, the methods, the conclusions of the Sciences one and all, and this even in view of establishing their own contentions. And more and more of the territory formerly assigned to Metaphysics or Religion seems in process of being conquered by Science: in Metaphysics, by experimental psychology, and by the simple history of the various philosophical systems, ideas, and technical terms, and of the local and temporal, racial and cultural antecedents and environments which gave rise to them; in Religion, by an analogous observation and study of man in the past and present, of man studied from within and from without.

Now this scientific spirit has hitherto, since its birth at the Renaissance, ever tended to the ever-increasing development of three main characteristics, which are indeed but several aspects of one single aim and end. There was and is, for one thing, the passion for Clearness, which finds its expression in the application of Mathematics and of the Quantitative view and standard to all and every subject-matter, in so far as the latter is conceived as being truly knowable at all. There was and is, for another, the great concept of Law, of an iron Necessity running through and expressing itself in all things, one great Determinism, before which all emotion and volition, all concepts of Spontaneity and Liberty, of Personality and Spirit, either Human or Divine, melt away, as so many petty subjective wilfulnesses of selfish, childish, "provincial" man, bent on fantastically humanising this great, cold thing, the Universe, into something responsive to his own profoundly unimportant and objectively uninteresting sensations and demands. There was and is, for a third thing, a vigorous Monism, both in the means and in the end of this view. Our sources of information are *but one*,—the reasoning, reckoning Intellect, backed up by readily repeatable, directly verifiable Experiment. The resultant information is *but one*,—the Universe within and without, a strict unbroken Mechanism.

If we look at the most characteristically modern elements of Descartes, and, above all, of Spinoza, we cannot fail to find throughout, as the reaction of this Scientific spirit upon Philosophy, the passion for those three things: for Clearness and ready Transferableness of ideas; for one universal, undeniable Common Element and Measure for all knowledge of every degree and kind; and for Law, omnipresent and inexorable. That is, we have here a passion for Thing as over against, as above, Person; for the elimination of all wilfulness, even at the cost of will itself, of all indetermination, obscurity and chance, even at the cost of starving and drying up whole regions of our complex nature, whole sources of information, and of violently simplifying and impoverishing the outlook on to reality both within us and without.

And yet how unjust would he be who failed to recognise, in the case of Spinoza especially, the noble, and at bottom deeply religious, motives and aspirations underlying such excesses; or the new problems and necessities, the permanent growth and gain, which this long process of human thought has brought to Religion itself, especially in indirect and unintentional ways!

For as to the motives, it ought not to be difficult to anyone who knows human history and human nature to see how the all but complete estrangement from Nature and Physical Fact which (from Socrates onwards, with the but very partial exception of Aristotle) had, for well-nigh two thousand years, preceded this reaction; how the treatment of Matter and the Visible as more or less synonymous with Non-Being and Irrationality, as a veil or even a wall, as a mere accident or even a positive snare, lying everywhere between us and Reality, could not fail to require and produce a swing of the pendulum in the opposite direction. And the feeling and the perception of how superficial and unreal, how oppressively confined, how intolerably fixed and ultimate, how arrogant

E

and cold and fruitless, such persistent neglect of the Data of Sense had somehow, at last, rendered philosophy, gave now polemical edge to men's zealous study and discovery of *this* world. This study was perceived, even by the shallower thinkers, to be fair and rational and fruitful in itself; and it was found, by some few deep spirits, to be a strangely potent means of purifying, enlarging, "deprovincialising" man himself. The severe discipline of a rigorous study of man's lowly, physical conditions and environment, things hitherto so despised by him, was now at last to purify him of his own childish immediacy of claim. The pettily selfish, shouting Individual was to pass through the broad, still, purgatorial waters of a temporary submergence under the conceptions, as vivid as though they were direct experiences, of ruthless Law, of Mechanism, of the Thing; so as to pass out, purified and enlarged, a Person, expressive of the Universal and Objective, of Order and of Law.

It is especially in Spinoza that this deeper, universally human and ethical, indeed we can say religious, implication and ideal of the rigorously scientific spirit is present in all its noble intuition and aspiration, and that at the same time, alas! this deep truth is forced into a ruinously inappropriate method and formulation. For the original end of the entire quest, an end which is still emotionally dominant and which furnishes the hidden dialectic of the whole,—Man, his nobility and interior purification and beatitude,—has here, intellectually, become but a means; Man, in the real logic of this system, is, hopelessly and finally, but a wheel in the huge mechanism of that *natura naturata* which Spinoza's own richness and nobility of character transcends with potent inconsistency. And this very system, which is so nobly human and Christian in its ethical tone and in its demand of a Conversion of the whole man, in its requiring man to lose and sacrifice his petty self that he may gain his true self and become a genuine constituent of the Universe and Thought of God, is also the very one which, by its ruthless Naturalism and Determinism of Doctrine and its universally Mathematical and Quantitative form and method, logically eliminates all such qualitative differentiation and conversion as impossible and futile.

The prima facie view of life as it presents itself to the clarifying, Scientific Intellect, namely the omnipresence of the determinist mechanism, has never been more impressively felt and pictured than by Spinoza; the dispositions and happiness of the purified, disinterested soul have rarely been experienced and described with more touching elevation and power. But there is no real transition, indeed no possibility of such, in his system, from that first aspect to this latter state; for that first aspect, that apparent determinism, is for his logic *not* merely apparent or secondary, but the very truth of truths, the very core and end of things.

And this bondage of mind to matter, this enslavement of the master to the servant, this narrow, doctrinaire intellectualism and determinism, is more hidden than cured in Leibniz, who, if he brings the immense improvement because enrichment of a keen sense and love of the Historical, loses, on the other hand, Spinoza's grandly Conversional tone and temper. A cheerful, easy, eminently sane but quite inadequate bustle of manifold interests; a ready, pleasant optimism; an endless laboriousness of the reasoning faculty; all this, even though carried out on a scale unique since the days of Aristotle, is necessarily unequal to face and bear "the burthen of all this unintelligible world."

9. THE ACHIEVEMENT OF SCIENCE

WE take it then that mankind has, after endless testings and experiences, reached the following conclusions. We encounter everywhere, both within us and without, both in the physical and mental world, in the first instance, a whole network of phenomena; and these phenomena are everywhere found to fall under certain laws, and to be penetrable by certain methods of research, these laws and methods varying indeed in character and definiteness according to the subject-matter to which they apply, but in each case affording to man simply indefinite scope for discovery without, and for self-discipline within.

And all this preliminary work and knowledge does not directly require religion nor does it directly lead to it; indeed we shall spoil both the knowledge itself, and its effect upon our souls and upon religion, if religion is here directly introduced. The phenomena of Astronomy and Geology, of Botany and Zoology, of human Physiology and Psychology, of Philology and History are, and ought to be, in the first instance, the same for all men, whether the said men do or do not eventually give them a *raison d'être* and formal rational interest by discovering the metaphysical and religious convictions and conclusions which underlie and alone give true unity to them and furnish a living link between the mind observing and the things observed. Various as are these phenomena, according to the department of human knowledge to which they severally belong, yet they each and all have to be, in the first instance, discovered and treated according to principles and methods immanent and special to that department.

And the more rigorously this is accomplished, both by carrying out these principles and methods to their fullest extent, and by conscientiously respecting their limits of applicability and their precise degree of truth and of range in the larger scheme of human activity and conviction, the more will such science achieve three deeply ethical, spiritually helpful results.

Such science will help to discipline, humble, purify the natural eagerness and wilfulness, the cruder forms of anthropomorphism, of the human mind and heart. This turning to the visible will thus largely take the place of that former turning away from it; for only since the Visible has been taken to represent laws, and, provisionally at least, rigorously mechanical laws characteristic of itself, can it be thus looked upon as a means of spiritual purification.

Such science again will help to stimulate those other, deeper activities of human nature, which have made possible, and have all along preceded and accompanied, these more superficial ones; and this, although such science will doubt-less tend to do the very opposite, if the whole nature be allowed to become exclusively engrossed in this one pheno-menal direction. Still it remains true that perhaps never has man turned to the living God more happily and humbly, than when coming straight away from such rigorous, dis-interested phenomenal analysis, as long as such analysis is felt to be both other than, and preliminary and secondary to, the deepest depths of the soul's life and of all ultimate Reality.

And finally, such science will correspondingly help to give depth and mystery, drama and pathos, a rich spirituality, to the whole experience and conception of the soul and of life, of the world and of God. Instead of a more or less abstract picture, where all is much on the same plane, where all is either fixed and frozen, or all is in a state of feverish flux, we get an outlook, with foreground, middle distances, and back-ground, each contrasting with, each partially obscuring, partially revealing, the other; but each doing so, with any freshness and fullness, only in and through the strongly willing, the fully active and gladly suffering, the praying, aspiring, and energising spiritual Personality, which thus both gives and gets its own true self ever more entirely and more deeply.

10. THE "RELATIONS" OF SCIENCE AND RELIGION

In such a conception of the place of Science, we have per-manently to take Science, throughout life, in a double sense and way. In the first instance, Science is self-sufficing, its own end and its own law. In the second instance, which alone is ever final, Science is but a part of a whole, but a function, a necessary yet preliminary function, of the whole of man; and it is but part, a necessary yet preliminary part, of his outlook. Crush out, or in any way mutilate or de-autonomise, this part, and all the rest will suffer. Sacrifice the rest to this part, either by starvation or attempted sup-pression, or by an impatient assimilation of this immense remainder to that smaller and more superficial part, and the whole man suffers again, and much more seriously.

And the danger, in both directions,—let us have the frankness to admit the fact,—is constant and profound: even to see it continuously is difficult; to guard against it with effect, most difficult indeed. For to starve or to suspect, to cramp or to crush this phenomenal apprehension and investigation, in the supposed interest of the ulterior truths, must ever be a besetting temptation and weakness for the religious instinct, wherever this instinct is strong and fixed, and has not yet itself been put in the way of purification.

For Religion is ever, *qua* religion, authoritative and absolute. What constitutes religion is not simply to hold a view and to try to live a life, with respect to the Unseen and the Deity, as possibly or even certainly beautiful or true or good: but precisely that which is over and above this,—the holding this view and this life to proceed somehow from God Himself, so as to bind my innermost mind and conscience to unhesitating assent. Not simply that I think it, but that, in addition, I feel bound to think it, transforms a thought about God into a religious act.

Now this at once brings with it a double and most difficult problem. For Religion thus becomes, by its very genius and in exact proportion to its reality, something so entirely *sui generis*, so claimful and supreme, that it at once exacts a twofold submission, the one simultaneous, the other successive; the first as it were in space, the second in time. The first regards the relations of religion to things non-religious. It might be parodied by saying: "Since religion is true and supreme, religion is all we require: all things else must be bent or broken to her sway." She has at the very least the right to a primacy not of honour only, but of direct jurisdiction, over and within all activities and things. The second regards the form and concept of religion itself. Since religion always appears both in a particular form at a particular time and place, *and* as divine and hence authoritative and eternal; and since the very strength and passion of religion depend upon the vigorous presence and close union of these two elements: religion will ever tend either really to oppose all change within itself, or else to explain away its existence. Religion would thus appear doomed to be either vague and inoperative, or obscurantist and insincere.

And it is equally clear that the other parts of man's nature and of his outlook cannot simply accept such a claim, nor could religion itself flourish at all if they could and did accept it. They cannot accept the claim of religion to be immediately and simply all, for they are fully aware of being themselves something also. They cannot accept her claim to dictate to them their own domestic laws, for they are fully aware that they each, to live truly at all, require their own laws and their own, at least relative, autonomy. However much man may be supremely and finally a religious animal, he is not *only* that; but he is a physical and sexual, a fighting and an artistic, a domestic and social, a political and philosophical animal as well.

Nor can man, even simply *qua* religious man, consent to a simple finality in the experience and explication, in the apprehension and application of religion, either in looking back into the past; or in believing and loving, suffering and acting in the present; or in forecasting the future, either of the race or of himself alone. For the *here and now*, the concrete "immediacy," the unique individuality of the religious experience for *me*, in this room, on this very day, its freshness, is as true and necessary a quality of living religion as any other whatsoever. And if all life sustains itself only by constant, costing renovation and adaptation of itself to its environment, the religious life, as the most intense and extensive of all lives, must somehow be richest in such newness in oldness, such renovative, adaptive, assimilative power.

Now it is deeply instructive to observe all this at work historically. For here we find every variety of attitude towards this very point. There are men of Religion who attempt to do without Science, and men of Science who attempt to do without Religion. Or again, men of Religion attempt to *level up*,—to assimilate the principles and results of the various sciences directly to religion, or at least to rule those scientific principles and results directly by religion. Or men of Science attempt to *level down*, to make religion into a mere philosophy or even a natural history. Yet we find also,—with so persistent a recurrence in all manner of places and times, as itself to suggest the inherent, essential, indestructible truth of the view,—another, a far more costing attitude. This attitude refuses all mutilation either of normal human nature or of its outlook, all oppression of one part by the other; for it discovers that these various levels of life have been actually practised in conjunction by many an individual in the past and in the present.

11. CHRISTIANITY, THE REVELATION OF PERSONALITY AND DEPTH

Now the whole of this clear, conceptual, abstractive Greek method, in as far as it identified abstractions with realities, and names with things, and reasoning with doing, suffering, and experience; and sought for Unity outside of Multiplicity, for Rest outside of Energising, for the Highest outside of Personality and Character as these are developed and manifested in the permeation and elevation of the lower; has in so far been succeeded and superseded by two other great world-moving experiences of the human race, experiences apparently even more antagonistic to each other than either appears to be to the Greek view: Christianity and Scientific Method.

As to Christianity, it is really impossible to compare it directly with Hellenism, without at once under-stating its originality. For its originality consists not so much in its single doctrines, or even in its teaching as a whole, and in the particular place each doctrine occupies in this teaching, as in its revelation, through the person and example of its Founder, of the altogether unsuspected depth and inexhaustibleness of human Personality, and of this Personality's

source and analogue in God, of the simplicity and yet difficulty
and never-endingness of the access of man to God, and of
the ever-preceding condescension of God to man. Hence if
Christianity is thus throughout the Revelation of Personality;
and if Personality is ever a One in Many (and more deeply
One and more richly Many, in proportion to the greatness
of that spiritual reality): then we need not wonder at the
difficulty we find in pointing out any one particular doctrine
as constitutive of the unique originality of Christianity.

For a Person came, and lived and loved, and did and
taught, and died and rose again, and lives on by His Power
and His Spirit for ever within us and amongst us, so unspeakably rich and yet so simple, so sublime and yet so
homely, so divinely above us precisely in being so divinely
near,—that His character and teaching require, for an ever
fuller yet never complete understanding, the varying study,
and different experiments and applications, embodiments
and unrollings of all the races and civilisations, of all the
individual and corporate, the simultaneous and successive
experiences of the human race to the end of time. If there
is nothing shifting or fitful or simply changing about Him,
there are everywhere energy and expansion, thought and
emotion, effort and experience, joy and sorrow, loneliness and
conflict, interior trial and triumph, exterior defeat and
supplantation: particular affections, particular humiliations,
homely labour, a homely heroism, greatness throughout in
littleness. And in Him, for the first and last time, we find an
insight so unique, a Personality so strong and supreme, as
to teach us, once for all, the true attitude towards suffering.

Not one of the philosophers or systems before Him had
effectually escaped falling either into Pessimism, seeing the
end of life as trouble and weariness, and seeking to escape
from it into some aloofness or some Nirvana; or into Optimism, ignoring or explaining away the suffering and trial
which, as our first experience and as our last, surround us on
every side. But with Him, and alone with Him and those
who still learn and live from and by Him, there is the union
of the clearest, keenest sense of all the mysterious depth and

breadth and length and height of human sadness, suffering, and sin, *and*, in spite of this and through this and at the end of this, a note of conquest and of triumphant joy.

And here, as elsewhere in Christianity, this is achieved not by some artificial, facile juxtaposition: but the soul is allowed to sob itself out; and all this its pain gets fully faced and willed, gets taken up into the conscious life. Suffering thus becomes the highest form of action, a divinely potent means of satisfaction, recovery, and enlargement for the soul,—the soul with its mysteriously great consciousness of pettiness and sin, and its immense capacity for joy in self-donation.

And again, His moral and spiritual idealism, whilst indefinitely higher than that of any of the philosophers or prophets before Him, has nothing strained or restless, nothing rootless or quietistic, nothing querulous or disdainful, or of caste or sect about it: the humblest manual labour, the simplest of the human relations, the universal elemental faculties of man as man, are all entered into and developed, are all hallowed in smallest detail, and step by step.

And finally His teaching, His life, are all positive, all constructive, and come into conflict only with worldly indifference and bad faith. No teacher before Him or since, but requires, if we would not be led astray by him, that we should make some allowances, in his character and doctrine, for certain inevitable reactions, and consequent narrowness and contrarinesses. Especially is this true of religious teachers and reformers, and generally in exact proportion to the intensity of their fervour. But in Him there is no reaction, no negation, no fierceness, of a kind to deflect His teaching from its immanent, self-consistent trend. His very Apostles can ask Him to call down fire from heaven upon the unbelieving Samaritans; they can use the sword against one of those come out to apprehend Him; and they can attempt to keep the little ones from Him. But He rebukes them; He orders Peter to put back the sword in its scabbard; and He bids the little ones to come unto Him, since of such is the Kingdom of Heaven. Indeed St. Mark's Gospel tells us how the disciples begged Him to forbid a man who did not follow them from casting out devils in His name; and how He refused to do so, and laid down the great universal rule of all-embracing generosity: "He that is not against us, is for us."

Now it is this very reality and depth, and hence the rich Unity, the growth, variety, and manifold fruitfulness of His life and teaching, which explain, as a necessity and an advantage, that we should have those successive pictures and conceptions of Him which already the New Testament presents. *Because* Socrates was so great and impressive, we have the two successive, remarkably divergent, portraits of him: the external, historical, by Xenophon; the internal, typical one, by Plato; and *that* is all. *Because* our Lord is so unspeakably greater, and continues, with inexhaustible freshness, to be the very life of the lives of Christians, we have three or four classical portraits of Him in the New Testament; and, in a certain true manner and degree, each successive age, in a measure each single soul, forms, and has to form, its own picture of Him.

We can roughly classify these pictures under the three successive types of the "Petrine," the "Pauline," and the "Johannine," provided we do not forget that the precise limits of the first of these divisions are difficult to draw, and that there are growths and diversities of aspect to be found within the Pauline type. For the Petrine type will here be sought in the Synoptic Gospels, and in particular in those accounts and sayings there which appear to give us the closest reproductions of our Lord's very acts and words and of the impressions produced by these upon the original witnesses. The Pauline type will embrace four main stages or developments: that of the four or five of the earlier Epistles—the two to the Thessalonians and those to the Galatians, Corinthians and Romans; that of the Epistles of the Captivity, Colossians, Philippians, Ephesians; that of the Pastoral Epistles; and that of the Epistle to the Hebrews. And even in the least diversified, the Johannine type, there is the variation between the Gospel and Epistles on the one hand, and the Apocalypse on the other.

But taking these three types as each a unity, we shall hardly be guilty of an empty schematisation, if the Petrine or Primitive-Apostolic group represents to us mainly the simplest statement of the external facts, and especially of the traditional, the Jewish side of our Lord's teaching; and if the Pauline and Johannine groups each mainly represent to us, in various degrees and combinations, the two manners in which the hidden significance of these facts, as intended for all men and for all time, can be penetrated, viz. by thought and speculation, and by feeling and operative experience.

Of course none of the three groups is without a large element common to it and to the other two: it is the same facts that are looked at and loved, by means of the same powers of the soul, and within the same great common principles and convictions. Only the precise antecedents, point of view, temper of mind; the selection, presentation, and degree of elaboration of the facts and of their spiritual meaning; the preponderance of this or that mental activity; the reasons and connections sought and seen, are often widely different in each, and produce a distinctiveness of impression which can be taken to correspond roughly to the three main powers of the soul: to the range of sense-perception and of memory; to that of reasoning; and to that of intuition, feeling, and will. If each group had *only* that element which can be taken as being its predominant one, then any single group would be of little value, and each group would imperatively require ever to be taken in conjunction with the other two. But, as a matter of fact, neither are the "Petrine" writings free from all reasoning and mystical affinities; nor are the "Pauline" free from the historic, positive spirit, or, still less, from the mystical habit; nor the "Johannine" free from the deepest teaching as to the necessity of external facts, or from some argument and appeals to reason. Hence each group, indeed each writing even singly, and still more all three groups if taken together, profoundly embody and proclaim, by the rich variety of their contents and spirit, the great principle and measure of all life and truth: unity in and through variety, and steadfastness in and through growth.

Specially easy is it to find in all three types the two chief among the three modalities of all advanced religion: the careful reverence for the external facts of nature (so far as these are known), and for social religious tradition and institutions; and the vivid consciousness of the necessity and reality of internal experience and actuation, as the single spirit's search, response and assimilation of the former.

Thus the Petrine group gives us, as evidence for the observation and love of the external world: "Behold the birds of the heaven, how they sow not, neither do they gather into barns"; "Consider the lilies of the field how they grow; they toil not, neither do they spin: yet I say unto you, that even Solomon in all his glory was not arrayed like one of these"; "The seed springeth up and grows, the man knoweth not how; the earth beareth fruit of itself, first the blade, then the ear, then the full corn in the ear"; "When the fig-tree's branch is become tender and putteth forth its leaves, ye know that the summer is nigh"; and, "When it is evening, ye say: 'It will be fair weather: for the heaven is red.' And in the morning: 'It will be foul weather to-day: for the heaven is red and lowring.'"

And as to reverence for tradition we get: "Think not that I came to destroy the law or the prophets; I came not to destroy but to fulfil." And this respect extends to existing religious practices: "Take heed," He says, "that ye do not your righteousness before men, to be seen of them," but then describes the spirit in which they are to practise their "*sedaka*," this "justice" which they are to do, with its three quite traditional divisions of alms-deeds, prayer, fasting, the three Eminent Good Works of Judaism. And again: "If thou offer thy gift upon the altar," the doing so is in nowise criticised.

Indeed there is no shrinking from the manifestation, on the part of the crowd, of new and even rude forms of trust in the visible and external: "A woman which had an issue of blood twelve years, . . . came in the crowd behind, and touched His garment. For she said: 'If I touch but His garments, I shall be made whole.' And straightway the fountain of her blood was dried up"; and the crowds generally "laid the sick in the marketplaces, and besought Him that they might touch if it were but the border of His garment; and as many as touched Him were made whole"; and this "border" consisted doubtless in the blue tassels, the Zizith, worn by every religious Jew at the four corners of his cloak.

And the twelve Apostles, whom He sends out with special instructions, "And they went out, and preached that men should repent. And they cast out many devils, and anointed with oil many that were sick, and healed them." Indeed there is, as the act preliminary to His public ministry, His baptism in the Jordan; and there is, as introductory to His Passion, the supremely solemn, visible, and audible act which crowns the Last Supper.

But this same group of documents testifies also to a mystical, interior element in Our Lord's temper and teaching. "Blessed are the poor in spirit: for theirs is the kingdom of heaven," "Blessed are the pure in heart: for they shall see God," are Beatitudes which cannot be far from the *ipsissima verba* of Our Lord. "At that season Jesus answered and said, 'I thank Thee, O Father, Lord of Heaven and earth, that Thou didst hide these things from the wise and understanding, and didst reveal them unto babes: yea, Father, for so it was well-pleasing in Thy sight.' . . . 'Come unto Me, all ye that labour and are heavy laden, and I will give you rest. Take My yoke upon you, and learn of Me; for I am meek and lowly of heart: and ye shall find rest unto your souls. For My yoke is easy, and My burden is light.'" This deeply mystical passage doubtless expresses with a vivid exactitude the unique spiritual impression and renovation produced by Him within the souls of the first generations of His disciples. And the three Synoptists give us five times over the great fundamental mystical paradox: "If any man would come after Me, let him deny himself, and take up his cross, and follow Me. For whosoever would save his life shall lose it; and whosoever shall lose his life for My sake and the gospel's, shall save it." And the great law of interiority is recorded in St. Mark: "Hear Me all of you, and understand: there is nothing from without the man, that going into him can defile him: but the things which proceed out of the man are those that defile the man."

And we get in Mark the fundamental interior virtue of childlikeness, and the immanence of Christ in the childlike soul: "If any man would be first, he shall be last of all, and minister of all." "And he took a little child and set him in the midst of them: and taking him in His arms, He said unto them, 'Whosoever shall receive one of such little children in My name, receiveth Me: and whosoever receiveth Me, receiveth not Me, but Him that sent Me.'" "Suffer the little children to come unto Me; forbid them not: for of such is the kingdom of heaven."

And the spirituality of the soul's life in heaven, and the eternal *Now* of God, as the Living and Vivifying Present, are given in all three Synoptists: "When they shall rise from the dead, they neither marry, nor are given in marriage; but are as angels in heaven. But as touching the dead, . . . have ye not read . . . how God spake unto him, saying, 'I am the God of Abraham, and the God of Isaac, and the God of Jacob'? He is not the God of the dead, but of the living."

The Pauline group furnishes by far the greater amount of the explicit reasoning to be found in the New Testament; where, e.g. does the New Testament furnish a parallel to the long and intricate argument of chapters third to eleventh of the Epistle to the Romans, with its constant "therefores" and "buts" and "nows"? Yet this same group of writings also emphasises strongly, though more rarely, the external-act side of religion, and is deeply penetrated by the intuitive-emotional, the mystical spirit of Christianity.

The external, historical side is represented by the careful description and chronological arrangement observable in the account of six successive apparitions of the Risen Christ; and by the reference back to the acts and words used in the Eucharistic act at the Last Supper.

Yet throughout the writings of St. Paul and of his school, it is the mystical, interior, experimental element that permeates the argumentative-speculative and the historical constituents. The chief manifestations of this mystical spirit and conviction, which really penetrates and knits together the whole of the Pauline teaching, can perhaps best be taken in a logical order. First then it is St. Paul who, himself or through writers more or less dependent on him, gives us by far the most definite and detailed presentation of by far the most extraordinary experiences and events to be found in the New Testament outside of the Gospels themselves. For the author of the Acts of the Apostles gives us the lengthy description of the Pentecostal Visitation, and, three times over, the most vivid account of Our Lord's apparition to Saul on the way to Damascus. And St. Paul himself describes for us, at the closest first hand, the ecstatic states of the Christian communities in their earliest charismatic stage; he treats the apparition on the way to Damascus as truly objective and as on a complete par with the earlier apparitions accorded to the chosen Apostles in the first days after the Resurrection; and he gives us the solemn reference to his own experience of rapture to the third Heaven. We should, however, note, in the next place, as the vital complement, indeed as the necessary prerequisite, to this conviction and to the effectiveness of these facts,—facts conceived and recorded as external, as temporal and local,—St. Paul's profound belief that all external evidences, whether of human reasoning and philosophy or of visible miracle, fail to carry conviction without the presence of certain corresponding moral and spiritual dispositions in those to whom they are addressed. "The word of the Cross," the very same preaching, "is to them that are perishing foolishness; but unto us which are being saved it is the power of God." And the external, taken alone, can so little convince, that even the seeking after the external, without requisite dispositions, will but get us farther away from its hidden function and meaning. "Jews ask for signs (miracles), and Greeks seek after wisdom (philosophy); but we preach Christ crucified, unto Jews a stumbling-block, and unto Gentiles foolishness; but unto them that are called, both Jews and Greeks, Christ the power of God and the wisdom of God. Because the foolishness of God is wiser than men; and the weakness of God is stronger than men." And the cause of this difference of interpretation is shown to lie in the various interior dispositions of the hearers: "The natural man receiveth not the things of the Spirit of God: for they are foolishness unto him; and he cannot know them, because they are spiritually judged; but he that is spiritual judgeth all things."

And yet this mystery of religion has to be externally offered, to be preached to us, and is preached to all men; it is intended by God to be known by all, and hence it is He who stimulates men to external preaching and external hearing, as to one of the prerequisites of its acceptance: "The mystery which hath been hid from all ages and genera- tions: but now hath it been manifested"; he desires the Colossians to be strengthened in "the knowledge of the mystery of God and Christ"; and has to "speak the mystery of the Christ," to "make it manifest."

And since this preaching, to be effective, absolutely requires, as we have seen, interior dispositions and interior illumin- ation of the hearers, and since these things are different in different men, the degrees of initiation into this identical mystery are to be carefully adapted to the interior state of those addressed. "We speak wisdom among the perfect (τέλειοι)," the technical term in the heathen Greek Mysteries for those who had received the higher grades of initiation. "I, brethren, could not speak unto you as unto spiritual, but (only) as unto carnal, as unto babes in Christ. I fed you with milk, not with meat; for ye were not yet able."

And since all good, hence also the external preaching, comes from God, still more must this all-important interior appre- hension of it come from Him. In a certain real sense the Spirit is thus organ as well as object of this interior light. "But unto us God revealed" the wisdom of God "through the Spirit; for the Spirit searcheth all things, yea, the deep things of God. For who among men knoweth the things of a man, save the spirit of the man which is in him? even so the things of God none knoweth, save the Spirit of God."

But further, the mystery revealed in a unique degree and form in Christ's life, is really a universal spiritual-human law;

F

the law of suffering and sacrifice, as the one way to joy and possession, which has existed, though veiled till now, since the foundation of the world. "The mystery of Christ, which in other generations was not made known unto the sons of men, as it hath now been revealed to His holy apostles and prophets in the spirit." And this law, which is Christ's life, must reappear in the life of each one of us. "We have been buried together with Him through Baptism unto death, in order that, as Christ rose again from the dead through the glory of the Father, so we also may walk in the newness of life"; "We know that our old man was crucified with Him. . . . But if we have died with Christ, we believe that we shall also live with Him"; "If the Spirit of him that raised up Jesus from the dead dwelleth in you, He that raised Jesus from the dead shall quicken also your mortal bodies through His Spirit that dwelleth in you."

Christ's life can be thus the very law of all life, because "He is the first-born of all creation, for in Him were all things created, in the heavens and upon the earth," "all things have been created through Him"; "and He is before all things, and in Him all things consist"; "all things are summed up in Christ"; "Christ is all in all." So that in the past, before His visible coming, the Jews in the desert "drank of a spiritual rock that followed them: and the rock was Christ." And as He Himself is the perfect image of God, so all things are, in varying degrees, created in the image of Christ: "(Christ) who is the image of the invisible God"; "in Him were all things created." And since man is, in his original and potential essence, in a very special sense "the image and glory of God," his perfecting will consist in a painful reconquest and development of this obscured and but potential essence, by becoming, as far as may be, another Christ, and living through the successive stages of Christ's earthly life. We are bidden "all attain . . . unto a full-grown man, unto the measure of the stature of the fullness of Christ," so that, in the end, we may be able to say with the Apostle himself: "I live; and yet no longer I, but Christ liveth in me"; a consummation which appears so possible to St. Paul's mind, that he eagerly, painfully longs for it: "My little children, of whom I am again in travail, until Christ be formed in you." And indeed "we all, with unveiled face reflecting as a mirror the glory of the Lord, are transformed into the same image from glory to glory, even as from the Lord the Spirit."

We have then in St. Paul not only a deeply mystical element, but mysticism of the noblest, indeed the most daringly speculative, world-embracing type.

And finally the Johannine group furnishes us with an instance, as strong as it is conceivable within the wide pale of a healthy Christian spirit, of the predominance of an interior and intuitive, mystical, universalistic, spiritual and symbolic apprehension and interpretation both of external fact and of explicit reasoning.

The Visible and Historical is indeed emphasised, with a full consciousness of the contrasting Gnostic error, in the culminating sentence of the solemn Prologue of the Gospel, "And the Word became Flesh, and dwelt amongst us (and we beheld His glory)," and in the equally emphatic opening sentence of the First Epistle: "That which was from the beginning, that which we have heard, that which we have seen with our eyes, that which we beheld, and our hands handled, . . . we announce unto you." Hence too the Historical, Temporal Last Judgment, with its corporal resurrection, remains as certainly retained in this Gospel as in St. Matthew: "The hour cometh, in which all that are in the tombs shall hear His voice; shall come forth; they that have done good, unto the resurrection of life; and they that have done ill, unto the resurrection of judgment."

And Reasoning of a peculiarly continuous, rhythmically recurrent pattern, is as present and influential everywhere, as it is difficult to describe or even to trace. For it is here but the instrument and reflex of certain Mystical conceptions and doctrines, of a tendency to see, in everything particular and temporal, the Universal and Eternal; to apprehend Unity, a changeless Here and Now, in all multiplicity and succession, and hence to suppress explicit reasoning and clear distinctions, movement, growth and change, as much as may be, both in the method of presentation and in the facts presented. If the Synoptists give us the successive, and write, unconsciously but specially, under the category of Time: the Fourth Gospel consciously presents us with simultaneity, and works specially under the category of Space.

The Successive is here conceived as but the appearance of the Simultaneous, of the Eternal and Abiding. Hence the historical development in the earthly experiences, teachings, and successes of Christ is ignored: His Godhead, that which *is*, stands revealed from the first in the appearances of His earthly life. Hence too the various souls of other men are presented to us as far as possible under one eternal and changeless aspect; they are types of various abiding virtues and iniquities, rather than concrete, composite mortals.

God appears here specially as Light, as Love, and as Spirit. Yet these largely thing-like attributions co-exist with personal qualities, and with real, ethical relations between God and the world: "God so loved the world, that He gave His only begotten Son, that whosoever believeth on Him shall not perish, but have eternal life." The Father "draws" men, and "sends" his Son into the world.

And this Son has eternally pre-existed with the Father; is the very instrument and principle of the world's creation; and "is the true Light that lighteth every man coming into the world." And this Word which, from the first, was already the Light of all men, became Flesh specially to manifest fully this its Life and Light. Indeed He is the only Light, and Way, and Truth, and Life; the only Door; the Living Bread; the true Vine.

This Revelation and Salvation is indeed assimilated by individual souls and is received by them at a given moment, by a birth both new and from above, and is followed by a new knowledge. But this knowledge is not absolute nor unprogressive. Everywhere the Evangelist has indeed the verb γιγνώσκω, but nowhere the noun Gnosis; and the full meaning of the Revelation of the Father by the Son is to be only gradually revealed by the Holy Spirit. And this special new knowledge is not the cause but the effect of an ethical act on the part of the human soul,—an act of full trust in the persons of God and of His Christ, and in the intimations of the moral conscience as reflections of the divine will and nature. "If any man willeth to do His will, he shall know of the teaching, whether it be of God, or whether I speak from myself"; "He that doeth the truth, cometh to the light."

And this trust, and the experimental knowledge which flows from it, lead to an interior conviction so strong as to make us practically independent of external evidences. Hence in the First Epistle, this "we *know*" is repeatedly emphasised: "We *know* that, if He shall be manifested, we shall be like Him"; "Ye *know* that He was manifested to take away sins." And this knowledge is communicated by the Spirit of God to man's soul; the spirit bearing witness, there within, to the truth of Christ's words, communicated from without. "It is the Spirit that beareth witness, because the Spirit is the Truth."

External signs (miracles), and a certain un-ethical assent given to them and their implications, these things are, even at their best, but preliminary, and, of themselves, insufficient. Hence Our Lord can find "many who believed in His name, seeing His signs (miracles) which He did"; and yet could "not trust Himself to them." Nicodemus indeed can come to Our Lord, moved by the argument that "thou hast come a teacher from God, for no man can do the signs (miracles) that thou doest, unless God be with him." But then Our Lord's whole conversation with him renders clear how imperfect and ignorant Nicodemus is so far,—he had come by night, his soul was still in darkness. So also "many Samaritans believed in Him," because of His sign,—His miraculous knowledge of her past history, shown to the Woman at the Well; but more of them believed because of His own words to them: "We have (now) heard for ourselves, and *know* that this is indeed the Saviour of the world." Hence He can Himself bid the Apostles, in intimation of their full and final privilege and duty, "believe in Me" (that is, My words and the Spirit testifying within you to their Truth), "that I am in the Father, and the Father in Me"; and, only secondarily and failing that fullness, "but if not, then believe, because of the very works." And the whole Johannine doctrine as to the object and method of Faith is dramatically presented and summed up in the great culminating scene and saying of the Fourth Gospel: "Thomas" (the Apostle who would see a visible sign first, and would then build his Faith upon that sight) "saith to Him: 'My Lord and my God.' Jesus saith to him: 'Because thou hast seen Me, thou hast believed; blessed are they that have not seen, and yet have believed."

And this Faith and Knowledge arising thus, in its fullness, at most only on occasion, and never because, of spatial and temporal signs, are conceived as a timeless, Eternal Life, and as one which is already, here and now, an actual present possession. "He that believeth on the Son hath eternal life"; "He that heareth My word, and believeth Him that sent Me, hath eternal life"; "We know that we have passed from death unto life"; "We know Him that is true, and we are in Him that is true, even in His Son Jesus Christ. This is the true God and eternal life." There is then a profound immanence of Christ in the believing soul, and of such a soul in Christ; and this mutual immanence bears some likeness to the Immanence of the Father in Christ, and of Christ in the Father. "In that day" (when "the Father shall give you the Spirit of Truth") "ye shall know that I am in My Father, and ye in Me, and I in you."

12. CHRISTIANITY: PESSIMIST AND OPTIMIST

Now I think it is Professor Ernst Troeltsch who has most fully explicated the precise centre of this difficulty, which, in its acuteness, is a distinctly modern one, and the direction in which alone the problem's true solution should be sought.

(1) "The chief problem of Christian Ethics," he says, "is busy," not with the relation between certain subjective means and dispositions, but "with the relation between certain objective ends, which have, in some way, to be thought

together by the same mind as so many several objects, and
to be brought by it and within it to the greatest possible
unity. And the difficulty here lies in the fact, that the sub-
lunar among these ends are none the less moral ends, bearing
the full specific character of moral values,—that they are
ends-in-themselves, and necessary for their own sakes, even
at the cost of man's natural happiness; and yet that they
operate in the visible world, and adhere to historical form-
ations which proceed from man's natural constitution, and
dominate his earthly horizon; whilst the Super-worldly End
cannot share its rule with any other end. Yet the special
characteristic of modern civilisation resides precisely in such
a simultaneous insistence upon the Inner-worldly Ends, as
possessing the nature of ends-in-themselves, and upon the
Religious, Super-worldly End: it is indeed from just this
combination that this civilisation derives its peculiar richness,
power and freedom, but also its painful, interior tension and
its difficult problems."

(2) The true solution of the difficulty surely is that "Ethical
life is not, in its beginnings, a unity but a multiplicity: man
grows up amidst a number of moral ends, whose unification is
not his starting-point but his problem. And this multiplicity
can be still further defined as the polarity of two poles,
inherent in man's nature, of which the two chief types proceed
respectively from the religious and from the inner-worldly
self-determination of the soul,—the polarity of Religious, and
that of Humane Ethics, neither of which can be dispensed
with without moral damage, yet which cannot be brought
completely under a common formula. On this polarity
depends the richness, but also the difficulty, of our life, since
the sub-lunar ends remain, to a large extent, conditioned by
the necessities and prerequisites of their own special subject-
matters, and since only on condition of being thus recognised
as ends in themselves, can they attain to their morally
educative power."

Or, to put the same matter from the point of view of
definitely Christian experience and conviction: "The formula,
for the specific nature of Christianity, can only be a complex

conception,—the special Christian form," articulation and correction, "of the fundamental thoughts concerning God, World, Man and Redemption which," with indefinite variations of fullness and worth, "are found existing together in all the religions. And the tension present in this multiplicity of elements thus brought together is of an importance equal to that of the multiplicity itself; indeed in this tension resides the main driving-force of Religion. Christianity" in particular "embraces a polarity within itself, and its formula must be dualistic; it resembles, not a circle with one centre, but an ellipse with two focuses. For Christianity is," unchangeably, "an Ethics of Redemption, with a conception of the world both optimistic and pessimistic, both transcendental and immanental, and an apprehension both of a severe antagonism and of a close interior union between the world and God. It is, in principle, a Dualism, and yet a Dualism which is ever in process of abolition by Faith and Action. It is a purely Religious Ethic, which concentrates man's soul, with abrupt exclusiveness, upon the values of the interior life; and yet, again, it is a Humane Ethic, busy with the moulding and transforming of nature, and through love bringing about an eventual reconciliation with it. At one time the one, at another time the other, of these poles is prominent: but neither of them may be completely absent, if the Christian outlook is to be maintained.—And yet the original germ of the whole vast growth and movement ever remains an intensely, abruptly Transcendent Ethic, and can never simply pass over into a purely Immanental Ethic. The Gospel ever remains, with all possible clearness and keenness, a Promise of Redemption, leading us, away from the world, from nature and from sin, from earthly sorrow and earthly error, on and on to God; and which cannot allow the last word to be spoken in this life. Great as are its incentives to Reconciliation, it is never entirely resolvable into them. And the importance of that classical beginning ever consists in continuously calling back the human heart, away from all Culture and Immanence, to that which lies above both."

We thus get at last a conception which really covers, I

think, all the chief elements of this complex matter. But the reader will have noted that it does so by treating the whole problem as one of Spiritual Dynamics, and not of Intellectual Statics. For the conception holds and requires the existence and cultivation of three kinds of action and movement in the soul. There are, first, the various centres of human energy and duty of a primarily This-world character, each of which possesses its own kind and degree of autonomy, laws and obligations. There is, next, the attempt at organising an increasing interaction between, and at harmonising (whilst never emasculating or eliminating), these various, severally characteristic, systems of life and production into an ever larger ultimate unity. And, lastly, there is as strong a turning away from all this occupation with the Contingent and Finite, to the sense and apprehension of the Infinite and Abiding. And this dynamic system is so rich, even in the amount of it which can claim the practice of the majority of souls, as to require definite alternations in the occupations of such souls, ranging thus, in more or less rhythmic succession, from earth to Heaven and from Heaven back again to earth.

And so great and so inexhaustible is this living system, even by mankind at large, that it has to be more or less parcelled out amongst various groups of men, each group possessing its own predominant *attrait*,—either to work out one of those immanental interests, say Art, Natural Science, Politics; or to fructify one or more of these relatively independent interests, by crossing it with one or more of the others; or to attempt to embrace the whole of these intra-mundane interests in one preliminary final system; or to turn away from this whole system and its contents to the Transcendent and Infinite; or finally to strive to combine, as far as possible, this latter Fleeing to the Infinite with all that former Seeking of the Finite.—We shall thus get specialists within one single domain; and more many-sided workers who fertilise one Science by another; and philosophers of Science or of History, or of both, who strive to reach the *rationale* of all knowledge of the Finite and Contingent: and Ascetics and Contemplatives who, respectively, call forth and dwell upon the sense and presence of the Infinite and Abiding, underlying and accompanying all the definite apprehensions of things contingent; and finally, the minds and wills that feel called to attempt as complete a development and organisation as possible of all these movements.

13. THE SCIENTIFIC HABIT AND MYSTICISM

IN one of Trendelenburg's most penetrating essays, he shows us how, between blind Force and conscious Thought,—if we presuppose any tendency towards unity to exist between them,—there can be but three possible relations. "Either Force stands before Thought, so that Thought is not the primitive reality, but the result and accident of blind Force; or Thought stands before Force, so that blind Force is not itself the primitive reality, but the effluence of Thought; or finally, Thought and Force are, at bottom, only one and the same thing, and differ only in our mind's conception of them." And only one of these three positions can, by any possibility, be the true one: hence their internecine conflict.

Now Religion, in its normal, central stream, stands most undoubtedly for Thought before Force, the second, the Theistic view. And yet it would be profoundly impoverishing for our outlook and practice, and would but prepare a dangerous reaction in ourselves or others, were we ever to ignore the immense influence, in the history, not only of philosophical speculation, but even of religious feeling and aspiration, not indeed of the first, the Materialist, view (which owes all its strength to non-religious causes or to a rebound against religious excesses), but of the third, the Pantheistic, Monistic, view, whose classical exponent Spinoza will probably remain unto all time.

If we examine into what constitutes the religious plausibility and power of this view, we shall find, I think, that it proceeds, above all, from the fact that, only too often, the second, the Theistic view and practice, leaves almost or quite out of sight the purification and slow constitution of the Individual into a Person, by means of the Thing-element, the apparently blind Determinism of Natural Law and Natural Happenings. Yet nothing can be more certain than that we must admit and place this undeniable, increasingly obtrusive, element and power *somewhere* in our lives: if we will not own it as a means, it will grip us as our end. The unpurified, all but merely natural, animal, lustful and selfish individual man, is far too like to the brutes and plants, indeed even to the inorganic substances that so palpably surround him, for it not to be a fantastic thought to such thinkers as Spinoza (and indeed it would be an excessive effort to himself) to believe that he is likely, taken simply in these condition, to outlast, and is capable of dominating, the huge framework of the visible world, into which his whole bodily and psychical mechanism is placed, and to which it is bound by a thousand ties and closest similarities: his little selfish thinkings cannot but seem mere bubbles on a boundless expanse of mere matter; all creation cannot, surely, originate in, depend from, and move up to, a Mind and Spirit in any way like unto this trivial ingenuity.

It is true, of course, that Spinoza ended,—as far as the logic of his system went,—by "purifying" away not only this animal Individualism, but Spiritual Personality as well, and this because he takes Mathematico-Physical concepts to be as directly applicable and as adequate to Ultimate Reality as are the Ethico-Spiritual categories. We have then to admit that even so rich and rare, so deeply religious a spirit as Spinoza could insist upon purification by the "preliminary Pantheism," and yet could remain, in theory, the eager exponent of an ultimate Pantheism. Like the Greeks, he not only passes through a middle distance, a range of experience which appears dominated by austere Fate and blind Fortune, but finds Fate even in ultimate Reality. Whilst, however, the Greeks often thought of Fate as superior even to the Gods, Spinoza finds Ultimate Reality to be neither Nature nor Spirit, but simply Being in General, with a Law which is neither Natural nor Spiritual Law, but Law in general. This

General Being and General Law then bifurcate, with the most rigorous determinism and complete impartiality, step by step, into parallel and ever co-present manifestations of Nature and of Spirit, and of their respective laws, which, though different, are also each strictly determined within their own series.

But Spinoza's error here undoubtedly lies in his *de facto* violent bending (in spite of this theoretical Parallelism) of all Knowledge, Reality and Life, under the sole Mathematico-Physical categories and method; and in the insistence upon attaining to ultimate Truth by one single bound and with complete adequacy and clearness. And the greatness here consists in the keen and massive sense of three profound truths. He never forgets that Mathematico-Physical Science is rigidly determinist, and that it stands for a certain important truth and penetrates to a certain depth of reality. He never ceases to feel how impure, selfish, petty is the natural man, and how pure, disinterested, noble, can and should be the spiritual personality. And he never lets go the sense that, somehow, that science must be able to help towards this purification.

Now these three truths must be preserved, whilst the Mathematico - Physical one - sidedness and the "one - step" error must be carefully eliminated. And indeed it is plain that only by such elimination can those truths operate within a fully congenial system. For only thus, with a dissimilarity between the Ultimate, Libertarian, Spiritual Reality, and the Intermediate, Determinist, Physico-Mathematical Range, can we explain and maintain the pain, not only of the selfish but also of the true self, in face the Mere Thing; and only thus is all such pain and trouble worth having, since only thus it leads to the fuller development and the solid constitution of an abiding, interior, mental and volitional Personality.

Professor H. J. Holtzmann has got an eloquent page concerning the kind of Dualism which is more than ever desirable for souls, if they would achieve a full and virile personality in this our day. "It would appear to be the wiser course for us to recognise the incompatibility between merely natural existence and truly personal life, just as it is, in its whole acute non-reconciliation; to insert this conflict into our complete outlook on to Life in its full breadth and depth, and to find the harmonisation in God the Infinite, in whom alone such parallels can meet, and not deliberately to blind our right eye or our left, in order to force that outlook into one single aspect,—a degree of unification which, when achieved in this violent manner, would mean for us, at the same time, a point of absolute inertia, of eternal stagnation." And he then shows how it is precisely the interaction within our minds, feelings, and volitions, of, on the one hand, the boundless world of nature, with its majestic impersonality, and on the other hand, the inexhaustible, indefinitely deeper realm of personal life, as it appears within the stream of human history, which is best adapted to give us some fuller glimpses of the greatness of God and of the specific character of religion.

The religious imagination, mind, heart and will,—that is to say, the complete, fully normal human being at his deepest, —has thus been more and more forced, by an increasingly articulated experience of the forces and requirements of actual life, to hold and to practise, with ever-renewed attempts at their most perfect interstimulation and mutual supplementation, a profoundly costing, yet immensely fruitful, trinity in unity of convictions on this point.

In every time, place and race, man will continue to be or to become religious, in proportion to his efficacious faith in, and love of, the overflowing reality and worth of the great direct objects of religion,—God and the soul, and their interrelation in and through the Kingdom of God, the Church, and its Divine-Human Head,—the whole constituting God's condescension towards and immanence in man, and man's response and orientation towards the transcendent God.

And again, in every age, place and race, man will be or will become deeply religious, in proportion to the keenness with which he realises the immense need of spiritual growth and purification for his, at best, but inchoate personality.

But,—and this third point we must admit, in the precise extension and application given to it here, to be characteristically modern,—man will (if he belongs to our time and to our Western races, and is determined fully to utilise our special circumstances, lights and trials, as so many means towards his own spiritualisation) have carefully to keep in living touch with that secondary and preliminary reality, the Thing-world, the Impersonal Element, Physical Science and Determinist Law. He will have to pass and repass beneath these Caudine forks; to plunge and to replunge into and through this fiery torrent; and, almost a merely animal individual at the beginning and on this side of such docile bendings and such courageous plungings, he will (if he combines them with, and effects them through, those two other, abiding and ultimate, directly religious convictions) straighten himself up again to greater heights, and will come forth from the torrent each time a somewhat purer and more developed spiritual person than he was before such contraction and purgation.

14. SOCIAL RELIGION AND MYSTICISM

Let us take first the relation of the single human soul to its fellow-souls.

Now Kierkegaard tells us: "the Absolute is cruel, for it demands *all*, whilst the Relative ever continues to demand *some* attention from us." And the Reverend George Tyrrell, in his stimulating paper, *Poet and Mystic*, shows us that, as regards the relations between man's love for man and man's love for God, there are two conceptions and answers in reply to the question as to the precise sense in which God is "a jealous God," and demands to be loved alone. In the first, easier, more popular conception, He is practically thought of as the First of Creatures, competing with the rest for Man's love, and is here placed alongside of them. Hence the inference that whatever love they win from us by reason of their inherent goodness, is taken from Him: He is not loved perfectly, till He is loved alone. But in the second, more difficult and rarer conception, God is placed, not alongside of creatures but behind them, as the light which shines through a crystal and lends it whatever lustre it may have. He is loved here, not apart from, but through and in them. Hence if only the affection be of the right kind as to mode and object, the more the better. The love of Him is the "form," the principle of order and harmony; our natural affections are the "matter" harmonised and set in order; it is the soul, they are the body, of that one Divine Love whose adequate object is God in, and not apart from, His creatures. Thus we have already found that even the immensely abstractive and austere St. John of the Cross tells us: "No one desires to be loved except for his goodness; and when we love in this way, our love is pleasing unto God and in great liberty; and if there be attachment in it, there is greater attachment to God." And this doctrine he continuously, deliberately practises, half a century after his Profession, for he writes to his penitent, Donna Juana de Pedraças in 1589: "All that is wanting now, is that I should forget you; but consider how that is to be forgotten which is ever present to the soul."

But Father Tyrrell rightly observes: "To square this view with the general ascetic tradition of the faithful at large is exceedingly difficult." Yet I cannot help thinking that a somewhat different reconciliation, than the one attempted by him, really meets all the substantial requirements of the case.

I take it, then, that an all-important double law or twin fact, or rather a single law and fact whose unity is composed of two elements, is, to some extent, present throughout all characteristically human life, although its full and balanced realisation, even in theory and still more in practice, is ever, necessarily, a more or less unfulfilled ideal: viz. that not only there exist certain objects, acts and affections that are simply wrong, and others that are simply right or perfect, either for all men or for some men: but that there exist simply no acts and affections which, however right, however obligatory, however essential to the perfection of us all or of some of us, do not require, on our own part, a certain alternation of interior reserve and detachment away from, and of familiarity and attachment to, them and their objects. This general law applies as truly to Contemplation as it does to Marriage.

And next, the element of detachment which has to penetrate and purify simply all attachments,—even the attachment to detachment itself,—is the more difficult, the less obvious, the more profoundly spiritual and human element and movement, although only on condition that ever some amount of the other, of the outgoing element and movement, and of attachment, remains. For here, as everywhere, there is no good and operative yeast except with and in flour; there can be no purification and unity without a material and a multiplicity to purify and to unite.

And again, given the very limited power of attention and articulation possessed by individual man, and the importance to the human community of having impressive embodiments and examples of this, in various degrees and ways, universally ever all-but-forgotten, universally difficult, universally necessary, universally ennobling renunciation: we get the reason and justification for the setting apart of men specially drawn and devoted to a maximum, or to the most difficult kinds, of this renunciation. As the practically universal instinct, or rudimentary capacity, for Art, Science and Philanthropy finds its full expression in artists, scientists, philanthropists, whose specific glory and ever necessary corrective it is that they but articulate clearly, embody massively and, as it were, precipitate what is dimly and intermittingly present, as it were in solution, throughout the consciousness and requirements of Mankind; and neither the inarticulate instinct, diffused among all, would completely suffice for any one of the majority, without the full articulation by a few, nor the full articulation by this minority could thrive, even for this minority itself, were it not environed by, and did it not voice, that dumb yearning of the race at large: so, and far more, does the general religiosity and sense of the Infinite, and even its ever-present element and requirement of Transcendence and Detachment, seek and call forth some typical, wholesomely provocative incorporation,—yet, here, with an even subtler and stronger interdependence, between the general demand and the particular supply.

And note that, if the minority will thus represent a maximum of "form," with a minimum of "matter," and the majority a maximum of "matter," with a minimum of "form": yet some form as well as some matter must be held by each; and the ideal to which, by their mutual supplementations, antagonisms and corrections, they will have more and more to approximate our corporate humanity will be a maximum of "matter," permeated and spiritualised by a maximum of "form." If it is easy for the soul to let itself be invaded and choked by the wrong kind of "matter," or even simply by an excess of the right kind, so that it will be unable to stamp the "matter" with spiritual "form"; the opposite extreme also, where the spiritual forces have not left to them a sufficiency of material to penetrate or of life-giving friction to overcome, is ever a most real abuse.

15. ETERNAL LIFE GIVEN IN EXPERIENCE

ETERNAL Life, in its pregnant, concrete, ontological sense, —the operative conviction of its reality,—is not, primarily, a matter of Speculation and Philosophy, but reveals itself clearly only in the course of ages, and even then only to riper, deeper souls, as having been all along (in some manner and degree) experienced and postulated in all that men feel, will, do, and are of a characteristically human kind. It is only Religion that, in this matter, has furnished man with a vivid and concrete experience and conviction of permanent ethical and spiritual value. Philosophy, as such, has not been able to do more than analyse and clarify this religious conviction, and find, within its own domain and level, certain intimations and requirements converging towards such a conviction. It has not itself been able vividly to experience, or unshakably to affirm, a corresponding Reality as actually present and

G

ever operative in the production of these very intimations and requirements.

Eternal Life, as thus operative in man's life and discovered for us there by Religion, is not an ultimate cause, a self-subsisting entity, which (accidentally or necessarily) evolves a living subject or subjects; but it is simply the effect, the action, of a living Reality, or the effect, the interaction, of several such realities. Hence Eternal Life is no substitute for either God or man; but it is the activity, the effect, of God, or of man, or of both.

Eternal Life, in the fullest thinkable sense, involves three things—the plenitude of all goods and of all energisings that abide; the entire self-consciousness of the Being Which constitutes, and Which is expressed by, all these goods and energisings; and the pure activity, the non-successiveness, the simultaneity, of this Being in all It has, all It is. Eternal Life, in this sense, precludes not only space, not only clock-time —that artificial chain of mutually exclusive, ever equal moments,—but even *duration*, time as actually experienced by man, with its overlapping, interpenetrating successive stages. But Eternal Life precludes space and clock-time because of the very intensity of its life. The Simultaneity is here the fullest expression of the Supreme Richness, the unspeakable Concreteness, the overwhelming Aliveness of God; and is at the opposite pole from all empty unity, all mere being— any or all abstractions whatsoever.

Eternal Life, in a real, though not in the fullest sense, is attributable to man. This lesser eternal life appears to have its range between the pure Simultaneity of God, and mere Clock-Time, and to have its true form in *Duration*—an ever more or less overlapping succession, capable of being concentrated into quasi-simultaneities. And this lesser eternal life, although unending, is never boundless; nor does it (here below at least) ever become entirely actual.

Now, owing to this our likeness in unlikeness to It, the Eternal Living Spirit (though necessarily incomprehensible by our own) can be, and is, continuously apprehended by us—since that Spirit really penetrates us and all Its creatures.

And this our apprehension occurs, not separately, abstractively, clearly, statically; but ever more or less in, or contrasting with, finite, contingent, changing things; and it does so obscurely, yet with an immensely far-reaching dynamic operativeness. From hence alone can spring our unquenchable thirst after the Eternal and Abiding, the Objective, the Final; and our intolerable pain at the very idea of being entirely confined to the merely fleeting, subjective, momentary —a pain which persists even if we extend the validity and permanence of our life's experience to all humanity, taken simply as such. For this thirst and pain could not be so ineradicable and so profoundly operative, and could not constitute so decidedly the very flower and test of our fullest manhood, did it not proceed from a Reality or Realities deeper than any exclusively human projection or analysis whatsoever.

Nor will it suffice to refer this experience to the operation, within us, of Spirit in the making—to the gradual and painful coming to self-consciousness of the one concrete Universe (of which we form an integral part) precisely through our spirits and their growth. For we have no other instance of an unrealised perfection producing such pain and joy, such volitions, such endlessly varied and real results; and all by means of just this vivid and persistent impression that this Becoming is an already realised Perfection. Religion would thus deceive us precisely in the conviction and act which are central in all its higher forms and stages—Adoration. And the noblest root and flower of the Jewish-Christian religion and of European civilisation,—the sense of *Givenness*, of grace, of dependence upon a Reality other and higher than ourselves, singly or collectively—would also have to go. For such a habit of mind requires (logically, and in the long run also practically) my belief in a Reality not less but more self-conscious than myself—a Living One Who lives first and lives perfectly, and Who, touching me, the inferior, derivative life, can cause me to live by His aid and for His sake.

Thus such a sense of the Divine Eternity or Simultaneity will be developed by man within, and in contrast to, *duration*.

And it will be strengthened in proportion as man effects, in others and in himself, results spiritually real within this (for him) real duration; and as he collects his spirit (in alternation to such action) away from all particular strivings, and concentrates it, more exclusively, upon the Divine Living One —the ever-present Background and Support of his little life. *Time* then, in the sense of *duration* (with the spiritual intercourse and the growth in spiritual character which we develop and consolidate in such time), is, for us men, not a barrier against Eternal Life, but the very stuff and means in and by which we vitally experience and apprehend that Life. Man's temporal life is thus neither a theory nor even a vision; nor something that automatically unrolls itself. Nor, on the other hand, is it, even at its deepest, itself the Ultimate experienced by man. But man's life is one long, variously deep and wide, rich and close, tissue of (ever more or less volitional) acts and habits—instinctive, rational, emotive; of strivings, shrinkings, friction, conflict, suffering, harmony and joy; and of variously corresponding permanent effectuations in and by the spirit thus active. And hence man's life is full of cost, tension and drama. Yet such an individual life never experiences, indeed never is constituted by, itself alone; but it is ever endlessly affected by the environment and stimulation of other realities, organisms, spirits; and it ever itself correspondingly affects such other realities. And the whole of this inter-connected realm of spirits is upheld, penetrated, stimulated, and articulated by the one Infinite Spirit, God. Thus a real succession, real efforts, and the continuous sense of limitation and inadequacy are the very means in and through which man apprehends increasingly (if only he thus loves and wills) the contrasting yet sustaining Simultaneity, Spontaneity, Infinity, and pure Action of the Eternal Life of God.

But also *spatial* concepts and imagery play two important rôles in the full and normal consciousness of Eternal Life. For whether or no the spatial category abides with man in the Beyond, in this earthly life at least he cannot persistently and vividly apprehend even the most spiritual realities, as distinct and different from each other, except by picturing them as disparate in space. Now a vivid consciousness of the deep distinction and difference (within all their real affinity and closeness of intercourse) between God and man, and the continuous, keen sense that all man has, does, and is of good is ever, in its very possibility, a free gift of God, constitutes the very core of religion. Hence the spatial imagery, which, by picturing God as *outside* the soul and Heaven as *above* the earth, helps to enforce this fundamental truth, is highly valuable—as valuable, indeed, as the imagery (spatial still) which helps to enforce the complementary truth of God's likeness to the soul and His penetration of it, by picturing God as *within* the soul and Heaven as *in* this room.

And again, the principles, ideals and picturings of Mathematics and Physics (with their insistence upon ruthless law, utter interchangeableness of all individual instances, and flawless determinism) have a very certain place and function in the full spiritual life of the soul. For they provide that *preliminary* Pantheism, that transition through fate and utter dehumanisation, which will allow the soul to affirm, ultimately and as ultimate, a Libertarianism and Personalism free from all sentimentality or slovenliness, and immune against the attacks of *ultimate* Pantheism, which can *now* be vanquished as only the caricature of the poorer half of a far richer whole. Yet for the sufficient operativeness of that Mathematico-Physical world and outlook, vivid pictures of space and of quasi-space—clock-time—are absolutely necessary.

Finally, *material* things (however dead or seemingly dead) and abstract propositions (however empty if taken alone) can, and do, continually thwart or stimulate human spirits —within this life at least. Because God is Spirit, and because man is spirit and is more and more to constitute himself a personality, it does not follow that man is to effect this solely by means of spirits and personalities, divine and human. Nor does man require material things only for the expression and communication of a personality already developed independently of such material things. But, as in all mental apprehension and conviction there is always, somewhere, the element of the stimulation of the senses, so also does the spirit awaken to its own life and powers, on occasion of contact and conflict with material things. Hence Eternal Life will (here below at least) not mean for man aloofness from matter and the bodily senses, nor even a restriction of their use to means of spiritual self-expression; but it will include also a rich and wise contact with, and an awakening by means of, matter and *things*.

All this costly acceptance and affirmation of Eternal Life will be found to form the sole self-consistent alternative to a (more or less obscure, but none the less real and immensely operative) refusal of man's true call, and the election of the (always easier) course of evading the soul's deepest longings and requirements. This evasion will strengthen the animal instincts and chaotic impulsions of the man's complex being; and will weaken those higher claims of human reason and of spiritual organisation and transfiguration. And the soul may at last arrive at an abiding disintegration and self-contradiction, and be alive only in a superficial, distracted degree and way. And this shrinkage and pain of self-contradiction and self-stultification, which the soul itself has (at least indirectly) willed, would be the soul's death.

In any case, it seems clear that, with regard to a self-stultifying soul, neither Total Annihilation nor a consciousness equal, though contrary, to that of the soul which practises and experiences Eternal Life, meets the various facts as well as does the doctrine that the effects of such full self-determinations indeed abide both for good and for evil, but that they differ not only in quality, but also in intensity. Thus, though no soul would ever cease completely, and none of its fullest spiritual and moral self-determinations would ever, in their effects upon such a soul itself, be as though they had not been, the contrast between the saved and the lost soul would be between two different quantities, as well as qualities, of life. And whereas the sense of Time, in the most fully *eternalised* of human spirits, would be so *Durational* as almost to lapse into Simultaneity, the sense of Time with *pheno-*

menalised human souls would lose almost all Duration and be quite close to Clock-Time—to the mechanical movement of soulless matter. This is certainly the case in this life; here we are merely assuming that what already *is*, as the deepest of our experiences, will continue to obtain as long as we last at all.

Eternal Life, conceived as above, will be found to include and to require a deep sense of human Weakness and of man's constant need of the Divine Prevenience, and again of the reality of Sin and of our various inclinations to it; but also to exclude all conceptions of the total corruption of human nature, of the essential impurity of the human body, or of the utter debilitation of the will. The Pauline, Augustinian, Lutheran, Calvinist, Jansenist trend, impressive though it is, will have to be explained, in part, as a good and necessary (or at least as an excusable, temporary) corrective of some contrary excess; and, for the rest, it will have to suffer incorporation within a larger whole, which, in appearance more commonplace, is yet in reality indefinitely richer — the doctrine and practice of Jesus Christ Himself. "In my flesh abideth no good thing," will have somehow to be integrated within "the spirit indeed is willing, but the flesh is weak."

And lastly, Eternal Life will not be simply a Moralism, with just the addition of a theoretical or practical reference to God, as the sanction and source of morality. Such a Religion has, fortunately, never existed except in the heads of some Philosophers. In its central consciousness and action, this Life will be indeed religious, hence Adoration, a Cultus —a deep, rich, spiritual Cultus, but a Cultus still. This for the ingoing, recollective movement. And the outgoing movement will not only discover God as hidden in the deepest ideals, necessities and impulsions of Ethics, but also in the fullest strivings of Art and in the widest and most delicate attempts of the speculative and analytical reason. God is no less truly the ultimate Source, Sustainer and End of perfect Beauty and of utter Truth than of complete Goodness and of the purest Self-Donation.

The sense, then, of Eternal Life requires, for its normal,

general, and deepest development, *Duration*, history; Space, institutions; Material Stimulations, and symbols, something sacramental; and Transcendence, a movement away from all and every culture and civilisation, to the Cross, to asceticism, to interior nakedness and the Beyond. Thus our very sense of, and search for, Eternal Life will, apparently, re-enforce or re-instate all the exclusive ecclesiastical claims, the dread oppressions and persecutions of the past. The bitterest of all earthly hatreds would thus seem to be an essential condition of heavenly love. Yet Religion, taken as here supposed, would, in three ways, powerfully counteract these very certain and most grave dangers.

Religion is here assumed, on the evidence of undeniable history, to exist and to function in various stages and degrees of depth, purity and articulation, and with variously intense and true revelations from God through prophets inspired by Himself. And men who are in the fuller, truer, purer stages and degrees may increasingly learn to recognise, in the positive and fruitful constituents and effects of other religions, something good and from God — fragments and preparations for such fuller truth as they themselves possess.

Again Religion, even in its totality, is here supposed to be indeed the deepest, yet not the only activity of man's spirit; and each of these several activities is taken to possess its own immanental laws, duties and rights. And Religion has the difficult, yet quite feasible and supremely fruitful, task of ever respecting, whilst ever more and more harmonising, purifying, and utilising, each and all of these various realms, under penalty of finding, otherwise, that itself is more and more bereft of necessary material and stimulation, and that all the other activities of man's many-levelled nature escape more and more into a wilderness of rank secularism.

And finally, in this scheme of life the first cause, and the ultimate unity, of all things is found in God, as the supremely rich, self-revealing, self-giving Eternal Life. This ultimate Living Unity is trusted, and, in the long run, is mysteriously found, to permeate all, and to bring fruitfulness to any one good activity, from the other levels and kinds of goodness, even though apparently most distant or most contrary. And it is just because of this fundamental, ineradicable inter-connection, and of the soul's conviction of it, that man's spirit can drive home this or that research or interest, and can remain sure of contributing (in proportion to his selfless attention to the immanent necessities and prophetic hints of its subject-matter) something of abiding value to the other departments and levels of man's energisings, and, ultimately, to his further seeking and finding of Eternal Life.

The many requirements thus articulated cannot fail to appear intolerably complex both to those who attempt to stand aloof from all Religion, and to those who, with little or no analysis or theory, are directly absorbed in its practice. Like all living realities, living Religion possesses a sovereign spontaneity and rich simplicity which seem to render all attempts at analysis an insult. Indeed, Religion in particular possesses three essentials, which continually bring expansion and simplicity to its tension and complexity.

Religion is essentially Social *horizontally*; in the sense that each several soul is *therefore* unique because intended to realise just *this* post, function, joy, effect within the total organism of all souls. Hence no soul is expected to be a "jack-of-all-trades," but only to develop fully its own special gifts and *attraits*, within and through, and for, that larger organism of the human family, in which other souls are as fully to develop their own differing gifts and *attraits*, as so many supplements and compensations to the others. The striving of any one soul can thus be peaceful, since limited in its range to what this particular soul, at its best, most really wants and loves.

And Religion is essentially Social *vertically*—indeed here is its deepest root. It is unchangeably a faith in God, a love of God, an intercourse with God; and though the soul cannot abidingly abstract itself from its fellows, it can and ought frequently to recollect itself in a simple sense of God's presence. Such moments of direct preoccupation with God alone bring a deep refreshment and simplification to the soul.

And Religion, in its fullest development, essentially requires, not only this our little span of earthly years, but a life beyond. Neither an Eternal Life that is already fully achieved here below, nor an Eternal Life to be begun and known solely in the beyond, satisfies these requirements. But only an Eternal Life already begun and truly known in part here, though fully to be achieved and completely to be understood hereafter, corresponds to the deepest longings of man's spirit as touched by the prevenient Spirit, God. And hence, again, a peace and simplification. For that doubly Social life I try to lead here (though most real, and though itself already its own exceeding great reward) constitutes, after all, but the preliminary practice, the getting ready, for ampler, more expansive, more utterly blissful energisings in and for man, the essentially durational, quasi-eternal, and God, the utterly Abiding, the pure Eternal Life.

16. THE SENSE OF ETERNAL LIFE

THE complex of vivid, operative convictions connected with Eternal Life is fundamentally fivefold. And each of these convictions awakens and feeds special habits and capacities, which are so many true and potent antidotes to the evils considered above.

There is, first, a keen yet double sense of *Abidingness*—an absolute Abidingness, pure Simultaneity, Eternity, in God; and a relative abidingness, a quasi-eternity, Duration, in man (*qua* personality). And the Eternity is always experienced by man only within, together with, and in contrast to, the Duration. And both Eternity and Duration stand out, in man's deepest consciousness, with even painful contrast, against all mere Succession, all sheer flux and change.

Here the special value lies in the double sense that we are indeed actually touched, penetrated, and supported by the purely Eternal; and yet that we ourselves shall never, either here or hereafter, be more than quasi-eternal, durational. For only this double sense will save us from the perilous alternatives of an uncreaturely sheer fixity and an animal mere flux and change. We thus gain a perennial source of continuity and calm.

There is, next, the keen sense of *Otherness in Likeness*. We are genuinely like, and we are genuinely unlike, God, the Realised Perfection. Hence there is ever a certain tension, a feeling of limitation or of emptiness, a looking for a centre outside of, or other than, our own selves.

Here again this double sense will be profoundly helpful in our troubles. For thus we are never free to lose reverence for the deepest of what we are, since it is like God, and actually harbours God. And yet we may never lose humility and a thirst for purification, since even the deepest and best of ourselves never is, never will be, God; and since all that we actually are is full of weakness and of manifold sins and faulty habits. And so we find a continual reason for self-respect, humility, contrition, each aiding and penetrating the other; and for a faith and certainty, which will never be arrogant, and for a diffidence, which will never be sceptical.

There is, thirdly, the keen sense of *Other-Worldliness in contrast with This-Worldliness*. There is here a lively conviction that our spiritual personality, and its full beatitude, can never be attained in this life, but only in the other life, after death; and yet that the other life can be begun in this life, indeed that we are, all of us, more or less solicited, here and now, by that other life, and that we cannot consummate it *there*, unless we begin it *here*. And, in this case, as everywhere, the greater and ultimate has to awake and to grow within us, in and through, and in contrast with, the lesser and (eventually) secondary.

This double sense is, again, a deep help in all our trials. For thus we are pricked on to labour energetically at the improvement of man's earthly lot, in all its stages and directions; but we do so without philistinism, impatience, or fanaticism, since we are fully convinced (even before beginning) that these attempts, could they all succeed, would not, could not, ever satisfy man, when once he is fully awake. And this applies, in its degree, even to our spirituality, even

to the Church. Even these are, in considerable part, preparatory, educative, during this our short schooltime, our
years of training, upon earth—a necessary and noble function,
and one that is fundamentally rooted in Him Who Abides
and in the quasi-eternal within ourselves; yet one which
(taken as it stands here on earth) is not throughout an end,
the end, but is a means, or, at best, *the* means. We thus find
perpetual escape from all pedantry or feverishness, and this
through the gain of an unconquerable, because sober,
optimism.

There is, fourthly, the keenest sense of *Reality*. Our analyses,
theories, hypotheses, our very denials and scepticisms, all
presuppose realities which environ and influence us, real
beings; realities which, together with us real men, constitute
one real world. And throughout, and within, and over
against, all these realities is *the* Reality of realities, the Eternal
Spirit, God. Indeed, this Source and Sustenance of the other
realities is apprehended by us ever with, and in, and through,
and over against, those other, various realities that impinge
upon our many-levelled lives, And thus our highest certainties
awaken with, and require, our lower and lowest ones.

This double sense again will greatly aid us. For it will
make us profoundly concrete, historical, incarnational,
ontological, real; yet all this without a touch of inflation. And
it will fill us with dauntless faith, courage and joy, yet ever
also with the creaturely temper—with respect for the body,
for things, for matter: and will keep us ever averse to all
abstract and subjectivist schemes.

And finally, there is the keen sense of *Unity in Multiplicity
and of Multiplicity in Unity*—of the Organism. Everywhere we
find in the real world only such organisms—systems, families,
complexes; nowhere sheer, mere unity or units. God
Himself (in the deep rich Christian orthodoxy) is a Trinity
of Persons; Christ is a Duality of Natures; the Humanity
of Christ and of all men is a Trinity of Powers. Our bodies
are wondrous organisms, our minds are still more wonder-
fully organic; and the two together form an organisation of
an even more marvellous unity in multiplicity. And yet it

is not even such a single man who is the true, fundamental social unit, but the family, in which the father, mother and child are each *sui generis* and essential, as non-interchangeable parts of this rich organism. Thus from a lichen or seaweed up to God Himself — the unspeakable Richness (because the incomprehensibly manifold Unity and complete Organisation)—we find ever increasingly rich, organised unities. And the great social complexes of Society and the State, of Economics, Science, Art, are all similarly possessed of specific laws of organisation. They are strong and beneficent only as special wholes possessed of special parts, which wholes again have to grow and fructify in contact, contrast and conflict with other such complexes without, and the ever more or less disorderly elements within, themselves.

Here, again, we find an immense help. For thus we are all taught Reverence for each other's spiritual individuality, and for the characteristics of all the great organisms; since each is necessary for all the others. And we gain in Public Spirit; since we feel keenly that no individual or organisation, however essential and sacred, can live fully and fruitfully except by living also with and for other individuals and organisations. And, perhaps above all, the religious passion can thus, at last, more and more require and seek the scientific, and the other noble, passions of mankind. For here man has to grow with and through other men and other things, never simply within and through himself. And thus his very religion here drives him to find checks and obstacles even to his standards and ideals—sure, as he is, that he requires purification even in the best of what he is and has, and that God, who has ordered all things to co-operate towards the good of those who seek and love Him, will ever help his soul to find His Peace and Eternity in even the severest storms and wreckage of its earthly times.

With regard to specially precious manifestations of the experience and conviction of Eternal Life, of God with man, within the authoritative Institutions, in these our times, we can again point to the impartial testimony of Sir Charles Booth. In general, "the clergy and ministers" amongst the

London poor, he tells us, "have no authority that is recognised, but their professional character remains . . . and their
manner is somewhat resented. In the case of the Roman
Catholic priesthood alone do we find the desired combination of professionalism and authority, resting not on the
individual but on the Church he serves; and where most
nearly approached, it is by the lives of some of the High
Church clergy" (op. cit., p. 428). And in English literature
generally we find poignant expressions of this Other-Worldliness fostered (in various yet everywhere real ways) by Religious
Traditions and Institutions. Thus we get Claude Monte-
fiore's moving pages upon Prayer, in his *Liberal Judaism*,
1907; Frederick Robertson's great sermon on "The Loneliness
of Christ"; Dean Church's study of the sense of God in the
Psalms, as contrasted with the Vedas; and many an address
in J. H. Newman's *Parochial and Plain Sermons* and *Sermons
to Mixed Congregations*. Then for the Russian Church, we
have the striking extracts from the Diary of Father John
(Sergieff) of Cronstadt, published in English as *My Life
in Christ*, in 1897.

And for deep spirituality and heroism in the Roman
Catholic Church, the present writer's mind dwells ever
specially upon four examples.

There is the rough uncultured Belgian, Father Damien,
deliberately contracting and dying the loathsome, slow death
of a leper, from love of God in men utterly without claims
of any other kind upon him, away in an island lost in the
ocean at the Antipodes, as Robert Louis Stevenson has
unforgettably described the simple, splendid life.

And there is, again, Jean Baptiste Vianney, the now
canonised simple peasant Curé of Ars. How impressive are
the accounts by the Abbé Monnin, an eye-witness of the
Curé's utter absorption in God and in souls, each ever
inciting the other, and the joyous expansion of his entire
nature through this keen sense and love! (*Le Curé d'Ars*,
12th ed., 2 vols., 1874, is before me). And in the *Spirit of
the Curé d'Ars*, chronicled by the same, we find numberless
deeply spontaneous sayings, such as the following: "Time

never seems long in prayer. I know not whether we can
even wish for heaven!" Yet "the fish swimming in a little
rivulet is well off, because it is in its element; but it is still
better in the sea." "When we pray, we should open our
heart to God, like a fish when it sees the wave coming."
"Do you see, my children, except God, nothing is solid—
nothing, nothing! If it is life, it passes away; if it is fortune,
it crumbles away; if it is health, it is destroyed; if it is repu-
tation, it is attacked. We are scattered like the wind." "You
say it is hard to suffer? No, it is easy; it is happiness. Only
we must love while we suffer, and suffer whilst we love. On
the way of the cross, you see, my children, only the first step
is painful. Our greatest cross is the fear of crosses" (English
translation, pp. 28, 40, 114).

And then there is Eugénie Smet, the daughter of a burgher
of Lille (1825–71), who, as Mère Marie de la Providence,
founded an Order of devoted women, at work, even before
her death, as far as India and China; who insisted upon
remaining in Paris throughout the siege and the Commune,
1870–1; and who slowly died there, in agonies of cancer,
utterly absorbed with joy in God, the Eternal and utterly
Real, and with tender and unceasing activity towards His
poor and sick around her. In the midst of these immense
trials she was wont to say: "Let us feel that Eternity is begun;
whatever pain we are going through, let us make joy out of
that thought." And: "In all things I can only see God alone;
and, after all, that is the only way to be happy. If once we
begin to look at secondary causes, there is an end of peace"
(Lady Georgiana Fullerton, *Life of Mère Marie de la Providence*,
4th ed., 1904, pp. 241, 237).

And finally, there is before my mind, with all the vividness
resulting from direct personal intercourse and deep spiritual
obligations, the figure of the Abbé Huvelin, who died only
in 1910. A gentleman by birth and breeding, a distinguished
Hellenist, a man of exquisitely piercing, humorous mind, he
could readily have become a great editor or interpreter of
Greek philosophical or patristic texts, or a remarkable Church
historian. But this deep and heroic personality deliberately

preferred "to write in souls," whilst occupying, during thirty-five years, a supernumerary, unpaid post in a large Parisian parish. There, suffering from gout in the eyes and brain, and usually lying prone in a darkened room, he served souls with the supreme authority of self-oblivious love, and brought light and purity and peace to countless troubled, sorrowing, or sinful souls. His Curé, of St. Augustin, has spoken well of this great figure; Adeline, Duchess of Bedford, a devoted Anglican, has published a vivid, and almost entirely accurate, sketch of him; and now three volumes have been issued containing the careful reports, taken down by certain of his hearers, of familiar addresses which are full (at least for those who knew and loved the saintly speaker) of sudden gleams of the deepest spiritual insight and love.

Thus, in the "Conferences on some of the Spiritual Guides of the Seventeenth Century," he says, in connection with St. François de Sales: "When once we desire a thing to be true, we are very near to finding it true"; and "a spirituality of the little-by-little is not an enfeebled spirituality." And, in criticism of Jansenism: "There exist families of souls which are determined to find the principle of tranquillity within their own selves; they want to cast anchor within their own depths. But we have to cast anchor, not below, but above; it is in God, in His goodness, that we have to found our hope." And finally: "God, who might have created us directly, employs, for this work, our parents, to whom He joins us by the tenderest ties. He could also save us directly, but He saves us, in fact, by means of certain souls, which have received the spiritual life before ourselves, and which communicate it to us, because they love us."

Of Père de Condren, Abbé Huvelin says: "He has hardly written any books; he wrote in souls"; "he experienced great interior derelictions and strange obscurities—a man is not called to form other souls without having to suffer much"; and "his call was not to live for himself, but to live utterly for Him who gave him all things."

In speaking of M. Olier, M. Huvelin exclaims: "Strip yourself of self, love God, love men; what are all these other things that seem of such importance to you?" And he declares: "The world sees, in this or that soul, the passions, the bitter waters which fill it; but we priests, we seek, beneath these bitter waters, the little spring of sweet waters, Arethusa, that little thread of grace, which, though deeper down and more hidden, is nevertheless most truly there." And again: "The true means to attract a soul, is not to attenuate Christian doctrine, but to present it in its full force, because then we present it in its beauty. For beauty is one of the proofs of truth."

As to St. Vincent de Paul, he tells us: "See the reason why, in this life so devoted to his fellow-creatures, you will find something austere, and shut up in God: it is that the Saint feels the necessity, for himself and for others, thus to re-immerse, to temper anew his soul in the source of all love."

And lastly, with respect to the great Trappist Abbé de Rancé, he observes: "When something very high and in-accessible is put before human nature it feels itself impelled to attain to that height, by something mysterious and divine which God infuses into the soul." And: "There is ever something mysterious in every conversion; we never succeed in fully understanding even our own"; nevertheless, "the voice of God does not speak in moments of exaltation. Such converted souls would say: 'It was in the hour when I was most mistress of myself, most recollected, least agitated, that I heard the voice of God.'"

Thus souls, who live an heroic spiritual life within great religious traditions and institutions, attain to a rare volume and vividness of religious insight, conviction and reality. They can, at their best, train other souls, who are not all unworthy of such training, to a depth and tenderness of full and joyous union with God, the Eternal, which utterly surpasses, not only in quantity but in quality, what we can and do find amongst souls outside all such Institutions, or not directly taught by souls trained within such traditions. And thus we find here, more clearly than in any philosopher as such, that Eternal Life consists in the most real of relations

H

between the most living of realities—the human spirit and the Eternal Spirit, God; and in the keen sense of His Perfection, Simultaneity and Prevenience, as against our imperfection, successiveness and dependence. And we find that this sense is awakened in, and with, the various levels of our nature; in society as well as in solitude; by things as well as by persons. In such souls, then, we catch the clearest glimpses of what, for man even here below, can be and is Eternal Life.

BOOK II

THE SOUL OF A SAINT

BOOK II

THE SOUL OF A SAINT

17. ST. CATHERINE OF GENOA

QUITE special disadvantages attach to the study of this
particular Saint. Her character, for one thing, is distinctly
wanting in humour, in that shrewd mother-wit which is so
marked a feature in some of the great Spanish Mystics, in
St. Teresa especially, but which is not quite absent even in
the less varied and very austere St. John of the Cross. There
is, on the contrary, a certain monotony, a somewhat wearying
vehemence, about our Genoese. Her experience, again, is
without the dramatic vicissitudes of the reform of an Order
or the foundation of Monasteries, as with St. Teresa; or of
contact and even conflict with the temporal and spiritual
officiality of her time, as with St. Catherine of Siena. Nor
is her life lit up by the beautiful warmth of happy, requited
domestic affection, nor is it varied and extended by the rich
possession of children of her own. And again her life is obscured
and complicated, at least for our comprehension of it, by a
nervous ill-health which it is impossible for us to care about,
in itself. And, finally, special difficulties attach to the understanding of her. Unlike St. Teresa, St. John of the Cross,
and many other Saints, she did not herself write one line of
her so-called "Writings"; and yet it is these, mostly very
abstruse and at times all but insuperably difficult, "Writings,"
records which did not attain their present form and bulk till
a good forty years after her death, that contain the most
original part of her legacy to the Church.

Yet all this is balanced if not exceeded by a rare and stimulating combination of characteristics. The very ordinariness

of her external lot,—a simple wife and widow, at no time belonging to any Religious Order or Congregation; the apparently complete failure of her earthly life, which gives occasion to the birth within her of the heavenly one; the rich variety and contrasts of her princely birth and social position, and the lowly, homely activity and usefulness of her forty years of devotedness; the unusually perfect combination of a great external action and administrative capacity with a lofty contemplation; the apparent suddenness and whole-hearted swiftness of her Conversion, succeeded by the long years of interior conflict and painful growth, unhelped, practically unknown, by anyone but God's inspiring Spirit, and these years again followed by a period of requiring and practising the ordinary mediate docilities; the strange nervous health of especially her later years, so carefully and truthfully recorded for us, a psychic condition interesting if but for her own lofty superiority to attaching any direct importance or necessarily miraculous meaning to it: all this, even if it were all, helps to give an extraordinary richness and instructiveness to her life.

But stimulating, transfiguring, embracing all this, appears her special spiritual apprehension and teaching, of a quite extraordinary depth, breadth and balance, distinction and refinement. The central oneness of the soul's nature and sufferings and joys here and hereafter, and the resultant psychological character and appeal, to be found in all true experience of forecasting of such things; the never-ceasing difference between Spirit and Matter; the incomprehensibility, but indefinite apprehensibleness, for the clean of heart, of God and spiritual realities; the pure disinterestedness of His love for us, and the corresponding distinterestedness of all true love for Him; the universality of His light and love, and the excess of His mercy above His justice; the innate affinity between every human soul and Him, and the immanence of Himself within us; the absence of all arbitrary or preternatural action in the forces and realities constitu-tive of the spiritual world and life; the constant union of right suffering with deep peace, and the final note of joy and of self-conquering triumph issuing from complete self-renunciation: all this and much more appears in her teaching with a spontaneity, breadth and balance peculiarly its own.

No wonder then that, from the contemporary circle of her devoted friends and disciples onwards, Catherine should have attracted, throughout the centuries and in many lands, a remarkable number of deep minds and saintly characters. The ardent young Spaniard, St. Aloysius Gonzaga, and the shrewd and solid Savoyard Bishop, St. François de Sales, love to quote and dwell upon her example and her doctrine. Mature theologians, such as Cardinal Bellarmine, the hard-headed controversialist; Cardinal Bona, the liturgical and devotional writer; and Cardinal de Berulle, the mystical-minded founder of the French Oratory; and again, such varied types of devotedness as Madame Acarie, the foundress of the French Reformed Carmelites; the Baron de Renty, that noble Christian soldier; Bossuet, the hard and sensible; and Fénelon, the elastic and exquisite,—all love her well. Such thoroughly representative ascetical writers again as the Spanish Jesuits Francisco Arias and Alfonzo Rodriguez; the French ones, Saint-Jure and Jean Joseph Surin; the Italian, Paolo Segneri; the Pole, Lancisius; and the German, Drexel, all drew food and flame from her character and doctrine. Then at the beginning of the nineteenth century, Friedrich von Schlegel, the penetrating, many-sided leader of the German Romantic school, translated her *Dialogue*. In our own time Father Isaac Hecker, that striking German-American, loved her as a combination of contemplation and external action; Father Faber strongly endorsed her conception of Purgatory; Cardinal Manning occasioned and prefaced an admirable translation of her *Treatise*; and Cardinal Newman has incorporated her Purgatorial teaching in the noblest of his poems, *The Dream of Gerontius*. Indeed, General Charles Gordon also can not unfairly be claimed as her unconscious disciple, since her teaching, embodied in Cardinal Newman's poem, was, besides the Bible and *Imitation*, his one written source of strength and consolation during that noble Christian captain's heroic death-watch at Khartoum. And among recent writers, Mr. Aubrey de Vere has given us a refined poetic paraphrase of her *Treatise*, and Father George Tyrrell has developed its theme in one of his most striking Essays.

I too have, in my own way, long cared for her example and teaching, and for the great questions and solutions suggested by both. A dozen times and more have I visited and lingered over the chief scenes of her activity; and the literary sources of all our knowledge of her life have been dwelt upon by me for twenty years and more.

I have but very few new details and combinations to offer, in so far as her external life is concerned. It is with regard to the growth of her historic image and the curious vicissitudes which I have been able to trace in the complication of her "Writings"; as to her spirit and teaching; and as to the place and function to be allotted in the religious life to such realities and phenomena as those presented by her, that I hope to be able to contribute something of value. For although the substance and the primary phenomena of religion are eternal, they appear in each soul with an individuality and freshness pathetically unique; and their attempted analysis and apprehension, and their relations to the other departments of human life, necessarily grow and vary. Indeed it would be truly sad, and would rightly tempt to disbelief in an overruling Providence and divine education of the human race, if the four centuries that intervene between our Saint and ourselves had taught us little or nothing of value, in such matters of borderland and interpretation as nervous health, the psychology of religion, and the distinguishing differences between Christian and Neo-Platonic Mysticism. Whole Sciences, indeed the Scientific, above all the Historic spirit itself, have arisen or have come to maturity since her day. Hence the realities of her life, as of every religious life, remain fresh indeed with the deathless vitality of love and grace, and but very partially explicable still; and yet the highest intellectual honour of each successive period should be found in an ever-renewed attempt at an ever less inadequate apprehension and utilisation of these highest and deepest manifestations of Authority, Reason and Experience, —of the Divine in our poor human life.

18. THE MARRIAGE OF CATHERINE

The Convent Chaplain was Catherine's Confessor, and through him she attempted to gain the permission of the Nuns to enter their Community. But whilst they hesitated and put her off, on the very reasonable ground of her unusual youth, her father died (end of 1461); and a particular combination, from amongst the endless political rivalries and intrigues of Genoa, soon closed in upon the beautiful girl, member of the greatest of the Guelph families of that turbulent time. It was a bad and sorry business, and one likes to think that the father, had he lived, would not thus have sacrificed his daughter. For if in Shakespeare's *Romeo and Juliet* we have two youthful lovers joining hands and hearts, in spite of the secular enmity of their respective houses; here, alas! in real life, we have the contrary spectacle, the deep because dreary tragedy of two great rival factions making— rather, hoping to make—peace, by the enforced union of two mutually indifferent and profoundly unsuited young people.

Not but that socially the two were admirably matched. For Giuliano Adorno belonged to a family hardly inferior in antiquity and splendour to Catherine's own. Six different Adorni had been Doges of Genoa in 1363, 1385, 1413, 1443, 1447, 1461; and the one of 1413 had been Giuliano's own grandfather. They were Lords of the Greek Island of Chios (Scio), which they had helped to conquer for Genoa in 1349.

And now the last Doge of the family, Prospero Adorno, had just been driven from the Ducal throne by Paolo Campofregoso, the strong-willed representative of the great rival, though also Ghibelline, family of the Fregosi. Campofregoso was now both Duke and Archbishop of Genoa. By an alliance with the Fieschi, the most powerful of the Guelph families, the Adorni could hope, in their turn, to oust the Fregosi, and to reinstate themselves at the head of the great Republic. The ideals, antipathies or indifference of a girl of sixteen were not allowed to stand in the way; and so the contract was signed on 13 January, 1463.

The marriage was celebrated soon afterwards in the Cathedral of San Lorenzo, in the Chapel of St. John the Baptist, since the Campanaro family, which had built it in 1299, and the Adorni, who had married into and succeeded the Campanaro, were excepted from the rule prohibiting the access of women to this Chapel. Since Cardinal Giorgio Fieschi had recently died, Bishop Napoleone Fieschi, of Albenga, presided at the ceremony.

Giuliano's father was dead; only his widowed mother, Tobia dei Franchi, remained. It was, however, with Catherine's mother, in the old Palazzo near the Cathedral, that the young couple were to live, and actually stayed, during the first two years.

Giuliano was young and rich; his two elder brothers occupied high naval posts; his first cousin, Agostino Adorno, was a man of noble character and great initiative; and a descendant of this cousin, also Agostino, was later on Beatified. But Giuliano himself did at first worse than nothing, and never did much throughout his life. A man of an undisciplined, wayward, impatient and explosive temper; selfish and self-indulgent; a lover of obscure and useless, in one instance criminal, squandering of his time, money, health and affections, he did not deserve the rare woman who had been sold to him; and would possibly indeed have managed to be a better man with a wife he had really loved, or with one of a temperament and outlook more ordinary and nearer to his own. As it was, he was hardly ever at home, and, according to his own later penitent admission and testamentary provisions, he was, some time during the first ten years of his marriage, gravely unfaithful to his wife.

Catherine, on her part, spent the first five of these dreary years in sad and mournful loneliness, at first in her mother's house, and afterwards, at least in the winter-time, in Giuliano's own palace, a building which stood exactly where now stands the Church of St. Philip Neri, in the Via Lomellina (at that time, Via Sant' Agnese), and near the Piazza Annunziata. In the summer-time she would stay, mostly alone again, at Giuliano's country seat at Prà on the Western Riviera, just beyond Pegli, and six English miles from Genoa.

This latter property is still in existence, but was, some twenty years ago, on the extinction of the male line of the Adorni, sold to the Piccardo family. The present moderate-sized house, standing close to the high-road and sea-beach, although evidently rebuilt (probably on a considerably smaller scale) since Catherine's time, no doubt occupies part at least of the old site. But the Chapel which, in the Saint's days, adjoined the house, was described by Vallebona (in 1887) as turned into a stable; and in April 1902 an elderly servingman of the Piccardo family showed me the precise spot, on a now level meadow expanse closely adjoining the house, where he himself, some fifteen years since, had helped to pull down this chapel-stable. He showed me the (probably seventeenth-century) picture representing the scene of the Saint's conversion, which had, at that time, been still in this building, and which is now hung up in a small Confraternity-Chapel near by in Prà.

19. THE THEOLOGICAL VALUE OF CATHERINE'S SPIRIT

Now it is a well-known principle of Catholic theology, propounded with classic clearness and finality by Pope Benedict XIV., in his standard work *On the Beatification and Canonisation of the Servants of God*, that such an approbation of their sayings or writings binds neither the Church nor her individual members to more than the two points, which are alone necessary with respect to the possibility and advisability of the future Beatification and Canonisation of the author of the sayings or writings in question. The Church and her individual members are thus bound only to hold the perfect

orthodoxy and Catholic piety of such a saintly writer's intentions, and again the (at least interpretative) orthodoxy of
these his writings, and their spiritual usefulness for some class
or classes of souls. But every kind and degree of respectful
but deliberate criticism and of dissent is allowed, if only
based upon solid reasons and combined with a full acceptance
of those two points.

And indeed it is plain that heroism in action and suffering
is one thing, and philosophical genius, training and balance
is another; and even, again, that deep and delicate experiences
on the one hand, and the power of their at all adequate
analysis and psychological description, are two things and not
one. Still, it is also evident that in proportion as a Saint's
doctrine is, professedly or at all events actually, based upon
or occasioned by his own experience will it rightly demand a
double measure of respectful study. For, in such a case, we
can be sure not only of the saintly intentions of the teacher,
but also of his doctrines being an attempt, however partially
successful, at expressing certain first-hand, unusually deep
and vivid experiences of the religious life, experiences which,
taken in their substance and totality, constitute the very
essence of his sanctity.

Now this is manifestly the case with Catherine. And hence
she furnishes us with those very conditions of fruitful discussion, so difficult to get in religious matters. On the one
hand, her undoubted sanctity and the personal experimental
basis of her doctrine gain for her our willingness, indeed
determination, first of all patiently to study and assimilate
and sympathetically to reconstruct her special spiritual world
from her own inner starting- and growing-point, and all this,
at this first stage, without any question as to the completeness or final truth and value of the intellectual analyses and
syntheses of these experiences elaborated by herself. And,
on the other hand, we find ourselves driven, at our second
stage, to examine the literary sources and philosophical and
theological implications of this her teaching—if pressed;
and to make various respectful, but firm and free distinctions
and reservations, with regard to these sources and affinities.

For here, in these her analyses and syntheses, a special quality of her own temperament is ever at work, and causes her to express, as best she can, a concentration of a whole host of the strongest feelings concerning just the one point of that one moment's experience, with a momentary complete exclusion of all the rest. Here, again, her dependence, for her categories of thought and general language, imagery and scheme of doctrine, upon Fra Jacopone da Todi and upon the Pseudo-Dionysian writings is readily traceable,— the latter, compositions which we have only now succeeded in tracing, with final completeness and precision, to their predominantly Neo-Platonist source. And here we cannot but carefully consider the impressive series of Church pronouncements which have occurred since Catherine spoke and her devotees wrote.

It was a rare combination of numerous special circumstances,—several of them unique,—which rendered possible the retention and indeed solemn approbation of the difficult and daring doctrine and language not rarely to be met with in the *Vita* (in contradistinction to the so-called *Opere*).

For one thing, the originator, the subject-matter and form, above all the school of her doctrine, all combined to secure it the largest possible amount of liberty and sympathetic interpretation. The originator, the soul from whom the doctrine had proceeded, had not herself written down one word of it; but she had spoken it all, warm from the very heart which loved and lived it: the cold and chilling process of deliberate composition had but little part in the whole matter, and that part was not hers. The subject-matter was not primarily dogmatic, and not at all political or legal; it dealt not with theological systems or visible institutions, but with the experiences of single souls: and at all times a great latitude has been allowed in such subject-matter, when proceeding, as here, from some saintly soul as the direct expression of its own experience. The form was not systematic, and aimed at no completeness; all was incidentally addressed to a few devoted disciples, in short monologues or homely conversations. The title *Trattato*, given later on to the collection of

her detached thoughts on Purgatory, is thoroughly mis-
leading; her whole spirit and form were precisely not that of
the treatise. And the school to which she so obviously belonged
was probably her chief protection. Indeed, the doctrinally
difficult passages are, in a true sense, the least personal of
her sayings: we shall find all their doctrinal presuppositions,
—as to the immobility, indefectibility, deification of the
soul; the possession by the soul of God without means or
measure; and the like,—to go back to the writings which,
purporting to be by the Areopagite Dionysius, the Convert
of St. Paul, but composed in reality between A.D. 490 and
520, so profoundly influenced all mystical thinking and
expression for one thousand years and more of the Church's life.

And again, the period during which the corpus of Catherine's doctrine was in process of formation was specially
favourable to such large toleration. For if she died in 1510,
ten years before the outbreak of the Protestant Reformation,
with its inevitable reaction, her chief chronicler, the saintly
philanthropist Vernazza, did not die, a true martyr to that
boundless love of souls which he had derived from his great-
souled friend, till 1524; and her Confessor Marabotto did not
depart till 1528. Thus her doctrine would remain substantially
untouched and treasured up till some twenty years after her
death, and thirteen years after the great upheaval.

We have already noted that (somewhere about 1528, and
on to 1551) her teaching *did* meet with some opposition.
It would be interesting to study how the objection arose
and was met. Here it must suffice to point out that,
whereas Catherine's Purgatorial doctrine is free from any
final difficulty on the score of orthodoxy, it is just that doctrine
which was hedged in and glossed before all the rest; and
that whereas other parts of her teaching, in the form given in
the *Vita*, are full of such difficulty, they remain strangely
unmodified to this very day. It will appear that the *Dialogo*
was in part composed to perform an office towards those
doctrinal chapters of the *Vita*, similar to that performed by
the glosses in and towards the text of the *Trattato*.

20. SOURCES OF CATHERINE'S DOCTRINE

WE have evidence, as regards literary influences, that
Catherine fed her mind on three books or sets of books:
the Bible, the Pseudo-Dionysian Treatises, and the *Lode* of
Jacopone da Todi.

The allusions to passages of Scripture are continual, but
mostly of a swiftly passing, combinatory, allegorising kind.
Direct quotations and attempts at penetrating the objective
sense of particular passages are rare, for most of the direct
quotations are clearly due to her historians, not to herself;
yet they exist and put her direct study of Scripture beyond
all doubt. Her favourite Bible books were evidently Isaiah
and the Psalms, and the Pauline and Johannine writings.
Some touches (remarkably few for a mystic) are derived from
the Canticle of Canticles, and many less obvious ones from
the Synoptic Gospels; but there are no certain traces, I think,
of any other Old Testament books, nor, in the Pauline group,
of any passage from the Pastoral Epistles.

The evidence for her direct knowledge and use of Dionysius
is, it is true, but circumstantial. But the following three facts
seem, conjoined as they are in her case, sufficient to prove
this knowledge. (i.) We may be aware that her cousin
and close spiritual friend, Suor Tommasa, wrote a devotional
treatise on Denys the Areopagite, presumably before Catherine's death, since Tommasa was sixty-two years of age in
that year 1510; it would be strange indeed if Catherine did
not, even if but from this quarter, get to know some of the
Dionysian writings, perhaps even whilst they could still only
be read in MS. form. (ii.) Marsilio Ficino published in
Florence, in 1492, his Latin translation of the *Mystical
Theology* and of the *Divine Names*, with a copious commentary;
and the book, dedicated to Giovanni de' Medici, Archbishop
of Florence and future Pope Leo X., found its way at once
to all the larger centres of life, learning and devotion in
Italy. Thus Catherine lived still eighteen years after the
publication of this, the first printed, edition of any part of

Denys (original or translation); even if she did not know these writings before, it seems again very unlikely that she would not get to know them now. (iii.) There are, it is true, no direct quotations from Denys, nor does his name appear in the *Vita ed Opere*, except in that account of Suor Tommasa. But numerous sayings of Catherine bear, as we shall see later on, so striking a resemblance to passages in those two books of Denys, that it is difficult to explain them by merely mediate infiltration; and that those sayings ultimately, as to their literary occasion, go back to the Areopagite, is incontestable. I quote Denys from the usually careful translation of the Rev. John Parker: *The Works of Dionysius the Areopagite*, Pt. I., London, Oxford, 1897, with certain corrections of my own.

The proofs for her knowledge and love of Jacopone da Todi's Italian "Praises" is, on the other hand, direct and explicit. The *Vita*, p. 37, makes her say: "Listen to what Fra Jacopone says in one of his *Lode*, beginning: 'O amor di povertade,'" and then gives her word-for-word commentary on verse 23 of this his *Loda* LVIII. Words from this same verse are again quoted by her on p. 62; the opening line of this *Loda* is put into her mouth on p. 83; and another verse, the sixth, is quoted by her, as by the Blessed Jacopone, on p. 92. I have been able to find many other sayings of hers which are hardly less directly suggested by the great Umbrian than these. Here, again, she probably knew the *Lode* in MS. form before they appeared in print in 1490; but will in any case have known them in this their printed form. I have carefully studied in this, the first printed edition (Florence: Bonaccorsi), all the *Lode* bearing upon subjects and doctrines dear to Catherine. They are twenty in all, from among the hundred and two numbers of that collection.

21. GOD AND CREATION

First, then, we will take the sayings about Creation, and the original, substantially indelible character of all created beings. "I saw a sight which satisfied me much. I was shown the Living Fountain of Goodness, which was (as yet) all within Itself alone, without any kind of participation. And next I saw that It began to participate with the creature, and made that very beautiful company of Angels, in order that this company might enjoy His ineffable glory, without asking any other return from the Angels than that they should recognise themselves to be creatures created by His supreme goodness. . . . And hence, when they were clothed in sin by their pride and disobedience, God suddenly subtracted from them the participation of His goodness. . . . Yet He did not subtract it all, for in that case they would have remained still more malign than they (actually) are, and they would have had Hell infinite in pain, as they now have it in time." . . . "When we ourselves shall depart from this life,—supposing we are in mortal sin,—then God would subtract from us His goodness and would leave us in our own selves, yet not altogether, since He wills that in every place there should be found His goodness accompanied by His justice. And if any creature could be found that did not participate in His goodness, that creature would be as malignant as God is good."

From her sayings as to Creation and Pure Love, Creation's cause, we come to those as to the Natural Conformity between God and Rational Creatures; His constant care for the human soul; and the consequent law of imitative love incumbent upon us. "I see God to have so great a conformity with the rational creature, that if the Devil himself could but rid himself of those garments of sin, in that instant God would unite Himself to him, and would make him into that which he, the Devil, attempted to achieve by his own power. So too with regard to man: lift off sin from his shoulders, and then allow the good God to act,—God who seems to have nothing

I

else to do than to unite Himself to us."—"It appears to me, indeed, that God has no other business than myself."—"If man could but see the care which God takes of the soul, he would be struck with stupor within himself."—"I see that God stands all ready to give us all the aids necessary for our salvation, and that He attends to our actions solely for our good. And, on the contrary, I see man occupied with things that are opposed to his true self and of no value. And at the time of death God will say to him: 'What was there that I could do for thee, O man, that I did not do?' And man himself will then see this clearly."—"When God created man, He did not put Himself in motion for any other reason than His pure love alone. And hence, in the same way as Love Itself, for the welfare of the loved soul, does not fail in the accomplishment of anything, whatever may be the advantage or disadvantage that may accrue from thence to the Lover, so also must the love of the loved soul return to the Lover, with those same forms and modes with which it came from Him. And then such love as this, which has no regard for aught but love itself, cannot be in fear of anything."

We can take next her teachings as to the relations between the love of God, love of our true self, and false self-love. "The love of God is our true self-love, the love characteristic of and directed to our true selves, since these selves of ours were created by and for Love Itself. The love, on the other hand, of every other thing deserves to be called self-hatred, since it deprives us of our true self-love, which is God. Hence 'Him love, Who loveth thee,' that is, Love, God; and 'him leave who doth not love thee,' that is, all other things, from God downwards."

"God so loves the soul, and is so ready to give it His graces, that, when He is impeded by some sin, then men say: 'Thou hast offended God,' that is, thou hast driven away God from thee, Who, with so much love, was desiring to do thee good. And men say this, although it is really man who then suffers the damage and who offends his own true self. But because God loves us more than we love our own selves, and gives more care to our true utility than we do ourselves, therefore does He get designated as the one who is offended. And, indeed, if God could be the recipient of suffering, it would be when, by sin, He is driven away by and from us." "This corrupt expression: 'Thou hast offended God.'" "Thou couldst discover, (O soul,) that God is continually willing whatsoever our true selves are wishing; He is ever aiming at nothing but at our own true spiritual advantage."

Hence happiness and joy, different from all mere pleasure, ever accompany this reconquest of our true self-love and this our re-donation of it to its true source. "Man was created for the end of possessing happiness. And having deviated from this his end, he has formed for himself a false, selfish self, which in all things struggles against the soul's true happiness." "This divine love is our proper and true love." "Man can truly know, by continual experience, that the love of God is our repose, our joy and our life; and that (false) self-love is but constant weariness, sadness and a (living) death of our true selves, both in this world and in the next." "All sufferings, displeasures and pains are caused by attachment to the false self. And although adversities many a time seem to us to be unreasonable, because of certain considerations which we believe to be true and indeed quite evident; yet the fact remains that it is our own imperfection which is preventing us from seeing the truth, and this it is which causes us to feel pains, suffering and displeasure." "O Love! if others feel an obligation to observe Thy commandments, I, on my part, freely will to have them all ten, because they are all delightful and full of love. . . . This is a point which is understandable only to him who himself experiences it; for in truth the divine precepts, although they are contrary to our sensuality, are nevertheless according to our own spirit which, of its very nature, is ever longing to be free from all bodily sensations, so as to be able to unite itself to God through love."

The sayings as to the close correspondence between the true self and God lead us on easily to those about the true self's instinctive recognition of God, and its hunger for the possession, for the *interiorisation* of God. "If I were to see the whole court of heaven all robed in one and the same manner, so

that there would be no apparent difference between God and
the Angels; even then the love which I have in my heart
would recognise God, in the same manner as does a dog his
master. Love knows how, without means, to discover its End
and ultimate Repose." "If a consecrated Host were to be
given me together with other non-consecrated ones I would,
I think, distinguish It by the taste, as wine from water."—
"When she saw the Sacrament upon the Altar in the hand of
the priest, she would exclaim within herself (as it were,
addressing the priest): 'O swiftly, swiftly speed It to the
heart, since It is the heart's own food.'"

Catherine's hunger for the interiorisation of all the external
helps of religion, even, indeed specially, of the Holy Eucharist
Itself, leads us on to her statements as to the superiority of
interior graces and dispositions over all exterior manifestations and sensible consolations, and as to the nature of acts
produced by the false self or apart from the grace of God.
"If we would esteem the operations of God" as they truly
deserve, "we should attend more to things interior than
to exterior ones. . . . The true light makes me see and
understand that we must not look to what proceedeth from
God to aid us in some special necessity and for His glory,
but that we must look solely to the pure love with which
He performs His work with regard to us. When the soul
perceives how direct and pure are the operations of love, and
that this love is not intent upon any benefit that we could
confer upon It, then indeed the soul also desires, in its turn,
to love with a pure love, and from the motive of the divine
love alone."

"This not-eating of mine is an operation of God, independent of my will, hence I can in nowise glory in it; nor
should we marvel at it, for to Him such an operation is as
nothing."—And to her Confessor Don Marabotto she says
reprovingly, when he too wanted to smell the strange,
strengthening odour which she smelt on his hand: "Such
things as God alone can give" (i.e. states and conditions in
the production of which the soul does not co-operate) "He
does not give to him who seeks them; indeed, He gives them

only on occasion of great need, and in order that we may draw great spiritual profit from them."

"If I do anything that is evil, I do it myself alone, nor can I attribute the blame to the Devil or to any other creature but only to my own self-will, sensuality, and other such malign movements. And if all the Angels were to declare that there was any good in me, I would refuse to believe them, because I clearly recognise how that all good is in God alone, and that in me, without divine grace, there is nothing but deficiency."—"I would not that, to my separate self, even one single meritorious act should ever be attributed, even though I could at the same time be certified of no more falling from henceforward and of being saved; because such an attribution would be to me as though a Hell." "Rather would I remain in danger of eternal damnation than be saved by, and see, such an act of the separate self." "The one sole thing in myself in which I glory is that I see in myself nothing in which I can glory."

"Yet it is necessary that we should labour and exercise ourselves, since divine grace does not give life nor render pleasing unto God except that which the soul has worked; and without work on our part grace refuses to save."—"We must never wish anything other than what happens from moment to moment, all the while, however, exercising ourselves in goodness. And to refuse to exercise oneself in goodness, and to insist upon simply awaiting what God might send, would be simply to tempt God."

The passages concerning the close relations between man's pure love and instinct for God, and Pure Love, God Himself, easily lead us on to those in which Pure Love, Peace, Grace, the True Self, indeed the Essence of all things are positively identified with God. "Hearing herself called" to any office of her state or of charity, "she would," even though apparently absorbed in ecstatic prayer, "arise at once, and go without any contention of mind. And she acted thus, because she fled all self-seeking as though it were the devil. And she felt at such times as though she could best express her feelings by means of the glorious Apostle's words: 'Who

then shall separate me from the love of *God*?' and the remainder of the great passage. And she would say: 'I seem to see how that immovable mind of St. Paul extended much farther than he was able to express in words; since Pure Love is God Himself; who then shall be able to separate Him from Himself?'" Elsewhere and on other occasions we find her declaring: "Love is God Himself"; "Pure Love is no other than God"; "the Divine love is the very God, infused by His own immense Goodness into our hearts."

She also declares that: "Grace is God"; that "Peace is God,"—"wouldest thou that I show thee what thing God is? Peace,—that peace which no man finds, who departs from Him." And further still: "The proper centre of every one is God Himself"; "my *Me* is God, nor do I recognise any other *Me*, except my God Himself"; "my Being is God, not by simple participation but by a true transformation of my Being." "God is my Being, my *Me*, my Strength, my Beatitude, my Good, my Delight." Indeed "the glorious God is the whole essence of things both visible and invisible."

All these startling statements are but so many expressions of one of the most characteristic moods and attitudes of her mind and heart. For in her vehemence of love and thirst for unification she would exclaim: "I will have nothing to do with a love that would be *for* God or *in* God; this is a love which pure love cannot bear: since pure love is (simply) God Himself"; "I cannot abide to see that word *for*, and that word *in*, since they denote to my mind a something that can stand between God and myself."

All this doctrine would be summed up by her in certain favourite expressions. "She was wont often to pronounce these words: 'Sweetness of God, Fullness of God, Goodness of God, Purity of God'"; and at a later time "she had continually on her lips the term '(clear) Fullness'" (Self-adequation, *nettezza*).

22. THE SIN OF SELF-LOVE

CATHERINE's extreme sensitiveness is no doubt a chief cause of the peculiar form in which she experiences her sinfulness and faults and their actually slow purification, as expressed in those of her sayings which refer to the growth of love and to the continuous imperfections of the soul. "From the time when I began to love Him, that love has never failed me"; "indeed it has continually grown unto its consummation in the depths of my heart." This growth takes place only step by step; and is in reality never complete, and never without certain imperfections. "The creature is incapable of knowing anything but what God gives it from day to day. If it could know (beforehand) the successive degrees that God intends to give it, it would never be quieted." "When from time to time I would advert to the matter, it seemed to me that my love was complete; but later, as time went on and as my sight grew clearer, I became aware that I had had many imperfections. . . . I did not recognise them at first, because God-Love was determined to achieve the whole only little by little, for the sake of preserving my physical life, and so as to keep my behaviour tolerable for those with whom I lived. For otherwise, with such other insight, so many excessive acts would ensue, as to make one insupportable to oneself and to others." "Every day I feel that the motes are being removed, which this Pure Love casts out (*cava fuori*). Man cannot see these imperfections; indeed, since, if he saw these motes, he could not bear the sight, God ever lets him see the work he has achieved, as though no imperfections remained in it. But all the time God does not cease from continuing to remove them." "From time to time, I feel that many instincts are being consumed within me, which before had appeared to be good and perfect; but when once they have been consumed, I understand that they were bad and imperfect. . . . These things are clearly visible in the mirror of truth, that is of Pure Love, where everything is seen crooked which before appeared straight."

And yet the slowness of this purification is, in the last resort, caused, if not by the incomplete purity of her love, at least by the deep-rootedness and evasive character of the wrong self-love that has to be extirpated. "This our self-will is so subtle and so deeply rooted within our own selves, and defends itself with so many reasons, that, when we cannot manage to carry it out in one way, we carry it out in another. We do our own wills under many covers (pretexts),—of charity, of necessity, of justice, of perfection." But pure love sees through all these covers: "I saw this love to have so open and so pure an eye, its sight to be so subtle and its seeing so far-reaching, that I stood astounded." "True love wills to stand naked, without any kind of cover, in heaven and on earth, since it has not anything shameful to conceal." And "this naked love ever sees the truth; whilst self-love can neither see it nor believe in it." "Pure love loves God without any *for* (any further motive)."

And man, every man, is capable of this pure love and of the truth which such love sees: "I see every one to be capable of my tender Love." "Truth being, by its very nature, communicable to all, cannot be the exclusive property of any one."

23. CATHERINE AND PURE LOVE

The next group of sayings deals with the purity of Love, and the severity with which this purity progressively eliminates all selfish motives and attachments, whilst itself becoming increasingly its own exceeding great beatitude. "Pure Love loves God without why or wherefore (*perchè*)." "Since Love took over the care of everything, I have not taken care of anything, nor have I been able to work with my intellect, memory and will, any more than if I had never had them. Indeed every day I feel myself more occupied in Him, and with greater fire." "I had given the keys of the house to Love, with ample permission to do all that was necessary, and determined to have no consideration for soul or body, but to see that, of all that the law of pure love required, there should not be wanting the slightest particle (*minimo chè*). And I stood so occupied in contemplating this work of Love, that if He had cast me, body and soul, into hell, hell itself would have appeared to me all love and consolation."

Yet the corresponding, increasing constraint of the false self is most real. "I find myself every day more restricted, as if a man were (first) confined within the walls of a city, then in a house with an ample garden, then in a house without a garden, then in a hall, then in a room, then in an ante-room, then in the cellar of the house with but little light, then in a prison without any light at all; and then his hands were tied and his feet were in the stocks, and then his eyes were bandaged, and then he would not be given anything to eat, and then no one would be able to speak to him; and then, to crown all, every hope were taken from him of issuing thence as long as life lasted. Nor would any other comfort remain to such an one, than the knowledge that it was God who was doing all this, through love with great mercy; an insight which would give him great contentment. And yet this contentment does not diminish the pain or the oppression."

There is next a group of sayings as to the immense, blinding and staining effect of even slight self-seekings, and as to how God gradually transforms the soul. "God and Sin, however slight, cannot live peaceably side by side (*stare insieme*). Since some little thing that you may have in your eye does not let you see the sun, we can make a comparison between God and the sun, and then between intellectual vision and that of the bodily eye." "After considering things as they truly are, I find myself constrained to live without self." "Since the time when God has given the light to the soul, it can no more desire to operate by means of that part of itself which is ever staining all things and rendering turbid the clear water of God's grace. The soul then offers and remits itself entirely to Him, so that it can no more operate except to the degree and in the manner willed by tender Love Himself; and henceforth it does not produce works except such as are pure, full and sincere; and these are the works that please God-Love."

"I will not name myself either for good or for evil, lest this my (selfish) part should esteem itself to be something." "Being determined to join myself unto God, I am in every manner bound to be the enemy of His enemies; and since I find nothing that is more His enemy than is self in me, I am constrained to hate this part of me more than any other thing; indeed, because of the contrariety that subsists between it and the spirit, I am determined to separate it from all the goods of this world and of the next, and to esteem it no more than if it were not."

"When she saw others bewailing their evil inclinations, and forcing themselves greatly to resist them, and yet the more they struggled to produce a remedy for their defects, the more did they commit them, she would say to them: 'You have subjects for lamentation (*tu hai li guai*) and bewail them, and I too would be having and bewailing them; you do evil and bewail it, and I should be doing and be bewailing it as you do, if God Almighty were not holding me. You cannot defend yourself, nor can I defend myself. Hence it is necessary that we renounce the care of ourselves unto Him, Who can defend this our true self; and He will then do that which we cannot do."

"As to the annihilating of man, which has to be made in God, she spoke thus: 'Take a bread, and eat it. When you have eaten it, its substance goes to nourish the body, and the rest is eliminated, because nature cannot use it at all, and indeed, if nature were to retain it, the body would die. Now, if that bread were to say to you: "Why dost thou remove me from my being? If I could, I would defend myself to conserve myself, an action natural to every creature": you would answer: "Bread, thy being was ordained for a support for my body, a body which is of more worth than thou; and hence thou oughtest to be more contented with thine end than with thy being. Live for thine end, and thou wilt not care about thy being, but thou wilt exclaim (to the body): 'Swiftly, swiftly draw me forth from my being, and put me within the

operation of that end of mine, for which I was created.' . . .
The soul, by the operation of God, eliminates from the body
all the superfluities and evil habits acquired by sin, and retains
within itself the purified body, which body thenceforth performs its operations by means of these purified senses. . . .
And, when the soul has consumed all the evil inclinations of
the body, God consumes all the imperfections of the soul."

In each particular instance, the process was wont to be as
follows: "When her selfish part saw itself tracked down by
Love, Catherine would turn to Him and say: 'Even though
it pain sense, content Thy will: despoil me of this spoil and
clothe me with Love full, pure and sincere.'"

We get next a set of apparently contrary sayings, concerning the suddenness of God's illumination; how the degree
of this light cannot be determined by man; and what are,
nevertheless, the conditions under which it will not act. In
some cases, "the soul is made to know in an instant, by means
of a new light above itself, all that God desires it to know,
and this with so much certainty that it would be impossible
to make the soul believe otherwise. Nor is more shown it
than is necessary for leading it to greater perfection." "This
light is not sought by man, but God gives it unto man when
He chooses; neither does the man himself know how he
knows the thing that he is made to know. And if perchance
man were determined to seek to know a little further than he
has been made to know, he would achieve nothing, but would
remain like unto a stone, without any capacity."

And she would pray: "Be Thou my understanding; (thus)
shall I know that which it may please Thee that I should
know. Nor will I henceforth weary myself with seeking; but
I will abide in peace with Thine understanding, which shall
wholly occupy my mind." "If a man would see properly in
spiritual matters, let him pluck out the eyes of his own presumption." "He who gazes too much upon the sun's orb,
makes himself blind; even thus, I think, does pride blind
many, who want to know too much." "When God finds a
soul that does not move, He operates within it in His own
manner, and puts His hand to greater things. He takes from

this soul the key of His treasures which He had given to it, so that it might be able to enjoy them; and gives to this same soul the care of His presence, which entirely absorbs it."

The next group can be made up of passages descriptive of the dealings adopted by God with a view to first winning souls as He finds them, and then raising them above mercenary hope or slavish fear; and of the childlike fearlessness inspired by perfect trust in God. As to the winning them, she says: "The selfishness of man is as contrary to God and rebellious against Him, that God Himself cannot induce the soul to do His will, except by certain stratagems (*lusinghe*): promising it things greater than those left, and giving it, even in this life, a certain consoling relish (*gusto*). And this He does, because He perceives the soul to love things visible so much, that it would never leave one, unless it saw four."

And, as to God's raising of the soul, she propounds the deep doctrine, which only apparently contradicts the divine method just enunciated, as to the necessary dimness of the soul's light with regard to the intrinsic consequences of its own acts, a dimness necessary, because alone truly purificatory, for the time that runs between its conversion, when, since it is still weak, it requires to see, and its condition of relative purity, when, since it is now strong, it can safely be again allowed to see. "If a man were to see that which, in return for his good deeds, he will have in the life to come, he would cease to occupy himself with anything but heavenly things. But God, desiring that faith should have its merit, and that man should not do good from the motive of selfishness, gives him that knowledge little by little, though always sufficiently for the degree of faith of which the man is then capable. And God ends by leading him to so great a light as to things that are above, that faith seems to have no further place.—On the other hand, if man knew that which hereafter he will have to suffer if he die in the miserable state of sin, I feel sure that, for fear of it, he would let himself be killed rather than commit one single sin. But God, unwilling as He is that man should avoid doing evil from the motive of fear, does not allow him to see so terrifying a spectacle, although He shows it in part to such souls as are so clothed and occupied by His pure love that fear can no more enter in."

And as to the full trust of pure love, we have the following: "God let her hear interiorly: 'I do not want thee henceforward to turn thine eyes except towards Love; and here I would have thee stay and not to move, whatever happens to thee or to others, within or without'; 'he who trusts in Me, should not doubt about himself.'"

And this Love gives of itself so fully to those that give themselves fully to It, that when asked by such souls to impetrate some grace for them she would say: "I see this tender Love to be so courteously attentive to these my spiritual children, that I cannot ask of It anything for them, but can only present them before His face." In other cases, as in those of beginners when sick and dying, she would be "drawn to pray for" a soul, and would "impetrate" some special "grace for it." "Lord, give me this soul," she would at times pray aloud, "I beg Thee to give it me, for indeed Thou canst do so." And "when she was drawn to pray for something, she would be told in her mind: 'Command, for love is free to do so.'"

24. CATHERINE'S SPIRITUAL SIGNIFICANCE

Before proceeding further to what is really still a necessary part and elucidation of Catherine's spiritual character and special significance,—her doctrine and the posthumous effect, extension, and application of her life and teaching upon and by means of her greatest disciples,—it may be well to pause a little, and to try to give, as far as the largely fragmentary and vague evidence permits, a short and vivid picture and summary, in part retrospective and in part prospective, of the special type, meaning and importance of Catherine's personality and spiritual attitude, and of the interrelation of the two. In so doing I propose to move, as far as possible, from the psycho-physical and temperamental peculiarities and determinisms of her case, up to the spiritual characteristics and ethical self-determinations; and to try to note everywhere what she was not as definitely as what she was. For only thus shall we have some adequate apprehension of the "beggarly elements" which she found, and of the spiritual organism and centre of far-reaching influence which she left. And only thus too will it be possible to see at all clearly the cost, the limitations, and the special functions, temporary and permanent, of her particular kind of soul and sanctity.

It is clear then, first, that in her we have to do with a highly nervous, delicately poised, immensely sensitive and impressionable psycho - physical organism and temperament. It was a temperament which, had it been unmatched by a mind and will at least its equals; had these latter not found, or been found by, a definite, rich and supernaturally powerful, historical and institutional religion; and had not the mind and will, with this religious help, been kept in constant operation upon it, would have spelt, if not moral ruin, at least lifelong ineffectualness. Yet, as a matter of fact, not only did this temperament not dominate her, with the apparently rare and incomplete exceptions of some but semi-voluntary, short impressions and acts during the last months of her life; but it became one of the chief instruments and materials of her life's work and worth. Only together with such a mind and will, is such a temperament not a grave drawback; and even with them it is an obvious danger, and requires their constant careful checking and active shaping.

And this temperament involved an unusually large subconscious life. All souls have some amount of this life, but many have it but slight and shallow: she had it of a quite extraordinary degree and depth. A coral reef, growing up from, and just peering above, a hundred-fathom-deep ocean, would be an appropriate picture of the large predominance of subconsciousness in this spacious soul. And even this circumstance alone would cause her spiritual lights and fully conscious experiences to come abruptly, and in the form of quasi-physical seizures and surprises. Continuous, and possibly long, incubations of ideas and feelings would thus be taking place in the subconscious region, and these feelings and ideas would then, when fully ripe, or on some slight stimulation from the conscious region or directly from the outer world, make sudden irruptions into that full consciousness. Nor would such natural suddenness of full consciousness really militate against the claim to supernaturalness of the ideas and feelings thus revealed. For they would still be most rightly conceived as the work of God's Spirit in and through the action of her own spirit: not their causation and their source, but simply the suddenness of their revelation and the channel of their outlet would lose in supernaturalness.

And hers was a soul with habitually large fields of consciousness. Apparently from her conversion onwards, and certainly during the last fourteen years of her life, the moments or days of narrow fields were, till quite the last weeks or even days, comparatively rare; and their narrowness was evidently always felt as most painful and oppressive. And the interior occupation was so intense; the several fields succeeded each other with such an apparent automatism and quality of even physical seizure; and they were either so entrancing by their largeness or so depressing by their narrowness: that to souls not in tune with hers, she must, in the former moods, have appeared as egoistic, as (in a sense) too much of a man, as one absorbed in great but purely general, super-personal ideas which were making her forget both her own and her fellow-creatures' minor wants; and, in the latter moods, as downrightly egotistic, as (in a way) too much of a woman, as one engrossed in her own purely individual, small and fanciful troubles and trials. Yet the "Egoism" is not dominant during her middle period, since it is certain that her charitable and administrative activities, and close affective interest in the daily, physical and emotional lot and demands of the poor and lowly, were most real and considerable. And, in her third period, it was this very "Egoism" which, as we shall see, was the form and means of the interior apprehension and exterior elaboration of her most original and suggestive doctrines, and became the occasion for her stimulation of other intensely active souls on to great nation-wide enterprises of the most practical, permanent and heroic kind. And the "Egoistic" moods are unapparent before the last two years or less of her life; and they then are clearly but the occasional, involuntary suspensions or partial yieldings of her normally iron will,—rare checks and intermittences, which, with little or no preventible faultiness on her own part, give us pathetically vivid glimpses of what that normal life of hers cost her to achieve and to maintain, and of what she would have been, if bereft of God's generosity ever awakening, deepening and operating through her own.

All this sensitiveness, subconsciousness, spaciousness, variety, and suddenness of apprehension and feeling; all this largely chaotic, mutually conflicting, raw material of her spiritual life, even if it had existed alongside of but feeble and inert powers of organisation and transformation, would not have failed to produce considerable suffering; although, in such a case, that suffering would have remained largely inarticulate, and would have left the soul checked and counter-checked by various tyrannous passions and fancies. The soul would thus have been less efficient and persuasive than the least subconscious and sensitive specimens of average and "common-sense" humanity. But, in her case, all this unusually turbulent raw material was in unusually close contiguity to powers of mind and of will of a rare breadth and strength. And this very closeness of apposition and width of contrast, and this great strength of mind and will, made all that disordered multiplicity, distraction and dispersion of her clamorous, many-headed, many-hearted nature, a tyranny impossible and unnecessary to bear. And yet to achieve the actual escape from such a tyranny, the mastering of such a rabble, and the harmonisation of such a chaos, meant a constant and immense effort, a practically unbroken grace-getting and self-giving, an ever-growing heroism and indeed sanctity, and, with and through all these things, a corresponding expansion and virile joy. It can thus be said, in all simple truth, that she became a saint because she had to; that she became it, to prevent herself going to pieces: she literally had to save, and actually did save, the fruitful life of reason and of love, by ceaselessly fighting her immensely sensitive, absolute and claimful self.

Catherine's mind was without humour or wit; and this was, of course, a serious drawback. And her temperament was of so excessive a mentality as to amount to something more or less abnormal. For not only is there no trace about her, at any time, of moral vulgarity of any kind, or of any tendency to it; and this is, of course, a grand strength; but she seems at all times to have been greatly lacking in that quite innocent and normal sensuousness, which appears to form a necessary element of the complete human personality. It is true that in the anecdotes of her impulsive and yet reverent affection for the pestiferous woman and the cancerous workman, with the finely self-oblivious sympathy which moves her to kiss the mouth of the first, and long to remain with her arms around the neck of the other, there is the beautiful tenderness and daring of a great positive purity, of the purity of flame and not of snow. And her love of her servants, Argentina in particular, and of poor Thobia, is exquisitely true and constant. Yet even all this can hardly be classed with the element referred to, with that love of children and of women as the bearers of them, that instinct of union with all that is pure and fruitful in the normal life of sex, such as is so beautifully present throughout St. Luke's Gospel, but which is, at least relatively, absent from St. John's.

Possibly her unhappy and childless marriage determined the non-development or the mortification of any tendencies to such a temper. But the absence referred to was more probably caused by her congenital psychical temperament and state themselves; and, if so, it would point to her as a person hardly intended for marriage, and as one who, through no fault of her own, could not satisfy the less purely mental of the perfectly licit requirements which make up the many-levelled wants of a normal, or at least ordinary, man's and husband's nature. Pompilia's dying words, in Browning's *Ring and the Book*, would, probably, at any time after her premature involuntary marriage, have found an appropriate place upon Catherine's lips, had she ever thought it loyal or

K

kind to utter them: "'In heaven there is neither marriage nor giving in marriage.' How like Jesus Christ to say that!"

Yet it is at least as difficult to think of her as really intended for the cloister. That early wish of hers to join a religious community, sincere and keen as it no doubt was at the time, evidently faded away completely, probably already before her conversion thirteen years later, and certainly before her widowhood. Perhaps she would have been best suited, throughout her adult years, to the life of an unmarried woman living in the world,—to the kind of life which she actually led during her widowhood, with such changes in it as her earlier, robuster health would have involved for those earlier years. She would thus, throughout her life, have divided her energies, in various degrees and combinations, between attention to the multiform, practical, physico-emotional wants of the poor; the give and take of stimulation and enlightenment to and from some few large-hearted, heroically operative friends; and, as source and centre of all such actual achievements and of indefinitely greater possibilities, indeed as a life already largely eternal and creative,—contemplative prayer of various degrees and kinds. But such a life, if it would have left out much disappointment and suffering, and not for herself alone, yet would also have been without the special occasions and incentives to her sudden conversion and long patience and detailed magnanimity. Her life, in appearing on the surface as less of a failure, would at bottom have been less of a spiritual success.

Indeed the failures and fragmentarinesses of her life, even if and where more than merely apparent to us or even to herself, helped and still help to give a poignant forcefulness to her example and teaching. There is nothing pre- or post-arranged, nothing artificial or stagy, nothing, in the deliberate occupations of her convert life, that is simple brooding about this woman: when she thinks or prays, she does so; when she acts, she acts; when she suffers, she suffers; and there is an end of it. The infinitely winning qualities of a simple veracity; of a successive livingness, because ever operative occupation with the actual real moment, and not with the after-shadow of the past nor with the fore-shadow of the future; and, through all this, of a healthy creatureliness are thus spread over all she does,—over her virtues, which are never reflected as such within her own pure mind, and over her very weaknesses and failings which, summed up in their source, her false self, are ever being acknowledged, feared, and fought, with a heroism not less massive because its methods are so wisely indirect.

It is plain that Catherine's temperament was naturally a profoundly sad one, although her acutest attacks of melancholy were generally succeeded by some unusually great expansion, illumination or consolation of soul. She had, to adopt a term of recent psychology, a very low "difference-threshold"; easily and swiftly would her consciousness be affected by every kind of irritant: even a slight stimulation would at once produce pain, anxiety, or oppression of mind or soul. She was thus evidently made for a few lifelong friends, for such as would deserve the privilege of giving much sympathy and patience, and of getting back helps and stimulations indefinitely greater both in quality and kind; and was not fitted for many acquaintances of the ordinary kind, with their hurry of disjointed, hand-to-mouth, half-awake thinking, feeling and doing.

And it is very noticeable that her friendships and attachments of all kinds were of a steadiness and perseverance to which there are no real exceptions. To Giuliano, markedly inferior in nature though he evidently was to her, and positively unfaithful during the early years of their long, ill-assorted marriage, she remained faithful even during those first years which she herself never ceased to condemn as her pre-conversion period; she behaved with true magnanimity towards himself and Thobia and Thobia's mother; and she even evinced a certain affective attachment to him and to his memory. And it would hardly be fair to quote the change in the dispositions as to her place of burial in proof of a change in her dispositions towards him. She whose affectionate interest in Thobia is shown, by irrefragable documentary proof, to have persevered, indeed increased, to the end of the poor young woman's life, will not have changed in her feelings towards her own dead husband. Towards her brothers and sister, her nephews and nieces, her numerous Wills and Codicils show that she entertained a constant and operative affection.

These same documents prove that her affection and gratitude towards Don Marabotto were equally sincere and provident. It is true that she twice broke off relations with him, although only for a day and three days respectively; and, at the last, this devoted friend of the last eleven years of her life was no more about her. Yet we have remarked that those two former absences were but caused by reasonable fears of getting spoilt by him; and that the final absence was no doubt in no way her doing. And perhaps the most impressive of all her attachments were that to the Hospital, as representative of the sick poor whom she had served, so actively and at such cost to self, for twenty-five years and more,—all her legal dispositions and her very domicile for the last thirty years of her life proclaim the permanent prominence of this interest; and her affection towards her servants, since nothing could be more considerate, thoughtful, equable and persevering than her care and love for Benedetta, Mariola and Argentina. Here again I cannot find any certain exceptions: for we know nothing of the history of the servant Antonietta except that, even on the one occasion of her mention, it appeared already doubtful whether the girl herself would care to remain with her mistress to the end.

There is but one apparent, and indeed a startling, exception to this unbroken continuity of affection. Ettore Vernazza, certainly the greatest and closest, the most docile and the most influential, of her disciples, he to whom we owe the transmission of the larger and the most precious part of her teaching and spirit, and who, as will be seen, became, after her death even more than before it, and more and more right up to his own heroic end, the living reproduction and extension of the very deepest and greatest experiences and influences of her life: Vernazza appears nowhere in her Wills, except as, on one occasion, the actual drawer of the document, and, on another, as a witness. And he was far away, and clearly not accidentally, at the time of her death. I take it to be quite certain that we have here not an exception, at the point of her fullest sympathy, to that gratitude and permanence of feeling which obtained demonstrably in the other, lesser cases; but that this silence and this departure are to be explained, the former entirely, and the latter in part, by the special character as much of Ettore as of Catherine, and by the special form which their friendship assumed in consequence. I shall return to this point in my chapter on Vernazza.

Catherine's states of absorption in prayer, such as we find ever since her conversion, were transparently real and sincere, and were so swift and spontaneous as to appear quasi-involuntary. They were evidently, together with, and largely on occasion of, her reception of the Holy Eucharist, the chief means and the ordinary form of the accessions of strength and growth to her spiritual life.

Possibly throughout the four years of the first period of her convert life, certainly and increasingly throughout the twenty-two years of the second, middle period, these absorptions occurred frequently, indeed daily; they were long, and lasted up to six hours at a stretch; and they were apparently timed by herself, and never rendered her incapable of hearing or attending to any call to acts of duty or of charity, and of breaking off then and there. And throughout these years she seems to have known but one kind of absorption, this primarily spiritual one, which appears to have been a particularly deep Prayer of Quiet; and she appears to have always been, if exercised, yet also profoundly sustained and strengthened, by it, even physically, for the large activity and numerous trials and sufferings awaiting her on her return to her ordinary life. And these were the years during which she lived with no mediate guidance.

During the last eleven, perhaps even thirteen years of her life, first one, and then, considerably later, a second change occurs in these respects. First these profound, healthy and fruitful absorptions, and the power to occasion or effect, to bear or endorse them, diminish greatly, though apparently gradually, in length, regularity and efficiency; indeed they do so almost as markedly as does the capacity for external work, their former complement and correlative. The spiritual life now breaks up into a greater variety of shorter and more fitful incidents and manifestations. The sympathy of friends, the sustaining counsel of priests, and the communication on her part of many spiritual thoughts and experiences take, in large part, the place of those long spells of the Prayer of Quiet or of Union, and still more of that external activity which are both now becoming more and more impossible to her. And next,—though not, as far as our evidence goes, before the last six months or so of her life,—there arises a second series of absorptions, externally closely similar, yet internally profoundly different. These latter absorptions are primarily psychical and involuntary, indeed psychopathic. And she herself shows and declares her knowledge of this their pathological character, her ability to distinguish them from their healthy rivals, her inability to throw them off unaided, her wish that others should rouse her from them, and her power to accept and second such initiation coming to her from a will-centre other than her own.

Now her attendants and biographers, possibly all of them and even during her lifetime, considered and called those healthy absorptions "ecstasies"; and though we have clear evidence of her ever having shrunk from so naming them herself, and though, here as everywhere, she habitually turned away from considering the form and psycho-physical concomitants of her spiritual experiences, and concentrated her attention on their content and ethico-religious truth and power, there seems to be no special reason for quarrelling with their application of this term. Yet it is of great importance to observe that none of her teaching can with propriety be called directly Pneumatic. For I can find nothing that even purports to have been spoken in a state of trance, nor anything authentic that claims to convey, during her time of ordinary consciousness, anything learnt during those states of absorption other than what, in a lesser degree, is probably experienced, during at least some rare moments, by all souls that have attained to the so-called Prayer of Quiet. It is quite clear, I think, that in all these authentic passages the states of absorption are treated substantially as times when the conscious region of her soul, a region always relatively shallow, sinks down into the ever-present deep regions of subconsciousness; and hence as experiences which can only be described indirectly,—in their effects, as traced by and in the conscious soul, after its rising up again, from this immersion in subconsciousness, to its more ordinary condition of so-called "full consciousness," i.e. as full a consciousness as is normal, for this particular soul, in the majority of moments as are not devoted to physical sleep.

But if apparently none of Catherine's contemplations are derived directly from things learnt during these times of absorption; those contemplations are, none the less, all indirectly influenced, in the most powerful and multiform manner, by these absorptions. For these absorptions constituted the moments of the soul's feeding and harmonisation, and they enriched and concentrated it, for the service of its fellows, and for other occasions of further self-enlargement. And these absorptions, with their combination of experienced fruitfulness and undeniable obscurity, for the very soul that has passed through them, when this soul has returned to ordinary consciousness, give to all, even to the most lucid of her sayings, a beautiful margin of mist and mystery, a never-ceasing sense of the incomprehensibility, and yet of the soul's capacity for an intellectual adumbration, of the realities and truths in which our whole spiritual life is rooted,—realities and truths which she is thus, without even a touch of inconsistency, ever struggling to apprehend and to communicate a little less inadequately than before.

25. THE TEACHING OF CATHERINE

CATHERINE's teaching, as we have it, is, at first sight, strangely abstract and impersonal. God nowhere appears in it, at least in so many words, either as Father, or as Friend, or as Bridegroom of the soul. This comes no doubt, in part, from the circumstance that she had never known the joys of maternity, and had never, for one moment, experienced the soul-entrancing power of full conjugal union. It comes, perhaps, even more, from her somewhat abnormal temperament, the (in some respects) exclusive mentality which we have already noted. But it certainly springs at its deepest from one of the central requirements and experiences of her spiritual life; and must be interpreted by the place and the function which this apparently abstract teaching occupies within this large experimental life of hers which stimulates, utilises, and transcends it all. For here again we are brought back to her rare thirst, her imperious need, for unification; to the fact that she was a living, closely knit, ever-increasing spiritual organism, if there ever was one.

This unification tended, in its reasoned, theoretic presentation, even to overshoot the mark: for it would be impossible to press those of her sayings in which her true self appears as literally God, or her state of quiet as a complete motionlessness or even immovability. Yet in practice this unification ever remained admirably balanced and fruitful, since, in and for her actual life, it was being ever conceived and applied as but a whole-hearted, constantly renewed, continuously necessary, costing and yet enriching, endeavour to harmonise and integrate the ever-increasing elements and explications of her nature and experience. And even on the two points mentioned, her theory gives an admirably vivid presentment of the prima facie impression produced by its deepest experiences upon every devoted soul.

And on other points her theory is, even as such, admirably sober, closely knit and stimulating. For, as to the cause of Evil, she ever restricts herself to finding it in her own nature, and to fighting it there: hence the personality of Evil, though nowhere denied, yet rarely if ever concerns her, and never does so directly in her strenuous and practical life. Yet, on the other hand, this fight takes, with her, the form not primarily of a conflict with this or that particular fault, these several conflicts then summing themselves up into a more or less interconnected warfare; but it makes straight for the very root-centre of all the particular faults, and, by constantly checking and starving that, suppresses these. And hence the Positive, Radical character of Evil is, in practice, continuously emphasised by her.

Yet this root-centre of Evil within her was most certainly not conceived by her as a merely general and abstract false self or self-seeking. Her biographers, mostly over-anxious to prove the innocence of her nature, even at the expense of the heroism of her life and of the reasonableness and truthfulness of her statements, are no doubt responsible for the constant air of would-be devout and amiable (!) exaggeration which she wears on all this self-fighting side of her. Yet we have, I think, but to take the simplest and most authentic of the rival accounts,—those which give us the smallest quantity of self-denunciation, and we can understand the quality of this self-blame, and can fix its special, entirely concrete and pressing, occasion and object. For considering the immense claimfulness, the cruel jealousy, the tyrannous fancifulness, the brooding inventiveness, the at last incurable absoluteness of the weak and bad side and tendency of a temperament and natural character such as hers, had it been allowed to have its way, there is, I think, nothing really excessive or morbid, nothing that is not most healthy and humble, and hence sensible and admirably self-cognitive and truthful, about this heroic strenuousness, this ever-watchful, courageous fear of self, and those declarations of hers that this false self was as bad as any devil. To such a temperament and *attrait* as hers only one master could be deliberately taken, or could be long borne, as centre of the soul: God *or* Self;—not two: God *and* Self. And hence all practice or even tolerance of, as it were, separate compartments of the soul; all "a little of this, and not too much of that" spirit; all "making the best of both worlds" temper; all treatment of religion as a means to other ends, or as so much uninterpreted inheritance and dead furniture or fixed and frozen possession of the mind, or as a respectable concomitant and condiment or tolerable parasite to other interests: all such things must have been more really impossible to her than would have been the lapse into self-sufficiency and self-idolatry, and the attempt to find happiness in such a downward unification.

And the one true divine root-centre of her individual soul is ever, at the same time, experienced and conceived as present, in various degrees and ways, simply everywhere, and in everything. All the world of spirits is thus linked together: and a certain slightest remnant of a union exists even between Heaven and Hell, between the lost and the saved. For there is no absolute or really infinite Evil existent anywhere; whilst everywhere there are some traces of and communications from the Absolute Good, the Source and Creator of the substantial being of all things that are. And to possess even God, and all of God, herself alone exclusively, would have been to her, we can say it boldly, a truly intolerable state, if this state were conceived as accompanied by any consciousness of the existence of other rational creatures entirely excluded from any and every degree or kind of such possession. It is, on the contrary, the apprehension of how she, as but one of the countless creatures of God, is allowed to share in the effluence of the one Light and Life and Love, an effluence which, identical in essential character everywhere, is not entirely absent anywhere: it is the abounding consciousness of this universal bond and brotherhood, this complete freedom from all sectarian exclusiveness and from all exhaustive appropriation of God, the Sun of the Universe, by any or all of the just or unjust, upon all of whom He shines: it is all this that constitutes her element of unity, saneness and breadth, the one half of her faith and the greater part of her spiritual joy.

And the other half of her faith constitutes her element of difference, multiplicity and depth, and is itself made up of two distinct convictions. No two creatures have been created by God with the same capacities; and, although they are each called by Him to possess Him to the full of their respective capability, they will necessarily, even if they all be fully faithful to their call, possess Him in indefinitely and innumerably various degrees and ways. And, so far, there is still nothing but joy in her soul. Indeed we can say that the previous element of unity and breadth calls for this second element of diversity and depth; and that only in and with the other can each element attain to its own full development and significance, and thus the two together can constitute a living whole.

But the second conviction as to difference is a sombre and saddening one. For she holds further that the diversity is not only one of degrees of goodness and a universal fullness of variously sized living vessels of life and joy; but that there is also a diversity in the degree of self-making or self-marring on the part of the free-willing, self-determining creatures of God. Here too she still, it is true, finds the omnipresent divine Goodness at work, and in a double fashion and degree. The self-marring of some, probably, in her view, of most souls, gets slowly and blissfully albeit painfully unmade by the voluntary acceptance, on the part of these souls, of the suffering rightly attaching, in a quite determinist manner, to all direct, deliberate and detached pleasure-seeking of the false self. And this is Purgatory, which is essentially the same whether thus willed and suffered in this world or in the next. And the self-marring of other, probably the minority of, sinful souls, though no longer capable of any essential unmaking, is yet in so far overruled by the divine Goodness (which, here as everywhere, is greater than the creature's badness), that even here there ever remains a certain residue of moral goodness, and that a certain mitigation of the suffering which necessarily accompanies the remaining and indeed preponderant evil is mercifully effected by God. And this is Hell, which is essentially the same, whether thus, as to its pain, not willed but suffered here or hereafter. Thus she neither holds an *Apocatastasis*, a Final Restitution of all ᴛhings,—what might be called a Universal Purgatory,—nor a Gradual Mitigation of the sufferings of the lost; but the eventual complete purgation and restitution applies only to some, though probably to most, souls, and the mitigation of this suffering, in the case of the lost, is not gradual but instantaneous.

Here again, then, we find her thirst for unification strikingly at work. For she discovers one single divine Goodness as active and efficient throughout the universe; and she everywhere finds spiritual pain to consist in the discordance felt by the rational creature between its actual contingent condition and its own indestructible ideal, and such pain to be everywhere automatically consequent upon deliberate acts of self-will. Hence the suffering is nowhere separately willed or separately sent by God; and, in all cases of restoration, the suffering, in proportion as it is freely willed by the sufferer, is ever medicinal and curative and never vindictive. It is these considerations which make her able to endure this sombre side of reality.

Now it is all this second set of beliefs, all this faith in diversity, multiplicity and depth, which prevents any touch of real Pantheism or Indifferentism from defacing the breadth of her outlook, and effectually neutralises any tendency to a sheer Optimism or Monism. She loves God's Light and Love so much, that she is indefatigable in seeking, and constantly happy in finding, and incapable of not loving, even the merest glimpses of it, everywhere. And yet, precisely on that same account, everywhere the central passion of her soul is given to fostering the further growth of this Light and Love, to already loving it even more as it will or may be than as it already is, and thus deeply loving it already, in order that it may be still more lovable by and by. And thus the universality, and what we may call the particularity, of God's self-communication and of the creature's response, are equally preserved, and in such wise that each safeguards, supplements, and stimulates the other. And thus her grace-stimulated craving, both for indefinite expansion and breadth and for indefinite concentration and depth, is met and nourished by this width and distance, this clarity and dimness of outlook on to the rich and awe-inspiring greatness of God and of His world of souls.

And union with this one Centre is, for all rational free-willing creatures, to be achieved, at any one and at every moment, by the whole-hearted willing and doing, by the full endorsing, of some one thing,—some one unique state and duty offered to the soul in that one unique moment. Thus life gets apparently broken up into so many successive steps and degrees of work, each to be attended to as though it were the first and last; and as so much special material and occasion for the practice of unification, ostensibly in the matter supplied and for the moment which supplies it, but really in the soul to which it is offered and for the totality of its life. Her soul is even if taken at any one moment, and still more, of course, if considered in its successive history, over-flowing with various acts, with (as it were) so many numberless waves and wavelets, currents and cross-currents of volition; and the warp and woof of her life's weaving is really close-knit with numberless threads of single willings, preceded and succeeded by single perceptions, conceptions and feelings of the soul. Yet the very fullness of this flow and the closeness of this weaving, their great and ever-increasing orderliness and spontaneity, such as we can and must conceive them to have been present during the majority of the moments of her convert and waking life, tended, during such times, to obliterate any clear consciousness of their different constituents, and to produce the impression of one single state, even one single act. And this very action, even inasmuch as thus felt to be simple and one, is furthermore experienced psychically as a surprise and seizure from without, rather than as a self-determination from within. And this psychic peculiarity is taken by her as but the occasion and emotional, quasi-sensible picturing of the ever-present and ever-growing experience and conviction that all right human action, the very self-donation of the creature, is the Creator's best gift, and that the very act of her own mind and heart, in all its complete inalienableness and spontaneity, is yet, in the last resort, but an illumination and stimulation coming from beyond the reaches of her own mind and will, from the mind and will of God. And thus Ethics are englobed by Religion, Having by Doing, and Doing by Being: yet not so that, in her fullest life, any of the higher things suppress the lower, but so that each stimulates the very things that it transcends.

We shall trace farther on how largely and spontaneously she has, from out of the many different possible types and forms of spirituality chosen out, assimilated and further explicated certain Platonic and especially certain Neo-Platonic conceptions. We shall be unable to suggest any likely intermediary, or to assume with certainty a direct derivation, for these conceptions from Plato, or indeed from Plotinus or Proclus; and shall nevertheless be obliged to postulate some now untraceable communication, on some most important points, between Plato and herself. Besides this, she derives one Platonic conception from the Book of Wisdom and a corresponding passage in St. Paul; and a certain general Platonic tone and imagery from the Johannine Gospel and First Epistle. Her Neo-Platonism, on the contrary, she derives, massively and all but pure, through two of the Pseudo-Dionysian books and her dearly loved Franciscan Mystic Poet, Jacopone da Todi. It is indeed to the Pauline, Johannine, Dionysian, and Jacopone writings that she owes, with the exception of a certain group of Platonic conceptions, practically all that she did not directly derive from her own psychical and spiritual experiences.

Now her assimilation of this particular strain of doctrine has remained but partial and theoretical with respect to those parts of Dionysian Neo-Platonism which were not borne out by the facts of her own Christian experience; but it has extended even to her emotional attitude and practice, in cases where the doctrine was borne out by these facts.

Thus we shall find that she often speaks theoretically of Evil as simply negative, as the varyingly great absence of Good. Yet, in practice and in her autobiographical picturings, she fights her bad self, to the very last, as a truly positive force. The force of God is everywhere conceived as indefinitely greater, as, indeed, alone infinite; yet the force of Evil is practically experienced and pictured as real and positive also, in its kind and degree.

Again, she often speaks as though her spiritual life had, at some one particular moment, simply arrived at its final culmination, and had attained God and perfection with complete finality,—such, at least, as this particular soul of hers can achieve. Yet, very shortly after, we find her unmistakably in renewed movement and conflict, and observe her mind to be now fully aware of that past "perfection" having been but imperfect, because that act or state is now seen from a height higher than that former level: hence that "perfection" was perfect, at most, in relation to its helps and opportunities in and for its own special movement.

Again, it is at times as though she conceived her body to be a sheer clog and prison-house to the soul, and as though the soul's weakness and sinfulness were essentially due to its union with the flesh. But here especially her later commentators have amplified and systematised her teaching almost beyond recognition; the authentic sayings of this kind, though too strong to be pressed, are few, and belong exclusively to the last stages of her illness; and, above all, these declarations are checked and entirely eclipsed by her normal and constant view as to the specific nature of Moral Evil. For this Evil consists, for her, essentially in the self-idolatry, the claimful self-centredness of the natural man, ever tending, in a thousand mostly roundabout ways, to make means and ends, centre and circumference, Sun and Planet change places, and to put some more or less subtle wilfulness and pleasure-seeking in the place of Duty, Happiness and God. Few, even amongst the Saints, can have realised and exemplified more profoundly the indelible difference between pleasure and happiness, between the false and the true self; and few have more keenly, patiently felt and taught that the soul's true life is, even eventually, not a keeping or a getting what the lower instincts crave: but that, on the contrary, a whole world of pleasures which, however base and short and misery-productive, can be intensely and irreplaceably pleasur-

able while they last, has successively to be sacrificed, for good
and all; and that what is retained has gradually to proceed
from other motives, to be grouped around other centres, and
be ever only a part and a servant, and never a master or the
whole. The gulf between every kind of Autocentricism
and the Theocentric life, between mere Eudæmonism
and Religion, could not be found anywhere more constant
or profound.

Again, it is at times as though the absence or suppression
of even the noblest of human fellow-feelings and of particular,
parental and friendly, attachments, and not their purification
and deepening, multiplication and harmonisation, were the
end and aim of perfection. But little or nothing of this
belongs, I think, to any deliberate and enduring theory of
hers, still less to her full and normal practice; and the impression of such inhumanity is, in so far as it is derived from
authentic documents, entirely caused by and restricted to
her early convert reaction, and her late over-strained or
worn-out psycho-physical condition.

Again, it is sometimes as though she believed indeed in an
energising and progress of the soul, yet held this progress to
be, after conversion, an absolutely unbroken, equable, necessary and automatic increase in perfection; and that such a
soul's last state is, necessarily and in all respects, better than
were its previous stages.—The Redactors of her life most
undoubtedly think this. Because, for instance, she was Matron
from 1490 to 1496, and could no more fill the post from 1496
to 1510:—therefore "not to give part of her activity to such
external work was more perfect than to give it," is the argument that underlies their scheme for these two periods.—
Yet I can find nothing in her teaching to show that she held
any such view. She was, indeed, ever too much absorbed,
by the experiences and duties of her successive moments,
to find even the leisure of mind requisite for the manufacture
of so doctrinaire a system. And indeed there is nothing in
the conception of sanctity, or in that of a gradual and general
increase in generosity and purity of the saintly soul's dispositions and intentions, which requires us to hold that such

a soul's last state and efficiency is, in every respect, better than the first. For the range and volume of the efficiency, wisdom, balance, appropriateness of even our goodness is not determined by our will and the graces given to our will alone. Physical and psychical health and strength, illness and weakness; helps and hindrances from friends and foes; the changing influences and limitations of growing age; and the ever-shifting combinations of all these and of similar things,—things and combinations which are all but indirectly attainable by our wills in any way: all this is ever as truly at work upon us as our wills and God's spiritual graces are in operation directly within ourselves. And if Catherine's richness, breadth and balance of soul are, considering her special and successive health and circumstances, remarkable up to the very end, and probably actually grew to some extent with the growing obstacles, yet those qualities hardly grew or could grow *pari passu* with these obstacles. The manifold efficiency and the unity in multiplicity were distinctly greater before 1496 than after. And thus the Saints too join their lowlier brethren in paying the pathetic debt of our common mortality. They too can be called upon to survive the culmination of their many-sided power, and to retain perpetual youth only as regards their intention and the central ideas and the spiritual substance of their soul.

Once more she seems as though, to make up for this apparent suppression of the element of time, unduly to press the category of space, at least in her contemplations. We shall see how often in these contemplations God Himself, and the soul, or at least its various states, appear as places; so that the whole spiritual life and world come thus to look rather like an atomic co-ordination, a projection on the space and a static mechanism, than an interpenetrative subordination, a production in time or at least in duration, and a dynamic organism.—Yet it will be found that all this imagery is consciously, though no doubt quite naturally, used only *as* imagery, and that it is thus used both because it was spontaneously presented to her mind by her psychic peculiarities and because it readily adapted itself as a vehicle to

L

express one of the deepest experiences and convictions of
her spirit.

For her psychic peculiarities involved, on the one hand, a
curiously rapid and complete change and difference of states
of consciousness, and, on the other hand, a remarkable
absence (or at least dimness) of consciousness as to this
transition itself, which, however abrupt, was of course as
truly a part of her inner life as were the several completed
states and outlooks. Now the apparently static element and
harmony in any one of these states could, of course, be at all
clearly presented in no other form than that of a spatial
image; whereas the changing element in all these states seems
to have accumulated chiefly in the subconscious region, to
have at last suddenly burst into the conscious sphere, and to
have there effected the change too rapidly to permit of, or
at least to require, the presentation of this element as such,
a presentation which could only have taken the form of a
consciousness of time or of duration. From all this it follows
that, to her immediate psychic consciousness, each of her
successive experiences presented itself as ever one spatial
picture, as one "place."

And the imagery, thus quasi-automatically presented to
her, could not fail to be gladly used and emphasised by her to
express the deepest experiences of her spiritual life. For it
was the element of simultaneity, of organic interpenetration,
of the God-like *Totum Simul*, which chiefly impressed her in
these deepest moments. And hence the soul is conceived by
her as, in its essence, eternal rather than as immortal—as, in
its highest reaches and moments, outside of time and not as
simply wholly within it; and as, on such occasions, vividly
though indirectly conscious of the fact. Heaven itself is
thought of not as eventually succeeding, with its own endless
succession, to the finite succession of these our fleeting earthly
days; but as already forming the usually obscure, yet ever
immensely operative, background, groundwork, measure and
centre of our being, now and here as truly as there and then.
And hence again, Heaven, Purgatory, and Hell are for her
three distinct states of the soul, already effected in their

essence here below, and experienced as what they are, in part and occasionally here, and fully and continuously hereafter. Thus the fundamental cleavage in the soul's life is not between things successive,—between the Now and the Then, and at the point of death; but between things simultaneous, between the This and the That, and at the point of sin and of self-seeking.

And finally, she seems at times to speak Greek-wise, as though the soul's life consisted essentially, or even exclusively, in an intellection, a static contemplation. Yet we have already seen how robust and constant is her ethical dualism, how essentially, here below at least, happiness consists for her in a right affection and attachment, in the continuous detaching of the true self from the false self, and the attaching of the true self unto God. And we should note how that intellection itself is conceived as ever accompanied by a keen sense of its inferiority to the Reality apprehended, and as both the result and the condition and the means of love and of an increase of love. And again we should note that this sense of inferiority does not succeed the intellection, as the result of any reasoning on the disparity between the finite and Infinite, but accompanies that intellection itself, and corresponds to the surplusage of her feelings over her mental seeings, and of her experience over her knowledge. And we should add the fact that, in the most emphatic of her sayings, she makes the essence of Heaven to consist in the union of the finite with the Infinite Will; and that this doctrine alone would seem readily to harmonise with her favourite teaching as to Heaven beginning here below.

If the Platonic and Neo-Platonic elements appear, at first sight, as massive and even excessive constituents of Catherine's doctrine, Historical and Institutional Christianity seems, on a cursory survey, to contribute strangely little even to her practice. Not one of her ordinary contemplations is directly occupied with any scene from Our Lord's life. The picture of the "Pietà," so impressive to her in her nursery-days; the great Conversion-Vision of the Bleeding Christ; and the slighter cases of the signing of herself with the sign of the

Cross and of her lying with outstretched arms, which occurred during the last stage of her illness, are the sole indications of any immediate occupation with the Passion; whilst the two cases of the Triptych "Maestà" and the painting representative of Our Lord at the well (cases which indicate an attraction to the Infancy and to at least one incident of the Public Life) complete the list of all direct attention to any incidents of Our Lord's earthly existence. As to occupation with or invocation of the Saints, inclusive of the Blessed Virgin, I can find but one instance, the invocation of St. Benedict, two days before her Conversion. We have seen, as to Sacramental Confession, how little there can have been of it, throughout the long middle period of her Convert Life; and how she was, during this time, simply without any priestly guidance. And she never was a Tertiary, nor did she belong to any Confraternity, nor did she attempt to gain Indulgences, nor did she practise popular devotions, such as the Rosary or Scapular.

Nor could these facts be quite fairly met, except to a certain relatively small extent with regard to Confession, by insistence upon the changing character of the Church's discipline, if we thus mean to assert that she did not, in these matters, act exceptionally with regard to the practice and theory of fervent souls of her own time. For, on all the points mentioned, the ordinary fervent practice was already, and had been for centuries, different; and, in the matter of priestly guidance, her chroniclers have not failed to transmit to us the wonders and murmurs of more than one contemporary.

Yet here again the prima facie impression is but very incompletely borne out by a closer study.

For first, none of these historical and institutional elements are ever formally excluded, or attacked, or slighted. Indeed, in the matter of Indulgences, we have seen how she arranged or allowed that monies of her own should be spent in procuring certain facilities for gaining them by others.

And next, special practices, more than equivalent in their irksomeness, are throughout made to take the place of ordinary practices, in so far and for so long as these latter are abstained from. An unusually severe ascetical penitential time, and then the rarest watchfulness and continuous self-renouncement, take thus, for a considerable period, the place of the sacramental forms of Penance.

And thirdly, if there is an unusual rarity in Confession there is an almost as rare frequency of Communion; and authentic anecdotes show us how she scandalised some good souls as truly by this frequency as by that rarity. Indeed throughout her convert life, an ardent devotion to the Holy Eucharist forms the very centre of her daily life; during probably thirty-five years she only quite exceptionally misses daily Communion; and she has the deepest attraction to the Mass, and a holy envy of priests for their close relation to the Blessed Sacrament. And though there are no contemplations of hers directly occupied with the Holy Eucharist, yet we shall find this experience and doctrine to have profoundly shaped and coloured teachings and apprehensions which, at first sight, are quite disconnected with It. We can already see how all-inclusive a symbol and stimulation of her other special attractions and conceptions this central devotion could not fail to be. She found here the Infinite first condescending to the finite; so that the finite may then rise towards the Infinite; the soul's life, a hunger and a satisfaction of that hunger, through the taste of feeling rather than through the sight of reason; God giving Himself through such apparently slight vehicles, in such short moments, and under such bewilderingly humble veils; and our poor *a priori* notions and *a posteriori* analyses thus proved inadequate to the living soul and the living God.—Extreme Unction also was highly esteemed: she spontaneously demanded it some four times and finally received it with great fervour. Church hymns too—witness the "Veni, Creator," chanted on her death-bed —and liturgical lights are spontaneously used.

And lastly, her practice in the matter of Confession and of priestly advice became, during her last thirteen years, identical in frequency with that of her devout contemporaries; and thus her life ended with the practice, on all the chief points, of the average, ordinary devotional acts and habits of her time. And this final practice of the ordinary means, together with her lifelong dislike of singularity and of notice; her humble misgivings in the midst of her most peaceful originalities, and the utter absence of any tendency to think her way, inasmuch as it was at all singular, the only way or even the best way, except just now and here for her own self alone; her complete freedom from the spirit of comparing self with others, of dividing off the sheep from the goats, or of having some short, sure and universal means or test for holiness: all this shows us plainly how Catholic and unsectarian, how truly free, not only from slavish fear and pusillanimous conformity, but also from all enthralment to merely subjective fancies, from all solipsism or conceit was her strong soul.

It has been well said that there are three stages of the spiritual life, and three corresponding classes of souls.

There are the souls that are characterised, even to the end of their earthly lives, by that, more or less complete, naturalistic Individualism, with which we all in various degrees begin. Catherine's own time and country were full of such thoroughly Individualistic, unmoral or even anti-moral men, who, however gifted and cultivated as artists, scholars, philosophers, and statesmen, must yet be counted as essentially childish and as clever animals rather than as spiritual men. And she herself had, during the five years which had preceded her conversion, tended, on the surface of her being, towards something of this kind.

Next come the souls that have recognised and have accepted Duty and Obligation, that are now striving to serve God as God, and that are attempting, with a preponderant sincerity, to live the common and universal life of the Spirit. These of necessity tend to suspect, or even to suppress and sacrifice, whatever appears to be peculiar to themselves, as so much individualistic subjectivity and insidious high treason to the objective law of Him who made their souls, and who now bids them save those souls at any cost. The large majority of the souls that were striving to serve God in Catherine's times belonged, as souls belong in these our days, and will necessarily

and rightly bel   e end, to this second, universalistic,
uniformative typ   ss. And Catherine herself evidently
belonged promine.   this type and class, during her first
four convert years.

And there are, finall , an ever relatively small number of
souls that are called, and a still smaller number that attain,
to a state in which the Universality, Obligation, Uniformity
and Objectivity, of the second stage and class, take the form
of a Spiritual Individuality, Liberty, Variety and Subjectivity: Personality in the fullest sense of the term has now
appeared. And this fullest Spiritual Personality is the profoundest opposite and foe of its naturalistic counterfeit, of
those spontaneous animal liberalisms which reigned, all but
unrecognised as such because all but uncontrasted by the true
ideal and test of life, prior to that prostration before absolute
obligation, that poignant sense of weakness and impurity,
and that gain of strength and purity from beyond its furthest
reaches, experienced by the soul at its conversion.

Yet that merely subjective, liberalistic Individualism of the
first stage can only be kept out, even at the third stage, by
retaining within the soul all the essential characteristics of the
second stage,—by a continuous passing and re-passing under
the Caudine Forks of the willed defeat of wayward, self-
pleasing wilfulness, and of the deliberate acceptance of an
objective system of ideas and experiences as interiorly binding
upon the self. For if the second stage excludes the first, the
third stage does not exclude the second. Yet now all this,
in these rare souls, leads up to and produces a living reality
bafflingly simple in its paradoxical, mysterious richness. For
now the universality, obligation and objectivity of the Law
become and appear greater, not less, because incarnated in
an eminently unique and unreproduceable, in a fully personal
form. And at this stage only do we find a full persuasiveness.

Catherine attained unmistakably, after her four years of
special penitence, to this rare third stage. For not only is
she essentially as individual and unique as if she were not
universal and uniform; and essentially as universal and
uniform as if she were not individual: but she is indefinitely

more truly original and subjective, because of her voluntary boundness and objectivity. Indeed she is solidly and really free and personal, because the continuous renunciation and expulsion of all naturalistic individuality remains, to the very end, one of the essential functions of her soul.

From all this it is clear how easy it would be to misread the lesson of her manifold life, and to turn such examples as hers from a help into a hindrance. For her melancholy temperament, her peculiar psychic health, her final external inefficiency: all this is too striking not to tempt the admiration, perhaps even the hopeless and ruinous imitation, of such crude and inexperienced souls as know not how to distinguish between the merely given materials and untransferable determinisms of each separate soul's psychical and temperamental native outfit, and the free, grace-inspired and grace-aided use made by each soul of these, its more or less unique, occasions and materials. Those materials were, of themselves, of no moral worth, and lent themselves only in part with any ease to the upbuilding and realisation of her spirit's ideal. And it is only this, her wise and heroic use of her materials,—though this also, of course, is not directly transferable,—that represents the spiritually valuable constituent of the life.

Similarly with the form, and the psychic occasions or accompaniments of her very prayer and spiritual absorptions, and with some of the constituents of her doctrine, if taken as speculative and analytic and final, rather than as psychological and descriptive and preliminary. These things again could easily be misused. For the former are largely quite special and, in themselves, morally indifferent peculiarities, transformed and utilised by quite special graces and lifelong spiritual heroisms. And the latter, we shall find, were never intended to be systematic, complete or ultimate; and indeed they owe their true force and value to their being the occasional, spontaneous and immediate expressions and adumbrations of an experience indefinitely richer and more ultimate than themselves.

And finally, it would of course be absurd to take the

limitations of her activity and interests, even if we were to restrict ourselves to those common to all the stages of her life, as necessarily admirable, or as universally inevitable. For there is, in the very nature of things, no equation between her one soul, however rich and stimulating, or even all the souls of her class and school, or of her age or country, on the one hand, and the totality of religious experience, and its means and incorporations, on the other hand, even if, by totality, we but mean that part of it already achieved and accepted by grace-impelled mankind.

26. WHAT WE MAY LEARN FROM CATHERINE

AND yet Catherine's life and teaching will be found full of suggestion and stimulation, if they are taken in their inter-penetration, and if due regard is paid to their fragmentary registration, to the necessary distinction between what, amongst all these facts, was mere means, occasion and temporal setting, and what amongst them was aim and end, utilisation and abiding import, and to the fact that all this experience is but one out of the indefinitely many applica-tions, extensions and mutually corrective and supplementary exemplifications of the spirit and life of Christ, as it lives itself out throughout the temperaments, races and ages of mankind. Above all it can teach us, I think, with a rare completeness, wherein lies the secret of a persuasive holiness. For Catherine lets us see, with unusual clearness, how this winningness lies in the pathetically dramatic spectacle and appeal presented by a life engaged in an ever-increasing ethical and spiritual energising,—whether in a slow shifting and pushing of its actual centre, down and in from the circumference of the soul to its true centre, and from this true centre enlarging and reorganising its whole ever-expanding being again and again; or in an apparently sudden finding itself placed, and loyally placing itself, in this true centre, and then from there prosecuting and maintaining the organisation and transformation of its varyingly peripheral life, a life treated at one time as central and complete. And this persuasiveness can here be discovered to be greater or less in proportion to the thoroughness and continuousness of this centralisation and purification; to the degree in which this issues in a new, spontaneously acting ethico-spiritual personality; and to the closeness and costingness of the connection between those means and this result. Such a soul will be persuasive because of its ever seeking and finding a purifying intermediacy, a river of death, to all its merely naturalistic self-seeking.

And it is this nobly ascetic requirement and search and end which no doubt explain what, at first sight, is strange, both in its presence and in its attractiveness, in her own case and more or less in that of all the mature and complete Saints,—I mean, the large predominance of an apparently Pantheistic element in her life, the strong emphasis laid upon an apparent Thing-Conception of God and of the human spirit.

It was clearly not alone because of the Neo-Platonist element and influence of the books she chiefly used that she, in true Greek fashion, finds and allows so large a place for conceptions of things, for images derived from the natural elements, and for mental abstractions, in her religious experiences and teachings: God appearing in them predominantly as Sun, Light, Fire, Air, Ocean; Beauty, Truth, Love, Goodness. For, after all, other elements could be found in these very books, and other writings were known to her besides these books: hence this her preference for just these elements still demands an explanation.

Nor was it ultimately because, nervously high-pitched and strained as she was by nature, she even physically craved and required an immense expansion for this her excessive natural concentration. She thus evidently longed first to move through, and to bathe and rest and spread out her psychic self, in an ample region, in an enduring state of quasi-unconsciousness, in an (as it were) innocently animal or even simply vegetative objectivity, indeed in an apparent bare element and mere Thing, before, thus rested, braced, and as it were now healthily reconcentrated, she more directly met the Infinite Concentration and Determination, the Personal Spirit, God. For, after all, hers was so heroic a spirit, and so self-distrustful, indeed self-suspecting, a heart, that a mere psychic affinity or requirement would have failed so permanently and deliberately to captivate her mind.

Nor, finally, was it ultimately because her domestic sorrows or inexperiences, or even her very psychic peculiarities and apparent lack of all even innocent sensuousness, left the images of Bride and Bridegroom, of Parent and Child, perhaps even of Friend, respectively painful, empty, or pale to her consciousness. For, even so, she could and did care, with a beautiful affectiveness of her own, for her brothers and sister, for Vernazza, her "spiritual son," and for many a humble toiler or domestic. And indeed her whole tendency is ultimately to find God's special home, the only one of His dwelling-places which we men really know, in the human heart of hearts.

The ultimate and determining reason was no doubt her deep spiritual experience and conviction (as vivid as ever was the psychic tendency which gave it form and additional emotional edge and momentum) that she must continuously first quench and drown her feverish immediacy, her clamorous, claimful false self, and must lose herself, as a merely natural Individual, in the river and ocean of the Thing, of Law, of that apparently ruthless Determinism which fronts life everywhere, before she could find herself again as a Person, in union with and in presence of an infinite Spirit and Personality.

Thus Greek Fate is here retained, but it is transformed through being transplaced. For Fate has here ceased to be ultimate and above the very gods, the poor gods who were so predominantly the mere projections of man's Individualism: Fate is here intermediate and a way to God—the great God, the source and ideal of all Personality. And indeed this Fate is not, ultimately, simply separate from God; it is indeed omnipresent, but everywhere only as the preliminary and subaltern, expression, for us men, of the Divine Freedom that lies hidden and operating behind it. And we men

attain to some of this Freedom only by the inclusion within
our spiritual life of that Fate-passage and of our actual
constant passing through it, on and on.

In the general tendency and form of her inner life and
conviction Catherine has, of course, substantially nothing but
what she shares with all the Mystics, in proportion as these
retain Law, Ethics and Personality; and she has much that
forms part of the convictions of all Christians, indeed of all
Theists. Yet in the degree and precise manner of her elaboration and application of those things, and again in the circumstances of their documentary transmission, Catherine will,
I think, be found in three points comparatively original, and
in a fourth point practically unique.

First she has, as we have seen, not only a strikingly persistent attitude of transcendence and detachment with regard
to her psycho-physical state in general (this is indeed an
attitude common to all ethically sound and fruitful Mystics:
witness in particular St. John of the Cross); but she has also
a most remarkable faculty and activity of discrimination
between her own healthy and morbid states. Even this latter
power she probably shares, in various degrees, with all such
ethical-minded Mystics as nevertheless suffered from a
partially *maladif* psycho-physical condition: witness especially
St. Teresa.—Yet contemporary documentary evidence, for
not only such actual variations between healthy and unhealthy
states, but also for the Mystic's knowledge of and witness to
the existence of both and to the difference between the two,
is necessarily rare. I know of no evidence more vivid and
final, although of much that is larger in amount, than the
evidence furnished by Catherine's *Vita*.

And next she has both a constant, deep sense that religion
never consists simply in ends but in means as well, and never
ceases to use and practise the latter; and a concomitant keen
apprehension of the difference between means and ends, and
ever illustrates this sense of difference by the striking variety
and liberty of the practical attitude which she is successively
moved to take, and actually does take, towards this or that of
the Institutional helps of the Church. Here again she but

exemplifies a principle which underlies the practice of all the Saints, in proportion to their maturity and full normality. And indeed our Lord Himself, the Model and the King of Saints, when asked which was the greatest of the Commandments, did not answer that He could not and would not tell, since to distinguish at all between greater and lesser Commandments would be liberalism; but, on the contrary, fully endorsed and canonised such a distinction and discrimination, by actually pointing out two Commandments as the greatest, and by declaring that from them depended all the law and the prophets. Hence to organise, and more and more to find and give their right, relative place and influence to all the different things practised and believed, is as important as is the corresponding practice and acceptance of all these different things. Yet, here again, full evidence both for such fidelity and docility and for such variety and liberty of soul, with regard to the means of religion, is rare: the records of the modern Saints mostly give us but the docility; those of the Fathers of the desert generally give us but the liberty; Catherine's *Vita* gives us both.

And thirdly, she is, amongst formally canonised Saints, a rare example of a contemplative and mystic who, from first to last, leads at the same time the common life of marriage and of widowhood in the world. Here again any misapprehension of the importance or significance of this fact would readily lead to folly. For it is undeniable that it has been the monastic life which, in however great variations of degree, form and lasting success, has furnished Christendom at large with an impersonation of self-renunciation sufficiently isolated, massive and continuous to be deeply impressive upon the sluggish spiritual apprehension of the average man. And indeed self-renunciation is so universally necessary and so universally difficult; upon its presence and activity religion, and all and every kind of rational human life depend so largely; without its tonic presence they are so necessarily but a dilettantism, a delusion or an hypocrisy: that to body it forth for all men must ever remain an honour and a duty specially incumbent upon some kind of Monasticism. For it is but right, and indeed alone respectful, to the Spirit of God, so manifold and mysterious in its gifts and inspirations, that every degree and kind of healthy and heroic self-renunciation should be practised and embodied; and that special honour should attach to its most massive manifestations.

Yet our general knowledge of poor, rarely balanced human nature and our detailed historical experience respectively anticipate and demonstrate how easy it is, on this point also, to confound the means with the end, and a part with the whole. And by such confusion either self-renunciation, that very salt of all truly human existence, gets actually stapled up in one corner of the wide world and of multiform life; or this apparent stapling becomes but a pedantic pretence and would-be monopoly, the salt meanwhile losing all its savour. And these two abuses and errors easily coalesce and reinforce each other. The fact is that the total work and duty of collective humanity,—the production of a maximum of true recollection, rest and detachment, effected in and through a maximum of right dispersion, action and attachment; above all a maximum of ethico-spiritual transformation of the world and, in and through such work, of each single worker,—is too high for any single soul, or even class or vocation, to hope to exhaust. Only by all and each joining hands and supplementing each other can all these numberless degrees and kinds of call and goodness, together, slowly, throughout the ages, get nearer and nearer to that inexhaustible ideal which lies so deep and ineradicable within the heart of each and all. And thus will the two fundamental movements of the soul, as it were its expiration and its inspiration, the going out to gather and the coming home to garner, be kept up, in various degrees, by every human soul, and each soul and vocation will as keenly feel the need of supplementation, as it will apprehend the beauty and importance of the special contribution it is called to make to the whole, a whole here, as everywhere, greater than any of its parts, although requiring them each and all.—Now Catherine suggests and illustrates such a doctrine with rare impressiveness: for the pure and efficient love of God and man, the one end and measure for us all, ever consciously dominates all and every means within her admirably balanced and unified mind; and the renunciative element is under mostly quite ordinary exterior forms, as complete and constant as it could be found anywhere.

And lastly, her doctrine contains one conviction, or group of convictions, as original as, in such matters, one can expect to find. We get here the soul's voluntary plunge into Purgatory, its seeking and finding relief, from the now painful pleasure of sin, in the now joy-producing pain of purification; and the soul's discovery and acquisition, if and when in predominantly good dispositions, of its ever-fuller peace and bliss, because its ever-increasing harmonisation, in freely willing the suffering intrinsically consequent upon its own past evil pleasures and the resulting present imperfections of its will. And this cycle of facts and laws here springs from, and begins with, the soul's life Here and Now, and is held to extend (on the ever-present assumption of the substantial persistence of the spirit's fundamental spiritual properties and laws) to the soul's life Then and There. Thus these two lives differ with her rather in extent and intensity than in kind.

27. CATHERINE'S INTERPRETATIVE RELIGION

Now, by Interpretative Religion, I do not mean to imply that there is anywhere, in *rerum natura*, such a thing as a religion which is not interpretative, which does not consist as truly of a reaction on the part of the believing soul to certain stimulations of and within it, as of these latter stimulations and actions. As every (even but semi-conscious) act and state of the human mind, ever embraces both such action of the object and such reaction of the subject,—a relatively crude fact of sensation or of feeling borne in upon it, and an interpretation, an incorporation of this fact by, and into, the living tissue and organism of this mind: so is it also, necessarily and above all, with the deepest and most richly complex of all human acts and states,—the specifically religious ones.—

But if this interpretative activity of the mind was present from the very dawn of human reason, and exists in each individual in the precise proportion as mind can be predicated as operative within him at all: this mental activity is yet the last element in the compound process and result which is, or can be, perceived as such by the mind itself. The process is too near to the observer, even when he is once awake to its existence; he is too much occupied with the materials brought before his mind and with moulding and sorting them out; and this moulding and sorting activity is itself too rapid and too deeply independent of those materials as to its form, and too closely dependent upon them as to its content, for the observation by the mind of this same mind's contributions towards its own affirmations of reality and of the nature of this reality, not ever to appear late in the history of the human race or in the life of any human individual, or not to be, even when it appears difficult, a fitful and an imperfect mental exercise.

And when the discovery of this constant contribution of the mind to its own affirmations of reality is first made, it can hardly fail, for the time being, to occasion misgivings and anxieties of a more or less sceptical kind. Is not the whole of what I have hitherto taken to be a solid world of sense outside me, and the whole of the world of necessary truth and of obligatory goodness within me,—is it not, perhaps, all a merely individual creation of my single mind—a mind cut off from all effective intercourse with reality,—my neighbour's mind included? For all having, so far, been held to be objective, the mind readily flies to the other extreme, and suspects all to be subjective. Or if all my apprehensions and certainties are the resultants from the interaction between impressions received by my senses and mind and reactions and elaborations on the part of this mind with regard to those impressions, how can I be sure of apprehending rightly, unless I can divide each constituent off from the other? And yet, how can I effect such a continuous discounting of my mind's action by means of my own mind itself?

And this objection is felt most keenly in religion, when the religious soul first wakes up to the fact that itself, of necessity and continuously, contributes, by its own action, to the constitution of those affirmations and certainties, which, until then, seemed, without a doubt, to be directly borne in upon a purely receptive, automatically registering mind, from that extra-, super-human world which it thus affirmed. Here also, all having for so long been assumed to be purely objective, the temptation now arises to consider it all as purely subjective. Or again, if we insist upon holding that, here too, there are both objective and subjective elements, we readily experience keen distress at our inability clearly to divide off the objective, which is surely the reality, from the subjective, which can hardly fail to be its travesty.

And finally, this doubt and trouble would seem to find specially ready material in the mystical element and form of religion. For here, as we have already seen, psycho-physical and auto-suggestive phenomena and mechanisms abound; here especially does the mind cling to an immediate access to Reality; and here the ordinary checks and complements afforded by the Historical and Institutional, the Analytically Rational, and the Volitional, Practical elements of Religion are at a minimum. Little but the Emotional and the Speculatively Rational elements seems to remain; and these, more than any others, appear incapable of admitting that they are anything other than the pure and direct effects and expressions of spiritual Reality.

What, then, shall we think of all this?

We evidently must, in the first instance, guard against any attempt at doing a doctrinaire violence to the undeniable facts of our consciousness or of its docile analysis, by explaining all our knowledge, or only even all our knowledge of any single thing, as either of purely subjective or of purely objective provenance; for everywhere and always these two elements co-exist in all human apprehension, reason, feeling, will and faith. We find, throughout, an organisation, an indissoluble organism, of subjective and objective, hence a unity in diversity, which is indeed so great that (for our own experience and with respect to our own minds at all events)

M

the Subjective does not and cannot exist without the Objective, nor the Objective without the Subjective.

In the next place, we must beware against exalting the Objective against the Subjective, or the Subjective against the Objective, as if Life, Reality and Truth consisted in the one rather than the other. Because the subjective element is, on the first showing, a work of our own minds, it does not follow (as we shall see more clearly when studying the ultimate problems) that its operations are bereft of correspondence with reality, or, at least, that they are farther from reality than are our sense-perceptions. For just as the degree of worth represented by these sense-perceptions can range from the crudest delusion to a stimulation of primary importance and exquisite precision, so also our mental and emotional reaction and penetration represent almost any and every degree of accuracy and value.

And, above all, as already implied, the true priority and superiority lies, not with one of these constituents against the other, but with the total subjective-objective interaction and resultant, which is superior, and indeed gives their place and worth to, those ever interdependent parts.

Catherine herself, although delightfully free from the long scale of mediations between the soul and God which forms one of the predominant doctrines of the Areopagite, continues and emphasises most of what is common, and much of what is special to, all and each of these four writers [1]; she is a reflective saint, if ever there was one. And of her too we shall have to say that she is great by what she possesses, and not by what she is without: great because of her noble embodiment of the reflective and emotional, the mystical and volitional elements of Christianity and Religion generally. Religion is here, at first sight at least, all but entirely a thought and an emotion; yet all this thought and emotion is directed to, and occasioned by, an abiding Reality which originates, sustains, regulates and fulfils it. And although this Reality is in large part conceived, in Greek and specially in Neo-Platonist fashion, rather under its timeless and spaceless,

[1] St. Paul, Pseudo-Dionysius, St. John and Jacopone da Todi.

or at least under its cosmic aspect, rather as Law and Substance, than as Personality and Spirit: yet, already because of the strong influence upon her of the noblest Platonic doctrine, it is loved as overflowing Love and Goodness, as cause and end of all lesser love and goodness; and the real, though but rarely articulated, acceptance and influence of History and Institutions, above all the enthusiastic devotion to the Holy Eucharist with all its great implications, gives to the whole a profoundly Christian tone and temper.

True, the Church at large, indeed the single soul (if we would take such a soul as our standard of completeness), requires a larger proportion of those crisp, definite outlines, of those factual, historical and institutional elements; a very little less than what remains in Catherine of these elements, and her religion would be a simple, even though deep religiosity, a general aspiration, not a definite finding, an explicit religion. Yet it remains certain, although ever readily forgotten by religious souls, especially by theological apologists, that without some degree and kind of those outgoing, apprehending, interpreting activities, no religion is possible. Only the question as to what these activities should be, and what is their true place and function within the whole religious life, remains an open one. And this question we can study with profit in connection with such a life and teaching as Catherine's, which brings out, with a spontaneous, childlike profundity and daring, the elemental religious passion, the spiritual hunger and thirst of man when he is once fully awake; the depths within him anticipating the heights above him; the affinity to and contact with the Infinite implied and required by that nobly incurable restlessness of his heart, which finds its rest in Him alone Who made it.

28. CATHERINE'S FASTS

AND a little later on, again on the Feast of the Annunciation (25 March, 1476), another change took place, a change primarily concerned with her health, but one which brought out also the deep spirituality of her religion. On this day she experienced one of those interior locutions, which are so well authenticated in the lives of so many interior souls; and "her Love said that He wanted her to keep the Forty Days, in His company in the Desert. And then she began to be unable to eat till Easter; on the three Easter Days she was able to eat; and after these she again did not eat, till she had fulfilled as many days as are to be found in Lent." Similarly with regard to Advent. "Up to Martinmas" (12 November) "she would eat like all the world; and then her fast would begin, and would continue up to Christmas Day." Her subsequent Lenten fasts are described as beginning with Quinquagesima Monday and ending on Easter Sunday morning.

I take it that there can be no reasonable doubt as to the substantial accuracy of this account. But the following three facts must be borne in mind as regards the physical aspect of the matter.

The fast, for one thing, is not an absolute one. The account itself declares that she now and then drank a tumblerful of water, vinegar and pounded rock-salt. And to this must be added both the daily reception of wine—I suppose as much as a wineglassful—which was, according to a Genoese custom of that time, received by her, as a kind of ablution, immediately after her Communion; and such slight amount of solid food as, when in company, she would force herself to take and would sometimes, though rarely, manage to retain.

Again, the fast varies partly, in different years, in the date of its inception; and partly it does not synchronise with the beginning of the ecclesiastical fast. In the first year her Lenten fast begins on Lady Day, in the following years on Quinquagesima Sunday; her Advent fast begins throughout on Martinmas, 12 November.

And finally, the number of such fasts cannot be more than twenty-three Lents and twenty-two Advents. The MS. of 1547 has preserved the right tradition of a difference in the numbers of the Lenten and Advent fasts, but has raised the number of the former to a round, symmetrical one. It gives twenty-five Lents and twenty-two Advents. The printed *Vita* of 1551 levels the numbers respectively down and up to twenty-three Lents and as many Advents. Some further minor physical points will be considered in a later chapter.

But two other matters are here of direct spiritual interest: the effect of these fasts on her spiritual efficiency, and her own two-fold attitude towards them. For we are told, again I think quite authentically, that during these fasts she was more active in good works, and felt more bright and strong in health, than usual; answering thus to one of the tests put forward by Pope Benedict XIV., for discriminating super-natural, spiritually valuable fasts from simply natural ones. But with him we can find our surest tests in what is altogether beyond the range of the physical and psychical: in her own moral estimate of all these matters. For one thing, there appears here again that noble shrinking from any singularity of this kind within herself, and from all notice on the part of others. "This inability to eat gave her many a scruple at first, ignorant as she was as to its cause, and ever suspecting some delusion; and she would force herself to eat, considering that nature required it. And though this invariably produced vomiting, yet she would make the attempt again and again." "She would go to table with the others, and would force herself to eat and drink a little, so as to escape notice and esteem as much as possible." And again here, as in all matters visible and tangible, she shows an impressive loneliness in the midst of her more carnal-minded disciples. "She would say within herself, in astonishment" at their stopping to wonder at things so much on the surface: "If you but knew another thing, which I feel within myself!" And she would declare: "If we would rightly estimate the operations of God, we should wonder more at interior than at exterior things. This incapacity to eat is indeed an operation of

God, but one in which my will has no part; hence I cannot glory in it. Nor is there cause for our wondering at it, since for God this is as though a mere nothing."

These fasts, although beginning within her first period, are not characteristic of it; and her biographers rightly put them into a chapter distinct from her penances, properly speaking. These penances will have continued alongside of, and in between, these fasts for about a year after the beginning of the latter. And then at last, at the end of this first period of four years, "all thought of such (active) mortifications was, in an instant, taken from her mind in such guise that, even had she wished to carry out such mortifications, she would have been unable." For "the sight of her sins was now taken from her mind, so that she henceforth did not catch a glimpse of them,—as though they had all been cast into the depths of the sea."

29. CATHERINE AND THE PLAGUE

It must have been after she had thus shown a rare devotedness and talent in an ordinary Nurse's work, and had next, as Matron, manifested, for some years, a remarkable administrative ability, that, in 1493, she rose, in both capacities, to the very height of heroism and efficiency.

Early in January of that year, quite exceptionally cold weather visited the city: the harbour was frozen over; and early in the spring the Plague broke out so fiercely, and raged so long—till the end of August—that of those who remained in the stricken city, four-fifths succumbed to the terrible disease. Most of the rich and noble, all those that did not occupy any official post, fled from the town. But Catherine not only remained at her post, but she it was no doubt who organised, or helped to organise, the out-of-door ambulance and semi-open-air wards which we know to have been instituted at this juncture on the largest scale. The great open space immediately at the back of and above the Hospital, where now still stretch the public gardens of the Acquasola, she managed to cover with rows of sailcloth tents, and appointed special Doctors (mostly Lombards), Nurses, and Priests and Franciscan Tertiaries, for the physical and spiritual care of their occupants. Throughout the weeks and months of the visitation she was daily in the midst, superintending, ordering, stimulating, steadying, consoling, strengthening this vast crowd of panic-stricken poor and severely strained workers.

And "on one occasion, she found" here, "a very devout woman, a Tertiary of St. Francis, dying of" this "pestilential fever. The woman lay there in her agony, speechless for eight days. And Catherine constantly visited her, and would say to her, 'Call Jesus.' Unable to articulate, the woman would move her lips; and it was conjectured that she was calling Him as well as she could. And Catherine, when she saw the woman's mouth thus filled, as it were, with Jesus, could not restrain herself from kissing it with great and tender affection. And in this way she herself took the pestilential fever, and very nearly died of it. But, as soon as ever she had recovered, she was back again at her work, with the same great attention and diligence."

How much there is in this little scene! Beautiful, utterly self-oblivious impulsiveness; a sleepless sense of the omnipresence of Christ as Love, and of this Love filling all things that aspire and thirst after it, as spontaneously as the liberal air and the overflowing mother's breast fill and feed even the but slightly aspiring or the painfully labouring lungs and the eager, helpless infant mouth; swift, tender, warm, wholehearted affection for this outwardly poor and disfigured, but inwardly rich and beautiful fellow-creature and twin-vessel of election; an underlying virile elasticity of perseverance and strenuous, cheerful, methodical laboriousness; all these things are clearly there.

30. THE THREE CATEGORIES AND THE TWO WAYS

THERE is, first, the great category of *in, within, down into*; that is, recollection, concentration. "The love which I have within my heart." "Since I began to love It, never again has that Love diminished; indeed It has ever grown to Its own fullness, within my innermost heart." Hence she would say to those who dwelt in admiration of her psycho-physical peculiarities: "If you but had experience (*sapeste*) of another thing which I feel within me!" And again, "If we would esteem (aright) the operations of God, we must attend more to interior than to exterior things." And, with regard to the Holy Eucharist, she would whisper, when seeing at Mass the Priest about to communicate: "O swiftly, swiftly speed It down to the heart, since it is the heart's own food"; and she would declare, with regard to her own Communion: "In the same instant in which I had It in my mouth, I felt It in my heart."

There is, next, the category of *out, outside, outwards*; that is, liberation, ecstasy. "The soul which came out from God pure and full has a natural instinct to return to God as full and pure (as it came)." "The soul finds itself bound to a body entirely contrary to its own nature, and hence expects with desire its separation from the body." "God grants the grace, to some persons, of making their bodies into a Purgatory (already) in this world." "When God has led the soul on to its last stage (*passo*), the soul is so full of desire to depart from the body to unite itself with God, that its body appears to it a Purgatory, keeping it far apart from its (true) object." "The prison, in which I seem to be, is the world; the chain is the body"; "to noble (*gentili*) souls, death is the end of an obscure prison; to the remainder, it is a trouble,—to such, that is, as have fixed all their care upon what is but so much dung (*fango*)." And, whilst strenuously mortifying the body, she would answer its resistances, as though so many audible complainings, and say: "If the body is dying, well, let it die; if the body cannot bear the load, well, leave the body in the lurch (O soul)."

And all this imprisonment is felt as equivalent to being outside of the soul's true home. "I seem to myself to be in this world like those who are out of their home, and who have left all their friends and relations, and who find themselves in a foreign land; and who, having accomplished the business on which they came, stand ready to depart and to return home,—home, where they ever are with heart and mind, having indeed so ardent a love of their country (*patria*), that one day spent in getting there would appear to them to last a year."

And this feeling of outsideness, seen here with regard to the relations of the soul to the body and to the world, we find again with regard to sanctity and the soul. In this latter case also the greater is felt to be (as it were) entrapped, and contained only very partially within the lesser; and as though this greater could and did exist, in its full reality, only outside of the lesser. "I can no more say 'blessed' to any saint, taken in himself, because I feel it to be an inappropriate (*deforme*) word"; "I see how all the sanctity which the saints have, is outside of them and all in God." Indeed she sums this up in the saying: "I see that anything perfect is entirely outside of the creature; and that a thing is entirely imperfect, when the creature can at all contain it." Hence "the Blessed possess (*hanno*) blessedness, and yet they do not possess it. For they possess it, only in so far as they are annihilated in their own selves and are clothed with God; and they do not possess it, in so far as they remain (*si trovano*) in their particular (*proprio*) being, so as to be able to say: '*I* am blessed.'"

There is, in the third place, the category of *over*, *above*, *upwards*; that is elevation, sublimation. We will begin with cases where it is conjoined with the previous categories, and will move on into more and more pure aboveness. "I am so placed and submerged in His immense love, that I seem as though in the sea entirely under water, and could on no side touch, see, or feel anything but water." And "if the sea were the food of love, there would exist no man nor woman that would not go and drown himself (*affogasse*) in it; and he who was dwelling far from this sea, would engage in nothing else but in walking to get to it and to immerse himself within it." The soul here feels the water on every side of it, yet evidently chiefly above it, for it has had to plunge in, to get *under* the water.

"Listen to what Fra Jacopone says in one of his Lauds, which begins, 'O Love of Poverty.' He says: 'That which appears to thee (to be), is not; so high above is that which *is*. (True) elevation (*superbia*) is in heaven; earthy lowness (*umiltà*) leads to the soul's own destruction.' He says then: 'That which appears to thee,' that is, all things visible, 'are not,' and have not true being in them: 'so high' and great 'is He who *is*,' that is, God, in whom is all true being. 'Elevation is in heaven,' that is, true loftiness and greatness is in heaven and not on earth; 'earthy lowness leads to the soul's own destruction,' that is, affection placed in these created things, which are low and vile, since they have not in them true being, produces this result."—"I feel," she says in explanation of what and how she knows, "a first thing above the intellect; and above this thing I feel another one and a greater; and above this other one, another, still more great; and so up and up does one thing go above the other, each thing ever greater (than its predecessors), that I conclude it to be impossible to express even a spark (*scintilla*) as to It" (the highest and greatest of the whole series, God). Here it is interesting still to trace the influence of the same passage of Jacopone (again referred to in this place by the *Vita*), and to see why she introduced "greatness" alongside of "loftiness" into her previous paraphrase.

Now this vivid impression of a strong upward movement, combined with the feeling of being in and under something, gives the following image, used by her during her last illness: "I can no longer manage to live on in this life, because I feel as though I were in it like cork under water." And this "above," unlike to "outside," is accompanied by the image, not of clothing but of nakedness; the clothes are left below. "This vehement love said to her, on one occasion: 'What art thou thinking of doing? I want thee all for myself. I want to strip thee naked, naked. The higher up thou shalt go, however great a perfection thou mayest have, the higher will I ever stand above thee, to ruin all thy perfections ' "—this, of course, inasmuch as she is still imperfect and falls short of the higher and higher perfections to which her soul is being led.

And as to man's faculties, she says: "As the intellect reaches higher (*supera*) than speech, so does love reach higher than intellect." And again, as a universal law: "When pure love speaks, it ever speaks above nature; and all the things which it does and thinks and feels are always above nature."

Now these three categories of within and inward, outside and outward, above and upward position and movement, can lead, and do actually lead in Catherine's case, to two separate lines of thought and feeling. And these lines are each too much a necessary logical conclusion from the constant working of these categories, and they are each again far too much, and even apart from these categories, expressive of two rival but complementary experiences, for either of them to be able to suppress or even modify the other. Each has its turn in the rich, free play of Catherine's life. I will take the negative line first, and then the positive, so as to finish up with affirmation, which will thus, as in her actual experience and practice, be all the deeper and more substantial, because it has passed, and is ever repassing, through a process of limitation and purification.

First, then, if grace and God are only within, *and* only without, *and* only above, she will and does experience contradiction and paradox in all attempts at explaining reality; she will thus find things to be obscure instead of clear; and she will end by affirming the unutterableness, the unthinkableness of God, indeed of all reality. "I see without eyes, I understand without understanding, I feel without feeling, and I taste without taste." "When the creature is purified, it sees the True; and such a sight is not a sight." "The sight of how it is God" who sends the soul its purifying trials "gives the soul a great contentment; and yet this contentment does not diminish the pain." Still, "pure love cannot suffer; nor can it understand what is meant by pain or torment." "The sun, which at first seemed so clear to me, now seems obscure; what used to seem sweet to me, now seems bitter: because all beauties and all sweetness that have an admixture of the creature are corrupt and spoilt." "As to Love, only this can we understand about It, that It is incomprehensible to the mind." "So long as a person can still talk of things divine, and can relish, understand, remember and desire them, he has not yet come to port." For indeed "all that can be said about God is not God, but only certain smallest fragments which fall from (His) table."

And yet those experiences of God's presence as, apparently, in a special manner within us, and without us, and above us, also lead, by means of another connection of ideas, to another, to a positive result. For those experiences can lead us to dwell, not upon the difference of the "places," but upon the apparent fact that He is in a "place" of some sort, in space somewhere, the exact point of which is still to find; and, by thus bringing home to the mind this underlying paradox of the whole position, they can help to make the soul shrink away from this false clarity, and to fall back upon the deep, dim, true view of God as existing, for our apprehension, in certain states of soul alone, states which have all along been symbolised for us by these different "places" and "positions." And thus what before was a paradox and mystery *qua* space, because at the same time within and without, and because not found by the soul "within" unless through getting "without" itself, becomes now a paradox and mystery *qua* state, because the soul at one and the same time attains to its own happiness and loses it, indeed attains happiness only through deliberately sacrificing it. And we thus come to the great central secret of all life and love, revealed to us in its fullness in the divine paradox of our Lord's life and teaching.

God, then, first seems to be in a place, indeed to be a place. "I see all good to be in one only place, that is God." "The spirit can find no place except God, for its repose."

If God be in a place, we cannot well conceive of Him as other than outside of and above the soul, which itself, even

God being in a place, will be in a place also. "God has created the soul pure and full, with a certain God-ward instinct which brings happiness in its train (*istinto beatifico*)." And "the nearer the soul approaches" (is joined, *si accosta*) "to God, the more does the instinct attain to its perfection." Here the instinct within pushes the soul "onwards, outwards, upwards." And the nearer the soul gets to God in front, outside and above of it, the happier it becomes: because, the more it satisfies this its instinct, the less it suffers from the distance from God, and the more does it enjoy His proximity.

This approach is next conceived of as increasingly conveying a knowledge to the soul of God's desire for union with it; but such an approach can only be effected by means of much fight against and through the intervening ranks of the common enemies of the two friends; and, as we have already seen, chief amongst these enemies is the soul's false self. "The nearer man approaches to (*si accosta*) God, the more he knows that God desires to unite Himself with us." "Being determined to approach God, I am constrained to be the enemy of His enemies."

And then, that "place" in which God was pictured as being, is found to be a state, a disposition of the soul. Now as long as the dominant tendency was to think God with clearness, and hence to picture Him as in space, that same tendency would, naturally enough, represent this place He was in as outside and above the soul. For if He is in space, He is pictured as extended, and hence as stretching farther than, and outside of, the soul, which itself also is conceived as spatially extended; and if He is in a particular part of space, that part can only, for a geocentric apprehension of the world, be thought of as the upper part of space. But in proportion as the picture of physical extension and position gives way to its prompting cause, and the latter is expressed, as far as possible, un-pictorially and less clearly, but more simply as what it is, viz. a spiritual intention and disposition, she is still driven indeed, in order to retain some clearness of speech, to continue to speak as of a place and of a spatial movement, but she has now no longer three categories but only one, viz. *within* and *inwards*. For a physical quantity can be and move in different places and directions in space; but a spiritual quality can only be experienced within the substance of the spirit. "God created the soul pure and full, with a certain beatific instinct of Himself" (i.e. of His actual presence). And hence, "in proportion as it (again) approaches to the conditions of its original creation, this beatific instinct ever increasingly discovers itself and grows stronger and stronger."

And God being thus not without, nor indeed in space at all, she can love Him everywhere: indeed the *what* she is now constitutes the *where* she is; in a camp she can love God as dearly as in a convent, and heaven itself is already within her soul, so that only a change in the soul's dispositions could constitute hell for that soul, even in hell itself. "O Love," she exclaims, after the scene with the Friar, who had attempted to prove to her that his state of life rendered him more free and apt to love God, "who then shall impede me from loving Thee? Even if I were in the midst of a camp of soldiers, I could not be impeded from loving Thee." She had, during the interview, explained her meaning: "If I believed that your religious habit would give me but one additional glimpse" (spark, *scintilla*) "of love, I would without doubt take it from you by force, were I not allowed to have it otherwise. That you may be meriting more than myself, I readily concede, I am not seeking after that; let those things be yours. But that I cannot love Him as much as you can do, you will never succeed in making me even understand." "I stood so occupied in seeing the work of Love (within my soul), that if it had thrown me with soul and body into hell, hell itself would have appeared to me to be nothing but love and consolation." And, on another occasion, she says to her disciples: "If, of that which this heart of mine is feeling, one drop were to fall into hell, hell itself would become all life eternal"; and she accepts with jubilation this interpretation of her words, on the part of one of them (no doubt Vernazza): "Hell exists in every place where there is rebellion against Love, God; but Life Eternal, in every place where there is union with that same Love, God."

And she now cannot but pray to possess all this love,—love being now pictured as a food, as a light, or as water, bringing life to the soul. "O tender Love, if I thought that but one glimpse of Thee were to be wanting to me, truly and indeed I could not live." "Love, I want Thee, the whole of Thee." "Never can love grow quiet, until it has arrived at its ultimate perfection." And, in gaining all God, she gains all other things besides: "O my God, all mine, everything is mine; because all that belongs to God seems all to belong to me."

But if she loves all God, she can, on the other hand, love only Him: how, then, is she to manage to love her neighbour? "Thou commandest me to love my neighbour," she complains to her Love, "and yet I cannot love anything but Thee, nor can I admit anything else and mix it up with Thee. How, then, shall I act?" And she received the interior answer: "He who loves me, loves all that I love."

But soon her love, as generous as it is strong, becomes uneasy as to its usual consequences,—the consolations, purely spiritual or predominantly psychical or even more or less physical, which come in its train. And even though she is made to understand that at least the first are necessarily bound up with love, in exact proportion to its generosity, she is determined, to the last, to love for love itself, and not for love's consequences, battling thus to keep her spirituality free from the slightest, subtlest self-seeking. "This soul said to its Love: 'Can it really be, O tender Love, that Thou art destined never to be loved without consolation or the hope of some advantage in heaven or on earth' accruing to Thy lover?" "And she received the answer, that such an union could not exist without a great peace and contentment of the soul." And yet she continues to affirm: "Conscience, in its purity, cannot bear anything but God alone; of all the rest, it cannot suffer the least trifle."

And she practises and illustrates this doctrine in detail. "One day, after Communion, God gave her so great a consolation that she remained in ecstasy. When she had returned to her usual state, she prayed: 'O Love, I do not wish to follow Thee for the sake of these delights, but solely from the motive of true love.'" On another similar occasion she prays: "I do not want that which proceedeth from Thee; I want Thyself alone, O tender Love." And again, "on one occasion, after Communion, there came to her so much odour and so much sweetness that she seemed to herself to be in Paradise. But instantly she turned towards her Lord and said: 'O Love, art Thou perhaps intending to draw me to Thee by means of these sensible consolations (*sapori*)? I want them not; I want nothing except Thee alone.'"

31. THE OTHER WORLDS

Now here especially is it necessary ever to bear in mind her own presupposition, which runs throughout and sustains all her doctrine. For she is sure, beyond ever even raising a question concerning the point, that her soul and God, her two great realities and experiences, remain substantially the same behind the veil as before it, and hence that the most fundamental and universal of the soul's experiences *here* can safely be trusted to obtain *there* also. Hence, too, only such points in the Beyond are dwelt on as she can thus experimentally forecast; but these few points are, on the other hand, developed with an extraordinary vividness and fearless, rich variety of illustration. And it is abundantly clear that this assumption of the essential unity and continuity of the soul's life here and hereafter, is itself already a doctrine, and a most important one. We will then take it as such, and begin with it as the first of her teachings as to the Beyond.

"This holy soul," says the highly authoritative prologue to the *Trattato*, in close conformity with her constant assumptions and declarations, "finding herself, whilst still in the flesh, placed in the Purgatory of God's burning love,—a love which consumed (burnt, *abbrucciava*) and purified her from whatever she had to purify, in order that, on passing out of this life, she might enter at once into the immediate presence (*cospetto*) of her tender Love, God: understood, by means of this furnace

of love, how the souls of the faithful abide in the place of
Purgatory, to purge themselves of every stain of sin that,
in this life, had been left unpurged. And as she, placed in
the loving Purgatory of the divine fire, abode united to the
divine Love, and content with all that It wrought within
her, so she understood it to be with the souls in Purgatory."

The details of her doctrine as to the Beyond we can group
under three heads: the unique, momentary experience and
solitary, instantaneous act of the soul, at its passing hence and
beginning its purgation there; the particular dispositions, joys
and sufferings of the soul during the process of purification
as well as the cause and manner of the cessation of that process; and (generally treated by her as a simple contrast to
this her direct and favourite purgatorial contemplation) the
particular dispositions, sufferings and alleviations of lost souls.
Since her teachings on the last-named subject are more of an
incidental character, I shall take them first, and make them
serve, as they do with her, as a foil to her doctrine of the
Intermediate State: whilst her conception of Heaven, already
indicated throughout her descriptions of Pure Love, is too
much of a universal implication, and too little a special department of her teaching, to be capable of presentation here.

As to the cause of Hell, she says: "It is the will's opposition
to the Will of God which causes guilt; and as long as this evil
will continues, so long does the guilt continue. For those,
then, who have departed this life with an evil will there is no
remission of the guilt, neither can there be, because there can
be no more change of will." "In passing out of this life, the
soul is established for good or evil, according to its deliberate
purpose at the time; as it is written, 'where I shall find thee,'
that is, at the hour of death, with a will either determined to
sin, or sorry for sin and penitent, 'there will I judge thee.'"
Or, in a more characteristic form: "There is no doubt that
our spirit was created to love and enjoy: and it is this that it
goes seeking in all things. But it never finds satiety in things
of time; and yet it goes on hoping, on and on, to be at last
able to find it. And this experience it is that helps me to
understand what kind of a thing is Hell. For I see that man,

N

by love, makes himself one single thing with God, and finds there every good; and, on the other hand, that when he is bereft of love, he remains full of as many woes as are the blessings he would have been capable of, had he not been so mad."

And yet, and this is her own beautiful contribution to the traditional doctrine on this terrible and mysterious subject, neither are the sufferings of the lost infinite in amount, nor is their will entirely malign. And both these alleviations evidently exist from the first: I can find no trace anywhere in her teaching of a gradual mitigation of either the punishment or the guilt. Indeed, although she always teaches the mitigation of the suffering, it is only occasionally that she teaches the persistence of some moral good. Thus her ordinary teaching is: "Those who are found, at the moment of death, with a will determined to sin, have with them an infinite degree of guilt, and the punishment is without end"; "the sweet goodness of God sheds the rays of His mercy even into Hell: since He might most justly have given to the souls there a far greater punishment than He has." "At death God exercises His justice, yet not without mercy; since even in Hell the soul does not suffer as much as it deserves." But occasionally she goes farther afield, and insists on the presence there, not only of some mercy in the punishment, but also of some good in the will. "When we shall have departed from this life in a state of sin, God will withdraw from us His goodness, and will leave us to ourselves, and yet not altogether: since He wills that in every place His goodness shall be found and not His justice alone. And if a creature could be found that did not, to some degree, participate in the divine goodness, that creature would be, one might say, as malignant as God is good." There can be no doubt, as we shall see farther on, that this latter is her full doctrine and is alone entirely consistent with her general principles.

Certain details of her Hell doctrine which appear in immediate contrast to, or in harmony with, some special points of her Purgatorial teaching, had better appear in connection with the latter.

Let us now take, in all but complete contrast to this doctrine as to Hell, what she has to say about Purgatory. And here we have first to deal with the initial experience and act, both of them unique and momentary, of the soul destined for Purgatory. As to that experience, only one description has been preserved for us. "Once, and once only, do the souls (that are still liable to, and capable of, purgation) perceive the cause of (their) Purgatory that they bear within themselves,—namely in passing out of this life: then, but never again after that: otherwise self would come in (*vi saria una proprietà*)."

And this unique and momentary experience is straightway followed by as unique and momentary an act, free and full, on the part of the experiencing soul. Catherine has described this act in every kind of mood, and from the various points of view, already drawn out by us, of her doctrine, so that we have here again a most impressive and vivid summing-up and pictorial representation of all her central teaching.

"The soul thus seeing" (its own imperfection) and, "that it cannot, because of the impediment" (of this imperfection) "attain (*accostarsi*) to its end, which is God; and that the impediment cannot be removed (*levato*) from it, except by means of Purgatory, swiftly and of its own accord (*volontieri*) casts itself into it." Here we have the continuation of the outward movement: the soul is here absolutely impeded in that, now immensely swift, movement, and is brought to a dead stop, as though by something hard on the soul's own surface, which acts as a barrier between itself and God; it is offered the chance of escaping from this intolerable suffering into the lesser one of dissolving this hard obstacle in the ocean of the purifying fire: and straightway plunges into the latter.

"If the soul could find another Purgatory above the actual one, it would, so as more rapidly to remove from itself so important (*tanto*) an impediment, instantly cast itself into it, because of the impetuosity of that love which exists between God and the soul and tends to conform the soul to God." Here we have an extension of the same picturing, interesting because the addition of an upwards to the outwards introduces a conflict between the image (which evidently, for the soul's plunge, requires Purgatory to lie beneath the soul), and the doctrine (which, taking Purgatory as the means between earth and heaven, cannot, if any spatial picturing be retained at all, but place Heaven at the top of the picture, and Purgatory higher up than the soul which is coming thither from earth). The deep plunge has become a high jump.

"I see the divine essence to be of such purity, that the soul which should have within it the least mote (*minimo chè*) of imperfection, would rather cast itself into a thousand hells, than find itself with that imperfection in the presence of God." Here the sense of touch, of hardness, of a barrier which is checking motion, has given way to the sense of sight, of stain, of a painful contrast to an all-pure Presence; and the whole picture is now devoid of motion. We thus have a transition to the immanental picturing, with its inward movement or look.

"The soul which, when separated from the body, does not find itself in that cleanness (*nettezza*) in which it was created, seeing in itself the stain, and that this stain cannot be purged out except by means of Purgatory, swiftly and of its own accord casts itself in; and if it did not find this ordination apt to purge that stain, in that very moment there would be spontaneously generated (*si generebbe*) within itself a Hell worse than Purgatory." Here we have again reached her immanental conception, where the soul's concern is with conditions within itself, and where its joys and sorrows are within. Its trouble is, in this case, the sense of contrast, between its own original, still potential, indeed still actual though now only far down, hidden and buried, true self, and its active, obvious, superficial, false self. In so far as there is any movement before the plunge, it is an inward, intro-spective one; the soul as a whole is, for that previous moment, not conceived as in motion, but a movement of her self-observing part or power takes place within her from the surface to the centre; and only then, after her rapid journey from this her surface-being to those her fundamental in-eradicable requirements, and after the consequent intolerably painful contrast and conflict within herself, does she cast herself, with swift wholeheartedness, with all she is and has, into the purifying place and state.

And, in full harmony with this immanental conception, the greater suffering which would arise did she abide with this sight of herself and yet without any moral change is described as springing up spontaneously within herself. "The soul, seeing Purgatory to have been ordained for the very purpose of purging away its stains, casts itself in, and seems to find a great compassion (on the part of God) in being allowed (able) to do so." This appears to be only a variety of the immanental view just given.

We have finally to give her doctrine as to the particular dispositions, joys and sufferings of the soul during the process of its purgation, and as to the cause and manner of the cessation of that process.

As to the dispositions, they are generally the same as those which impelled the soul to put itself in this place of condition. Only whereas then, during that initial moment, they took the form of a single act, an initiation of a new condition, now they assume the shape of a continuous state. Then the will freely tied itself; now it gladly though painfully abides by its decision and its consequences. Then the will found the relief and distraction of full, epoch-making action; now it has but to will and work out the consequences involved in that generous, all-inclusive self-determination. The range and nature of this, its continuous, action will thus be largely the very reverse of those of that momentary act. "The souls that are in Purgatory are incapable of choosing otherwise than to be in that place, nor can they any more turn their regard (*si voltare*) towards themselves, and say: 'I have committed such and such sins, for which I deserve to tarry here'; nor can they say, 'Would that I had not done them, that now I might go to Paradise'; nor yet say, '*That* soul is going out before me'; nor, 'I shall go out before *him*.' They are so completely satisfied that He should be doing all that pleases Him, and in the way it pleases Him, that they are incapable of thinking of themselves." Indeed they are unable even to see themselves, at least directly, for "these souls do not see anything, even themselves in themselves or by means of themselves, but they (only) see themselves in God." Indeed we have already seen that to do, or to be able to do, otherwise, would now "let self come in (*sarebbe una proprietà*)."

And the joys and sufferings, and the original, earthly cause of the latter, are described as follows. "The souls in Purgatory have their (active) will conformed in all things to the will of God; and hence they remain there, content as far as regards their will." "As far as their will is concerned, these souls cannot find the pain to be pain, so completely are they satisfied with the ordinance of God, so entirely is their (active) will one with it in pure charity. On the other hand, they suffer a torment so extreme, that no tongue could describe it, no intellect could form the least idea of it, if God had not made it known by special grace." And indeed she says: "I shall cease to marvel at finding that Purgatory is" in its way as "horrible as Hell. For the one is made for punishing, the other for purging: hence both are made for sin, sin which itself is so horrible and which requires that its punishment and purgation should be conformable to its own horribleness." For in Purgatory too there still exist certain remains of imperfect, sinful habits in the will. "The souls in Purgatory think much more of the opposition which they discover in themselves to the will of God," than they do of their pain. And yet, being here with their actual will fully at one with God's purifying action (an action directed against these remains of passive opposition), "I do not believe it would be possible to find any joy comparable to that of a soul in Purgatory, except the joy of the Blessed in Paradise."

Now the sufferings of the soul are represented either as found by it, under the form of an obstacle to itself, whilst in motion to attain to God, a motion which in some passages is outward, in others inward; or as coming to it, whilst spatially at rest. Only in the latter case is there a further attempt at pictorially elucidating the nature of the obstacle and the cessation of the suffering. It is fairly clear that it is the latter set of passages which most fully suits her general teaching and even imagery. For, as to the imagery: after that one

movement in which the soul determines its own place, we
want it to abide there, without any further motion. And,
as to doctrine: more and more as the soul's history is unfolded,
should God's action within it appear as dominating and
informing the soul's action towards God, and should change
of disposition supplant change of place.

First, then, let us take the clearer but less final conception,
and see the soul in movement, in a struggle for outward
motion. "Because the souls that are in Purgatory have an
impediment between God and themselves, and because the
instinct which draws the soul on to its ultimate end is unable
as yet to attain to its fulfilment (*perfezione*), an extreme fire
springs up from thence (within them), a fire similar to that of
Hell." We have here an application and continuation of the
transcendental imagery, so that the impediment is outside or
on the surface of the soul, and God is outside and above this
again: but the whole picture here, at least as regards the fire,
is obscure and tentative.

Or the soul is still conceived as in movement, but the
motion is downwards from its own surface to its own centre,
a centre where resides its Peace, God Himself. "When a
soul approaches more and more to that state of original
purity and innocence in which it had been created, the instinct
of God, bringing happiness in its train (*istinto beatifico*), reveals
itself and increases on and on, with such an impetuousness of
fire that any obstacle seems intolerable." Here we have the
immanental picturing, the soul moving down, under the
influence of its instinct for God, to ever fuller masses of this
instinct present within the soul's own centre. But the extreme
abstractness and confusion of the language, which mixes up
motion, different depths of the soul, and various dispositions
of spirit, and which represents the soul as capable of approaching a state which has ceased to exist, cast doubts on the
authenticity of this passage. In both these sets where the soul
is in motion, we hear only of an impediment in general and
without further description; and, in both cases, the fire springs
up because of this impediment, whereas, as we shall see, in
the self-consistent form of her teaching the Fire, God, is

always present: the impediment simply renders this Fire painful, and that is all.

And next we can take the soul as spatially stationary, and as in process of qualitative change. Here we get clear and detailed pictures, both of what is given to the soul and of what is taken away from it. The images of the positive gain constitute the beautiful sixth chapter of the *Trattato*. But its present elaborate text requires to be broken up into three or four variants of one and the same simile, which are probably all authentic. I give them separately.

"If in the whole world there existed but one loaf of bread to satisfy the hunger of every creature: in such a case, if the creature had not that one bread, it could not satisfy its hunger, and hence it would remain in intolerable pain." Note how, so far, the nature of the possession of the bread is not specified, it is simply "had"; and how the pain seems to remain stationary.

"Man having by nature an instinct to eat: if he does not eat, his hunger increases continually, since his instinct to eat never fails him." Here all is clearer: man now takes the place of the creature in general; the possession is specified as an eating; the pain is a hunger; and this hunger is an ever-increasing one.

"If in all the world there were but one loaf of bread, and if only through seeing it could the creature be satisfied: the nearer that creature were to approach it (without seeing it and yet knowing that only the said bread could satisfy it), the more ardently would its natural desire for the bread be aroused within it (*si accenderebbe*),—that bread in which all its contentment is centred (*consiste*)." Here the image for the nature of the appropriation has been shifted from the least noble of the senses, taste and touch, to the noblest, sight: there is still a longing, but it is a longing to see, to exercise and satiate fully the intellectual faculties. And yet the satiety is evidently conceived not as extending to these faculties alone, but as including the whole soul and spirit, since bread would otherwise cease to be the symbol here, and would have been replaced by light. Note too the subtle complication intro-duced by the presentation, in addition to the idea of an increase of hunger owing to lapse of time, of the suggestion that the increase is caused by a change in the spatial relations between the hungering creature and its food, and by an ever-increasing approach of that creature to this food.

"And if the soul were certain of never seeing the bread, at that moment it would have within it a perfect Hell, and become like the damned, who are cut off from all hope of ever seeing God, the true Bread. The souls in Purgatory, on the other hand, hope to see that Bread, and to satiate themselves to the full therewith; whence they suffer hunger as great as will be the degree to which they will (eventually) satiate themselves with the true Bread, God, our Love." Here it is noticeable how the specific troubles of Hell and Purgatory are directly described, whereas the corresponding joys of Heaven are only incidentally indicated; and how the full sight is not preceded by a partial sight, but simply by a longing for this full sight, so that, if we were to press the application of this image, the soul in Purgatory would not see God at all. And yet, as we have seen above, souls there see, though not their particular sins, yet their general sinful habits; for what are the "impediment," the "imperfection," the "stain," which they go on feeling and seeing, but these habits? And they see themselves, though not in themselves, yet in God. But, if so, do they not see God?

The answer will doubtless be that, just as they do not see their sins any more in their specific particularity, but only feel in themselves a dull, dead remainder of opposition and imperfection, so also they do not, after the initial moment of action and till quite the end of their suffering, see God clearly, —as clearly as they do when the process is at an end. During one instant at death they had seen (as in a picture) their sins and God, each in their own utterly contrasted concrete particularity; and this had been the specific cause of their piercing pain and swift plunge. And then came the period of comparative dimness and dulness, a sort of general sub-consciousness, when their habits of sin, and God, were felt rather than seen, the former as it were in front of the latter, but both more vaguely, and yet (and this was the unspeakable

alleviation) now in a state of change and transformation.
For the former, the blots and blurs, and the sense of contrariety are fading gradually out of the outlook and consciousness; and the latter, the light and life, the joy and harmony of
the soul, and God, are looming clearer, nearer, and larger,
on and on. And even this initial feeling, this general perception,
this semi-sight and growing sight of God, is blissful beyond
expression; for "every little glimpse that can be gained of
God exceeds every pain and every joy that man can conceive
without it."

The imagery illustrative of what is taken from the soul,
and how it is taken, is twofold, and follows in the one case a
more transcendental, in the other case a more immanental,
conception, although in each case God is represented as in
motion, and the soul as abiding in the same place and simply
changing its qualitative condition under the influence of that
increasing approach of God and penetration by Him.

The illustration for the more transcendental view is taken
from the sun's light and fire's heat and a covering. It is, as
a matter of fact, made up of three sayings: one more vague
and subtle, and two more clear and vivid, sayings. "The joy
of a soul in Purgatory goes on increasing day by day, owing
to the inflowing of God into the soul, an inflowing which
increases in proportion as it consumes the impediment to its
own inflowing."—God's action upon the imperfect soul is as
the sun's action upon "a covered object. The object cannot
respond to the rays of the sun which beat upon it (*reverbera-
zione del sole*), not because the sun ceases to shine,—for it
shines without intermission,—but because the covering inter-
venes (*opposizione*). Let the covering be consumed away,
and again the object will be exposed to the sun and will
answer to the rays in proportion as the work of destruction
advances."—Now "Sin is the covering of the soul; and in
Purgatory this covering is gradually consumed by the fire;
and the more it is consumed, the more does the soul correspond and discover itself to the divine ray. And thus the one
(the ray) increases, and the other (the sin) decreases, till the
time (necessary for the completion of the process) is over."

It is clear that we have here three parallel passages, each with its own characteristic image, all illustrative of an identical doctrine: namely, the persistent sameness of God's action, viewed in itself, and of the soul's reaction, in its essential, central laws, needs and aspirations; and the accidental, superficial, intrinsically abnormal, inhibitory modification effected by sin in that action of God and in the corresponding reaction of the soul.—The first, dimmer and deeper saying speaks of an inflowing of God, with her usual combination of fire-and-water images. We seem here again to have the ocean of the divine fire, Itself pressing in upon the soul within It, yet here with pain and oppression, in so far as the soul resists or is unassimilated to It; and with peace and sustaining power, in so far as the soul opens out to, and is or becomes similar to, It. We hear only of an "impediment" in general, perhaps because the influx which beats against it is imaged as taking place from every side at once.—The second saying, the most vivid of the three, speaks of sunlight, and of how, whilst this sunlight itself remains one and the same, its effect differs upon one and the same object, according as that object is covered or uncovered. Here we get a "covering," since the shining is naturally imaged as coming from one side, from above, only. But here also it is the same sun which, at one time, does not profit, and, at another time, gives a renewed life to one and the same object; and it is clear, that either Catherine here abstracts altogether from the question as to what consumes the covering, or that she assumes that this consumption is effected by the sun itself.—The third saying is the least simple, and is indeed somewhat suspicious in its actual form. Yet here again we have certainly only one agent, in this case fire, which again, as in the case of the influx and of the sunlight, remains identical in itself, but varies in its effects, according as it does or does not meet with an obstacle. The ray here is a ray primarily of heat and not of light, but which is felt by the soul at first as painful, destructive flame, and at last as peaceful, life-giving warmth.

Now, amongst these three parallel sayings, it is that concerning the inflowing, which leads us gently on to the more immanental imagery—that of fire and dross. And this image is again given us in a number of closely parallel variants which now constitute one formally consecutive paragraph, —the third of Chapter X. of the *Trattato*. "Gold, when once it has been (fully) purified, can be no further consumed by the action of fire, however great it be; since fire does not, strictly speaking, consume gold, but only the dross which the gold may chance to contain. So also with regard to the soul. God holds it so long in the furnace, until every imperfection is consumed away. And when it is (thus) purified, it becomes impassible; so that if, thus purified, it were to be kept in the fire, it would feel no pain; rather would such a fire be to it a fire of Divine Love, burning on without opposition, like the fire of life eternal." Here the imperfection lies no more, as a covering, on the surface, nor does the purifying light or fire simply destroy that covering and then affect the bare surface; but the imperfection is mixed up with the soul, throughout the soul's entire depth, and the purification reaches correspondingly throughout the soul's entire substance. Yet, as with the covering and the covered object, so here with the dross and the impure gold, sin is conceived of as a substance alien to that of the soul. And, so far, God appears distinct from the fire: He applies it, as does the goldsmith his fire to the gold. But already there is an indication of some mysterious relation between the fire of Purgatory and that of Heaven. For if the very point of the description seems, at first sight, to be the miraculous character of the reward attached, more or less arbitrarily, to the soul's perfect purification, a character indicated by the fact that now not even fire can further hurt the soul, yet it remains certain that, the more perfect the soul, the more must it perceive and experience all things according to their real and intrinsic nature.

Another conclusion to the same simile is: "Even so does the divine fire act upon the soul: it consumes in the soul every imperfection. And, when the soul is thus purified, it abides all in God, without any foreign substance (*alcuna cosa*) within itself." Here God and the fire are clearly one and the same. And the soul does not leave the fire, nor is any question raised as to what would happen were it to be put back into it; but the soul remains where it was, in the Fire, and the Fire remains what it was, God. Only the foreign substance has been burnt out of the soul, and hence the same Fire that pained it then, delights it now. Here too, however, God and the soul are two different substances; and indeed this Fire-and-Gold simile, strictly speaking, excludes any identification of them.

32. CATHERINE AND THE BLESSED SACRAMENT

SINCE Holy Communion was the great source and centre of her love and strength, and the one partially external experience and practice which was thus renewed day by day throughout her life, and in the spiritual apprehension and effect of which we cannot trace any distinct periods, I shall dwell here, once for all, upon the characteristics of this devotion of hers, which were at all special to herself.

For one thing, even her ardent love of Holy Communion did not suppress a bashful dislike of being noticed or distinguished in the matter: "At the beginning of her conversion she had at times a feeling as of envy towards Priests, because they communicated on as many days as they would without any one wondering at it." "Once when, for a few days, the city was under an interdict, she went every morning a mile's distance outside of the city walls, so as to communicate; and she thought that she would not be seen by any one."

Next, there is a most characteristic eagerness for interior-isation, for turning the Holy Eucharist, perceived without, into the heart's food within; and a corresponding intensity of consciousness and tenderness at the moment of reception. "When she saw the Sacrament on the altar in the hands of the priests, she would say within herself: 'Now swiftly, swiftly convey it to the heart, since it is the heart's true food.'" And "one night she dreamt that she would be unable to communicate during the coming day, and waking up, she found that tears were dropping from her eyes, at which she wondered, since hers was a nature very slow to weep." And "when at Mass, she was often so occupied with her Lord interiorly, as not to hear one word of it; but when the time for Communion arrived, at that instant she would become conscious of exterior things." And she would say: "O Lord, it seems to me, that if I were dead, I should return to life to receive Thee; and that if an unconsecrated host were given to me, I should recognise it to be such by the mere taste alone, as one discerns water from wine."

Again, her Communion practice bears upon it the stamp of a staunch virility; of a constant emulation between her own generous turning-away from its sensible consolations and the divine action, which seems to have maintained these consolations throughout her life; and of a determination to abstain even from such deeply consoling Communions, if such abstention were the more perfect practice for her. "One day, when she had communicated, there came to her so much odour and so much sweetness, that she felt as though in Paradise. But turning at once towards her Love she said: 'O Love, wouldest thou perchance draw me to Thee with these savours (*sapori*)? I desire them not, since I desire but Thee, and Thee whole and entire!'" And "one day a holy Friar,"—it was probably the Observant Franciscan, Father Angelo of Chiavasso (near Genoa), beatified later on,—"said to her: 'You communicate every day: what kind of satisfaction do you derive from it?' And she answered him simply, explaining to him all her desires and feelings. But he, to test the purity of her intention, said: 'There might possibly be some imperfection in such very frequent Communion,' and then left her. And Catherine having heard this, fearing such imperfection, at once suspended her Communions, but at the cost of great distress. And the Friar, hearing a few days later of how she cared more not to do wrong than to have all the consolation and satisfaction of Communion, sent her word by all means to return to her daily Communions; and she did so."

And finally, her Communions produced effects direct and indirect, spiritual and psychical. The indirect, psycho-physical effects being variable, and related to the varying conditions of her health, will be noted as far as possible under the different periods of her life and, collectively, in the chapter on such psycho-physical questions. The spiritual effects no doubt grew, but this growth we have no sufficient materials for pursuing in detail. Yet they have throughout this peculiarity, that, central and all-permeating as this Eucharistic influence no doubt was, yet it nowhere takes the form of any specially Eucharistic devotion or directly Eucharistic meditation or doctrine, outside of Holy Communion itself and of the immediate occupation with *it*.

33. SOME PECULIARITIES OF DEVOTION

THREE items of information are furnished by the *Vita*, on one and the same half-page.

"She had such a hatred of self," says the *Vita*, "that she did not hesitate to pronounce this sentence: 'I would not have grace and mercy, but justice and vengeance shown to the malefactor. . . .'"

"For this reason it seemed that she did not even care to gain the Plenary Indulgences. Not as though she did not hold them in great reverence and devotion, and did not consider them to be most useful and of great value. But she would have wished that her own self-seeking part (*la sua propria parte*) should rather be chastised and punished as it deserved, than to see it pardoned (*assoluta*), and, by means of such satisfaction, liberated in the sight of God."

"She saw the Offended One to be supremely good, and the offender quite the opposite. And hence she could not bear to see any part of herself which was not subjected to the divine justice, with a view to its being thoroughly chastised. And hence, so as not to give this part any hope of being liberated from the pains due to it, she abstained from the Plenary Indulgences and also from recommending herself to the intercession of others, so as ever to be subject to every punishment and condemned as she deserved."

Here I would note three things.

For one thing, there can be no serious doubt as to the authenticity of the saying that opens out this group of communications and as to the substantial accuracy of the two parallel, and (I think) mutually independent, reports as to her practice: since the saying belongs to the class of short declarations given in *oratio directa*, which we shall find to be remarkably reliable throughout the *Vita*; and the reports testify to something so unusual, so little sympathetic to the hagiographical mind, so much in keeping with the remainder of her doctrine and practice, that we cannot believe them misinformed. The author of the *Dialogo* evidently fully accepted these three passages, when, in about 1549, she paraphrases them thus: "She therefore made no account of her sins, with respect to their punishment, but only because she had acted against that 'immense Goodness'"; "She found herself to be her who alone had committed all the evil, and alone she wanted to make satisfaction, as far as ever she could, without the help of any other person."

For another thing, we have absolutely final contemporary documentary evidence of the importance attached by herself both to Indulgences, and the gaining of them (at least by other people), and to Masses and prayers for the Dead, inclusive of herself when she should be gone. For as to Indulgences, we have entries in the Cartulary of the Hospital (under the dates of 11 March, 10 April, 29 May and 23 August, 1510) of various considerable sums, amounting in all to over £300, paid by the Hospital, at the first date, for Catherine's nephew Francesco, at all the other dates for herself, for the withdrawal of a suspension of the Indulgences attached to the Hospital Church, and for the transference, in that year, of the day appointed for their acquisition. Both these matters were carried out in Rome by means of Catherine's second nephew, Cardinal Giovanni Fiesco. This, it is true, is evidence that only covers the last six months of her life.

But as to Masses and Prayers for her own soul after death, we have (1) her second Will, of 19 May, 1498, where she leaves one share in the Bank of St. George (£100) to the Observant Franciscans of the Hospital Church, "who shall be bound to

celebrate Masses and Divine Offices for the soul of Testatrix";
(2) her Codicil, of 5 January, 1503, where she leaves (in
addition) £3 apiece to two Monasteries "for the celebration
of Masses for her own soul"; (3) her third Will, of 18 May,
1506, which confirms all this; and (4) her last Will, of 18
March, 1509, where she leaves £3 each to three Monasteries,
which are each to "celebrate thirty Masses for her soul," £3
to a fourth Monastery for Prayers for her soul, and £25 to
the Franciscans of the Hospital Church for the celebration of
Masses to the same effect.

The reader will at once perceive that these facts are fully
compatible with the attitude so emphatically ascribed to her
in the *Vita*, only if we take these latter statements as expressive
of certain intense, emotional moods; or of some relatively
short penitential period; or of what she did and felt with
regard to herself alone and for whilst she was to live here
below, not of what others should do for themselves at all
times and for herself when she was gone.

And finally, we know exactly how and why the doctrine
and practice described in those passages in the *Vita* were
accepted by the Congregation of Rites, as forming no obstacle
to her canonisation. Pope Benedict XIV., in his great classical
work on Beatification and Canonisation, says, "After I had
ceased to hold the office of Promoter of the Faith" (the
date will have been between 1728 and 1733), "I know that a
controversy arose as to the doctrine of a certain *Beata*, with
regard to the truth of which it was possible to have different
opinions." And after giving this *Beata's* doctrine and practice
as these are presented by Catherine's *Vita*, and citing the
arguments used against their toleration, he proceeds: "But
the Postulators answered (1) that this *Beata* had not omitted
to gain Plenary Indulgences from any contempt for them,
since her veneration for them was demonstrated by most
unambiguous documents" (no doubt Cardinal Fiesco's
action, in her name and at her expense, in Rome in 1510,
is meant); "(2) that it is the doctrine of very many theologians, that those do not sin, who do not labour to gain
Indulgences because they desire to make satisfaction in their

o

own persons in this world or to suffer in the next; (3) that we should not confound safety with perfection: it appears indeed to be safer to atone for one's fault both by one's own good works *and* by Indulgences; but not more perfect, supposing that a man abstains from Indulgences because his love of God and his detestation of having offended Him are so great that he desires to make satisfaction to Him, by bearing the whole of the merited punishment; and (4) that examples are not wanting of perfect souls, that have, for a while, desired to bear, even for the sins of others, the pains of Hell itself, although without falling away from the friendship and grace of God. And hence the Congregation of Sacred Rites considered that this doctrine did not militate against the holiness of the said *Beata* or against the approbation of her virtues as heroic." [1]

And a third and last peculiarity is particularly instructive as showing how entirely an unusual, at first sight quietistic, practice is not restricted, in her case, to specifically Catholic habits.

This peculiarity has already appeared in part in the second of the two accounts as to her attitude towards Indulgences. "She abstained from recommending herself to the intercession of others." And this is borne out, but (as we shall find) with certain unforeseeable restrictions, by the rest of the *Vita*. As regards even the Saints, one only invocation of any one of them is on record,—that of St. Benedict in 1474, already given.

And if she did not ask others for prayers for herself in her own lifetime, her own prayers for others were evidently rare, were apparently always concerned with their spiritual welfare, and were generally produced only under some special interior impulsion. Hence when asked, in 1496 or later, by Vernazza, in the name of several of her spiritual children, to pray that God might grant them "some little drops of His Love," she answers that "for these I cannot ask anything from this tender Love; I can but present them in His presence." This

---

[1] *Benedicti XIV. de servorum Dei Beatificatione et Beatorum Canonisatione*, ed. Padua, 1743, vol. ii., p. 239a.

is, no doubt, because she sees them to be already full of the love of God. Whereas in 1495 the poor working man, Marco del Sale, is dying of a cancer in the face, and is in a state of wild impatience: so she prays most fervently for him. It is true that the *Vita* adds that she did so, "having had an interior movement to this effect. For she never could turn to pray for a particular object, unless she had first felt herself called interiorly by her Love." Still, this did not prevent her, in 1497, from praying most fervently for patience for her husband (who was dying from a painful complaint), simply "because she feared that he might lose his soul," and without any other more peculiar incentive than this.

Evidently here again, as with the Confessions and Indulgences, her life and practice were indefinitely varied and spontaneous, and incomparably richer than the preconceptions and logic of at least some of her biographers will admit, or indeed than many of her own fervent sayings, so vividly expressive of certain moments or sides of her career or character, suggest or even seem to leave possible. But the underlying meaning and ultimate harmonisation of these apparent inconsistencies between her doctrine and her practice, we can only gradually hope to find.

34. HER GENERAL AFTER-LIFE CONCEPTIONS

Now Catherine's general After-Life Conceptions in part bring into interesting prominence, in part really meet and overcome, the perplexities and mutually destructive alternatives which we have just considered. I shall here again leave over to the next chapter the simply ultimate questions, such as that of the pure Eternity versus the Unendingness of the soul; but shall allow myself, as to one set of her general ideas, a little digression as to the probability of their ultimate literary suggestion by Plato.—These Platonic passages probably reached her too indirectly, and by means and in forms which I have too entirely failed to discover, for me to be able to discuss them in my chapter devoted to her assured and demonstrably direct literary sources. But these sayings of Plato greatly help to illustrate the meaning of her doctrine. —I shall group these, her general, positions and implications under four heads, and shall consider three of these as, in substance, profoundly satisfactory, but one of them, the second, as acceptable only with many limitations, although this second has obviously much influenced the form given by her to several of those other conceptions.

First, then, we get, as the fundamental presupposition of the whole Eschatology, a grandly sane, simple and profound doctrine formulated over and over again and applied throughout, with a splendid consistency, as the key and limit to all her anticipations and picturings. Only because of the fact, and of our conviction of the fact, of the unbroken continuity and identity of God with Himself, of the human soul with itself, and of the deepest of the relations subsisting between that God and the soul, across the chasm formed by our body's death, and only in proportion as we can and do experience and achieve, during this our earthly life, certain spiritual laws and realities of a sufficiently elemental, universal, and fruitful, more or less time- and space-less character, can we (whilst ever remembering the analogical nature of such picturings even as to the soul's life here) safely and profitably forecast certain general features of the future which is thus already so largely a present. But, given these conditions in the present, we can and should forecast the future, to the extent implied. And as Plato's great imaginative projection, his life-work, the *Republic*, achieves its original end (of making more readily understandable, by objectivising, on a large scale, the life of the inner city of our own soul) in so far as he has rightly understood the human soul and has found appropriate representations of its powers, laws and ideals in his future commonwealth, even if we cannot accept this picture for political purposes and in all its details: so is it also with Catherine's projection, which, if bolder in its subject-matter, is, most rightly, indefinitely more general in its indications than is Plato's great diagram of the soul. Man's spiritual personality being held by her to survive death;—to retain its identity and an at least equivalent consciousness, of that identity,—the deepest experiences of that personality before the body's death are conceived as re-experienced by it, in a heightened degree and form, after death itself. Hence these great pictures, of what the soul will experience then, would remain profoundly true of what the soul seeks and requires now, even if there were no *then* at all.

And note particularly how only with regard to one stage and condition of the spirit's future life,—that of the purification of the imperfect soul,—does she indulge in any at all direct doctrine or detailed picturing; and this, doubtless, not only because she has experienced much concerning this matter in her own life here, but also because the projection of these experiences would still give us, not the ultimate state, but more or less only a prolongation of our mixed, joy-in-suffering life upon earth. As to the two ultimate states, we get only quite incidental glimpses, although even these are strongly marked by her general position and method.

And next, coming to the projection itself, we naturally find it to present all the strength and limitations of her own spiritual experiences which are thus projected: her attitude towards the body and towards human fellowship (two subjects which are shown to be closely inter-related by the continuous manner in which they stand and fall together throughout the history of philosophy and religion) thus constitutes the second general peculiarity of her Eschatology. We have already noted, in her life, her strongly ecstatic, body-ignoring, body-escaping type of religion; and how, even in her case, it tended to starve the corporate, institutional conceptions and affections. Here, in the projection, we find both the cause and the effect again, and on a larger scale. Her continuous psycho-physical discomforts and keen thirst for a unity and simplicity as rapid and complete as possible, the joy and strength derived from ecstatic habits and affinities, would all make her, without even herself being aware of it, drop all further thought as to the future fate of that oppressive "prison-house" from which her spirit had at last got free.

Now such non-occupation with the fate of the body and of

her fellow-souls may appear quite appropriate in her Purga-torial Eschatology, yet we cannot but find that, even here, it already possesses grave disadvantages, and that it persists throughout all her After-life conceptions. For in all the states and stages of the soul we get a markedly unsocial, a *sola cum solo* picture. And yet there is, perhaps, no more striking difference, amongst their many affinities, between Platonism and Christianity than the intense Individualism which marks the great Greek's doctrine, and the profoundly social concep-tion which pervades Our Lord's own teaching,—in each case as regards the next life as well as this one. Plotinus's great culminating commendation of "the flight of the alone to the Alone" continues Plato's tradition; whereas, if even St. Paul and the Johannine writings speak at times as though the indi-vidual soul attained to its full personality in and by direct intercourse with God alone, the Synoptic Gospels, and at bottom also those two great lovers of Our Lord's spirit, never cease to emphasise the social constituent of the soul's life both here and hereafter. The Kingdom of Heaven, the Soul of the Church, as truly constitutes the different personalities, their spirituality and their joy, as they constitute it,—that great Organism which, as such, is both first and last in the Divine thought and love.

Here, in the at least partial ignoring of these great social facts, we touch the main defect of most mystical outlooks; yet this defect does not arise from what they possess, but from what they lack. For solitude, and the abstractive, unifying, intuitive, emotional, mystical element is also wanted, and this element and movement Catherine exemplifies in rare perfection. Indeed, in the great classical, central period of her life she had, as we know, combined all this with much of the outward movement, society, detailed observation, attach-ment, the morally *en-static*, the immanental type. Unfortun-ately the same ill-health and ever-increasing predominance of the former element, which turned her, quite naturally, to these eschatological contemplations, and which indeed helped to give them their touching tone of first-hand experience, also tended, of necessity, to make her drop even such slight and lingering social elements as had formerly coloured her thought. It is, then, only towards the understanding and deepening of the former of these two necessary movements of religion, that these, her latter-day enlargements of some of her deepest experiences and convictions, will be found true helps.

Yet if the usual *ad extra* disadvantages of such an abstractive position towards the body are thus exemplified by her, in this her unsocial, individualistic attitude, it is most interesting to note how entirely she avoids the usual *ad intra* drawbacks of this same position. For if her whole attention, and, increasingly, even her consciousness are, in true ecstatic guise, absorbed away from her fellows and concentrated exclusively upon God in herself and herself in God, yet this consciousness consists not only of *Nous*, that dry theoretic reason which, already by Plato, but still more by Aristotle, is alone conceived as surviving the body, but contains also the upper range of *Thumos*,—all those passions of the noblest kind,—love, admiration, gratitude, utter self-donation, joy in purifying suffering and in an ever-growing self-realisation as part of the great plan of God,—all the highest notes in that wondrous scale of deep feeling and of emotionally coloured willing which Plato made dependent, not for its character but for the possibility of its operation, upon the body's union with the soul.—And thus we see how, in her conception of the soul's own self within itself and of its relation to God, the Christian idea of Personality, as of a many-sided organism in which Love and Will are the very flower of the whole, has triumphed over the Platonic presentation of the Spirit, in so far as this is taken to require and achieve an ultimate sub-limation free from all emotive elements. Thus in her doctrine the whole Personality survives death, although this Personality energises only, as it were upwards, to God alone, and not also sideways and downwards, towards its fellows and the lesser children of God.

Catherine's third peculiarity consists in a rich and profound organisation of two doctrines, the one libertarian, the other determinist; and requires considerable quotation from Plato, whose teachings, bereft of all transmigration-fancies, seem clearly to reappear here (however complex may have been the mediation) in Catherine's great conception.

The determinist doctrine maintains that virtue and vice, in proportion as they are allowed their full development, spontaneously and necessarily attain to their own congenital consummation, a consummation which consists, respectively, in the bliss inseparable from the final and complete identity between the inevitable results upon itself of the soul's deliberate endeavours, and the indestructible requirements of this same soul's fundamental nature; and in the misery of the, now fully felt but only gradually superable, or even, in other cases, insuperable, antagonism between the inevitable consequences within its own self of the soul's more or less deliberate choosings, and those same, here also ineradicable, demands of its own truest nature.

As Marsilio Ficino says, in his *Theologia Platonica*, published in Florence in 1482: "Virtue is reward in its first budding, reward is virtue full-grown. Vice is punishment at the moment of its birth; punishment is vice at its consummation. For, in each of these cases, one and the same thing is first the simple seed and then the full ear of corn; and one and the same thing is the full ear of corn and then the food of man. Precisely the very things then that we sow in this our (earthly) autumn, shall we reap in that (other-world) summer-day." It is true that forensic terms and images are also not wanting in Catherine's sayings; but these, in part, run simply parallel to the immanental conception without modifying it; in part, they are in its service; and, in part, they are the work of theologians' arrangements and glosses.

And the libertarian doctrine declares that it is the soul itself which, in the beyond and immediately after death, chooses the least painful, because the most expressive of her then actual desires, from among the states which the natural effects upon her own self of her own earthly choosings have left her interiorly free to choose.

Now it is in this second doctrine especially that we find so detailed an anticipation by Plato of a whole number of highly original and characteristic points and combinations of points, as to render a fortuitous concurrence between Catherine and Plato practically impossible. Yet I have sought in vain, among Catherine's authentic sayings, actions, possessions, or friends, for any trace of direct acquaintance with any of Plato's writings. But Ficino's Latin translation of Plato, published, with immense applause, in Florence in 1483, 1484, must have been known, in those intensely Platonising times, to even non-professed Humanists in Genoa, long before Catherine's death in 1510, so that one or other of her intimates may have communicated the substance of these Platonic doctrines to her. Plotinus, of whom Ficino published a Latin translation in 1492, contains but a feeble echo of Plato on this point. Proclus, directly known only very little till much after Catherine's time, is in even worse case. The Areopagite, who has so continuously taken over whole passages from all three writers, although directly almost exclusively from Proclus, contains nothing more immediately to the purpose than his impressive sayings concerning Providence's continuous non-forcing of the human personality in its fundamental constitution and its free elections with their inevitable consequences; hence Catherine cannot have derived her ideas, in the crisp definiteness which they retain in her sayings, from her cousin the Dominican nun and the Areopagite. And it is certain, as we have seen, how scattered and inchoate are the hints which she may have found in St. Paul, the Johannine writings, and Jacopone da Todi. St. Augustine contains nothing that would be directly available,—an otherwise likely source considering Catherine's close connection with the Augustinian Canonesses of S. Maria delle Grazie.

In Plato, then, we get five conceptions and symbolic pictures that are practically identical with those of Catherine.

First we get the conception of souls having each, in exact accordance with the respective differences of their moral and spiritual disposition and character, as these have been constituted by them here below, a "place" or environment, expressive of that character, ready for their occupation after the body's death. "The soul that is pure departs at death, herself invisible, to the invisible world,—to the divine, immortal and rational: thither arriving, she lives in bliss. But the soul that is impure at the time of her departure and is . . . engrossed by the corporeal . . . , is weighed down and drawn back again into the visible place (world)."

And this scheme, of like disposition seeking a like place, is then carried out, by the help of the theory of transmigration, as a re-incarnation of these various characters into environments, bodies, exactly corresponding to them: gluttonous souls are assigned to asses' bodies, tyrannous souls to those of wolves, and so on: in a word, "there is no difficulty in assigning to all 'a whither' (a place) answering to their general natures and propensities." [1] For this corresponds to a law which runs throughout all things,—a determinism of consequences which does not prevent the liberty of causes. "The King of the universe contrived a general plan, by which a thing of a certain nature found a seat and place of a certain kind. But the formation of this nature, he left to the wills of individuals."

Or, with the further spatial imagery of movements up, level, or down, we get: "All things that have a soul change . . . and, in changing, move according to law and the order of destiny. Lesser changes of nature move on level ground, but great crimes sink . . . into the so-called lower places . . .; and, when the soul becomes greatly different and divine, she also greatly changes her place, which is now altogether holy." The original, divinely intended "places" of souls are all high and good, and similar to each other though not identical, each soul having its own special "place"; and for this congenital "place" each soul has a resistible yet ineradicable home-sickness. "The first incarnation" of human souls which "distributes each soul to a star," is ordained to be similar for all. . . . "And when they have been of necessity implanted in bodily forms, should they master their passions . . . they live in righteousness; if otherwise, in unrighteousness. And he who lived well through his allotted time shall be conveyed once more to a habitation in his kindred star,

[1] *Phaedo*, 81a–82a.

and there shall enjoy a blissful and congenial life; but failing
this he shall pass into . . . such a form of (further) incarnation as fits his disposition . . . until he shall overcome,
by reason, all that burthen that afterwards clung around
him." [1]

If from all this we exclude the soul's existence before any
beginning of its body, its transmigration into other bodies,
and the self-sufficiency of reason; and if we make it all to be
penetrated by God's presence, grace and love, and by our
corresponding or conflicting emotional and volitional as
well as intellectual attitude: we shall get Catherine's position
exactly.

But again, in at least one phase of his thinking, Plato
pictures the purification of the imperfect soul as effected, or
at least as begun, not in a succession of "places" of an
extensionally small but organic kind, bodies, but in a "place"
of an extensionally larger but inorganic sort,—the shore of a
lake, where the soul has to wait. "The Acherusian lake is
the lake to the shores of which the many go when they are
dead; and, after waiting an appointed time, which to some is
longer and to others shorter, they are sent back to be born as
animals." Here we evidently get a survival of the conception,
predominant in Homer, of a pain-and-joyless Hades, but
limited here to the middle, the imperfect class of souls, and
followed, in their case, by transmigration, to which alone,
apparently, purification is directly attached.

In the same Dialogue we read later on: "Those who
appear to have lived neither well nor ill . . . go to the river
Acheron, and are carried to the lake; and there they dwell
and are purified of their evil deeds . . . and are absolved
and receive the rewards of their good deeds according to their
deserts." Here we have, evidently, still the same "many"
and the same place, the shores of the Acherusian lake, but
also an explicit affirmation of purification effected there, for

---

[1] *Timaeus*, 41*d*, *e*; 42*b*, *d*. I have, for clearness' sake, turned Plato's
indirect sentences into direct ones; and have taken the *Timaeus* after the
Laws, although it is chronologically prior to them, because the full balance
of his system (which requires the originally lofty "place" of each individual
soul) is, I think, abandoned in the *Laws*: see 904*a*.

this purification is now followed directly, not by reincarnation, but by the ultimate happiness in the soul's original and fundamentally congenial "place." And this scheme is far more conformable to Plato's fundamental position: for how can bodies, even lower than the human, help to purify the soul which has become impure precisely on occasion of its human body?—We can see how the Christian Purgatorial doctrine derives some of its pictures from the second of these parallel passages; yet that the "longer or shorter waiting" of the first passage also enters into that teaching,—especially in its more ordinary modern form, according to which there is, in this state, no intrinsic purification.

And lower down we find: "Those who have committed crimes which, although great, are not unpardonable,—for these it is necessary to plunge (ἐμπεσεῖν) into Tartarus, the pains of which they are compelled to undergo for a year; but at the end of the year they are borne to the Acherusian lake. But those who appear incurable by reason of the greatness of their crimes . . . such their appropriate destiny hurls (ῥίπτει) into Tartarus, whence they never come forth." Here we get a Purgatory, pictured as a watery substance in which the more gravely impure of the curable souls are immersed before arriving at the easier purification, the waiting on the dry land alongside the lake; this Purgatory is, as a "place" and, in intensity, identical with Hell; and into this place the curable souls "plunge" and the incurable ones are "hurled." Of this third passage Catherine retains the identification of the pains of Purgatory and those of Hell; the "plunge," or "hurling," of two distinct classes of souls into these pains; and the mitigation, after a time, previous to complete cessation, of the suffering in the case of the curable class. But the "plunge," with her, is common to all degrees of imperfectly pure souls; there is, for all these souls, no change of "place" during their purgation, but only a mitigation of suffering; and this mitigation is at work gradually and from the first. And the ordinary modern Purgatorial teaching is like this passage, in that it keeps the curable souls in Tartarus, say, for one year, and lets them suffer there, apparently without mitigation, throughout that time: and that, in the case of both classes of souls, it conceives the punishment as extrinsic, vindictive and inoperative.

And a fourth *Phaedo* passage tells us: "Those who are remarkable for having led holy lives are released from this earthly prison, and go to their pure home, which is above, and dwell in the purer earth," the Isles of the Just, in Oceanus. "And those, again, amongst these who have duly purified themselves with philosophy, live henceforth altogether without the body, in mansions fairer far than these." Here we get, alongside of the two Purgatories and the one Hell, two Heavens, of which the first is but taken over from Homer and Pindar, but of which the second is Plato's own conception. Catherine, in entire accord with the ordinary teaching, has got but one "place" of each kind; and her Heaven corresponds, apart from his formal and final exclusion of every sort of body, to the second of these Platonic Heavens; whilst, here again, the all-encompassing presence of God's love for souls as of the soul's love for God, which, in her teaching, is the beginning, means and end of the whole movement, effects an indefinite difference between the two positions.

Yet Plato, in his most characteristic moods, explicitly anticipates Catherine as to the intrinsic, ameliorative nature and work of Purgatory: "The proper office of punishment is twofold: he who is rightly punished ought either to become better . . . by it, or he ought to be made an example to his fellows, that they may see what he suffers and . . . become better. Those who are punished by Gods and men and improved, are those whose sins are curable . . . by pain and suffering:—for there is no other way in which they can be delivered from evil, as in this world so also in the other. But the others are incurable—the time has passed at which they can receive any benefit themselves. . . . Rhadamanthus," the chief of the three nether-world judges, "looks with admiration on the soul of some just one, who has lived in holiness and truth . . . and sends him" without any intervening suffering "to the Isles of the Blessed. . . . I consider how I shall present my soul whole and undefiled before the Judge, in that day." Here the last sentence is strikingly like in form as well as in spirit to many a saying of St. Paul and Catherine.

But the following most original passages give us a sentiment and an image which, in their special drift, are as opposed to St. Paul, and indeed to the ordinary Christian consciousness, as they are dear to Catherine, in this matter so strongly, although probably unconsciously, Platonist, indeed Neo-Platonist, in her affinities. "In the time of Kronos, indeed down to that of Zeus, the Judgment was given on the day on which men were to die," i.e. immediately *before* their death; "and the consequence was, that the judgments were not well given,—the souls found their way to the wrong places. Zeus said: 'The reason is, that the judged have their clothes on, for they are alive. . . . There are many, having evil souls, who are apparelled in fair bodies or wrapt round in wealth and rank. . . . The Judges are awed by them; and they themselves too have their clothes on when judging: their eyes and ears and their whole bodies are interposed, as a veil, before their own souls. What is to be done? . . . Men shall be entirely stript before they are judged, for they shall be judged when dead; the Judge too shall be naked, that is, dead: he, with his naked soul, shall pierce into the other naked soul immediately *after* each man dies . . . and is bereft of all his kith and kin, and has left behind him all his brave attire upon earth, and thus the Judgment will be just.'"—If we compare this with St. Paul's precisely contrary instinct and desire to be "clothed upon" at death, "lest we be found naked," i.e. without the protection of any kind of body; and then realise Catherine's intense longing for "nudità,"—to strip herself here, as far as possible, from all imperfection and self-delusion before the final stripping off of the body in death, and to appear, utterly naked, before the utterly naked eye of God, so that no "clothes" should remain requiring to be burnt away by the purifying fires, the profound affinity of sentiment and imagery between Catherine and Plato—and this on a point essentially Platonic, —is very striking.

But, above all, in his deep doctrine as to the soul's spon-

taneous choice after death of that condition, "place," which,
owing to the natural effects within her of her earthly willings
and self-formation, she cannot but now find the most congenial to herself, Plato appears as the ultimate source of a
literary kind for Catherine's most original view, which
otherwise is, I think, without predecessors. "The souls,"
he tells us in the *Republic*, "immediately on their arrival in
the other world, were required to go to Lachesis," one of the
three Fates. And "an interpreter, having taken from her
lap a number of lots and plans of life, spoke as follows: 'Thus
saith Lachesis, the daughter of Necessity. . . . "Your
destiny shall not be allotted to you, but you shall choose it
for yourselves. Let him who draws the first lot, be the first
to choose a life which shall be his irrevocably. . . . The
responsibility lies with the chooser, Heaven is guiltless."'"
"No settled character of soul was included in the plans of
life, because, with the change of life, the soul inevitably
became changed itself." "It was a truly wonderful sight, to
watch how each soul selected its life. . . . When all the souls
had chosen their lives, Lachesis dispatched with each of them
the Destiny he had selected, to guard his life and satisfy his
choice." And in the *Phaedrus* Plato tells us that "at the end
of the first thousand years" (of the first incarnation) "the
good souls and also the evil souls both come to cast lots
and to choose their second life; and they may take any that
they like."

In both the dialogues the lots are evidently taken over from
popular mythology, but are here made merely to introduce a
certain orderly succession among the spontaneous choosings
of the souls themselves, whilst the lap of the daughter of
Necessity, spread out before all the choosers previous to their
choice, and the separate, specially appropriate Destiny that
accompanies each soul after its choice, indicate plainly that,
although the choice itself is the free act and pure self-expression of each soul's then present disposition, yet that this
disposition is the necessary result of its earthly volitions and
self-development or self-deformation, and that the choice now
made becomes, in its turn, the cause of certain inevitable

consequences,—of a special environment which itself is then productive of special effects upon, and of special occasions for, the final working out of this soul's character.—Plotinus retains the doctrine: "the soul chooses there" in the Other world,—"its Daemon and its kind of life." But neither Proclus nor Dionysius has the doctrine, whilst Catherine, on the contrary, reproduces it with a penetrating completeness.

And under our last, fourth head, we can group the simplifications characteristic of Catherine's Eschatology.

One simplification has, of course, for now some fifteen hundred years, been the ordinary Christian conception: I mean the elimination of the time-element between the moment of death and the beginning of the three states. Yet it is interesting to note how by far the greatest of the Latin Fathers, St. Augustine, who died in 430 A.D., still clings predominantly to the older Christian and Jewish conception of the soul abiding in a state of shrunken, joy-and-painless consciousness from the moment of the body's death up to that of the general resurrection and judgment. "After this short life, thou wilt not yet be where the saints will be," i.e. in Heaven. "Thou wilt not yet be there: who is ignorant of this? But thou canst straightway be where the rich man descried the ulcerous beggar to be a-resting, far away," i.e. in Limbo. "Placed in that rest, thou canst await the day of judgment with security, when thou shalt receive thy body also, when thou shalt be changed so as to be equal to an Angel." Only with regard to Purgatory, a state held by him, in writings of his last years, 410–30 A.D., to be possible, indeed probable, does he make an exception to his general rule: for such purification would have to take place "in the interval of time between the death of the body and the last day of condemnation and reward."

It is doubtless the still further fading away of the expectation, so vivid and universal in early Christian times, of the proximity of Our Lord's Second Advent, and the tacit prevalence of Greek affinities and conceptions concerning the bodiless soul, that helped to eliminate, at last universally, this interval of waiting, in the case of souls too good or too bad for purgation, from the general consciousness of at least Western Christendom. The gain in this was the great simplification and concentration of the immediate outlook and interest; the loss was the diminished apprehension of the essentially complex, concrete, synthetic character of man's nature, and of the necessity for our assuming that this characteristic will be somehow preserved in this nature's ultimate perfection.

There is a second simplification in Catherine which, though here St. Augustine leads the way, is less common among Christians: her three other-world "places" are not, according to her ultimate thought, three distinct spatial extensions and localities, filled, respectively, with ceaselessly suffering, temporarily suffering, and ceaselessly blessed souls; but they are (notwithstanding all the terms necessitated by such spatial picturings as "entering," "coming out," "plunging into") so many distinct states and conditions of the soul, of a painful, mixed, or joyful character. We shall have these her ultimate ideas very fully before us presently. But here I would only remark that this her union of a picturing faculty, as vivid as the keenest sense-perception, and of a complete non-enslavement to, a vigorous utilisation of, these life-like spatial projections, by a religious instinct and experience which never forgets that God and souls are spirits, to whom our ordinary categories of space and extension, time and motion, do not and cannot in strictness apply, is as rare as it is admirable; and that, though her intensely anti-corporeal and non-social attitude made such a position more immediately easy for her than it can be for those who remain keenly aware of the great truths involved in the doctrines of the Resurrection of the Body and the Communion of Saints, this her trend of thought brings into full articulation precisely the deepest of our spiritual apprehensions and requirements, whilst it is not her fault if it but further accentuates some of our intellectual perplexities.

We get much in St. Augustine, which he himself declares to have derived, in the first instance, from "the writings of the

P

Platonists," which doubtless means above all Plotinus (that keen spiritual thinker who can so readily be traced throughout this part of the great Convert's teaching), as to this profound incommensurableness between spiritual presence, energising, and affectedness on the one hand, and spatial position, extension and movement on the other. "What place is there within me, to which my God can come? . . . I would not exist at all, unless Thou already wert within me." "Thou wast never a place, and yet we have receded from Thee; and we have drawn near to Thee, yet Thou art never a place." "Are we submerged and do we emerge? Yet it is not places into which we are plunged and out of which we rise. What can be more like to places and yet more unlike? For here the affections are in case,—the impurity of our spirit, which flows downwards, oppressed by the love of earthly cares; and the holiness of Thy Spirit, which lifts us upwards with the love of security." For, as he teaches, "the spiritual creature can only be changed by times,"—a succession within a duration: "by remembering what it had forgotten, or by learning what it did not know, or by willing what it did not will. The bodily creature can be changed by times and places, by spatial motion, "from earth to heaven, from heaven to earth, from east to west." "That thing is not moved through space which is not extended in space . . . the soul is not considered to move in space, unless it be held to be a body."

In applying the doctrine just expressed to eschatological matters, St. Augustine concludes: "If it be asked whether the soul, when it goes forth from the body, is borne to some corporeal places, or to such as, though incorporeal, are like to bodies, or to what is more excellent than either: I readily answer that, unless it have some kind of body, it is not borne to bodily places at all, or, at least, that it is not borne to them by bodily motion. . . . But I myself do not think that it possesses any body, when it goes forth from this earthly body. . . . It gets borne, according to its deserts, to spiritual conditions, or to penal places having a similitude to bodies."

The reader will readily note a curiously uncertain frame of mind in this last utterance. I take it that Plotinian influences are here being checked by the Jewish conception of certain, definitely located, provision-chambers (*promptuaria*), in which all souls are placed for safe keeping, between the time of the body's death and its resurrection. So in the Fourth Book of Esra (of about 90 A.D.), "the souls of the just in their chambers said: 'How long are we to remain here?'"; and in the Apocalypse of Baruch (of about 150–250 A.D.), "at the coming of the Messiah, the provision-chambers will open, in which the" whole, precise "number of the souls of the just have been kept, and they will come forth."

But it is St. Thomas Aquinas who, by the explicit and consistent adoption and classification of these *promptuaria receptacula*, reveals to us more clearly the perplexities and fancifulnesses involved in the strictly spatial conception. "Although bodies are not assigned to souls (immediately after death), yet certain bodily places are congruously assigned to these souls in accordance with the degree of their dignity, in which places they are, as it were, locally, in the manner in which bodiless things can be in space: each soul having a higher place assigned to it, according as it approaches more or less to the first substance, God, whose seat, according to Scripture, is Heaven." "In the Scriptures God is called the Sun, since He is the principle of spiritual life, as the physical sun is of bodily life; and, according to this convention, . . . souls spiritually illuminated have a greater fitness for luminous bodies, and sin-darkened souls for dark places." "It is probable that, as to local position, Hell and the Limbo of the Fathers constitute one and the same place, or are more or less continuous." "The place of Purgatory adjoins (that of) Hell." "There are altogether five places ready to receive (*receptanda*) souls bereft of their bodies: Paradise, the Limbo of the Fathers, Purgatory, Hell, and the Limbo of Infants."

No doubt all these positions became the common scholastic teaching. But then, as Cardinal Bellarmine cogently points out: "no ancient, as far as I know, has written that the Earthly Paradise was destroyed . . . and I have read a large number who affirm its existence. This is the doctrine of all the Scholastics, beginning with St. Thomas, and of the

Fathers . . . St. Augustine indeed appears to rank this truth amongst the dogmas of faith." We shall do well, then, not to press these literal localisation - schemes, especially since, according to St. Augustine's penetrating analysis, our spiritual experiences, already in this our earthly existence, have a distinctly non-spatial character. Catherine's position, if applied to the central life of man here, and hence presumptively hereafter, remains as true and fresh and unassailable as ever,

And her last simplification consists in taking the Fire of Hell, the Fire of Purgatory, and the Fire and Light of Heaven as profoundly appropriate symbols or descriptions of the variously painful or joyous impressions produced, through the differing volitional attitudes of souls towards Him, by the one God's intrinsically identical presence in each and all. In all three cases, throughout their several grades, there are ever but two realities, the Spirit-God and the spirit-soul, in various states of inter-relation.

Here again it is Catherine's complete abstraction from the body which renders such a view easy and, in a manner, necessary for her mind. But here I would only emphasise the impressive simplicity and spirituality of view which thus, as in the material world it finds the one sun-light and the one fire-heat, which, in themselves everywhere the same, vary indefinitely in their effects, owing to the varying condition of the different bodies which meet the rays and flames; so, in the Spiritual World it discovers One supreme spiritual Energy and Influence which, whilst ever self-identical, is assimilated, deflected, or resisted by the lesser spirits, with inevitably joyous, mixed, or painful states of soul, since they can each and all resist, but cannot eradicate that Energy's impression within their deepest selves. And though, even with her, the Sun-light image remains quasi-Hellenic and Intellectual, and the Fire-heat picture is more immediately Christian and Moral: yet she also frequently takes the sunlight as the symbol of the achieved Harmony and Peace, and the Fire-heat as that of more or less persisting Conflict and Pain. She is doubtless right in keeping both symbols, and in ever thinking of each as ultimately implying the other, for God is Beauty and Truth, as well as Goodness and Love, and man is made with the indestructible aspiration after Him in His living completeness.

And here again Catherine has a complicated doctrinal history behind her.

We have already considered the numerous Scriptural passages where God and His effects upon the soul are symbolised as light and fire; and those again where joy or, contrariwise, trial and suffering are respectively pictured by the same physical properties. And Catherine takes the latter passages as directly explanatory of the first, in so far as these joys and sufferings are spiritual in their causes or effects.

Among the Greek Fathers, Clement of Alexandria tells us that "the Fire" of Purgatory,—for he has no Eternal Damnation,—"is a rational," spiritual, "fire that penetrates the soul"; and Origen teaches that "each sinner himself lights the flame of his own fire, and is not thrown into a fire that has been lit before that moment and that exists in front of him. . . . His conscience is agitated and pierced by its own pricks." Saints Gregory of Nyssa and Gregory of Nazianzus are more or less influenced by Origen on this point. And St. John Damascene, who died in about 750 A.D., says explicitly that the fire of Hell is not a material fire, that it is very different from our ordinary fire, and that men hardly know what it is.

Among the Latins, St. Ambrose declares: "Neither is the gnashing, a gnashing of bodily teeth; nor is the everlasting fire, a fire of bodily flames; nor is the worm, a bodily one."— St. Jerome, in one passage, counts the theory of the non-physical fire as one of Origen's errors; but elsewhere he mentions it without any unfavourable note, and even enumerates several Scripture-texts which favour it, and admits that "'the worm which dieth not and the fire which is not quenched,' is understood, by the majority of interpreters (a plerisque), of the conscience of sinners which tortures them." —St. Augustine, in 413 A.D., declares: "In the matter of the pains of the wicked, both the unquenchable fire and the intensely living worm are interpreted differently by different commentators. Some interpreters refer both to the body, others refer both to the soul; and some take the fire literally, in application to the body, and the worm figuratively, in application to the soul, which latter opinion appears the more credible." Yet when, during the last years of his life, he came, somewhat tentatively, to hold an other-world Purgatory as well, he throughout assimilated this Purgatory's fire to the fire of this-world sufferings. Thus in 422 A.D.: "Souls which renounce the wood, hay, straw, built upon that foundation (1 Cor. iii. 11–15), not without pain indeed (since they loved these things with a carnal affection), but with faith in the foundation, a faith operative through love . . . arrive at salvation, through a certain fire of pain. . . . Whether men suffer these things in this life only, or such-like judgments follow even after this life—in either case, this interpretation of that text is not discordant with the truth." "'He shall be saved yet so as by fire,' because the pain, over the loss of the things he loved, burns him. It is not incredible that some such thing takes place even after this life . . . that some of the faithful are saved by a certain purgatorial fire, more quickly or more slowly, according as they have less or more loved perishable things."

St. Thomas, voicing and leading Scholastic opinion, teaches that the fire of Purgatory is the same as that of Hell; and Cardinal Bellarmine, who died in 1621, tells us: "The common opinion of theologians is that the fire of Purgatory is a real and true fire, of the same kind as an earthly fire. This opinion, it is true, is not of faith, but it is very probable,"—because of the "consent of the scholastics, who cannot be despised without temerity," and also because of "the eruptions of Mount Etna." Yet the Council of Florence had, in 1439, restricted itself to the quite general proposition that "if men die truly penitent, in the love of God, before they have satisfied . . . for their sins . . . their souls are purified by purgatorial pains after death"; thus very deliberately avoiding all commitment as to the nature of these pains. Cardinal Gousset, who died in 1866, tells us: "The more common opinion amongst theologians makes the sufferings of Purgatory to consist in the pain of fire, or at least in a pain analogous to that of fire." This latter position is practically identical with Catherine's.

As to the fire of Hell, although here especially the Scholastics, old and new, are unanimous, it is certain that there is no definition or solemn judgment of the Church declaring it to be material. On this point again we find St. Thomas and those who follow him involved in practically endless difficulties and in, for us now, increasingly intolerable subtleties, where they try to show how a material fire can affect an immaterial spirit. Bossuet, so severely orthodox in all such matters, preaching, before the Court, about sin becoming in Hell the chastisement of the sinner, does not hesitate to finish thus: "We bear within our hearts the instrument of our punishment. 'Therefore have I brought forth a fire from the midst of thee, it hath devoured thee' (Ezek. xxviii. 18). I shall not send it against thee from afar, it will ignite in thy conscience, its flames will arise from thy midst, and it will be thy sins which will produce it."—And the Abbé F. Dubois, in a careful article in the Ecclesiastical *Revue du Clergé Français* of Paris, has recently expressed the conviction that "the best minds of our time, which are above being suspected of yielding to mere passing fashions, feel the necessity of abandoning the literal interpretation, judged to be insufficient, of the ancient symbols; and of returning to a freer exegesis, of which some of the Ancients have given us the example." Among these helpful "Ancients" we cannot but count Catherine, with her One God Who is the Fire of Pain and the Light of Joy to souls, according as they resist Him or will Him, either here or hereafter.

35. CATHERINE AND ETERNAL PUNISHMENT

TAKING now the three great after-life conditions separately, in the order of Hell, Purgatory and Heaven, I would first of all note that some readers may be disappointed that Catherine did not, like our own English Mystic, the entirely orthodox optimist, Mother Juliana of Norwich—her *Revelations* belong to the year 1373 A.D.—simply proclaim that, whilst the teaching and meaning of Christ and His Church would come true, all, in ways known to God alone, would yet be well. In this manner, without any weakening of traditional teaching, the whole dread secret as to the future of evil-doers is left in the hands of God, and a beautifully boundless trust and hope glows throughout those contemplations.

Yet, as I hope to show as we go along, certain assumptions and conceptions, involved in the doctrine of Eternal Punishment, cannot be systematically excluded, or even simply ignored, without a grave weakening of the specifically Christian earnestness; and that, grand as is, in certain respects, the idea of the Apocatastasis, the Final Restitution of all Things and Souls—as taught by Clement and Origen—it is not, at bottom, compatible with the whole drift, philosophy and tone (even apart from specific sayings) of Our Lord. And this latter teaching—of the simply abiding significance and effect of our deliberate elections during this our one testing-time,—and not that of an indefinite series of chances and purifications with an ultimate disappearance of all difference between the results of the worst life and the best, answers to the deepest postulates and aspirations of the most complete and delicate ethical and spiritual sense. For minds that can discriminate between shifting fashions and solid growth in abiding truth, that will patiently seek out the deepest instinct and simplest implications underlying the popular presentations of the Doctrine of Abiding Consequences, and that take these implications as but part of a larger whole: this doctrine still, and now again, presents itself as a permanent element of the full religious consciousness.

It would certainly be unfair to press Catherine's rare and incidental sayings on Hell into a formal system. Yet those remarks are deep and suggestive, and help too much to interpret, supplement and balance her central, Purgatorial teaching, and indeed to elucidate her general religious principles, for us to be able to pass them over. We have already sufficiently considered the question as to the nature of the Fire; and that as to Evil Spirits is reserved for the next Chapter. Here I shall consider four doctrines and difficulties, together with Catherine's attitude towards them: the soul's final fate, dependent upon the character of the will's act or active disposition at the moment of the body's death; the total moral perversion of the lost; the mitigation of their pains; and the eternity of their punishment.

Now as to the soul's final fate being made dependent upon the character of that soul's particular act or disposition at the last moment previous to death, this teaching, prominent in parts of the *Trattato* and *Vita*, goes back ultimately to Ezekiel, who, as Prof. Charles interestingly shows, introduces a double individualism into the order, Social and Organic, of the Eschatology of the Hebrew Prophets. For Man is seen, by him, as responsible for his own acts alone, and as himself working out separately his own salvation or his own doom; and this individual man again is looked at, not in his organic unity, but as repeating himself in a succession of separate religious acts. The individual act is taken to be a true expression of the whole man at the moment of its occurrence: and hence, if this act is wicked at the moment of the advent of the Kingdom, the agent will rightfully be destroyed; but if it be righteous, he will be preserved.—Now the profound truth and genuine advance thus proclaimed, who can doubt them? And yet it is clear that the doctrine here is solidly true, only if taken as the explicitation and supplement, and even in part as the corrective, of the previously predominant teaching. Take the Ezekielian doctrine as complete, even for its own time, or as final over against the later, the Gospel depth of teaching (with its union of the social body and of individual souls, and of the soul's single acts and of the general disposition produced by and reacting upon these acts), and you get an all but solipsistic Individualism and an atomistic Psychology, and you offend Christianity and Science equally.

It is evident that Catherine, if she can fairly be taxed with what, if pressed, would, in her doctrine rather than in her life, be an excessive Individualism, is, in her general teaching and practice, admirably free from Psychological Atomism; indeed did any soul ever understand better the profound reality of habits, general dispositions, tones of mind and feeling and will, as distinct from the single acts that gradually build them up and that, in return, are encircled and coloured by them all? Her whole Purgatorial doctrine stands and falls by this distinction, and this although, with a profound self-knowledge, she does not hesitate to make the soul express, in one particular act after death,—that of the Plunge,—an even deeper level of its true attitude of will and of its moral character than is constituted by those imperfect habits of the will, habits which it will take so much suffering and acceptance of suffering gradually to rectify.

Thus the passages in which Catherine seems to teach that God can and does, as it were, catch souls unawares, calling them away, and finally deciding their fate on occasion of any and every *de facto* volitional condition at the instant of death, however little expressive of the radical determination of that soul such an act or surface-state may be, will have (even if they be genuine, and most of them have doubtlessly grown, perhaps have completely sprung up, under the pen of sermonising scribes) to be taken as hortatory, hence as partly hyperbolical. And such an admission will in nowise deny the possibility for the soul to express its deliberate and full disposition and determination in a single act or combination of acts; nor that the other-world effects will follow according to such deep, deliberate orientations of the character: it will only deny that, at any and every moment, any and every act of the soul sufficiently expresses its deliberate disposition. Certainly it is comparatively rarely that the soul exerts its full liberty, in an act of true, spiritual self-realisation; and an analogous rarity cannot but be postulated by religious philosophy for contrary acts, of an approximately equal fullness of deliberation and accuracy of representation, with regard to the soul's volitional state. And yet the operative influence towards such rare, fully self-expressive acts of the right kind, and the aid towards similar, massive and truly representative volitions of the wrong kind, afforded by even quite ordinary half-awake acts and habits of respectively good or evil quality are so undeniable, and it is so impossible to draw a general line as to where such wishes pass into full willings and deliberate states: that the prevalence of a hortatory attitude towards the whole subject is right and indeed inevitable.

As to Moral Perversion, the reprobate will of the lost, we find that Catherine approaches the question from two different, and at bottom, on this point, incompatible, systems; but some incidental and short sayings of hers give us suggestive hints towards a consistent position in this difficult matter.

Catherine has a double approach. For, consistently with the strong Neo-Platonist, Dionysian strain in her mind, she frequently teaches and implies that Evil is the absence of Good, of Love, and nothing positive at all. In this case Evil would not only be less strong than good—only Manichæans would maintain that they were equal—but, as against the constructive force of good, it would have no kind even of destructive strength. Varying amounts, degrees, and kinds of good, but good and only good, everywhere, would render all, even transitory, pollution of the soul, and all, even passing, purification of it, so much actual impossibility and theoretical superstition. All that survived at all, could but be good; and at most some good might be added, but no evil could be removed, since none would exist.—Yet all this is, of course, strongly denied and supplanted by the, at first sight, less beautiful, but far deeper and alone fully Christian, position of her specifically Purgatorial teaching. Here Evil is something positive, an active disposition, orientation, and attachment of the will; it is not without destructive force; and its cure is a positive change in that will and its habits, and not a mere addition of good. Yet it is plain that, even exclusively within the implications of this deeper conviction, there is no necessity to postulate unmixed evil in the dis-position of any soul. In some the evil would be triumphing over the good; in others good would be triumphing over evil, —each over the other, in every degree of good or of evil, up to the all but complete extinction of all inclinations to evil or to good respectively.

And Catherine has suggestive sayings. For one or two of them go, at least in their implications, beyond a declaration as to the presence of God's extrinsic mercy in Hell, a presence indicated by a mitigation of the souls' sufferings to below what these souls deserve; and even beyond the Areopagite's insistence upon the presence of some real good in these souls, since he hardly gets beyond their continuous possession of those non-moral goods, existence, intelligence, and will-power. For when she says, "The ray of God's mercy shines even in Hell," she need not, indeed, mean more than that extrinsic mercy, and its effect, that mitigation. But when she declares: "If a creature could be found that did not participate in the divine Goodness,—that creature would, as it were, be as malignant as God is good," we cannot, I think, avoid applying this to the moral dispositions of such souls.

Now I know that St. Thomas had already taught, in at first sight identical terms: "Evil cannot exist (quite) pure without the admixture of good, as the Supreme Good exists free from all admixture of evil. . . . Those who are detained in Hell, are not bereft of all good"; and yet he undoubtedly maintained the complete depravation of the will's dispositions in these souls. And, again, after Catherine's first declaration there follow (at least in the text handed down in the *Vita*) words which explain that extrinsic mercy, not as mitigating the finite amount of suffering due to the sinner, but as turning the infinite suffering due to the sinner's infinite malice, into a finite, though indefinite amount; and hence, in the second declaration, a corresponding interior mercy may be signified —God's grace preventing the sinner from being infinitely wicked.

But Catherine, unlike St. Thomas, expressly speaks not only of Good and Evil, but of Good and Malignancy; and

Malignancy undoubtedly refers to dispositions of the will. And even if the words, now found as the sequel to the first saying, be authentic, they belong to a different occasion, and cannot be allowed to force the meaning of words spoken at another time. In this latter saying the words "as it were" show plainly that she is not thinking of a possible infiniteness of human wickedness which has been changed, through God's mercy, to an actual finitude of evil; but is simply asking herself whether a man could be, not infinitely but wholly, malignant. For she answers that, were this possible, a man would "as it were" be as malignant as God is good, and thus shows that the malignancy, which she denies, would only in a sense form a counterpart to God's benevolence: since, though the man would be as entirely malignant as God is entirely good, God would still remain infinite in His goodness as against the finitude of Man's wickedness.

The difficulties of such a combination of convictions are, of course, numerous and great. Psychologically it seems hard to understand why this remnant of good disposition should be unable to germinate further and further good, so that, at last, good would leaven the whole soul. From the point of view of any Theodicy, it appears difficult to justify the unending exclusion of such a soul from growth in, and the acquirement of, a predominantly good will and the happiness that accompanies such a will. And the testimony of Our Lord Himself and of the general doctrine of the Church appear definitely opposed: for does not His solemn declaration: "Hell, where their worm dieth not" (Mark ix. 48), find its authoritative interpretation in the common Church teaching as to the utterly reprobate will of the lost? And indeed Catherine herself, in her great saying that if but one little drop of Love could fall into Hell (that is, surely, if but the least beginning of a right disposition towards God could enter those souls), Hell would be turned into Heaven, seems clearly to endorse this position.

And yet, we have full experience in this life of genuinely good dispositions being present, and yet not triumphing or even spreading within the soul; of such conditions being, in various degrees, our own fault; and of such defeat bringing necessarily with it more or less of keen suffering.—There would be no injustice if, after a full, good chance and sufficient aid had been given to the soul to actualise its capabilities of spiritual self-constitution, such a soul's deliberately sporadic, culpably non-predominant, good did not, even eventually, lead to the full satisfaction of that soul's essential cravings.— The saying attributed to Our Lord, which appears in St. Mark alone, is a pure quotation from Isaiah lxvi. 24 and Ecclesiasticus vii. 17, and does not seem to require more than an abiding distress of conscience, an eternal keenness of remorse.

Again, the common Church-teaching is undoubtedly voiced by St. Thomas in the words, "Since these souls are completely averse to the final end of right reason, they must be declared to be without any good will." Yet St. Thomas himself (partly in explanation of the Areopagite's words, "the evil spirits desire the good and the best, namely, to be, to live, and to understand") is obliged to distinguish between such souls' deliberate will and their "natural will and inclination," and to proclaim that this latter, "which is not from themselves but from the Author of nature, who put this inclination into nature . . . can indeed be good." And, if we would not construct a scheme flatly contradictory of all earthly experience, we can hardly restrict the soul, even in the beyond, to entirely indeliberate, good inclinations, and to fully deliberate, bad volitions, but cannot help interposing an indefinite variety of inchoative energisings, half-wishes, and the like, and thinking of these as mixed with good and evil. Indeed this conclusion seems also required by the common teaching that the suffering there differs from soul to soul, and this because of the different degrees of the guilt: for such degrees depend undoubtedly even more upon the degree of deliberation and massiveness of the will than upon the degree of objective badness in the deed, and hence can hardly fail to leave variously small or large fragments of more or less good and imperfectly deliberate wishings and energisings present in the soul.

And finally Catherine's "little drop of Love" would, she says, "at once" turn Hell into Heaven, and hence cannot mean some ordinary good moral disposition or even such supernatural virtues as theological Faith and Hope, but Pure Love alone, which latter queen of all the virtues she is explicitly discussing there. Thus she in no wise requires the absence from these souls of a certain remnant of semi-deliberate virtue of a less exalted, and not necessarily regenerative kind.

As to the Mitigation of the Suffering, it is remarkable that Catherine, who has been so bold concerning the source of the pains, and the dispositions, of the lost souls, does not more explicitly teach such an alleviation. I say "remarkable," because important Fathers and Churches, that were quite uninfected by Origenism, have held and have acted upon such a doctrine. St. Augustine, in his *Enchiridion* (423 A.D. (?)) tells us that "in so far as" the Offering of the Sacrifice of the Altar and Alms "profit" souls in the beyond, "they profit them by procuring a full remission (of the punishment), or at least that their damnation may become more tolerable." And after warning men against believing in an end to the sufferings of the lost, he adds: "But let them consider, if they like, that the sufferings of the damned are somewhat mitigated during certain intervals of time."—Saints John Chrysostom and John Damascene, thoroughly orthodox Greek Fathers, and the deeply devout hymn-writer Prudentius among the Latins, teach similar doctrine; and in many ancient Latin missals, ranging from the eleventh to the fourteenth century, prayers for the Mitigation of the Sufferings of the Damned are to be found.

Hence the great Jesuit Theologian Petau, though not himself sharing this view, can declare: "Concerning such a breathing-time (*respiratio*) of lost souls, nothing certain has as yet been decreed by the Catholic Church, so that this opinion of most holy Fathers should not temerariously be rejected as absurd, even though it be foreign to the common opinion of Catholics in our time." And the Abbé Emery, that great Catholic Christian, the second founder of St. Sulpice, who died in 1811, showed, in a treatise *On the Mitigation of the Pains of the Damned*, that this view had also been held by certain Scholastic Theologians, and had been defended, without any opposition, by Mark of Ephesus, in the Sessions of the Council of Florence (1439 A.D.); and concluded that this doctrine was not contrary to the Catholic Faith and did not deserve any censure. The most learned Theologians in Rome found nothing reprehensible in this treatise, and Pope Pius VII. caused his Theologian, the Barnabite General, Padre Fontana, to thank M. Emery for the copy sent by him to the Holy Father.

Catherine herself cannot well have been thinking of anything but some such Mitigation when she so emphatically teaches that God's mercy extends even into Hell. Indeed, even the continuation of this great saying in the present *Vita*-text formally teaches such Mitigation, yet practically withdraws it, by making it consist in a rebate and change, from an infinitude in degree and duration into a finitude in degree though not in duration. But, as we have already found, this highly schematic statement is doubtless one of the later glosses, in which case her true meaning must have been substantially that of the Fathers referred to, viz. that the suffering, taken as anyhow finite in its degree, gets mercifully mitigated for these souls.—And, if she was here also faithful to her general principles, she will have conceived the mitigation, not as simply sporadic and arbitrary, but as more or less progressive, and connected with the presence in these souls of those various degrees of semi-voluntary good inclinations and wishes, required by her other saying. Even if these wishings could slowly and slightly increase, and the sufferings could similarly decrease, this would in nowise imply or require a final full rectification of the deliberate will itself, and hence not a complete extinction of the resultant suffering. Hell would still remain essentially distinct from Purgatory; for in Purgatory the deliberate, active will is good from the first, and only the various semi-volitions and old habits are imperfect, but are being gradually brought into full harmony with that will, by the now complete willing of the soul; and hence this state has an end; whereas in Hell the deliberate, active will is bad from the first, and only various partially deliberate wishes and tendencies are good,

but cannot be brought to fruition in a full virtuous determination of the dominant character of the soul, and hence
this state has no end.

And lastly, as to the Endlessness of this condition of the
Lost, it is, of course, plain that Catherine held this defined
doctrine; and again, that "the chief weight, in the Church-
teaching as to Hell, rests upon Hell's Eternity."

Here I would suggest five groups of considerations:

(1) Precisely this Eternity appears to be the feature of all
others which is ever increasingly decried by contemporary
philosophy and liberal theology as impossible and revolting.
Thus it is frequently argued as though, not the indiscriminateness nor the materiality nor the forensic externality nor the
complete fixity of the sufferings, nor again the complete
malignity of the lost were incredible, and hence the unendingness of such conditions were impossible of acceptance; but,
on the contrary, as though,—be the degree and nature of those
sufferings conceived as ever so discriminated, spiritual, interior
and relatively mobile, and as occasioned and accompanied by
a disposition in which semi-voluntary good is present,—the
simple assumption of anything unending or final about them,
at once renders the whole doctrine impossible to believe. It
is true that Tennyson and Browning take the doctrine simply
in its popular Calvinistic form, and then reject it; and even
John Stuart Mill and Frederick Denison Maurice hardly consider the eternity separately. But certainly that thoughtful
and religious-minded writer, Mr. W. R. Greg, brings forward
the eternity-doctrine as, already in itself, "a *curiosa infelicitas*
which is almost stupidity on the part of the Church."

(2) Yet it is plain how strongly, even in Mr. Greg's case,
the supposed (local, physical, indiscriminate, etc.) nature of
the state affects the writer's judgment as to the possibility
of its unendingness,—as indeed is inevitable. And it is even
clearer, I think, that precisely this eternity-doctrine stands for
a truth which is but an ever-present mysterious corollary to
every deeply ethical or spiritual, and, above all, every specifically Christian view of life. For every such view comes, surely,
into hopeless collision with its own inalienable requirements if

Q

it *will* hold that the deepest ethical and spiritual acts and conditions are,—avowedly performed though they be in time and space—simply temporary in their inmost nature and effects; whereas every vigorously ethical religion, in so far as it has reached a definite personal-immortality doctrine at all, cannot admit that the soul's deliberate character remains without any strictly final and permanent results. The fact is that we get here to a profound ethical and spiritual postulate, which cannot be adequately set aside on the ground that it is the product of barbarous ages and vindictive minds, since this objection applies only to the physical picturings, the indiscriminateness, non-mitigation, and utter reprobation; or on the ground that a long, keen purification, hence a temporally finite suffering, would do as well, since, when all this has completely passed away, there would be an entire obliteration of all difference in the consequences of right and wrong; or that acts and dispositions built up in time cannot have other than finite consequences, since this is to naturalise radically the deepest things of life; or finally that "Evil," as the Areopagite would have it, "is not," since thus the very existence of the conviction as to free-will and sin becomes more inexplicable than the theoretical difficulties against Libertarianism are insoluble.—Against this deep requirement of the most alert and complete ethical and spiritual life the wave of any Apocatastasis-doctrine or -emotion will, in the long run, ever break itself in vain.

(3) The doctrine of Conditional Immortality has, I think, many undeniable advantages over every kind of Origenism. This view does not, as is often imputed to it, believe in the annihilation by Omnipotence of the naturally immortal souls of impenitent grave sinners; but simply holds that human souls begin with the capacity of acquiring, with the help of God's Spirit, a spiritual personality, built up out of the mere possibilities and partial tendencies of their highly mixed natures, which, if left uncultivated and untranscended, become definitely fixed at the first, phenomenal, merely individual level,—so that spiritual personality alone deserves to live on and does so, whilst this animal individuality does not deserve

and does not do so. The soul is thus not simply born as, but can become more and more, that "inner man" who alone persists, indeed who "is renewed day by day, even though our outward man perish."

This conception thus fully retains, indeed increases, the profound ultimate difference between the results of spiritual and personal, and of animal and simply individual life respectively,—standing, as it does, at the antipodes to Origenism; it eliminates all unmoralised, unspiritualised elements from the ultimate world, without keeping souls in an apparently fruitless suffering; and it gives full emphasis to a supremely important, though continually forgotten fact,—the profoundly expensive, creative, positive process and nature of spiritual character. No wonder, then, that great thinkers and scholars, such as Goethe, Richard Rothe, Heinrich Holtzmann, and some Frenchmen and Englishmen, have held this view.

Yet the objections against this view, taken in its strictness, are surely conclusive. For how can an originally simply mortal substance, force, or entity become immortal, and a phenomenal nature be leavened by a spiritual principle which, *ex hypothesi*, is not present within it? And how misleadingly hyperbolical, according to this, would be the greatest spiritual exhortations, beginning with those of Our Lord Himself!

(4) And yet the conception of Conditional Immortality cannot be far from the truth, since everything, surely, points to a lowered consciousness in the souls in question, or at least to one lower than that in the ultimate state of the saved. This conception of the shrunken condition of these souls was certainly held by Catherine, even if the other, the view of a heightened consciousness, appears in hortatory passages which just *may* be authentic; and indeed only that conception is conformable with her fundamental position that love alone is fully positive and alone gives vital strength, and that all fully deliberate love is absent from the lost souls. And if we consider how predominantly hortatory in tone and object the ordinary teaching on this point cannot fail to be; and, on the other hand, how close to Manichæism any serious equating

of the force and intensity of life and consciousness between the Saved and the Lost would be, we can hardly fail to find ourselves free, indeed compelled, to hold a lesser consciousness for the Lost than for the Saved. Whilst the joyful life of the Saved would range, in harmonious intensity, beyond all that we can experience here, the painful consciousness of the Lost would be, in various degrees, indefinitely less. The Saved would thus not be only *other* than the Lost, they would actually be *more*: for God is Life supreme, and, where there is more affinity with God, there is more life, and more consciousness.

(5) But, if the view just stated is the more likely one, then we cannot soften the sufferings of those souls, by giving them a sense of Eternity, of one unending momentary Now, instead of our earthly sense of Succession, as Cardinal Newman and Father Tyrrell have attempted to do, in a very instructive and obviously orthodox manner. I shall presently argue strongly in favour of some consciousness of Eternity being traceable in our best moments here, and of this consciousness being doubtless more extended in the future blessed life. But here I have only to consider whether for one who, like Catherine, follows the analogy of earthly experience, the Lost should be considered nearer to, or farther from, such a *Totum-Simul* consciousness than we possess now, here below, at our best. And to this the answer must, surely, be that they are farther away from it. Yet God in His Mercy may allow this greater successiveness, if unaccompanied by any keen memory or prevision, to help in effecting that mitigation of the suffering which we have already allowed.

36. CATHERINE AND PURGATORY

IN the matter of a Purgatory, a very striking return of religious feeling towards its normal equilibrium has been occurring in the most unexpected, entirely unprejudiced quarters, within the last century and a half. In Germany we have Lessing, who, in the wake of Leibniz, encourages the acceptance of "that middle state which the greater part of our fellow-Christians have adopted": Schleiermacher, who calls the overpassing of a middle state by a violent leap at death "a magical proceeding"; David F. Strauss, who entirely agrees; Carl von Hase, who, in his very *Manual of Anti-Roman Polemics*, admits that "most men when they die are probably too good for Hell, but they are certainly too bad for Heaven"; the delicately thoughtful philosopher Fechner who, in the most sober-minded of his religious works, insists upon our "conceiving the life beyond according to the analogy of this-life conditions," and refers wistfully to "the belief which is found amongst all peoples and is quite shrunken only among Protestants—that the living can still do something to aid the dead"; and Prof. Anrich, probably the greatest contemporary authority on the Hellenic elements incorporated in Christian doctrine, declares, all definite Protestant though he is, that "legitimate religious postulates underlie the doctrine of Purgatory." And in England that sensitively religious Unitarian, W. R. Greg, tells us: "Purgatory, ranging from a single day to a century of ages, offers that borderland of discriminating retribution for which justice and humanity cry out"; and the Positivist, John Stuart Mill, declares at the end of his life: "All the probabilities in case of a future life are that such as we have been made or have made ourselves before the change, such we shall enter into the life hereafter. . . . To imagine that a miracle will be wrought at death . . . making perfect every one whom it is His will to include among His elect . . . is utterly opposed to every presumption that can be adduced from the light of nature."

Indeed the general principle of ameliorative suffering is so obviously true and inexhaustibly profound that only many, long-lived abuses in the practice, and a frequent obscuration in the teaching, of the doctrine, can explain and excuse the sad neglect, indeed discredit, into which the very principle and root-doctrine has fallen among well-nigh one-half of Western Christendom. As to the deplorably widespread existence, at the time of the Protestant Reformation, of both these causes, which largely occasioned or strengthened each other, we have the unimpeachable authority of the Council of Trent itself: for it orders the Bishops "not to permit that uncertain doctrines, or such as labour under the presumption of falsity, be propagated and taught," and "to prohibit, as so many scandals and stones of stumbling for the faithful, whatever belongs to a certain curiosity or superstition or savours of filthy lucre." The cautious admissions of the strictly Catholic scholar-theologian, Dr. N. Paulus, and the precise documentary additions and corrections to Paulus furnished, directly from the contemporary documents, by the fair-minded Protestant worker at Reformation History, Prof. T. Brieger, now furnish us, conjointly, with the most vivid and detailed picture of the said subtleties and abuses which gave occasion to that Decree.

It is surely not a small recommendation of Catherine's mode of conceiving Purgatory, that it cuts, as we shall see, at the very root of those abuses. Yet we must first face certain opposite dangers and ambiguities which are closely inter-twined with the group of terms and images taken over, for the purpose of describing an immanental Purgation, by her and her great Alexandrian Christian predecessors, from the Greek Heathen world. And only after the delimitation of the defect in the suggestions which still so readily operate from out of these originally Hellenic ideas, can we consider the difficulties and imperfections peculiar to the other, in modern times the predominant, element in the complete teaching as to the Middle State, an element mostly of Jewish and Roman proven-ance, and aiming at an extrinsically punitive conception. Both currents can be properly elucidated only if we first take them historically.

It is admitted on all hands that, in the practical form of Prayers for the Dead, the general doctrine of a Middle State can be traced back, in Judaism, up to the important passage in the Second Book of Maccabees, c. xii. vv. 43–5, where Judas Maccabæus sends about two thousand drachms of silver to Jerusalem, in order that a Sin-offering may be offered up for the Jews fallen in battle against Gorgias, upon whose bodies heathen amulets had been found. "He did excellently in this . . . it is a holy and devout thought. Hence he instituted the Sin-Offering for the dead, that they might be loosed from their sins." That battle occurred in 166 B.C., and this book appears to have been written in 124 B.C., in Egypt, by a Jew of the school of the Pharisees.

Now it is difficult not to recognise, in the doctrinal comment upon the facts here given, rather as yet the opinions of a Judaeo-Alexandrian circle, which was small even at the time of the composition of the comment, than the general opinion of Judaism at the date of Judas's act. For if this act had been prompted by a clear and generally accepted conviction as to the resurrection, and the efficacy of prayers for the dead, the writer would have had no occasion or inclination to make an induction of his own as to the meaning and worth of that act; and we should find some indications of such a doctrine and practice in the voluminous works of Philo and Josephus, some century and a half later on. But all such indications are wanting in these writers.

And in the New Testament there is, with regard to helping the dead, only that curious passage: "If the dead are not raised at all, why then are they baptised for them?" [1] where St. Paul refers, without either acceptance or blame, to a contemporary custom among Christian Proselytes from Paganism, who offered up that bath of initiation for the benefit of the souls of deceased relatives who had died without any such purification. Perhaps not till Rabbi Akiba's time, about 130 A.D., had prayers for the dead become part of the regular Synagogue ritual. By 200 A.D. Tertullian speaks of the practice as of an established usage among the Christian communities: "We make oblations for the Dead, on their anniversary, every year"; although "if you ask where is the law concerning this custom in Scripture, you cannot read of any such there. Tradition will appear before you as its initiator, custom as its confirmer, and faith as its observer."

It is interesting to note how considerably subsequent to the practice is, in this instance also, its clear doctrinal justification.

[1] 1 Cor. xv. 29.

Indeed the Jews are, to this hour, extraordinarily deficient in explicit, harmonious conceptions on the matter. Certainly throughout Prof. W. Bacher's five volumes of Sayings of the Jewish Rabbis from 30 B.C. to 400 A.D., I can only find the following saying, by Jochanan the Amoræan, who died 279 A.D.: "There are three books before God, in which men are inscribed according to their merit and their guilt: that of the perfectly devout, that of the perfect evil-doers, and that of the middle, the uncertain souls. The devout and the evil-doers receive their sentence on New Year's day . . . the first, unto life; the second, unto death. As to middle souls, their sentence remains in suspense till the day of Atonement: if by then they have done penance, they get written down alongside of the devout; if not, they are written down alongside of the evil-doers."

Yet it is the Platonising Alexandrian Fathers Clement and Origen (they died, respectively, in about 215 A.D. and in 254 A.D.), who are the first, and to this hour the most important, Christian spokesmen for a state of true intrinsic purgation. We have already deliberately rejected their Universalism; but this error in no way weakens the profound truth of their teaching as to the immanental, necessary interconnection between suffering and morally imperfect habits, and as to the ameliorative effects of suffering where, as in Purgatory, it is willed by a right moral determination. Thus Clement: "As children at the hands of their teacher or father, so also are we punished by Providence. God does not avenge Himself, for vengeance is to repay evil by evil, but His punishment aims at our good." "Although a punishment, it is an emendation of the soul." "The training which men call punishments." And Origen: "The fury of God's vengeance profits unto the purification of souls; the punishment is unto purgation." "These souls receive, in the prison, not the retribution of their folly, but a benefaction in the purification from the evils contracted in that folly,—a purification effected by means of salutary troubles."

Now Clement is fully aware of the chief source for his formulation of these deeply spiritual and Christian instincts and convictions. "Plato speaks well when he teaches that 'men who are punished, experience in truth a benefit: for those who get justly punished, profit through their souls becoming better.'" But Plato, in contradistinction from Clement, holds that this applies only to such imperfect souls as "have sinned curable sins"; he has a Hell as well as a Purgatory: yet his Purgatory, as Clement's, truly purges: the souls are there because they are partially impure, and they cease to be there when they are completely purified.

And Plato, in his turn, makes no secret as to whence he got his suggestions and raw materials, viz. the Orphic priesthood and its literature, which, ever since the sixth century B.C., had been succeeding to and supplanting the previous Orgiastic Dionysianism. Plato gives us vivid pictures of their doings in Athens, at the time of his writing, in about 380 B.C. "Mendicant prophets go to rich men's doors, and persuade these men that they have a power committed to them of making an atonement for their sins, or for those of their fathers, by sacrifices and incantations . . . and they persuade whole cities that expiations and purifications of sin may be made by sacrifices and amusements which fill a vacant hour, and are equally at the service of the living and the dead." Yet from these men, thus scorned as well-nigh sheer impostors, Plato takes over certain conceptions and formulations which contribute one of the profoundest, still unexhausted elements to his teaching,—although this element is, at bottom, in conflict with that beautiful but inadequate, quite anti-Orphic, conception of his—the purely negative character of Evil. For the Orphic literary remains, fragmentary and late though they be, plainly teach that moral or ritual transgressions are a defilement of the soul, an infliction of positive stains upon it; that these single offences and "spots" produce a generally sinful and "spotted" condition; and that this condition is amenable to and requires purification by suffering,—water, or more frequently fire, which wash or burn out these stains of sin. So Plutarch (who died about 120 A.D.) still declares that the souls in Hades have stains of different colours according to the different passions; and the object of the purificatory punishment is "that, these stains having been worn away, the soul may become altogether resplendent." And Virgil, when he declares "the guilt which infects the soul is washed out or burnt out . . . until a long time-span has effaced the clotted stain, and leaves the heavenly conscience pure": is utilising an Orphic-Pythagorean Hades-book.

This conception of positive stains is carefully taken over by the Alexandrian Fathers: Clement speaks of "removing, by continuous prayer, the stains (κηλῖδας) contracted through former sins," and declares that "the Gnostic," the perfect Christian, "fears not death, having purified himself from all the spots (σπίλους) on his soul." And Origen describes "the pure soul that is not weighed down by leaden weights of wickedness," where the spots have turned to leaden pellets such as were fastened to fishing-nets. Hence, says Clement, "post-baptismal sins have to be purified out" of the soul; and, says Origen, "these rivers of fire are declared to be of God, who causes the evil that is mixed up with the whole soul to disappear from out of it."

In Pseudo-Dionysius the non-Orphic, purely negative, view prevails: "Evil is neither in demons nor in us as an existent evil, but as a failure and dearth in the perfection of our own proper goods." And St. Thomas similarly declares that "different souls have correspondingly different stains, even as shadows differ in accordance with the difference of the bodies which interpose themselves between the light."

But Catherine, in this inconsistent with her own general Privation-doctrine, again conceives the stain, the "macchia del peccato," as Cardinal Manning has acutely observed, not simply as a deprivation of the light of glory, but "as the cause, not the effect, of God's not shining into the soul": it includes in it the idea of an imperfection, weakness with regard to virtue, bad (secondary) dispositions, and unheavenly tastes.

Now precisely in this profoundly true conception of Positive Stain there lurk certain dangers, which all proceed from the original Orphic diagnosis concerning the source of these stains, and these dangers will have to be carefully guarded against.

(1) The conviction as to the purificatory power of fire

was no doubt, originally, the direct consequence from the Orphic belief as to the intrinsically staining and imprisoning effect of the body upon the soul. "The soul, as the Orphics say, is enclosed in the body, in punishment for the punishable acts"; "liberations" from the body, and "purifications" of the living and the dead, ever, with them, proceed together. And hence to burn the dead body was considered to purify the soul that had been stained by that prison-house: the slain Clytemnestra, says Euripides, "is purified, as to her body, by fire," for, as the Scholiast explains, "fire purifies all things, and burnt bodies are considered holy." And such an intensely anti-body attitude we find, not only fully developed later on into a deliberate anti-Incarnational doctrine, among the Gnostics, but, as we have already seen, slighter traces of this same tone may be found in the (doubtless Alexandrian) Book of Wisdom, and in one, not formally doctrinal passage, a momentary echo of it, in St. Paul himself. And Catherine's attitude is generally, and often strongly, in this direction.

(2) A careful distinction is evidently necessary here. The doctrines that sin defiles,—affects the quality of the soul's moral and spiritual dispositions, and that this defilement and perversion, ever occasioned by the search after facile pleasure or the flight from fruitful pain, can normally be removed, and corrected only by a long discipline of fully accepted, gradually restorative pain, either here, or hereafter, or both: are profound anticipations, and have been most rightly made integral parts, of the Christian life and conception. The doctrine that the body is essentially a mere accident or super-addition or necessary defilement to the soul, is profoundly untrue, in its exaggeration and one-sidedness: for if the body is the occasion of the least spiritual of our sins, it can and should become the chief servant of the spirit; the slow and difficult training of this servant is one of the most important means of development for the soul itself; and many faults and vices are not occasioned by the body at all, whilst none are directly and necessarily caused by it. Without the body, we should not have impurity, but neither should we have specifically human purity of soul; and without it, given the

persistence and activity of the soul, there could be as great, perhaps greater, pride and *solipsism*, the most anti-Christian of all the vices. Hence if, in Our Lord's teaching, we find no trace of a Gnostic desire for purification from all things bodily as essentially soul-staining, we do find a profound insistence upon purity of heart, and upon the soul's real, active "turning," conversion, (an interior change from an un- or anti-moral attitude to an ethical and spiritual dependence upon God), as a *sine qua non* condition for entrance into the Kingdom of Heaven. And the Johannine teachings re-affirm this great truth for us as a *Metabasis*, a moving from Death over to Life.

And this idea, as to intrinsic purgation through suffering of impurities contracted by the soul, can be kept thoroughly Christian, if we ever insist, with Catherine in her most emphatic and deepest teachings, that Purgation can and should be effected in this life, hence in the body,—in and through all the right uses of the body, as well as in and through all the legitimate and will-strengthening abstentions from such uses; that the subject-matter of such purgation are the habits and inclinations contrary to our best spiritual lights, and which we have largely ourselves built up by our variously perverse or slothful acts, but which in no case are directly caused by the body, and in many cases are not even occasioned by it; and, finally, that holiness consists primarily, not in the absence of faults, but in the presence of spiritual force, in Love creative, Love triumphant,—the soul becoming flame rather than snow, and dwelling upon what to do, give and be, rather than upon what to shun.—Catherine's predominant, ultimate tone possesses this profound positiveness, and corrects all but entirely whatever, if taken alone, would appear to render the soul's substantial purity impossible in this life; to constitute the body a direct and necessary cause of impurity to the soul; and to find the ideal of perfection in the negative condition of being free from stain. In her greatest sayings, and in her actual life, Purity is found to be Love, and this Love is exercised, not only in the inward, home-coming, recollective movement,—in the purifying of the soul's dispositions, but also in the outgoing, world-visiting, dispersive movement,—in action towards fellow-souls.

And this social side and movement brings us to the second element and current in the complete doctrine of a Middle State,—a constituent which possesses affinities and advantages, and produces excesses and abuses, directly contrary to those proper to the element of an intrinsic purgation.

(1) Here we get early Christian utilisations, for purposes of a doctrine concerning the Intermediate State, of sayings and images which dwell directly only upon certain extrinsic consequences of evil-doing, or which, again, describe a future historical and social event,—the Last Day. For already Origen interprets, in his beautiful *Treatise on Prayer*, xxix. 16, Our Lord's words as to the debtor: "And thou be cast into prison . . . thou shalt by no means come out thence, till thou hast paid the last farthing," Matt. v. 25, 26, as applying to Purgatory. And in his *Contra Celsum*, vii. 13, he already takes, as the Biblical *locus classicus* for a Purgatory, St. Paul's words as to how men build, upon the one foundation Christ, either gold, silver, gems, or wood, hay, stubble; and how fire will test each man's work; and, if the work remain, he shall receive a reward, but if it be burnt, he shall suffer loss and yet he himself shall be saved yet so as by fire, 1 Cor. iii. 10–15. It appears certain, however, that St. Paul is, in this passage, thinking directly of the Last Day, the End of the World, with its accompaniment of physical fire, and as to how far the various human beings, then on earth, will be able to endure the dread stress and testing of that crisis; and he holds that some will be fit to bear it and some will not.

Such a destruction of the world by fire appears elsewhere in Palestinian Jewish literature,—in the Book of Enoch and the Testament of Levi; and in the New Testament, in 2 Peter iii. 12: "The heavens being on fire shall be dissolved, and the elements shall melt with fervent heat." Josephus, *Antiquities*, XI. ii. 3, teaches a destruction by fire and another by water. And the Stoics, to whom also Clement and Origen appeal, had gradually modified their first doctrine of a simply cosmological Ekpyrōsis, a renovation of the physical universe by fire, into a moral purification of the earth, occasioned by, and applied to, the sinfulness of man. Thus Seneca has the double, water-and-fire, instrument: "At that time the tide" of the sea "will be borne along free from all measure, for the same reason which will cause the future conflagration. Both occur when it seems fit to God to initiate a better order of things and to have done with the old. . . . The judgment of mankind being concluded, the primitive order of things will be recalled, and to the earth will be re-given man innocent of crimes."

(2) It is interesting to note how—largely under the influence of the forensic temper and growth of the Canonical Penitential system, and of its successive relaxations in the form of substituted lighter good works, Indulgences,—the Latin half of Christendom, ever more social and immediately practical than the Greek portion, came, in general, more and more to dwell upon two ideas suggested to their minds by those two, Gospel and Pauline, passages. The one idea was that souls which, whilst fundamentally well-disposed, are not fit for Heaven at the body's death, can receive instant purification by the momentary fire of the Particular Judgment; and the other held that, thus already entirely purified and interiorly fit for Heaven, they are but detained (in what we ought, properly, to term a *Satisfactorium*), to suffer the now completely non-ameliorative, simply vindictive, infliction of punishment,—a punishment still, in strict justice, due to them for past sins, of which the guilt and the deteriorating effects upon their own souls have been fully remitted and cured.

In this way it was felt that the complete unchangeableness of the condition of every kind of soul after death, or at least after the Particular Judgment (a Judgment held practically to synchronise with death), was assured. And indeed how could there be any interior growth in Purgatory, seeing that there is no meriting there? Again it was thought that thus the vision of God at the moment of Judgment was given an operative value for the spiritual amelioration of souls which, already in substantially good dispositions, could hardly be held to pass through so profound an experience without intrinsic improvement, as the other view seemed to hold.— And, above all, this form of the doctrine was found greatly to favour the multiplication among the people of prayers, Masses and good-works for the dead; since the *modus operandi* of such acts seemed thus to become entirely clear, simple, immediate, and, as it were, measurable and mechanical. For these souls in their *Satisfactorium*, being, from its very beginning, already completely purged and fit for Heaven,— God is, as it were, free to relax at any instant, in favour of sufficiently fervent or numerous intercessions, the exigencies of his entirely extrinsic justice.

(3) The position of a purely extrinsic punishment is emphasised, with even unusual vehemence, in the theological glosses inserted, in about 1512 to 1529, in Catherine's *Dicchiarazione*. Yet it is probably the very influential Jesuit theologian Francesco Suarez, who died in 1617, who has done most towards formulating and theologically popularising this view. All the guilt of sin, he teaches, is remitted (in these Middle souls) at the first moment of the soul's separation from the body, by means of a single act of contrition, whereby the will is wholly converted to God, and turned away from every venial sin. "And in this way sin may be remitted, as to its guilt, in Purgatory, because the soul's purification dates from this moment";—in strictness, from before the first moment of what should be here termed the *Satisfactorium*. As to bad habits and vicious inclinations, "we ought not to imagine that the soul is detained for these": but "they are either taken away at the moment of death, or expelled by an infusion of the contrary virtues when the soul enters into glory." This highly artificial, inorganic view is adopted, amongst other of our contemporary theologians, by Atzberger, the continuator of Scheeben.

Now it is plain that the long-enduring Penitential system of the Latin Church, and the doctrine and practice of Indulgences stand for certain important truths liable to being insufficiently emphasised by the Greek teachings concerning an intrinsically ameliorative *Purgatorium*, and that there can

be no question of simply eliminating these truths. But neither
are they capable of simple co-ordination with, still less of
super-ordination to, those most profound and spiritually
central immanental positions. As between the primarily
forensic and governmental, and the directly ethical and
spiritual, it will be the former that will have to be conceived
and practised as, somehow, an expression and amplification
of, and a practical corrective and means to, the latter.

(1) The ordinary, indeed the strictly obligatory, Church
teaching clearly marks the suggested relation as the right one,
at three, simply cardinal points. We are bound, by the Confession of Faith of Michael Palæologus, 1267 A.D., and by the
Decree of the Council of Florence, 1429 A.D., to hold that
these Middle souls "are purged after death by purgatorial or
cathartic pains"; and by that of Trent "that there is a
Purgatory." Yet we have here a true *lucus a non lucendo*, if
this place or state does not involve purgation: for no theologian
dares explicitly to transfer and restrict the name "Purgatory"
to the instant of the soul's Particular Judgment; even Suarez,
as we have seen, has to extend the name somehow.

Next we are bound, by the same three great Decrees, to
hold indeed that "the Masses, Prayers, Alms and other pious
offices of the Faithful Living are profitable towards the relief
of these pains," yet this by mode of "suffrage," since, as the
severely orthodox Jesuit, Father H. Hurter, explains in his
standard *Theologiae Dogmaticae Compendium*, "the fruit of this
impetration and satisfaction is not infallible, for it depends
upon the merciful acceptance of God." Hence in no case
can we, short of superstition, conceive such good works as
operating automatically: so that the *a priori* simplest view
concerning the mode of operation of these prayers is declared
to be mistaken. We can and ought, then, to choose among
the conceptions, not in proportion to their mechanical simplicity, but according to their spiritual richness and to their
analogy with our deepest this-life experiences.

And we are all bound, by the Decree of Trent and the
Condemnation of Baius, 1567 A.D., to hold that Contrition
springing from Perfect Love reconciles man with God, even

before Confession, and this also outside of cases of necessity or of martyrdom. Indeed, it is the common doctrine that one single act of Pure Love abolishes, not only Hell, but Purgatory, so that, if the soul were to die whilst that act was in operation, it would forthwith be in Heaven. If then, in case of perfect purity, the soul is at once in heaven, the soul cannot be quite pure and yet continue in Purgatory.

(2) It is thus plain that, as regards Sin in its relation to the Sinner, there are, in strictness, ever three points to consider: the guilty act, the reflex effect of the act upon the disposition of the agent, and the punishment; for all theologians admit that the more or less bad disposition, contracted through the sinful act, remains in the soul, except in the case of Perfect Contrition, after the guilt of the act has been remitted. But whilst the holders of an Extrinsic, Vindictive Purgatory, work for a punishment as independent as possible of these moral effects of sin still present in the pardoned soul, the advocates of an Intrinsic, Ameliorative Purgatory find the punishment to centre in the pain and difficulty attendant upon "getting slowly back to fully virtuous dispositions, through retracing the steps we have taken in departing from it." And the system of Indulgences appears, in this latter view, to find its chief justification in that it keeps up a link with the past Penitential system of the Church; that it vividly recalls and applies the profound truth of the interaction, for good even more than for evil, between all human souls, alive and dead; and that it insists upon the readily forgotten truth of even the forgiven sinner, the man with the good determination, having ordinarily still much to do and to suffer before he is quit of the effects of his sin.

(3) And the difficulties and motives special to those who supplant the Intrinsic, Ameliorating Purgatory by an Extrinsic, Vindictive *Satisfactorium*, can indeed be met by those who would preserve that beautifully dynamic, ethical and spiritual conception. For we can hold that the fundamental condition,—the particular determination of the active will,— remains quite unchanged, from Death to Heaven, in these souls; that this determination of the active will requires more

R

or less of time and suffering fully to permeate and assimilate to itself all the semi-voluntary wishes and habits of the soul; and that this permeation takes place among conditions in which the soul's acts are too little resisted and too certain of success to be constituted meritorious. We can take Catherine's beautiful Plunge-conception as indicating the kind of operation effected in and by the soul, at and through the momentary vision of God. And we can feel convinced that it is ever, in the long run, profoundly dangerous to try to clarify and simplify doctrines beyond or against the scope and direction of the analogies of Nature and of Grace, which are ever so dynamic and organic in type: for the poor and simple, as truly as the rich and learned, ever require, not to be merely taken and left as they are, but to be raised and trained to the most adequate conceptions possible to each.—It is, in any case, very certain that the marked and widespread movement of return to belief in a Middle State is distinctly towards a truly Purgative Purgatory, although few of these sincere truth-seekers are aware, as is Dr. Anrich, that they are groping after a doctrine all but quite explained away by a large body of late Scholastic and Neo-Scholastic theologians.

(4) Yet it is very satisfactory to note how numerous, and especially how important are, after all is said, the theologians who have continued to walk, in this matter, in the footsteps of the great Alexandrines. St. Gregory of Nyssa teaches a healing of the soul in the beyond and a purification by fire. St. Augustine says that "fire burns up the work of him who thinketh of the things of this world, since possessions, that are loved, do not perish without pain on the part of their possessor. It is not incredible that something of this sort takes place after this life."

St. Thomas declares most plainly: "Venial guilt, in a soul which dies in a state of grace, is remitted after this life by the purging fire, because that pain, which is in some manner accepted by the will, has, in virtue of grace, the power of expiating all such guilt as can co-exist with a state of grace." "After this life . . . there can be merit with respect to some accidental reward, so long as a man remains in some manner in a state of probation: and hence there can be meritorious acts in Purgatory, with respect to the remission of venial sin."—Dante (d. 1321) also appears, as Father Faber finely notes, to hold such a voluntary, immanental Purgatory, where the poet sees an Angel impelling, across the sea at dawn, a bark filled with souls bent for Purgatory: for the boat is described as driving towards the shore so lightly as to draw no wake upon the water.

Cardinal Bellarmine, perhaps the greatest of all anti-Protestant theologians (d. 1621), teaches that "venial sin is remitted in Purgatory *quoad culpam*," and that "this guilt, as St. Thomas rightly insists, is remitted in Purgatory by an act of love and patient endurance." St. Francis of Sales, that high ascetical authority (d. 1622), declares: "By Purgatory we understand a place where souls undergo purgation, for a while, from the stains and imperfections which they have carried away with them from this mortal life."

And recently and in England we have had Father Faber, Cardinal Manning and Cardinal Newman, although differing from each other on many other points, fully united in holding and propagating this finely life-like, purgative conception of Purgatory.

One final point concerning a Middle State. In the Synoptic tradition there is a recurrent insistence upon the forgiveness of particular sins, at particular moments, by particular human and divine acts of contrition and pardon. In the Purgatorial teaching the stress lies upon entire states and habits, stains and perversities of soul, and upon God's general grace working, in and through immanently necessary, freely accepted sufferings, on to a slow purification of the complete personality. As Origen says: "The soul's single acts, good or bad, go by; but, according to their quality, they give form and figure to the mind of the agent, and leave it either good or bad, and destined for pains or for rewards."

The antagonism here is but apparent. For the fact that a certain condition of soul precedes, and that another condition succeeds, each act of the same soul, in proportion as this act is full and deliberate, does not prevent the corres-

ponding, complementary fact that such acts take the preceding
condition as their occasion, and make the succeeding condition into a further expression of themselves. Single acts
which fully express the character, whether good or bad, are
doubtless rarer than is mostly thought. Yet Catherine, in
union with the Gospels and the Church, is deeply convinced
of the power of one single act of Pure Love to abolish, not of
course the effects outward, but the reflex spiritual consequences
upon the soul itself, of sinful acts or states.

Catherine's picture again, of the deliberate Plunge into
Purgatory, gives us a similar heroic act which, summing up
the whole soul's active volitions, initiates and encloses the
whole subsequent purification, but which itself involves a
prevenient act of Divine Love and mercy, to which this act
of human love is but the return and response. Indeed, as we
know, this plunge-conception was but the direct projection, on
to the other-world-picture, of her own personal experience at
her conversion, when a short span of clock-time held acts
of love received and acts of love returned, which transformed
all her previous condition, and initiated a whole series of
states ever more expressive of her truest self.—Act and state
and state and act, each presupposes and requires the other:
and both are present in the Synoptic pictures, and both are
operative in the Purgatorial teaching; although in the former
the accounts are so brief as to make states and acts alike look
as though one single act; and, in the latter, the descriptions
are so large as to make the single acts almost disappear
behind the states.

37. CATHERINE AND HEAVEN

WE have found a truly Purgational Middle state, with its
sense of succession, its mixture of joy and suffering, and
its growth and fruitfulness, to be profoundly consonant with
all our deepest spiritual experiences and requirements. But
what about Heaven, which we must, apparently, hold to
consist of a sense of simultaneity, a condition of mere unpro-

ductiveness and utterly uneventful finality, and a state of unmixed, unchanging joy?—Here again, even if in a lesser degree, certain experiences of the human soul can help us to a few general positions of great spiritual fruitfulness, which can reasonably claim an analogical applicability to the Beyond, and which, thus taken as our ultimate ideals, cannot fail to stimulate the growth of our personality, and, with it, of further insight into these great realities. I shall here consider three main questions, which will roughly correspond to the three perplexities just indicated.

Our first question, then, is as to the probable character of man's happiest ultimate consciousness,—whether it is one of succession or of simultaneity: in other words, whether, besides the disappearance of the category of space (a point already discussed), there is likely to be the lapse of the category of time also.—And let it be noted that the retention of the latter sense for Hell, and even for Purgatory, does not prejudge the question as to its presence or absence in Heaven, since those two states are admittedly non-normative, whereas the latter represents the very ideal and measure of man's full destination and perfection.

Now it is still usual, amongst those who abandon the ultimacy of the space-category, simultaneously to drop, as necessarily concomitant, the time-category also. Tennyson, among the poets, does so, in his beautiful "Crossing the Bar": "From out our bourne of Time and Place, the flood may bear me far"; and Prof. H. J. Holtzmann, among speculative theologians, in criticising Rothe's conception of man as a quite ultimately spatial-temporal being, treats these two questions as standing and falling together.—Yet a careful study of Kant's critique of the two categories of Space and Time suffices to convince us of the indefinitely richer content, and more ultimate reality, of the latter. Indeed, I shall attempt to show more fully in the next chapter, with the aid of M. Henri Bergson, that mathematical, uniform clock-time is indeed an artificial compound, which is made up of our profound experience of a duration in which the constituents (sensations, imaginations, thoughts, feelings, willings)

of the succession ever, in varying degrees, overlap, inter-
penetrate, and modify each other, and the quite automatic
and necessary simplification and misrepresentation of this
experience by its imaginary projection on to space,—its
restatement, by our picturing faculty, as a perfectly equable
succession of mutually exclusive moments. It is in that interpenetrative duration, not in this atomistic clock-time, that
our deeper human experiences take place.

But that sense of duration, is it indeed our deepest apprehension? Dr. Holtzmann points out finely how that we are
well aware, in our profoundest experiences, of "that permanently incomprehensible fact,—the existence of, as it
were, a prism, through which the unitary ray of light, which
fills our consciousness with a real content, is spread out into
a colour-spectrum, so that what, in itself, exists in pure
unitedness" and simultaneity, "becomes intelligible to us
only as a juxtaposition in space and a succession in time.
Beyond the prism, there are no such two things." And he
shows how keenly conscious we are, at times, of that deepest
mode of apprehension and of being which is a Simultaneity,
an eternal Here and Now; and how ruinous to our spiritual
life would be a full triumph of the category of time.

But it is St. Augustine who has, so far, found the noblest
expression for the deepest human experiences in this whole
matter of Duration and Simultaneity, as against mere Clock-
Time, although, here as with regard to Space, he is deeply
indebted to Plotinus. "In thee, O my soul, I measure time,—
I measure the impression which passing events make upon
thee, who remainest when those events have passed: this
present impression then, and not those events which had to
pass in order to produce it, do I measure, when I measure
time." "The three times," tenses, "past, present and future
. . . are certain three affections in the soul, I find them there
and nowhere else. There is the present memory of past
events, the present perception of present ones, and the present
expectation of future ones." God possesses "the splendour
of ever-tarrying Eternity," which is "incomparable with
never-tarrying times," since in it "nothing passes, but the

content of everything abides simply present." And in the next life "perhaps our own thoughts also will not be flowing, going from one thing to another, but we shall see all we know simultaneously, in one intuition." St. Thomas indeed is more positive: "All things will," in Heaven, "be seen simultaneously and not successively."

If then, even here below, we can so clearly demonstrate the conventionality of mere Clock-Time, and can even conceive a perfect Simultaneity as the sole form of the consciousness of God, we cannot well avoid holding that, in the other life, the clock-time convention will completely cease, and that, though the sense of Duration is not likely completely to disappear (since, in this life at least, this sense is certainly not merely phenomenal for man, and its entire absence would apparently make man into God), the category of Simultaneity will, as a sort of strong background-consciousness, englobe and profoundly unify the sense of Duration. And, the more God-like the soul, the more would this sense of Simultaneity predominate over the sense of Duration.

Our second question concerns the kind and degree of variety in unity which we should conceive to characterise the life of God, and of the soul in its God-likeness. Is this type and measure of all life to be conceived as a maximum of abstraction or as a maximum of concretion; as pure thought alone, or as also emotion and will; as solitary and self-centred, or as social and outgoing; and as simply reproductive, or also as operative?

Now it is certain that nothing is easier, and nothing has been more common, than to take the limitations of our earthly conditions, and especially those attendant upon the strictly contemplative, and, still more, those connected with the technically ecstatic states, as so many advantages, or even as furnishing a complete scheme of the soul's ultimate life.

As we have already repeatedly seen in less final matters, so here once more, at the end, we can trace the sad impoverishment to the spiritual outlook produced by the esteem in which the antique world generally held the psycho-physical peculiarities of trances, as directly valuable or even as prophetic

of the soul's ultimate condition; the contraposition and
exaltation, already on the part of Plato and Aristotle, of a
supposed non-actively contemplative, above a supposed non-
contemplatively active life; the largely excessive, not fully
Christianisable, doctrines of the Neo-Platonists as to the
Negative, Abstractive way, when taken as self-sufficient, and
as to Quiet, Passivity and Emptiness of Soul, when understood literally; and the conception, rarely far away from the
ancient thinkers, of the soul as a substance which, full-grown,
fixed and stainless at the first, requires but to be kept free
from stain up to the end.

And yet the diminution of vitality in the trance, and even
the inattention to more than one thing at a time in Contemplation, are, in themselves, defects, at best the price paid
for certain gains; the active and the contemplative life are,
ultimately, but two mutually complementary sides of life, so
that no life ever quite succeeds in eliminating either element,
and life, *caeteris paribus*, is complete and perfect, in proportion
as it embraces both elements, each at its fullest, and the
two in a perfect interaction; the Negative, Abstractive way
peremptorily requires also the other, the Affirmative, Concrete
way; the Quiet, Passivity, Emptiness are really, when wholesome, an incubation for, or a rest from, Action, indeed they
are themselves a profound action and peace, and the soul
is primarily a Force and an Energy, and Holiness is a growth
of that Energy in Love, in full Being, and in creative, spiritual
Personality.

Now on this whole matter the European Christian Mystics,
strongly influenced by, yet also largely developing, certain
doctrines of the Greeks, have, I think, made two most profound contributions to the truths of the spirit, and have
seriously fallen short of reality in three respects.

The first contribution can, indeed, be credited to Aristotle,
whose luminous formulations concerning Energeia, Action (as
excluding Motion or Activity), we have already referred to.
Here to *be* is to *act*, and Energeia, a being's perfect functioning and fullest self-expression in action, is not some kind of
movement or process; but, on the contrary, all movement and

process is only an imperfect kind of Energeia. Man, in his life here, only catches brief glimpses of such an Action; but God is not so hampered,—He is ever completely all that He can be, His Action is kept up inexhaustibly and ever generates supreme bliss; it is an unchanging, unmoving Energeia. —And St. Thomas echoes this great doctrine, for all the Christian schoolmen: "A thing is declared to be perfect, in proportion as it is in act,"—as all its potentialities are expressed in action; and hence "the First Principle must be supremely in act," "God's Actuality is identical with His Potentiality," "God is Pure Action (*Actus Purus*)."—Yet it is doubtless the Christian Mystics who have most fully experienced, and emotionally vivified, this great truth, and who cease not, in all their more characteristic teachings, from insisting upon the ever-increasing acquisition of "Action," the fully fruitful, peaceful functioning of the whole soul, at the expense of "activity," the restless, sterile distraction and internecine conflict of its powers. And Heaven, for them, ever consists in an unbroken Action, devoid of all "activity," rendering the soul, in its degree, like to that Purest Action, God, who, Himself "Life," is, as our Lord declared, "not the God of the dead, but of the living."

And the second contribution can, in part, be traced back to Plato, who does not weary, in the great middle period of his writings, from insisting upon the greatness of the nobler passions, and who already apprehends a Heavenly Eros which in part conflicts with, in part transcends, the Earthly one. But here especially it is Christianity, and in particular Christian Mysticism, which have fully experienced and proclaimed that "God" is "Love," and that the greatest of all the soul's acts and virtues is Charity, Pure Love. And hence the Pure Act of God, and the Action of the God-like soul, are conceived not, Aristotle-like, as acts of pure intelligence alone, but as tinged through and through with a noble emotion.

But in three matters the Mystics, as such and as a whole, have, here especially under the predominant influence of Greek thought, remained inadequate to the great spiritual realities, as most fully revealed to us by Christianity. The three points are so closely interconnected that it will be best first to illustrate, and then to criticise them, together.

Aristotle here introduces the mischief. For it is he who in his great, simply immeasurably influential, theological tractate, Chapters VI. to X. of the Twelfth Book of his *Metaphysic*, has presented to us God as "the one first unmoved Mover" of the Universe, but Who moves it as desired by it, not as desiring it, as outside of it, not as also inside it. God here is sheer Pure Thought, Noēsis, for "contemplation is the most joyful and the best" of actions. And "Thought" here "thinks the divinest and worthiest, without change," hence "It thinks Itself, and the Thinking is a Thinking of Thought." We have here, as Dr. Caird strikingly puts it, a God necessarily shut up within Himself, "of purer eyes than to behold, not only iniquity but even contingency and finitude, and His whole activity is one act of pure self-contemplation." "The ideal activity which connects God with the world, appears thus as in the world and not in God."

Now we have already allowed that the Mystics avoid Aristotle's elimination of emotion from man's deepest action, and of emotion's equivalent from the life of God. But they are, for the most part, much influenced in their speculations by this intensely Greek, aristocratic, intellectualist conception, in the three points of a disdain of the Contingent and Historical; of a superiority to volitional, productive energising; and of a presentation of God as unsocial, and as occupied directly with Himself alone. We have already studied numerous examples of the first two, deeply un-Christian, errors as they have more or less influenced Christian Mysticism; the third mistake, of a purely Transcendental, Deistic God, is indeed never consistently maintained by any Christian, and Catherine, in particular, is ever dominated by the contrary great doctrine, adumbrated by Plato and fully revealed by Our Lord, of the impulse to give itself, intrinsic to Goodness, so that God, as Supreme Goodness, becomes the Supreme Self-giver, and thus the direct example and motive for our own self-donation to Him. Yet even so deeply religious a non-Christian as Plotinus, and such speculative thinkers as

Erigena and Eckhart (who certainly intended to remain Christians) continue all three mistakes, and especially insist upon a Supreme Being, Whose true centre, His Godhead, is out of all relation to anything but Himself. And even the orthodox Scholastics, and St. Thomas himself, attempt at times to combine, with the noblest Platonic and the deepest Christian teachings, certain elements, which, in strictness, have no place in an Incarnational Religion.

For, at times, the fullest, deepest Action is still not conceived, even by St. Thomas, as a Harmony, an Organisation of all Man's essential powers, the more the better. "In the active life, which is occupied with many things, there is less of beatitude than in the contemplative life, which is busy with one thing alone,—the contemplation of Truth"; "beatitude must consist essentially in the action of the intellect; and only accidentally in the action of the will." God is still primarily intelligence: "God's intelligence is His substance"; whereas "volition must be in God, since there is intelligence in Him," and "Love must of necessity be declared to be in God, since there is volition in Him." God is still, in a certain sense, shut up in Himself: "As He understands things other than Himself, by understanding His own essence, so He wills things other than Himself, by willing His own goodness." "God enjoys not anything beside Himself, but enjoys Himself alone."—And we get, in correspondence to this absorption of God in Himself, an absorption of man in God, of so direct and exclusive a kind, as, if pressed, to eliminate all serious, permanent value, for our soul, in God's actual creation of our fellow-creatures. "He who knoweth Thee and creatures, is not, on this account, happier than if he knows them not; but he is happy because of Thee alone." And "the perfection of Love is essentially to beatitude, with respect to the Love of God, not with respect to the Love of one's neighbour. If there were but one soul alone to enjoy God, it would be blessèd, even though it were without a single fellow-creature whom it could love."

And yet St. Thomas's own deeply Christian sense, explicit sayings of Our Lord or of St. Paul, and even, in part, certain

of the fuller apprehensions of the Greeks, can make the great
Dominican again uncertain, or can bring him to entirely
satisfactory declarations, on each of these points. For we get
the declaration that direct knowledge of individual things,
and quasi-creative operativeness are essential to all true
perfection. "To understand something merely in general
and not in particular, is to know it imperfectly"; Our Lord
Himself has taught us that "the very hairs of your head are
all numbered"; hence God must "know all other individual
things with a distinct and proper knowledge."—And "a thing
is most perfect, when it can make another like unto itself.
But by tending to its own perfection, each thing tends to
become more and more like God. Hence everything tends
to be like God, in so far as it tends to be the cause of other
things."—We get a full insistence, with St. Paul (in 1 Cor. xiii.),
upon our love of God, an act of the will, as nobler than our
cognition of Him; and with Plato and St. John, upon God's
forthgoing Love for His creatures, as the very crown and measure of His perfection. "Everything in nature has, as regards
its own good, a certain inclination to diffuse itself amongst
others, as far as possible. And this applies, in a supreme degree,
to the Divine Goodness, from which all perfection is derived."
"Love, Joy, Delight can be predicated of God"; Love which,
of its very essence, "causes the lover to bear himself to the
beloved as to his own self": so that we must say with Dionysius that "He, the very Cause of all things, becomes ecstatic,
moves out of Himself, by the abundance of His loving
goodness, in the providence exercised by Him towards all
things extant."

And we get in St. Thomas, when he is too much dominated by the abstractive trend, a most interesting, because
logically necessitated and quite unconscious, collision with
certain sayings of Our Lord. For he then explains Matt.
xviii. 10, "their," the children's, "Angels see without ceasing
the face of their Father who is in Heaven" as teaching that
"the action (*operatio*), by which Angels are conjoined to the
increate Good, is, in them, unique and sempiternal"; whereas his commentators are driven to admit that the text,

contrariwise, implies that these Angels have two simultaneous "operations," and that their succouring action in no wise disturbs their intellectual contemplation. Hence, even if we press Matt. xxii. 30, that we "shall be as the Angels of God," we still have an organism of peaceful Action, composed of intellectual, affective, volitional, productive acts operating between the soul and God, and the soul and other souls, each constituent and object working and attained in and through all the others.

Indeed all Our Lord's Synoptic teachings, as to man's ultimate standard and destiny, belong to this God-in-man and man-in-God type of doctrine: for there the two great commandments are strictly inseparable; God's interest in the world is direct and detailed,—it is part of His supreme greatness that He cares for every sparrow that falls to the ground; and man, in the Kingdom of God, will sit down at a banquet, the unmistakable type of social joys.—And even the Apocalypse, which has, upon the whole, helped on so much the conception of an exclusive, unproductive entrance-ment of each soul singly in God alone, shows the deepest emotion when picturing all the souls, from countless tribes and nations, standing before the throne,—an emotion which can, surely, not be taken as foreign to those souls themselves. But, indeed, Our Lord's whole life and message become unintelligible, and the Church loses its deepest roots, unless the Kingdom of God is, for us human souls, as truly a part of our ultimate destiny as is God Himself, that God who fully reveals to us His own deepest nature as the Good Shepherd, the lover of each single sheep and of the flock as a whole.

We shall, then, do well to hold that the soul's ultimate beatitude will consist in its own greatest possible self-reali-sation in its God-likeness,—an Action free from all Activity, but full of a knowing, feeling, willing, receiving, giving, effectuating, all which will energise between God and the soul, and the soul and other souls,—each force and element functioning in its proper place, but each stimulated to its fullest expansion, and hence to its deepest delight, by the corresponding vitalisation of the other powers and ends, and of other similar centres of rich action.

And our third, last question is whether our deepest this-life apprehensions and experiences give us any reason for holding that a certain equivalent for what is noblest in devoted suffering, heroic self-oblivion, patient persistence in lonely willing, will be present in the life of the Blessed. It would certainly be a gain could we discover such an equivalent, for a pure glut of happiness, an unbroken state of sheer enjoyment, can as little be made attractive to our most spiritual requirements, as the ideal of an action containing an element of, or equivalent for, devoted and fruitful effort and renunciation can lose its perennial fascination for what is most Christian within us.

It is not difficult, I take it, to find such an element, which we cannot think away from any future condition of the soul without making that soul into God Himself. The ultimate cause of this element shall be considered, as Personality, in our next chapter: here I can but indicate this element at work in our relations to our fellow-men and to God.—Already St. Thomas, throughout one current of his teaching, is full of the dignity of right individuality. "The Multitude and Diversity of natures in the Universe proceed directly from the intention of God, who brought them into being, in order to communicate His goodness to them, and to have it represented by them. And since it could not be sufficiently represented by one creature alone, He produced many and diverse ones, so that what is wanting to the one towards this office, should be supplied by the other." Hence the multiplication of the Angels, who differ specifically each from all the rest, adds more of nobility and perfection to the Universe, than does the multiplication of men, who differ only individually. And Cardinal Nicolas of Coes writes, in 1457 A.D., "Every man is, as it were, a separate species, because of his perfectibility." As Prof. Josiah Royce tells us in 1901, "What is real, is not only a content of experience and the embodiment of a type; but an individual content of experience, and the unique embodiment of a type."

Now in the future beatitude, where the full development of this uniqueness in personality cannot, as so often here, be stunted or misapplied, all this will evidently reach its zenith. But, if so, then it follows that, although one of the two greatest of the joys of those souls will be their love and understanding of each other,—this love and trust, given as it will be to the other souls, in their full, unique personality, will, of necessity, exceed the comprehension of the giving personalities. Hence there will still be an equivalent for that trust and venture, that creative faith in the love and devotion given by us to our fellows, and found by us in them, which are, here below, the noblest concomitants and conditions of the pain and the cost and the joy in every virile love and self-dedication.—There is then an element of truth in Lessing's words of 1773: "The human soul is incapable of even one unmixed emotion,—one that, down to its minutest constituent, would be nothing but pleasurable or nothing but painful: let alone of a condition in which it would experience nothing but such unmixed emotions."—For, as Prof. Troeltsch says finely in 1903, "Everything historical retains, in spite of all its relation to absolute values, something of irrationality,"—of impenetrableness to finite minds, "and of individuality. Indeed just this mixture is the special characteristic of the lot and dignity of man; nor is a Beyond for him conceivable in which it would altogether cease. Doubt and unrest can indeed give way to clear sight and certitude: yet this very clarity and assurance will, in each human soul, still bear a certain individual character," fully comprehensible to the other souls by love and trust alone.

And this same element we find, of course, in a still greater degree,—although, as I shall argue later on, our experimental knowledge of God is greater than is our knowledge of our fellow-creatures,—in the relations between our love of God and our knowledge of Him. St. Thomas tells us most solidly: "Individual Being applies to God, in so far as it implies Incommunicableness." Indeed, "*Person* signifies the most perfect thing in nature,"—"the subsistence of an individual in a rational nature." "And since the dignity of the divine nature exceeds every other dignity, this name of Person is applicable, in a supreme degree, to God." And again: "God, as infinite, cannot be held infinitely by anything finite"; and hence "only in the sense in which comprehension is opposed to a seeking after Him, is God comprehended, i.e. possessed, by the Blessed." And hence the texts: "I press on, if so be that I may apprehend that for which also I was apprehended" (Phil. iii. 12); "then shall I know even as also I have been known" (1 Cor. xiii. 12); and "we shall see Him as He is" (1 John iii. 2): all refer to such a possession of God. In the last text "the adverb 'as' only signifies 'we shall see His essence' and not 'we shall have as perfect a mode of vision as God has a mode of being.'"—Here again, then, we find that souls loving God in His Infinite Individuality, will necessarily love Him beyond their intellectual comprehension of Him; the element of devoted trust, of free self-donation to One fully known only through and in such an act, will thus remain to man for ever. St. John of the Cross proclaimed this great truth: "One of the greatest favours of God, bestowed transiently upon the soul in this life, is its ability to see so distinctly, and to feel so profoundly, that . . . it cannot comprehend Him at all. These souls are herein, in some degree, like to the souls in heaven, where they who know Him most perfectly perceive most clearly that He is infinitely incomprehensible; for those that have the less clear vision, do not perceive so distinctly as the others how greatly He transcends their vision." With this teaching, so consonant with Catherine's experimental method, and her continuous trust in the persistence of the deepest relations of the soul to God, of the self-identical soul to the unchanging God, we can conclude this study of her Eschatology.

38. CATHERINE AND HER DISCIPLES

It is probably during the next two years of her life that
occurred the beautiful scene and conversation,—so typical
of her relations with her disciples during this first part of
her last period (1499 to 1501),—which we can think of as
her spiritual Indian summer, her Aftermath. The scene has
been recorded for us by her chief interlocutor, Vernazza.
Probably Bartolommea, Ettore's wife, was present, and
possibly also Don Marabotto. "This blessed soul," he writes,
"all surrounded though she was by the deep and peaceful
ocean of her Love, God, desired nevertheless to express
in words, to her spiritual children, the sentiments that were
within her. And many a time she would say to them: 'O
would that I could tell what my heart feels!' And her children
would say: 'O Mother, tell us something of it.' And she
would answer: 'I cannot find words appropriate to so great
a love. But this I can say with truth, that if of what my heart
feels but one drop were to fall into Hell, Hell itself would
altogether turn into Eternal Life.'" "And one of these her
spiritual children, an interior soul (*un Religioso*),"—Vernazza,
present on this occasion,—"dismayed at what she was saying,
replied: 'Mother, I do not understand this; if it were possible,
I would gladly understand it better.' But Catherine answered:
'My son, I find it impossible to put it otherwise.' Then he,
eager to understand further, said: 'Mother, supposing we
gave your word some interpretation, and that this corre-
sponded to what is in your mind, would you tell us if it was
so?' 'Willingly, dear son,' rejoined Catherine, with evident
pleasure.

"And the disciple continued: 'The matter might perhaps
stand in this wise.' And he then explained how that the
love which she was feeling united her, by participation, with
the goodness of God, so that she no more distinguished herself from God. Now Hell stands for the very opposite, since
all the spirits therein are in rebellion against God. If then
it were possible for them to receive even a little drop of such

s

union, it would deprive them of all rebellion against God, and would so unite them with Love, with God Himself, as to make them be in Life Eternal. For Hell is everywhere where there is such rebellion; and Life Eternal, whereso-ever there is such union. And the Mother, hearing this, appeared to be in a state of interior jubilation; whence with beaming face she answered: 'O dear son, truly the matter stands as you have said; and hearing you speak, I feel it really is so. But my mind and tongue are so immersed in this Love, that I cannot myself either say or think these or other reasons.' And the Disciple then said: 'O Mother, could you not ask your Love, God, for some of these little drops of union for your sons?' She answered, and with increased joyousness: 'I see this tender Love to be so full of condescension to these my sons, that for them I can ask nothing of It, and can only present them before His sight.'"

I sincerely know not where to look for a doctrine of grander depth and breadth, of more vibrating aliveness; for one more directly the result of life, or leading more directly to it, than are those few half-utterances and delicately strong indications of an overflowing interior plenitude and radiant, all-conquering peace.

And even one such scene is sufficient to make us feel that the following passage of the *Dialogo* is, in its substance and tone, profoundly true to facts: "This soul remained hence-forth" (in this third period) "many a time in company with its many spiritual friends, discoursing of the Divine Love, in such wise that they felt as though in Paradise, both collectively, and each one in his own particular way. How delightful were these colloquies! She who spoke and he who listened, each one fed on spiritual food of a delicious kind; and because the time flew so swiftly, they never could attain satiety, but, all on fire within them, they would remain there, unable at last to speak, unable to depart, as though in ecstasy."

Five times the *Vita* compares her countenance, which, when she was deeply moved, had a flushed, luminous and transparent appearance, to that of an Angel or Cherub or

Seraph; and it even gives a story, which purports to explain how she came to be called the latter. And though this anecdote may be little more than a literary dramatisation of this popular appellation of Catherine; and although, even if the scene be historical, Catherine has no kind of active share in bringing it about; yet the passage is, in any case, of some real interest, since it testifies to and typifies Catherine's abundance of moral and mental sanity and strong, serene restorative influence over unbalanced or tempted souls, and this at a time when she herself had already been in delicate health for about five years.

The story is interesting also in that it shows how strikingly like the superficial psycho-physical symptoms of persons described as possessed by an evil spirit were, and were thought to be, to those of ecstasy, hence to Catherine's own. Thus when an attack seized this "spiritual daughter of Catherine, —a woman of large mind (*alto intelletto*), who lived and died in virginity, and under the same roof with Catherine" (no doubt Catherine's second, unmarried, servant Mariola Bastarda is meant, and each must have had experience of the other's powers and wants from or before 1490 till 1497, and again from 1500 onwards),—"she would become greatly agitated and be thrown to the ground. The evil spirit would enter into her mind, and would not allow her to think of divine things. And she would thus be as one beside herself, all submerged in that malign and diabolic will."—And similarly we are told that Catherine would "throw herself to the ground, altogether beside herself," "immersed in a sea,"—in this case, "of the deepest peace"; and "she would writhe as though she were a serpent."

Yet this superficial likeness between these two states,—a likeness apparent already in the similar double series of phenomena described in St. Paul's Epistles and in the Acts of the Apostles,—serves, here also, but to bring out in fuller relief the profound underlying spiritual and moral difference between the two conditions of soul. For it is precisely in Catherine's company that, when insufferable to her own self, the afflicted Mariola would recover her peace and self-possession, so that "even a silent look up to Catherine's face would help to bring relief."

It is in 1500, soon after Mariola's return to her mistress (I take the maid's state of health to have occasioned her absence from Catherine for two years or so), that this spiritual daughter is represented as declaring in the first stage of one of these attacks,—or rather "the unclean spirit" possessing her is said to have exclaimed to Catherine: "We are both of us thy slaves, because of that pure love which thou possess-est in thy heart"; and "full of rage at having made this admission, he threw himself on the ground, and writhed with the feet." And then when,—all this is supposed to take place in the presence of both Catherine and Don Marabotto,—the possessed one has stood up, the Confessor forces the spirit step by step to speak out and to declare successively that Catherine is "Caterina," "Adorna or Fiesca," and "Caterina Serafina," the latter being uttered amidst great torment.

39. CATHERINE'S DEATH

DURING the early night hours of "the 14th, she again lost much blood, and she weakened much in her speech. Yet she once more, and it was the last time, communicated as usual. And throughout this day she lay there, with her pulse so slight as to be unfindable." And "many devoted friends were present."

And as the subsequent night ceased to be Saturday and became Sunday, the 15th, "she was asked whether she wished to communicate. But she then pointed with her right index-finger towards the sky." And her friends understood that she wished to indicate by this that she had to go and communicate in heaven. "And at this moment, this blessed soul gently expired, in great peace and tranquillity, and flew to her tender and much desired Love."

BOOK III

THE PHILOSOPHY OF RELIGION

BOOK III.

THE PHILOSOPHERS' REBELLION.

BOOK III

THE PHILOSOPHY OF RELIGION

40. RESPONSIBILITY AND BELIEF

SOME thirty years ago a saintly French Cleric [1] was telling
me his recent experiences at the death-bed of a Positivist [2] of
European renown. The man was in his seventies, and for a
full half century had organised and systematised the most
aggressively negative of the followers and of the teachings of
Auguste Comte—teachings which reduce all religion to purely
human realities taken for more than human by a sheer mirage
of the human mind. The Cleric in question was then in his
middle forties, a man of the finest mental gifts and training,
and a soul of the deepest spirituality. He had been sitting, at
the express invitation of the Positivist leader, almost daily for
three months by the sick man, and had kept a most careful
diary of all and everything from day to day. Nothing could
be more emphatic than were this Cleric's convictions that
this Positivist had, three months before he called in this
Abbé, been touched by a most real divine grace. A sudden,
intense, persistent pain had then awakened in this philosopher's heart, without any doing of his own, a pain which,
during the first three months, he had not succeeded in driving
away as morbid, or in explaining away as an illusion. The pain
was a pain for all the Sins—this term alone was adequate—
the Sins of his entire past life. Again this same Cleric had
come to know, from the Positivist himself during the remaining
three months of his life, the general interior history of his
long past and the sort of acts which now so much pained
him; and this Cleric could not but marvel at the innocence

[1] The late Abbé Huvelin.　　　　　　　[2] Emile Littré.

247

(according to ordinary standards) of a life adulated from youth upwards and which, until these past three months, had remained without misgivings as to the truth, the unanswerableness, the necessity and the duty, of its intensive, propagandist unbelief. The Positivist died, now explicitly sure of two things—that the pain was no fancy, but, on the contrary, the most genuine of intimations, the most real effect of realities and forces ignored by himself up to now; and again, that he was not going to cease in death, but, on the contrary, would then see the realities and forces of which he was now experiencing this effect. Still worshipped by the few whom he still admitted to his presence, with half a century of intense virile labour and rare moral purity behind him, he was now dying broken-hearted (his own words), prostrate at the foot of that great altar stair of real experiences which was now leading him back to the God from whom they came. On the last day of his life his devotedly Catholic wife, seeing death on his face, asked him whether he would like to be baptised (his militantly unbelieving parents had opposed all such "superstition"), and he answered he would; he was consequently baptised shortly before he entered upon unconsciousness. But to the end this Positivist, if asked to affirm the Church, or Christ, or even simply God, would answer, "Pray do not press me; not yet, not yet." Apparently, then, a man can be in good faith, at least for many years, in the denial of even the very rudiments of Theism.

Some three years ago I was listening to the account, by a scholarly young High Anglican Cleric, of his recent experiences in an English Officers' hospital during the Great War. Many of these officers, young and middle-aged, had met his religious advances, however elementary and tentative—they were all nominally Anglican—with a seemingly prompt, frank and manly repudiation, and with a confident and apparently spontaneous distinction between any and every creed and dogma, as the affairs of a paid clergy and of dreamy bookworms, and a pure life, as what alone mattered. The Chaplain, much as he regretted this refusal of all creed and dogma, still, for something like a year, I think, persisted in thanks to God for this recognition and practice of purity. But at last, one day he came upon one of these very officers, in the act of some grave impurity. Upon the Chaplain upbraiding him, not only for this impurity, but for the long deceit this officer had practised upon him, the officer turned upon the Chaplain, again with that confident and apparently spontaneous manner, and said: "There now, once more I catch you out as the artificial paid Cleric, the man who *will* insist upon the obligation of what is far-fetched and unnatural, and who *will* be shocked at the like of this. I do nothing but what nature prompts me to do." Here we cannot but feel that men can be hardened in bad faith, and this with regard to the most fundamental facts and principles of the most elementary moral life.

We all of us, in various degrees and ways, even directly from the history of our own souls, can readily add further instances to the two great facts, currents, laws of real life, just illustrated—the amazing innocences and the no less amazing corruptions of our poor human minds and wills. But let us now press these great general facts so as to reach some five large discriminations and deep maxims, helps towards a right attitude and action in these very delicate, yet also very important, matters of real life.

41. THE INEQUALITY OF RELIGIOUS ENDOWMENT

OUR first discrimination is quite preliminary, but none the less important; it clears up a confusion very general in our days, and, with it, a perennial source of indifference. We shrink increasingly—upon the whole rightly, I think,—from attributing bad faith, or impure life, or selfish motives, to those who differ from us however largely, short of clear demonstration of the presence and operation within these persons of such debasing influences. But this right and proper suspension of judgment leads with ease to the assumption that we ourselves and others are, all and always and entirely, in good faith and in the earnest search and practice of the light. We thus soon come to see around us a world constituted of countless intelligences and wills, each as true and strong as, there and then, it is capable of being; they are all, so far, equally good—there is no difference either between the goodness of the one and the goodness of the other, or between the actual goodness and the possible goodness of any one of them. But thus we not only fly in the face of, and we rapidly weaken, the sense of folly, weakness, sin, as very real facts in our own life and in all human history: we even (and this is my momentary point) ignore and weaken a still more undeniable set of facts and of awarenesses. I mean that we thus sophisticate our sense of the deep importance of any and every increase of accurate, adequate insight and power, whether or no we be responsible, innocent or guilty, as regards our possession of more or less of these things. Who blames a Hottentot for not knowing Greek? Yet a full hold of Greek means power for any mind. Who condemns Birket Foster for not being Turner? Yet Turner is a genius of the first water, Foster a worthy little stippling talent. So with Milton and Eliza Cook: "I would not burn a man," says Matthew Arnold, "who prefers Eliza Cook to Milton; nevertheless Milton is greater than Eliza Cook." Much the greater part in the education of a people and in the training of individual souls, and a very large proportion of the immense value of such education and training, is quite independent of any moral blame attaching to such a people or such an individual, or of any moral praise due to their educators. Malaria has ravaged Greece for now some five centuries; this has been a curse for the country, even if no one was to blame for it. Malaria can now be eradicated there within ten years; this would be an immense blessing, even if the men who brought this blessing were not more virtuous men than are the malarial Greeks.

If we would keep this preliminary discrimination quite clear and fully active, we must cultivate a vivid sense of the difference between impartiality and neutrality, and we must beware against assuming that God, the one author of any

two souls, will have endowed them with an equal depth and
range of spiritual insight and of religious call. We do not
require to be on our guard against similar errors with regard
to the body. I meet two soldiers on my walk, both apparently
thoroughly good fellows, and certainly both children of the
same God; the one possesses both his legs, the other retains
only one leg. I am here in no danger of declaring the possession
of one leg to be equal to the possession of two legs; and, in
frankly recognising this serious inequality, I do not deserve
the charge of bigotry or Pharisaicalness. Dr. J. N. Farquhar,
in his fine *Crown of Hindooism*, has admirably discriminated
throughout against two erroneous extremes in favour of the
true mean amongst the three positions possible for us towards
the several religions of the world. Neither, Dr. Farquhar
insists, is any one religion alone true, in the sense that all the
others are merely so much sheer error; nor, again, are they
all equally true; but, whilst all contain *some* truth, they not
only differ each from the other in the points on which they
are true, but also in the amount and importance of the truth
and power thus possessed. Not the neutrality which would
stand equally outside and above these very unequal different
religions, and which would level them down to the constituent
common to them all, is what is truly fair and really sympathetic. A much more difficult, a never completed task is
alone adequate here—the impartiality which takes sides,
not in prejudice and with only imperfect, exterior knowledge,
but which does so according to the respective real content
and objective worth of the several religions, as these have
been ascertained after long, docile study and close sympathetic
observation of the devotees of these religions. This would
constitute an attempt to level up, it would mean an endeavour gradually to constitute a great ascending scale of religious
values and of their several increasingly adequate representatives. In such a scheme we can, and ought, clearly to
declare, say, the Sikh religion (in its pristine purity) to stand
higher than unreformed Hindooism, and Christianity to be
fuller and deeper than the Judaism it sprang from; and all
this, without any reasonable suspicion of partiality and

narrow-mindedness. And the advantages of one religion over another, and the recognition of these advantages would be well grounded and of great importance, even if no sin whatsoever were reasonably chargeable against Hindoos and Jews.

42. THE DUAL SOURCE OF DIFFICULTIES IN THE SPIRITUAL LIFE

AT this point I would ask you carefully to distinguish with me between what, I submit, are two really distinct and differing sources or occasions of difficulty in the spiritual life. Hence I pray you to refuse adhesion to the (ultimately single-source) theory of the Rev. Dr. F. R. Tennant, as propounded especially in his suggestive book upon the Origin and Propagation of Sin. Dr. Tennant there draws out in full the position that responsible, deliberately willing man is evolved from the irresponsible, impulsively striving animal, and that this is why man is so persistently tempted to lapse into what now, for man, is Sin—into his, man's, pre-human stage. Sin is thus essentially an *atavism*. Dr. Tennant also very strikingly elucidates how the presence, within us men, of animal impulses is a necessary condition for specifically human purity—a purity which is essentially a virtue within the human body and an orderer of its instincts. All this may be difficult of harmonisation even with the most moderate of the Church symbols, i.e. the Tridentine definition, concerning Original Sin; but it is in itself, I think, a position of great psychological interest and of much pædagogic help. The position explains and simplifies many pressing problems. But Dr. Tennant, very unhappily I believe, extends this his evolutionary explanation to all sin: sins of Pride and Self-Centredness are traced here as complications and subtilisations introduced by the sophisticating mind into the animal instincts. Pride and Self-centredness thus also depend, in the last resort, as truly upon the animal descent as do impurity, gluttonness and sloth. Now this single derivation, I submit, will simply not work; and indeed it involves a grave insensibility to the specifically Christian conception of Sin, and of the degrees of its heinousness. I take it that what specially distinguishes the Christian from the Stoic and other Philosophical outlooks on to human virtues and vices, is precisely the Christian sense that Pride and Self-sufficiency is the central, typical sin. Impurity may indeed be the viler sin, but even Impurity is instinctively felt here to be less deadly than Pride. And for this same outlook, whilst Impurity is occasioned by the body, Pride is not; the doctrine of the Fall of the Angels grandly illustrates this deep instinct. Indeed all sensitively spiritual observation of the human heart bears this out. I take the occasion to Pride and Self-centredness to spring from the double characteristic of all intelligent creatures—that they are finite and dependent upon God, for their very existence and for all their essentially finite powers; and yet that God has endowed them with a certain independence, a certain limited force of initiation, acceptance or revolt. It is, not the body, but the possession of this double characteristic, it is this capacity, not only for obedience and dependence, but also for revolt and defiance—it is this Imperfect Liberty which is the occasion of, at least, Pride and Self-Sufficiency. And the reason why all creatures, so far as we know, have been created thus with but imperfect liberty, may well be that even God cannot create a being possessed of Perfect Liberty—a being incapable, by his very nature, of falling away from his best lights — since such a being would no more be finite and a creature, but infinite and God.

Now this brings us to our third great discrimination and practical maxim. We thus insist that, as below the level of the natural human acts—the acts essentially characteristic of a human being—there are the aberrations of Impurity, Gluttony, Sloth—so there are aberrations above the level of these first, natural human acts. Here are Pride, Vanity, Self-sufficiency. I take it that many minds which see plainly enough the reality of the lower offences are nowadays in the dark concerning the very possibility of the higher sins. The t-cause of this blindness is doubtless the immense, visible and tangible predominance, and (within its own inexorably limited range) the immense triumph, of mathematical and mechanical, indeed generally of Natural, Science; and the inevitable tendency to regard Arithmetic and Geometry as the sole ultimate type and measure of all truth and knowledge attainable by man. With this assumption well fixed within our very blood it does certainly appear supremely ridiculous to blame anyone for denying anything that cannot, in any place and at any moment, be clearly, demonstratively, undeniably proved. How can I blame a man for sticking exclusively to the lucidity of twice two makes four, if this knowledge, in its full development, gives him everything he requires, and if all other supposed knowledge leads him but to fog and fancy? And yet, nothing is more certain than that the richer is any reality, the higher in the scale of being, and the more precious our knowledge of it, the more in part obscure and inexhaustible, the less immediately transferable, is our knowledge of that reality. So is the reality and knowledge of a daisy more difficult and obscure than is that of a quartz crystal, and this crystal again than "two and two makes four"; so is the sea anemone beyond the daisy, and my little dog far beyond both. And so on again to man, to the knowledge of any one human soul, my own or another, or further to the knowledge of any great past historical personage or to a great historical event or period, say, the Great War so recently with us all: the richness and the value, yet also the complexity and an obscurity which refuses to be completely banished, are together always on the increase. True knowledge of God is very certainly not a matter of great learning or of subtle metaphysics; yet if God be at all like what all religion proclaims Him to be, man's knowledge of Him must indeed be continuously re-beginning, and all attempts to render this vivid knowledge in terms of a clear science must always leave not a little obscurity.

It may be asked, however, where and how can responsibility and guilt enter here? The evidence for all these realities, from the crystal to God, is what it is: no good will in the world can increase or change it; no evil inclination can suppress or even diminish it. The answer is, that certain dispositions of the will very certainly enter into all deep and delicate apprehensions, be they of the life-history of a clematis-plant, or of the doings of a spider. A certain rare disoccupation with the petty self is here a *sine qua non* condition of any success; it is this noble freedom from self which makes the character, e.g. of a Charles Darwin so very great. And the answer is further that, if a certain parental temper, a loving humility which joyfully bends down and contracts itself into the life of creatures lower than man, be necessary for the understanding of the orchid or the earth-worm, so a certain filial temper, a loving humility which joyfully reaches up, and stretches itself out wide towards the life above it, is necessary for our apprehension of God. Indeed the apprehension of the Higher-than-man, of the Highest, the Ultimate, the Perfect,—the Beginner, Sustainer and Consummator of all that is good in us, especially of our very capacity to give ourselves to Him; this, very certainly, not only attracts our higher and best self, but also tries and tests our lower, our self-centred, our jealous and envious self. It is at this point especially that we ought, I believe, to look for and to find the presence and operation of *Radical Evil* such as Kant traced it in man's jealousy of the higher and highest as that same man sees them, or is capable of seeing them. True, such a life-story as that of the Positivist, sketched above, perhaps also that of John Stuart Mill, should warn us against explaining all and every Atheism by such perverse dispositions. Yet it can do but good if, whilst practising the greatest reserve in our judgment of individuals, we keep alive within us this sense that a certain pang accompanies, in the meanness and jealousy of the human heart (and any one human heart is liable to more or less of such meanness and jealousy), the full, persistent recognition of a perfection entirely not of our own making, a perfection we can never equal, and yet a perfection, the recognition of our utter dependence upon which constitutes the very centre, the inevitable condition, of our own (even then essentially finite) perfection. I believe that not to be aware of the costliness, to unspiritualised man, of the change from his self-centredness, from *anthropocentrism* to *theocentrism*, means not only a want of awakeness to the central demand of religion, but an ignorance or oblivion of the poorer, the perverse tendencies of the human heart. This then will be our third great discrimination — the ever possible, and the often actual faultiness of our attitude to what is above us.

43. THE SOCIAL DYNAMICS OF BELIEF

So far we have considered religion as though it demanded only purity with regard to what is below the soul, the body and humility with regard to what is above the soul, God; as though, in a word, religion were constituted simply by intercourse of the alone with the Alone—the one soul with the one God. Yet there is a further abiding characteristic of living religion, when taken upon the whole and in the long run, which produces a third great group of responsibilities—occasions of virtue and temptations to various excesses or defects. And this third great group is, of course, in actual life, inter-connected, in the most various ways, with the other two groups. This third group is generated by the great fact, so often and easily overlooked, that though the religion of any one soul is, where fully alive, the most profoundly personal conviction and life within it, and though the religion of any such single soul will always show a certain delicate pitch, temper, application more or less specific to itself: yet religion is a profoundly social force, which operates from one con-temporary man to other contemporaries and on from genera-tion to generation, largely by means of groups and organisa-tions, history and institutions. Even the most aggressively individualist of men, provided he be still religious at all, will always reveal, to any at all skilful analysis of the content of his religious belief and spiritual life, large indebtednesses to this social, traditional, institutional element of religion. This element—this influence not only of single persons but of Institutions and *things*—is readily traceable in Our Lord's own life, in that of St. Paul, in that of St. Francis, in George Fox, in William Law. And this can only change when man shall walk this planet without a body, when he shall have nothing to learn from the things of the senses, and when God has become the God of the individual alone, and not the God also of human society and of the great human associations—the Family, the Guild, the State, the Church. Indeed the paradox is, meanwhile, really true, that the more utterly independent a man thinks himself of all traditions and institutions, the more excessively, unwisely dependent he is usually, in reality, upon some tradition or institution, if only for the very simple reason that we cannot even begin to discriminate, and to use instead of being used, where we are unaware of an influence being present at all. It is, of course, true that a really blind obedience to any authority is never equal to enlightened adhesion, and that it is such adhesion which should always be the ideal of all spiritual training; and, again, that even the most adequate outlook ceases to have any genuine worth in the soul concerned, where this outlook is an affair of mere routine. Nevertheless it is equally true, and far less obvious, that what any one man can himself directly experience and exhaustively know at first hand, especially at the first start, in all subject-matters and especially also in religion, amazingly limited, sporadic and intermittent. Only by a preliminary trust in the wiser among the teachers and trainers that surround our youth and adolescence, has any such man any chance of escaping from, possibly life-long, self-imprisonment. It is by my not denying as false what I do not yet see to be true, that I give myself the chance of growing in insight. And certainly that man must be an amazing genius who, at twenty, and even at thirty or forty, has not very much to learn from even an average representative of any one of the long-tried institutional religions, in their positive constructive teachings and practices.

Now if all this be so, we have here a third immense field for wise or unwise docility, for humility, partisanship, generosity, shrewdness, for meanness, indifference, revolt, and for all

T

possible shades and combinations of such and similar dispositions. Three points appear here to be the most important. There is, first, no such thing *in rerum natura* as a religious institution which can dispense the individual soul from the duty of a wise, discriminating appropriation and detailed application of the teachings and genius of that institution. "A man may cease to be a Christian, and may yet remain a damned fool," is a well-known judgment attributed to the late Professor Huxley. Similarly, a man may become a Quaker, or a Presbyterian, or an Anglican, or a Roman Catholic, and may remain almost as unwise as he was before; he may even add new unwisdoms to the old ones, through an unconscious travesty of even the noblest doctrines he has now more or less mechanically gained. We can even truthfully go further, and can maintain that the richer the creed the greater is the experience and the many-sided aliveness needed by the soul for an at all adequate presentation of this same creed. There is, again, no such thing for man as a complete escape from history and institutions. Thus the Quakers, very wisely, possess the institution of the Meetings of the First Day and of their strict obligation. Indeed the minor religious bodies are generally characterised by the specially emphatic stress laid by them upon some, or all, of the few institutions retained by them. We can thus maintain without undue paradox, that, by appurtenance to a particular religious body, we really keep in touch with the great tradition of mankind at large, and with God's general action in individual souls. And there is, finally, no such thing as appurtenance to a particular religious body without cost—cost to the poorer side of human nature and cost even, in some degree and way, to the better side of that same nature. Hence the need of an increasingly wise discrimination—of a generous payment of the cost where it affects the poorer side, and of a careful limitation of the cost, and a resourceful discovery of compensation elsewhere, where the cost affects the better side of our nature. No religious institution, e.g., can, as such, be a society for research into the history and philosophy of religion at large; no religious institution can, as such, be asked to watch over the laws intrinsic to astronomy or anthropology; nor can the intellectually finest presentations, even of the particular religious institution, be expected usually to acquire more than a footing of toleration within such institution. Especially will all these limitations be at work in religions of a large popular appeal and following. All this will, however, be bearable, in proportion to the richness in religious history and in present religious life of the institution, and in proportion to the soul's perception and practice of the other divinely willed, fundamental human organisms and lives— the Family, the Guild, the State—science, philosophy and art. Such a soul will have to lead a life of tension and of many levels; yet the cost of it all will not be found excessive, if only the great central Christian realities and life become more and more the ultimate convictions and the all-pervading final motives of all our doings and aims. The omnipresence of God, His self-revelation in Jesus Christ, the need of all men for all other men, the organic character of the great complexes, especially of the Church, and the love for the occasions of filial, fraternal, paternal habits, also and especially in the spiritual world—these facts and dispositions must become more and more part of our very life. We shall thus be both old and new, derivative and original, supported and supporting— supporting, at the last, in our little measure, not only other individual souls, but the very institution itself.

44. PERFECT AND IMPERFECT LIBERTY

AND this brings us out of our three central discriminations— out of, as it were, the three associated clouds constitutive of responsibility in religious belief—into a final serene level, somewhat corresponding to, yet greatly exceeding in richness of content and in positive value, the opening serenity—the preliminary discrimination, which, as yet, was without responsibility for religious belief. For here at last we again come, or seem to come, to no responsibility—to, this time, something beyond responsibility. Nothing is grander, in the development of the human outlook, so long as such development is fully, finely Christian—from Our Lord's own teachings onwards to the general spiritual convictions and the greatest spiritual incorporations of the Golden Middle Age—Aquinas, Dante, St. Francis of Assisi—than the ineradicable implication, and the growing articulation, of the difference between Imperfect and Perfect Liberty. All through the great movement we can trace the operation of the twin facts that man is by his Nature constituted in Imperfect liberty, but that the same man is called by Grace to the love of, and the indefinite approximation to, the Perfect Liberty of God. St. Augustine tells us *"posse non peccare, magna est libertas; non posse peccare, maxima est"* (it is already a great liberty to be able to avoid sin; but the greatest liberty is to be unable to sin at all). This doctrine cannot but be true, unless God, Who cannot sin, is thereby a slave; and unless human souls which, in proportion to the length and depth of their devotedness, very certainly grow less liable to grave sin, thereby become less free. Thus the Liberty of Choice is an imperfect kind of liberty, and Perfect Liberty consists in willing fully and spontaneously the behests of a perfect nature, and in the incapacity to will otherwise. Hence the more arbitrary an act, the less really free it is. This great insight grew dim soon after Aquinas, amongst the thinkers who successively dominated the later prevalent positions: Duns Scotus and Occam; Luther; Descartes, Pascal, and many another since, have taught a sheer arbitrary will in God, answered by acts of sheer will in man. Thus religion becomes more and more something which hovers clear outside, which indeed intrinsically contradicts, the rationalities of life and of the world. So with Descartes; though for him the actual world order is within itself a rationally interconnected system, yet the original choice of just this system is held to have been a purely arbitrary act. So further back with Occam: the Commandments, although interconnected as they stand, might have been established by God quite different, indeed directly contrary, to what they actually are.

When we come to Kant we do indeed, in the doctrine of the Categorical Imperative, attain to something which God Himself could not have willed otherwise—to something expressive of His Nature. But Kant unfortunately, not merely ignores, but explicitly combats, the connection, already so nobly proclaimed by Plato and Aristotle, between Virtue and the Highest Good—between Morality and Happiness; and in Kant the sense of the Reality of God and of His inviolable Nature (a sense of God which, in all living religion, is, together with man's need of God and prayer to God, always primary and central) is, where not denied altogether reduced to hypotheses in aid of the moral life. The fact of the matter doubtless is that even Duty, and an entire life spent in Obedience to Duty, these convictions taken alone, are not live religious categories. So little is it true that perfect religion eliminates joy and spontaneity, as unworthy of itself, that only a life penetrated by spontaneity and joy, can be recognised by religion as of supreme religious perfection. The great Pope Benedict XIV., in his standard work *On the Beatification and Canonisation of the Servants of God*, points out that, for Canonisation, as distinct from Beatification, the Roman Church requires, not, as is usually supposed, three things, but, in addition, a very important fourth thing. The Roman Church requires for its formal Canonisations a spontaneous popular cultus of one hundred years; three well-authenticated miracles; three well-authenticated acts of heroic virtue; *and* the note of expansive joy in this saintly soul's life and influence, however melancholy may have been its natural temperament. As Matthew Arnold puts it, with delicate perception: what entrances Christendom in St. Teresa is not directly her long years of struggle and of suffering to be faithful to conscience; it is the rapt joy, the gracious spontaneity, the seeming naturalness of the supernatural, in the last years of her life-long service, a service which has at last become the fullest freedom.

Now if all this be true, the whole question of Responsibility in Religious belief seems utterly to disappear on the heights of the religious life. As well insist to Kepler on the duty carefully to consider the stars, or to Darwin on his obligation minutely to watch the fertilisation of orchids, or to Monica on her guilt if she does not love Augustine: as to preach responsibility for belief to a soul full of the love and of the joy of God. And yet, even here, indeed here especially, we have to guard against unreality and dangerous simplification. Here below no soul, sufficiently ordinary for us to classify it at all, attains to a love and joy ever unbroken and incapable of increase; and hence, at some times and in some measure, it has to revert to what were formerly its more ordinary motives. And again, even in the Beyond the perfection of the human soul, still joined to a body however spiritual, and, above all, still a finite creature, will not consist in the elimination of all motives except the most extensive and intensive of them all, but in the full actuation, allocation, super- and subordination of all motives variously good in their kind within an immense living system—in an immensely rich harmony, and not in a monotone, however sublime. And thus a chaste fear and filial reverence, a humble trust, a sense of duty, and acts of submission and of self-surrender, homely virtues as well as heroic joys: all will, somehow, not be superseded but included in man's eventual beatitude in God. A holy fear can and will be, even in heaven, the servant and watchman to our love; and hence there will still remain some place and function, through all eternity, for the sense of responsibility in our religious belief.

45. RELIGION AND REALITY

I now propose to concentrate more fully upon the deepest of the four religious peculiarities—upon the Evidential, Revelational quality of religion, its intimations of Super-human Reality, and to meet more systematically the chief objections to the trans-human validity of these intimations. But I want first to make plain how much this final exposition intends to cover, and in what way it intends to operate.

The following pages, then, will chiefly consider Revelation, but also, in some measure, Miracle, Creation and Personality, —since these four experiences or concepts are all closely connected with the points in need of elucidation against the Pure Immanentists. But this study excludes any equal consideration of Evil, Suffering, Sin. It excludes these great facts, because they do not directly obstruct, even if they do not directly aid, the question as to the evidential worth of the superhuman intimations. If the answer to the objections against the evidential value of these intimations, and against the reasonableness of the four experiences and concepts closely connected with these intimations, turns out successful, then, and only then, will it be worth while to study these great realities as objections to the Theism for which we have then found good grounds. Evil, Suffering, Sin, can then be taken as difficulties which are possibly incapable of any complete solution, yet which, even so, would not of themselves abolish the evidential value we have discovered in the superhuman intimations of religion.

It might indeed be contended that Evil, Suffering, Sin— that the awful reality and significance of these things—themselves form a large part of the superhuman intimations of religion. But such a contention is based, I believe, on several confusions of thought. The intimations we here study are of a Superhuman Ultimate Reality; and this ultimate reality, in proportion as religion grows deeply and delicately religious, is apprehended as good, happy and holy. All this doubtless is always apprehended in conjunction, and in contrast, with other, different qualities of the apprehending man himself; and these qualities, it may well be urged, are felt to be evil, painful, sinful. Yet the apprehension of the man's qualities by the man himself are, in any case, only the occasion and concomitant of the same man's apprehension of the Superhuman. It may even be questioned whether a man's apprehensions of the human which are in the most close contact and in the most constant contrast with the same man's apprehensions of the Superhuman, are indeed Evil, Suffering, Sin. I believe those closest and most constant concomitants of the superhuman intimations to be, in actual fact, the feelings of Weakness, Instability, Dependence. And these feelings and apprehensions are clearly involved, as concomitant contrasts, in the experiences and concepts of Revelation, Miracle, Creation and Personality, which we deliberately include in our study.

As to the form of the following exposition, it may well seem rather a clearing away of objections than a direct establishment of positive facts. But this would only be an appearance. For the exposition assumes throughout the actual, indeed the admitted, existence of these intimations, whether illusory or not. The exposition has as little the need, as it would have the power, to construct these intimations; it simply finds them and describes and analyses them as best it can. The argument gets under way only upon the admission that religion, in fact, is always penetrated by these intimations; and the argument reaches port the moment these intimations are allowed really to be what they themselves claim to be. This study has thus to be taken in direct connection with actual life; the two, thus taken together, are free from any indirectness or ingenuity. The claim to trans-human validity continues upon the whole as present, operative, clear, in the religious intimations, as it continues present, operative, clear, in the intimations of the reality of an external world. And as our removal of objections to the reality of an external world necessarily establishes its reality for us—because *there* is the vivid impression, the sense of a trans-human reality all around us, which clamours to be taken as it gives itself, and which was only refused to be thus taken because of those objections; so now our removal of objections to the reality of the Superhuman Reality necessarily establishes its reality for us—since *there*, again, is the vivid impression, the sense of a still deeper, a different, trans-human Reality which penetrates and sustains ourselves and all things, and clamours to be taken as It gives Itself.

46. THE CHARACTERISTICS OF THE OBJECT OF RELIGION

WE first take, then, the characteristics of the objects apprehended by the religious mind.

Here it seems clear that the apparently endless variations which exist simultaneously between one entire religion and another entire religion, and even between single mind and single mind, or which show successively in one and the same religion, and even in one and the same mind, indeed that the crude childishness of much that most individuals and most religions think and represent their experience and its Object to be, do not, of themselves, condemn the position that a great trans-subjective superhuman Reality is being thus, variously and ever inadequately, yet none the less actually, apprehended by such groups or persons. The Reality, extant and acting upon and within the world distinct from the human mind, and upon and within those human minds and spirits themselves, can indeed be taken as the determining occasion, object, and cause of man's long search for and continuous re-finding of God; of the gradual growth in depth and in delicacy of man's religious apprehensions; of man finding his full rest and abiding base in the religious experience and certainty alone; and of man simultaneously becoming ever more conscious both of the need of the best, and of the inadequacy of all, human categories and definitions to express this really experienced Reality.

There is nothing intrinsically unreasonable in this, unless we are to become simple sceptics also in Ethics and Politics, indeed in Natural Science itself, since, in these cases also, we readily find a closely similar, bewildering variation, both simultaneous and successive,—we find similar childish beginnings, and similar slow and precarious growth. In Natural Science the earth and the sun are assuredly really extant, and rocks, plants and animals have been with man since first man appeared upon the earth. Yet innumerable crude fancies, each variously contradicting the others, have been firmly

believed for ages about these very certain realities; nor are
these same realities, even now, free from mysteries greater
certainly by far than is all we know with certainty about
them. Indeed the reality of the external world in general
can be called in question, as certainly as can the reality of
the spiritual world and of God; the reality of both these
worlds can be argued or willed away, as a mere subjective
illusion or projection, by this or that person, or group of
persons, for a while. But neither of these worlds can, with
strict consistency, ever be thus dissolved by any single man;
and neither of these worlds will ever, consistently or not, be
thus dissolved in permanence by any considerable body of
men, for reasons to be given presently. And note that the very
closeness and interiority of the chief evidences and experiences
of religion render the clear perception and true explication
of their content and significance, in certain important respects,
indefinitely more difficult than is the analogous attempt with
regard to the external world; and that such greater difficulty
is characteristic of every advance in depth, richness and
reality in the subject-matters of whatsoever we may study.
Thus the science of the soul is indefinitely richer in content,
but far more difficult, than is the science of shells.

But we have also to face the widespread violation, in the
earlier religions (even where these are already above nature-
worship), of truthfulness, purity, justice, mercy, as these
fundamental moral and spiritual qualities and duties are
understood in the later religions; and the fact that much of
such improvement as occurs (in what, if not the very heart of
religion, is surely closely connected with it) appears to proceed, not from religion, but from the growth of civilisation,
of the humane spirit, and this largely in keen conflict with
the representatives of superhuman religion. These are doubtless grave objections. For if Religion be, at bottom, the fullest
self-revelation of the Infinite Perfect Spirit in and to man's
finite spirit, and if indeed this self-revelation takes place most
fully in Religion, how can this self-revealing Spirit, just here,
and precisely through the belief in the Superhuman, here
most operative, instigate, or at all events allow, and thus

often render at the least possible, terrible crimes of deception, lust, injustice, cruelty? How can It require the aid of man's non-religious activities against man's religious apprehensions? —Here if we care to remain equitable, we shall have to bear in mind the following.

Man's personality, the instrument of all his fuller and deeper apprehensions, is constituted by the presence and harmonisation of a whole mass of energies and intimations belonging to different levels and values; and not one of these can (in the long run and for mankind at large) be left aside or left unchecked by the others, without grave drawback to that personality. Religion is indeed the deepest of energisings and intimations within man's entirety, but it is not the only one; and though through Religion alone God becomes definitely revealed to man as Self-conscious Spirit, as an Object, as *the* Object, of direct, explicit adoration, yet those other energies and intimations are also willed by God and come from Him, and (in the long run and for mankind at large) are necessary to man's health and balance even in religion itself. So also the Æsthetic Sense alone conveys the full and direct intimations of the Beautiful; yet it nevertheless requires, for its healthy, balanced functioning, the adequate operation of numerous other energies and intimations, from the senses up to mental processes, in the man who apprehends the Beautiful.

Such an at all adequate and balanced development of any one group of energies and intimations, let alone of the entire personality, is of necessity, except in rare souls or in rare moments of ordinary souls, a difficult and a slow process. It has been so certainly with ethics and humaneness. It has been so still more with religion.

It is important too, throughout all these somewhat parallel growths, especially those of Ethics and Religion, always to compare the conviction, command, or practice of one time, race or country, not with those of much later times or of quite other races or communities, but with the, closely or distantly, preceding habits of one and the same race and community. Thus in Ethics, polygamy should be compared, not with monogamy, but with polyandry; and polyandry again with romiscuous intercourse. And in Religion the imprecatory Psalms and the divine order to exterminate the Canaanites should be compared, not with the Sermon on the Mount, but with purely private *vendetta*. We thus discover that, in many cases which now shock us, the belief that God had spoken was attached to genuine, if slight, moves or to con-firmations of moves in the right direction; and in all such cases the belief was, so far, certainly well founded.

Doubtless more or less self-delusion in religion must at all times have occurred, and must be still occurring, both in individuals and even in the larger groups; and doubtless, had religion never existed, certain special kinds of self-delusion would not have operated amongst men. Yet man cannot, without grave damage, do without Religion; for he cannot, in the long run, formally deny all Reality to a Subject in which man's highest inevitable ideals can find a persistent home and be harmoniously alive; nor can he attain to the vivid apprehension and steady affirmation of such a Reality except by Religion. Ethics, Philosophy, Science, all the other special strivings of man, have indeed the right and the duty persistently to contribute their share—a share indispensable (in the long run and in various, largely indirect, ways) in awakening, widening, sweetening man's imagination, mind, emotions, will; and thus to aid him also in his preparation for, and in his interpretation of, the visitations of God's Spirit. But (again in the long run and in various, often strangely unexpected, yet terribly efficacious ways) these various activities, though not directly religious, cannot fail themselves to suffer inevitably, if men *will* go farther,—if they will deny all reality to the persistent object of all living Religion. Our gratitude most rightly goes out to those men who, from what-soever quarter, have helped to awaken, widen, sweeten man in general, and in ethical, philosophical, scientific directions in particular, even though those men may have had but little specific Religion, indeed even if (often more sinned against than sinning) they have vehemently combated the only form of specific, hence superhuman, Religion which they knew. But a gratitude no less sincere is due to those men also who indeed failed to understand the worth, and who opposed the growth, of such other activities, yet who preserved the sense of the specific character of Religion,—that it deals primarily, not with ideas, but with realities, and that a certain super-humanness is of the very essence of all full Religion.

The points where the affirmations seemingly essential to all superhuman religion appear to be hopelessly contradicted by Philosophy or Science have been taken by us as four: the experiences of Revelation and of Miracle, and the conceptions of Creation and of Personality. The first two will be considered presently in connection with the philosophical problems.

As to Creation, it is plain that no sheer beginnings, however much we may attempt to conceive them in terms and images of the latest Natural Science, are picturable, or clearly thinkable, by us at all. Yet assuredly all the finite life, even all the ordering of matter, such as is directly known to us in our visible universe, are known to us only with marks of having had a beginning. Natural Science cannot indeed start otherwise than with already extant diffused matter, and cannot but tend to speak as though this matter, by its purely immanental forces, groups itself into such and such combinations, and proceeds to ever more complex and interior results. Yet that "already extant," that presupposition demanded for the purposes of Science, and so as to secure to Science a situation in which it begins to have a subject-matter at all—surely exhausts all that such Science requires, and all that it can confidently teach us, concerning the eternity or non-eternity of matter. Again, the successive advents of vegetable, animal, human life upon our planet introduce differences delicately, powerfully different in kind, especially when any one of these lives is compared with inorganic matter, yet also when any one such life is compared with any other of these several lives. And finally, the adaptation, in these several organisms, of their life to its environment (even if simply caused, at the observational level of Natural Science, by survival of the fittest amongst a mass of variations) always pre-supposes the original presence and the persistent repetition of variations deserving to be thus selected. We thus, still, get in Natural

Science, if not a clear and complete proof of an Eternal Wisdom creating and ever sustaining all things, yet many a fact and problem which indicate how largely modal, where at all certain, is Evolution. Evolution in reality still gives us, at most and at best, not the ultimate *why* but the intermediate *how*; whilst the points of central religious importance here appear to be, not so much the non-eternity, as the createdness, of all finite realities.

Thus St. Thomas can teach us that the Eternity of the material universe would not be incompatible with its Creation, and that only Creation is intrinsically essential to Theism; although the Jewish-Christian Revelation has now taught us that, as a matter of fact, the universe is not only a creature but a non-eternal one. And indeed it appears certain that what religion here centrally cares for is "the mysterious and permanent relation between the moving changes we know in part, and the Power (after the fashion of that operation, unknown) which is "Itself unmoved all motion's source."

As to the Personal God, it has now become a prevalent fashion angrily to proclaim, or complacently to assume, the utter absurdity of anything Personal about the Infinite; since Personality, of every degree and kind, essentially implies, indeed largely consists of, limitations of various kinds, and is a gross anthropomorphism the moment we apply it to anything but man himself. Yet it is interesting to note the readiness with which these same thinkers will hypostatise parts, or special functions, of our human personality, and will indeed do so largely with concepts which we know to be specially characteristic of spatially extended bodies. Thus Thought or Love or Law, or even Substance, nothing of all this is, for such thinkers, anthropomorphic or sub-human; but anything personal is rank anthropomorphism. Yet it is only self-conscious spirit that we know well, since it alone do we know from within. Self-conscious spirit is immensely rich in content; and self-conscious spirit is by far the widest and yet deepest reality known to us at all. True, Natural Science and even Philosophy do not, of themselves, fully find the Personal God, since Natural Science is not, as such, busy with the like ultimate questions, and since Philosophy (as we shall show presently) appears, of itself, to bring us indeed to certain more than human orders or laws, but hardly fully to the Orderer. But there is nothing intrinsically un-reasonable in thinking of the ultimate Cause, Ground and End of the world as certainly not less than, as somehow not all unlike, what we know our own self-conscious mind, feeling and will to be, provided we keep the sense that God is certainly not just one Object amongst other objects, or even simply one Subject amongst other subjects; and that, though variously present and operative in all subjects and objects, He is not only more perfect than, but distinct and different from, them all. In so thinking we find in, or we attribute to, the supreme Reality what we ourselves possess that is richest in content, that is best known to us, and that is most perfect within our own little yet real experience—we have done what we could; and life and history abound with warnings how easy it is here to go apparently further and to fare in fact very much worse.

Indeed we can safely hold with Lotze, not only that Person-ality is compatible with Infinitude, but that the personality of all finite beings can be shown to be imperfect precisely because of their finitude, and hence that "Perfect Personality is compatible only with the conception of an Infinite Being; finite beings can only achieve an approximation to it."

47. AN ANALYSIS OF EXPERIENCE

MAN'S actual experiences, the data with which he starts, are never (as a certain current in modern philosophy might easily lead us to believe) simply impressions which are felt by man at the time of his receiving them as purely subjective, or which are conclusively shown to be merely subjective by philosophical analysis, or which in reason man ought to assume to be merely subjective unless a strict demonstration of their trans-subjectivity be forthcoming. The data of man's actual experience, on the contrary, are subject *and* object, each giving to and taking from the other; the two, and not the one only, are (somehow and to some co-relative extent) included within the single human consciousness. And since only an outlook so purely *solipsistic* as to be destructive of the assumptions necessary to any and all coherent reasoning can, in the long run, deny the reality of something, indeed also of some mind or minds, other than, and distinct from, our own minds; and since these our minds are doubtless surrounded by and related to such other various realities: the rational presumption is that the spontaneous and universal testimony of these our minds (after deduction of such points or forms as can be clearly shown to be simply subjective) is truly indicative of the several trans-subjective realities which these experiences so obstinately proclaim. Kant's interestingly unconscious self-contradiction here, — that we can know nothing whatever about trans-subjective reality, yet that we know for certain it is in no sense like what even our deepest and most closely criticised experiences indicate it to be—can doubtless not be maintained as reasonable by any mind once vividly aware of the inconsistency. We shall have, on the contrary, to say that, by the very nature of things, we cannot indeed get clean out of our mind, so as to compare things as they are outside it with the same things as we experience them within it; yet that we have every solid reason for, and no cogent reason against, holding that the objects most persistently apprehended by our deeper experience as trans-subjectively real, and whose acceptance by us as thus real brings light, order and fruitfulness, in the most unexpected ways and into the most remote places of our life and work, are indeed trans-subjectively real and are, in themselves, not all unlike to, not disconnected with, what we thus apprehend them to be.

We doubtless know nothing completely, nothing adequately, not even ourselves; we know nothing directly from within except ourselves. Yet we do not know only ourselves, or other things only through reasoning them out from this our self-knowledge. But, in the endless contacts, friendly, hostile, of give, of take, between ourselves and the objects of all kinds which act upon us, and upon which we act in some degree or way, we do not obtain, of ourselves a real knowledge, and of the other things a merely subjective impression as to their mere appearance; but such contacts always simultaneously convey some real experience, some real knowledge, both of ourselves and of the objects thus experienced, and indeed of each precisely on occasion, and because, of the other.

But can I thus experience and know God? The question is, in the first instance, *not whether I can, but whether I do*. It is true that, outside the specifically religious life and apprehension, there is no vivid experience of God as a Distinct Reality, as the Supreme Subject, as Self-conscious Spirit. Nor, even in the religious life, is God so apprehended except on occasion of and in contrast to other, different, lesser realities. Yet even outside such specifically religious experiences, in all the larger human apprehensions and endeavours, wheresoever they become entirely serious and fully conscious of their own essential presuppositions and necessary ideals, there is found to exist, ineradicably, the sense of a More-than-merely-subjective, whether individually or even generally human, without which those larger apprehensions and endeavours would lose all ultimate worth and justification.

This More-than-merely-subjective was admirably brought out, as regards Ethics, by Fichte in 1800. "Let us suppose you go and sow seed in a field: so much as this may be reckoned as your own act alone. But you no doubt sow, not simply to sow, but that your seed may germinate and may bear fruit. The latter, the future harvest—however much your sowing may be a necessary condition for it—is no more your action, but the aim of your action. We have here two things, and not one." "Now in all your actions which show visibly in the world of sense, you always reckon in this way upon *two* things:—upon a first thing, which is solely produced by yourself, and upon a second thing, which exists and which acts entirely independently of yourself, and is simply *known* to you,—an eternal Order of Nature." And thus too in Ethics. "If a man here calls the law by which a special consequence necessarily follows from any particular determination of his will, an *Order*, and (in contradistinction from the Order of Nature) a Moral or Intelligible Order, whence a Moral or Intelligible Coherence, or System, or World, would arise; such a man would not, by this procedure, be placing the Moral Order within the finite moral beings themselves, but outside of [in distinction from] them; he would thus assume something in addition to these beings." "Now here is, according to me, the *place* of Religious Faith,—here, in this necessary thinking and demanding of an Intelligible Order, Law, Arrangement, or whatever else you may care to call it, by which all genuine morality, the interior purity of the heart, has necessary consequences." But the late Professor Windelband, in his *Präludien* (1903 and since), and Professor Eucken, in his *Der Wahrheitsgehalt der Religion* (1904 and since), have traced out in much detail precisely similar necessitations in the Theory of Knowledge and in Logic, and again in Æsthetics, where the worlds of the trans-subjectively True and the trans-subjectively Beautiful are as truly necessary presuppositions as is a world of the trans-subjectively Good a necessary presupposition in Ethics. And the late Professor Siegwart and Professor Volkelt have most thoroughly laid bare the ever-present working of this trans-subjective intimation and faith in Logic and the Theory of Knowledge.

Now even with these three more-than-simply-subjective worlds we have not, it is true, yet reached the Self-conscious Spirit experienced by Religion. But we have thus established important points. Man's general, human experience (wheresoever it is sufficiently wide, deep and earnest, sufficiently trustful of whatever may turn out to be its necessary prerequisites, and sufficiently pressed and analysed) reveals intimations and orders of more than merely human origin, truth and range. Man's general, human experience reveals this Trans-Subjective, Superhuman World in at least three specific forms, on three different sides of his experience. And whether or not there be still another legitimate form and side of human experience, a fourth revelation of the Trans-Subjective, Superhuman World which can bring further light and support to those three, it is certain that, having got as far as those three revelations, it is exceedingly difficult for men at large to retain a vivid faith in those three worlds, and yet deliberately to reject the revelation of Self-conscious Spirit offered to them by Religion. True, the same Fichte, continuously so sure of the reality and more than human character of the Moral World, tells us, in 1798 and 1800, that "this faith is faith full and entire. That living and active Moral Order is itself God; we do not require and we cannot apprehend any other. There is no ground in reason for going beyond such a Moral Cosmic Order, and, by means of a conclusion from the effect to the cause, to assume, in addition, a Particular Being as this cause." But then we are left thus at the surely strange, highly abstract, more or less mythical, conception of "an active Ordering." We are thus given an Order which is not a mere *Orderedness*, in which case God and world would be one, and there would be no God; but an Order which is an *active Ordering*, which is, in so far, distinct from the world it orders; and yet an Ordering which neither is, nor implies, an *Orderer*. But it is surely entirely doubtful (even apart from what the complete, hence also especially the religious, experience of mankind may convey and require) whether such a strange *intermezzo* of a conception is, in the long run, possible for the human mind. For we have here an active Ordering of a gigantic conflict and confusion, according to abiding, more than human, standards of Truth, Beauty and Goodness, standards not made by, yet recognisable by the human spirit; and nevertheless this Ordering and these standards are not to be the effects of Self-conscious Spirit, and are not to be apprehended by such a spirit.

Insistence upon this *intermezzo*, as the ultimate analysis of man's entire legitimate experience, becomes indeed something doctrinaire and contradicts the general method and temper which have led the mind to the point attained, if we *will* maintain it even after we have been brought face to face with the massive, varied, persistent witness of the religious sense and life. For only if we show how and why the logical, the æsthetic and the ethical life can alone be trusted and not the religious life also, where it supplies what those three lives all severally seek, can we consistently accept the deep-lying testimony of the logical, æsthetic and ethical lives, and, nevertheless, refuse or explain away the central witness of the religious life. Fichte indeed bids us "cease to listen to the demands of an empty system," and to beware lest, by our hypothesis of a personal God, we make the first of all objective cognitions, the most certain of all certainties, to depend upon "ingenious pleadings (*Klügelei*)." Yet the now immensely abundant testimony of Religion lies before us as a warning that Fichte here confounded philosophical thinking and the general idea of religiousness with the specifically religious experiences themselves. Theological deductions and speculations have indeed at times articulated or analysed, in "ingenious" ways, the deepest and most delicate experiences of living religion. Yet these experiences themselves always present their object as overflowingly existent; and, in proportion as spirituality becomes more conscious of its own requirements and more sensitively discriminating, this object is apprehended as perfect Self-conscious Spirit, as very Source of all existence and reality. We can indeed argue against Religion, as mistaken in so doing; but that Religion actually does so, and this, not in the form of deductive reasoning, but in that of intuitive experience, cannot seriously be denied.

And this Religious Experience is, in fact, interwoven, from first to last, with the sense of Revelation and the sense of Miracle.

As to Revelation, it is remarkable that men's latter-day pre-occupation with the apparent imperfections in the *content* of the various religions has frequently blinded them to the excellence of the *form*, the vehicle of all Religion. For the characteristic form of all Religion is Revelation; and the various activities and achievements of human life, wheresoever these are sufficiently deep to awaken and to hold the entire man and to lead him to some certitude, all possess, in various degrees and ways, something *revelational* about them.

It is true, of course, that the *naïf* Realism or Objectivism of classical and mediaeval times (so little conscious, upon the whole, of the always present, and often large, contribution furnished by the apprehending human Subject to this subject's apprehensions of the Object) led, by the excess of every reaction, to a sometimes equally one-sided Idealism or Subjectivism, in which the entire outer and inner world becomes the sheer projection, or at least the purely subjective elaboration, by mankind, into orders of beauty, truth and goodness, of what is intrinsically (or what at least is found by us analytically to be) a sheer *caput mortuum*—just so much dead matter or wild flux and chaotic impulsions. Yet it is equally true that the newer sciences of Biology, Sociology and History are now fast bringing us to a third stage where truth and life will more and more evidently be found to consist in the fullest and most manifold interaction between Subject and Object—and this in increasing degrees, according to the increase in the importance of the subject-matter experienced or studied. And everywhere in these newer sciences there is a sense of how much there is to *get*, how rich and self-communicative is all reality, to those who are sufficiently detached from their own petty subjectivisms. A keen yet reverent study of the *Given* appears here,—by a Darwin, be it of but the earth-worm, and by a Wilken, be it of but the scribblings on ancient potsherds. And then the greater *Givennesses* are found in those vast Intelligible Orders, which persistently show themselves anew, wheresoever human experience is sufficiently pressed, and which so entranced the great minds of a Kant and of a Fichte. In all these cases we have an absorption of the Subject in the Object, and a response—an assuredly gradual, ever only partial, yet a very real, self-revelation—of the Object to the Subject. In the cases of these Intelligible Orders we have already something more or less religious. Indeed the sense of *Givenness*, of *Prevenience*, of a *Grace*, of something transcendent having in part become Immanent to our human world as a Fact within this factual world, and of this Fact as alone rendering even possible that sense of Givenness—all these experiences are already present in the apprehension and affirmation of those Intelligible Orders as truly extant. And yet it is only the specifically religious experience which gives us Revelation at its fullest, not only as to Revelation's content but also as to Revelation's form. For Religion alone brings the vivid revelation of Spirit other than the human—a Spirit so perfect and so richly real as Itself to be the ultimate, overflowingly self-conscious cause of man's very capacity for apprehending It. Nevertheless, such a Self-manifestation of Perfect Spirit, once found and accepted, gives a base, a setting and a crown to all those other self-manifestations of the lesser realities— a base, a setting and a crown which their graduated series, taken as a whole, so greatly requires and which indeed it dimly and semi-consciously prepares yet cannot itself effectuate. And this same Self-manifestation of Spirit and the human spirit's response to It, render superfluous all attempts, always more or less hopeless, to construct God à priori, or even to demonstrate Him, from the facts of nature and of human life, by any single, deductive argument of a strictly constraining force. Because Spirit, God, works in our midst and in our depths, we can and we do know Him; because God has been the first to condescend to us and to love us, can we arise and love Him in return. "Do you wake?" asks St. Bernard. "Well, He too is awake. If you arise in the night time, if you anticipate to your utmost your earliest awaking, you will already find Him waking—you will never anticipate His own awakeness. In such an intercourse you will always be rash if you attribute any priority, any predominant share to yourself; for He loves both more than you love, and before you love at all." The prevenience of God becomes thus the crown and final guarantee of all the other, minor preveniences which variously bring us the materials and occasions for our other kinds of knowledge and conviction—from the crystal and the plant on to the animal and man.

The experience of Miracle, when discriminated in the higher religions and by maturely spiritual souls, appears to be composed, in its essence, of three, yet only of three, vivid, interdependent apprehensions. There is the vivid apprehension of something *unique* being experienced or produced, *hic et nunc*, in this particular experiencing soul. There is the vivid apprehension that this unique experience comes from the one Divine *Spirit* to this particular human spirit. And there is the vivid apprehension that this effect of Spirit upon spirit is not restricted to the human spirit alone, but that the Spirit can affect, and in any particular instance is actually affecting, in more or less striking, most real ways, the very *body* and its psychical, indeed even its physical conditions and environment, and the visible exterior conditions and history of mankind. All our previous considerations have prepared us thus to conceive Reality as, in proportion to its depth, an ever nearer and nearer approach to the Concrete Universal, to the unique embodiment of a universally valuable type; to discover, in this tendency, throughout the successive stages of realities, to ever increasing typical uniqueness, the increasingly large operation of the actually extant Concrete Universal, God; and to recognise, as we retrace these stages, that neither does God's Spirit live all aloof from man's spirit, nor does man's spirit live all aloof from man's body or from this physical body's physical environment. On the contrary, throughout reality, the greater works in and with and through the lesser, affecting and transforming this lesser in various striking degrees and ways. To at least this degree in these ways does Miracle, and the belief in Miracle, thoroughly belong to the permanent experience of mankind, and to the adequate analysis of this experience. Grave difficulties arise only when these three central experiences are interpreted as meaning that the spiritual or psychical or physical effects of Miracle constitute direct breaches within (as it were) the phenomenal rind and level of natural reality—breaches which can be strictly demonstrated to be such by Natural Science itself. This opinion, if pressed, requires of Natural Science (whose subject-matter is essentially limited to that level and that constituent of reality or appearance where strict continuity or repetitive law can be found or applied) to discover its object in what suspends or contradicts these characteristics, and hence is outside its special range and cognisance. Wherever such suspension or contradiction could be discovered, Science would have nothing to work upon, and could only wait till it again found something more or less continuous or repetitive.

48. ANTI-RELIGIOUS PSYCHOLOGY

IT is doubtless the practical difficulties which, more largely than all the other objections put together, explain the *doctrinaire* aloofness or the angry set-purpose to be found extant and operative, more or less in all times and places, against Religion, as soon as Religion appears in its full specific and articulate form—i.e. as a conviction and claim of the Superhuman. For as men look back into the past, or even carry the effects of the past within their very blood, they perceive or feel that, if not Religion in its roots, yet at least the various theologies and the various sects and churches have, in all sorts of times and places, ways and degrees, protected and perpetuated, or occasioned and increased, impoverishments, divisions, oppressions, obvious or obscure, yet very real, within men's inner lives, or as between man and man, or between one group of men and other groups. And in all such cases the sanction or stimulus to such grave inhibitions or complications appear to have sprung precisely from the supposed superhuman character of some revelation, command or institution. Such a work as Andrew White's *History of the Warfare of Science and Theology* (1903) shows, in full detail, how largely the Science, Philosophy, Medicine, Politics, Life generally, which we all practise or profit by, have been established at the price of conflict, more or less costly, with such Superhuman Claims. Hence we are bound to show how and why those blights or deadlocks were not produced by the Superhuman Claims as such, and indeed how and why a Superhuman Conviction, rightly understood and wisely practised, remains our sole ultimate guarantee against Fanaticism on the one hand and Scepticism on the other.

It is plain, for one thing, that this whole practical question is greatly complicated by the fact that (even more than the other circles of the higher human endeavours,—Science, Art, Ethics) Religion always brings with it, Religion indeed always more or less requires, such things as association, organisation, institutions. Religious Institutions indeed habitually insist upon two most precious principles and practices which the other, non-religious, circles do not and cannot thus vividly apprehend and directly inculcate; yet these same Institutions also tend to enforce these principles and practices by means which are accountable for certainly the greater amount of the bitterness felt by so many serious, clean-lived men against those very principles and practices themselves.

Such Institutions, then, most rightly maintain the Superhuman Claim as essential to Religion; they emphasise Religion as essentially Revelation, as man's deepest experience of the ultimate Reality through the action of that Reality Itself,—a Reality which both underlies and crowns all our other, lesser strivings and *givennesses*. And such Institutions, again, most rightly emphasise the great difference in amount, purity, and worth of the spiritual truth and life to be found even within the sincerest and most entirely positive convictions and practices of the several religions of mankind. Here we have two immense services rendered by the higher Religious Institutions to the abiding truths, to the ultimate basis of man's worth; services absolutely without serious parallel, as to their depth and range, in any other quarter.

Yet that superhuman, revelational Religion has, in the rough and tumble of life, and by and for the average institutionalist, been too often conceived as though arising *in vacuo*, and hence as though able, even in the long run, to dispense with, or to starve, the other activities and necessities of man; or, again, as though not only Religion but Theology were a divine communication—as though God Himself communicated intrinsically adequate, mathematically precise formulations of Religion. And thus we get a starving of all that is not directly religious in man or an arrest of theological improvement. We get an insistence upon a direct and decisive

jurisdiction, by a deductive theology and institutional admin-
istration, over the results of (indeed over the very methods
and necessities specific to) man's other activities and apprehensions, in Science and Æsthetics, in Historical Research,
Politics and Ethics, and in Philosophy. And in proportion
as this is actually effected, Religion becomes bereft of the
material, the friction, the witnesses so essential to the health
and fruitfulness of man in general and of Religion in particular. The material is lost; for man's full other experiences,
which, pressed, yield so firm a foundation for specific Religion,
are here prevented from being thus full and from being thus
pressed. The friction between Religion and Ethics, and
between Theology and Science and Philosophy, so necessary
to bring out the fullest powers of each and the deep underlying mutual need which, in the living man, each has of all
the others, is eliminated; since all these several activities,
except that of the official Theology, have, previous to all
possibility of wholesome clashing, been carefully deprived
of all their specific weapons of attack and of defence. And
the witnesses for religion disappear; for what is a witness who
has, by forcible suppressions or modifications of his testimony,
been rendered "safe" beforehand?

And again, as to all the religions of mankind other than
their own, such great Institutions tend, in their average
representatives and disciples, to speak and act as though it
were Indifferentism ever to discover *some* religious truth and
life as present in such other religions, in however various
degrees and ways. The whole conception of varyingly intense
and varyingly precious feelings after God; of stages of growth
and of light; of more or less error and corruption mixed with
more or less of truth and of health; of the test and measure
of such truth and health lying indeed within the deepest
practice and the fundamental convictions of the most richly
and most specifically religious of the great religious bodies
—with these as most fully explicating whilst exceeding the
previous illuminations and gropings of man's soul: such a
conception is clearly difficult to every fully organised Religious
Institution.

The all-important facts here are, however, that no Orthodoxy explicitly denies such a general position; and that no
Orthodoxy achieves its own deepest function except it explicitly admits and genially practises this its very genuine
implication. And is it really so difficult, precisely for men
so rightly concentrated upon the reality of God and of His
operativeness throughout the world at large, and especially
throughout the world of souls, to find thus His traces, though
doubtless in very different degrees of clearness and of worth,
even where their possessors are not awake to their source,
or even where they turn angrily against the bearers of a fuller
message? Unless the whole Christian Church is wrong in
insisting upon the Old Testament as the Word of God, unless
St. Paul was wrong in preaching God to the heathen Athenians
as "Him Whom they had ignorantly worshipped," and unless
our Lord Himself was wrong in coming, "not to be ministered
to, but to minister," some such attitude cannot but be the
right one, however difficult to our poor human passions it
may persistently remain.

Even amongst the rigorist Primitive Christians and amongst
harsh Mediaeval Churchmen, such mild and comprehensive
convictions and characters have as certainly occurred as the
fierce feelings and persecuting proceedings of others amongst
their contemporaries. And it would clearly be utterly à priori
and arbitrary to construe these convictions and characters as
springing from, or as leading to, indifference. The Church
Father Lactantius and the Popes St. Gregory the Great and
Alexander II. were no less certain of, and no less zealous for,
Superhuman Religion—for the supreme truth of Christianity
and of Catholicism, than were the Church Father St. Augustine or the Popes St. Pius V. and Paul IV. But the former
combined, with this their all-pervading and all-crowning
faith, a keen sense for the natural virtues, as the inviolable
pre-requisites, concomitants and consequences of the Supernatural Life; for the elements of truth and goodness present
in all men and in all religions; for the essentially free character
of the act and habit of faith; and for the irreplaceable persuasiveness of love; whereas the latter were all but exclusively

engrossed in the specifically religious virtues, in the completest religion, in this religion's scholastic and juridical
formulation, and in the influence and utility of pressure, fear,
commands, obedience. But both groups, in their several
ways, are equally discriminative, equally zealous, equally
superhuman.

The dispositions and acts of the mild and comprehensive
group appear now to be as true and as wise as ever, and to
require no more than certain further discriminations. We
religious men will have to develop, *as part of our religion*, the
ceaseless sense of its requiring the *nidus*, materials, stimulant,
discipline, of the other God-given, non-religious activities,
duties, ideals of man, from his physical and psychical necessities
up to his æsthetic, political and philosophical aspirations. The
autonomy, competition, and criticism of the other centres of
life will have thus to become welcome to religion for the sake
of religion itself. We religious men again will have to develop,
as part of our religion, a sense, not simply of the error and evil,
but also of the truth and the good, in any and every man's
religion. We will have to realise, with Cardinal John de
Lugo, S.J. (who died in 1660), that the members of the various
Christian sects, of the Jewish and Mohammedan communions,
and of the non-Christian philosophies, who achieved and
achieve their salvation, did and do so in general simply by
God's grace aiding their good faith instinctively to concentrate
itself upon, and to practise, those elements in the cultus and
teaching of their respective sect, communion or philosophy,
which are true and good and originally revealed by God.[1]
And, finally, we religious men, especially we Catholic Christians, will indeed never drop the noble truth and ideal of a
universal unity of cultus and belief, of one single world-wide
Church, but we will conceive this our deathless faith in
religious unity as being solidly realisable only if we are able
and glad to recognise the rudimentary, fragmentary, relative,
pædagogic truth and worth in religions other than our own,
—a worth which, as regards at least Judaism and Hellenism, the
Roman Church has never ceased to practise and to proclaim.

[1] *De Fide*, Disputatio xii., No. 50 seqq.

To conclude.

We have found reason to hold that all actually lived Religion is, in proportion to the depth and delicacy of its spirituality, always simultaneously conscious of two closely interconnected things: *the more than human reality of the Object of its experience*, which Object indeed Itself reveals Itself in, and makes real, this experience, AND *the abiding difference between even this its present experience and the great Reality thus experienced and revealed.* And, in this twin consciousness, living Religion is like every other truly live apprehension. No true scientist, artist, philosopher, no moral striver, but finds himself, at his best and deepest moments, with the double sense that some abiding, trans-subjective, other-than-human or even more-than-human reality, or force, or law, is manifesting itself in his experiences; and yet that these very experiences, and still more his reasoned abstracts of them, give but a very incomplete, ever imperfect, conception of those trans-subjective realities.

And now let us suppose that all such conviction of a real contact with Superhuman Reality were to be lost by humanity at large; and that neither general life, in its deepest necessities, nor the historical religions, in their special answers, would any longer be admitted as witnesses to anything but just so much sheer projection of merely human, although racial, fancies. Thus, the spiritual deeps, beckoning us on to their ever further, never exhaustible, exploration, and the spiritual atmosphere, in and through which mankind has ever, with varying degrees of consciousness as to this medium, perceived things finite, would go. And in lieu of Mysterious Reality, to be ever more closely pressed and more deeply penetrated, we should be environed by an importunate mystification which, surely, men would attempt to eliminate at any and every cost. Such men, bereft of all atmosphere, such "men of the moon," would, of necessity, end by being sure that they knew all there is to know, or, at least, that they or their fellow-men could thus know all there is to know: hence they would represent the very acme of intolerance. For, in truth, abstractions of his own mind and projections of his own wishes, if and where taken by man to be in very deed no more than himself, and to correspond to nothing outside of or higher than himself, will, in the long run, be incapable of satisfying man; and hence they will be unable to check his passions, good or evil. The Fanaticism which in man, as long as he is man, will always lurk within the folds of his emotions, and which in religious men springs, not from their superhuman belief as such, but from their ignorance or misunderstanding of certain pre-requisites and conditions essential to the healthy and fruitful working of Superhuman Religion (that gift and act and habit, so free and yet so firm, within poor yet rich, complex, many-levelled man)—will, in such a supposed attempt at a purely immanental life, no doubt at first (if it have no other man's supernatural belief to tilt against) roam about loose and restless. But Fanaticism, in such a case, would soon attach itself to some sheer Secularism—to what such a pure Immanentist would at first admit to be merely such; it would next attempt solemnly to proclaim and to believe such a Secularism to be somehow great or even unique, and to enforce it as such; and then, unless simple assent to the Trans-Subjective Intimations returned, even this kind and degree of conviction and Fanaticism would be succeeded by a Scepticism, more sincere but more destructive than even this Secularism itself.

Are cultivated West Europeans really coming, for good and all, to such a condition of alternate or of simultaneous irreligious fanaticism and utter scepticism? Surely, no. For if religious faith and hope and love are free gifts of God and free virtues of man, and if they are, in some respects, specially difficult for such Europeans, yet the present keenness of irritation, amongst so many of these men, against the very terms of Transcendence and the Superhuman, is demonstrably, in great part, a quite understandable reaction against still widely prevalent ways of conceiving and of applying (i.e. of enforcing) the Superhuman and Religion. The presence and pressure of the motives for General Religion, and the answering evidences and aids of Specific, Characteristic Religion (as these latter culminate, for us Europeans, in the Jewish-Christian Revelation and Spiritual Society) remain, on and on, too strongly rooted in the very nature and necessities of the spiritual world which environs and penetrates us all, for them not, more or less continuously, to keep or to raise us above such irritation and reactions against the Super-natural as such. And once a man is thus free from a specially dangerous, because inverted and hence unnoticed, dependence upon the faults and excesses of others, he will be able to find, to love and to practise (by means of and within the great Historical Institutions) deep Superhuman Religion, and this without repelling other souls, where these are sincere and serious in their own degree and kind.

Some years ago alarm grew rife concerning the safety of Winchester Cathedral, discovered to be undermined by water-courses; and expert divers, in full diving dress, plunged down through the springs to the swamps and sands—the foundations so daringly accepted by the original builders of the majestic edifice. The divers found the great oaken beams, as laid by those first builders upon those shifting natural foundations still, for the most part, serviceably sound. Yet some of these beams required replacing; and the guardian architects decided to replace them all by great concrete piers. We too, in this study, have been probing foundations—those of Religion. But here we have found the foundations to consist of rock—two interdependent, interclamped rock-masses: the general, dim and dumb Religiosity—the more or less slumbering sense and need of the Abiding and Eternal; and the concrete, precise and personal Religion—the clear answer to that confused asking, and, with this answer, the now keen articulation of that dim demand. And both that general dull sense and this special definite presentment were found by us in actual life,—found by us there as Givennesses of an evidential, revelational, an other-than-human, a more-than-human quality. Yet here also, in our own subject-matter, as there in the case of the Cathedral, some renovation or re-arrangement of the structure reared more or less directly upon the ancient and abiding foundations appeared to be demanded. Nevertheless in this, the religious case, the desir-able repairs turned out to consist essentially, not in preventing shifting, swampy foundations from spreading their sapping influence upwards, but, on the contrary, in eliminating, from the various stages of builders' work reared upon the sound and solid rock-foundations, whatsoever may impede those stages from full reception of this soundness and solidity. And we found the dispositions necessary for the unhampered spreading throughout the whole of life of the soundness resident in the deepest roots—in Superhuman Religion, to be three: the soberly autonomous development of the several non-religious faculties and of the non-religious associations of man; the ready recognition, by any one religion, of elements of worth variously present in the other religions, together with the careful avoidance of all attempts at forced conformity; and a careful respect for the methods intrinsic to history and philosophy, even where these analyse or theorise the documents and experiences of religion itself. Thus will all men of good faith be laid open to the appeal, so full of aid to the best that is in them, of Superhuman Religion in its profound life and reality.

to 299

49. THE VIVID DIMNESS OF RELIGIOUS BELIEF

As you doubtless know, even the reality of any outside world —especially the existence of material objects—of sun and moon, of rocks and rivers—their existence, or (at least) that we can at all know that they exist—has been denied by philosophers of distinction. And we have to admit that it is a complicated and tedious business to prove these philosophers to be wrong; that no one argument quotable against them is, taken alone, entirely clear and utterly irresistible.

Again, most philosophers deny that we, human individuals, possess any direct knowledge of the nature, the character of other human individuals, however near and dear to us; they maintain that our knowledge, in all such cases, is always of ourselves alone, and that we then get, beyond this our sole real knowledge, only our ever faulty and fallible interpretation of essentially ambiguous signs—of peculiarities of gesture, tone, look, which reach us, or seem to reach us, from those other beings. I believe myself that, where we love, we possess, or can develop, direct instinct and intuition in such matters. Nevertheless, however the case may really stand, the process, indeed the result itself, of our knowledge of our fellows, is not simple and clear. On the contrary, the process is most subtle and complex; and the result, at its best, is indeed most rich and vivid, but distinctly not simple and "clear"—it can be resisted even by ourselves, and it can only very rarely be transferred, with any ease, to others, however closely these others may be connected with us.

Certainly with regard to animals—even with respect to our dogs that we know and love best, we are often in the dark as to what is their momentary disposition and requirement. But how instructive it is to watch precisely such animals thus dear to us—I mean their knowledge and love of us, and their need of us and of our love! Our dogs know us and love us, human individuals, from amongst millions of fairly similar other individuals. Our dogs know us and love us thus most really, yet they doubtless know us only vividly, not clearly; we evidently strain their minds after a while—they then like to get away amongst servants and children; and, indeed, they love altogether to escape from human company, the rich and dim, or (at best) the vivid experiences—the company that is above them, to the company of their fellow-creatures, the company that affords so much poorer but so much clearer impressions—the level company of their brother-dogs. And yet, how wonderful! dogs thus require their fellow-dogs, the shallow and clear, but they also require us, the deep and dim; they require indeed what they can grasp; but they as really require what they can but reach out to, more or less—what exceeds, protects, envelops, directs them. And, after a short relaxation in the dog-world, they return to the bracing of the man-world.

Now pray note how if religion is right—if what it proclaims as its source and object, if God be real, then this Reality, as superhuman, *cannot possibly* be clearer to us than are the realities, and the real qualities of these realities, which we

x

nsidering. The source and object of religion, if
ue and its object be real, *cannot*, indeed, *by any
s clear to me even as I am to my dog.* For the cases
sidered deal with realities inferior to our own
rial objects, or animals), or with realities level
to our own reality (fellow human beings), or with realities
no higher above ourselves than are we, finite human beings
to our very finite dogs. Whereas, in the case of religion—if
religion be right—we apprehend and affirm realities indefinitely superior in quality and amount of reality to ourselves,
and which, nevertheless (or rather, just because of this),
anticipate, penetrate and sustain us with a quite unpicturable
intimacy. The obscurity of my life to my dog, must thus be
greatly exceeded by the obscurity of the life of God to me.
Indeed the obscurity of plant life—so obscure for my mind,
because so indefinitely inferior and poorer than is my human
life—must be greatly exceeded by the dimness, for my human
life, of God—of His reality and life, so different and superior,
so unspeakably more rich and alive, than is, or ever can be,
my own life and reality.

You may well ask here: "But what protection, then, do you
leave me against mere fancy and superstition? Will we not,
thus, come to believe, to pretend to believe, in reality *because*
the affirmations of it are obscure? And are not all sorts of
nonsense, of bogies, of chimeras, obscure? What evidence,
then, remains for these, the most sweeping and important
of all affirmations? Ought we not to be careful, indeed exacting
as to proof, exactly in proportion to the importance of the
matters that solicit our adhesion? And how otherwise can
we be careful than in demanding clearness for the proof, in
precise proportion to the importance of the subject-matter?"

The answer here is not really difficult, I think.

Note, pray, how Darwin acquired certainty, and remark
the nature of the certainty he acquired, concerning the
character, the habits, indeed (in part) the very existence of
fly-trap plants and of orchids, of earthworms and of humming-
birds. He was always loving, learning, watching; he was
always "out of himself," doubling himself up, as it were, so

as to penetrate these realities so much lowlier than himself, so different from himself. He had never done and finished; what he learnt to-day had to be re-learnt, to be supplemented and corrected to-morrow, yet always with the sense that what he had learnt was, not his own mind and its fancies and theories, but realities and their real qualities and habits. His life thus moved out into other lives. And what he thus discovered was, not clear, but vivid; not simple, but rich; not readily, irresistibly transferable to other minds, but only acquirable by them through a slow self-purification and a humble, loving observation and docility like unto his own. His own conclusions deserved, and indeed demanded credit, because so many different facts, facts often widely apart from each other, converged to these conclusions; and because, on the other hand, these same conclusions, once accepted, illumined so large a body of other facts—facts which, otherwise, remained quite dark or strange anomalies. Indeed these conclusions, once accepted, led on to the discovery of numerous facts which had been unknown, unsuspected until then. Yet these very conclusions, since this is the process and the nature of their proof, were not and are not irresistible at any one moment and because of any one single fact or argument. Indeed, to this hour, even the most reasonably assured of the conclusions of Darwin have certain clear objections against them, objections which we cannot solve. So also even Copernicanism—that mathematically clear doctrine concerning the rotation of the earth around the sun—has certain objections standing over against it, which we cannot solve.

So it always is, in various degrees, with all our knowledge and certainty concerning existences, realities, and concerning the real qualities and nature of these realities. We get to know such realities slowly, laboriously, intermittently, partially; we get to know them, not inevitably nor altogether apart from our dispositions, but only if we are sufficiently awake to care to know them, sufficiently humble to welcome them, and sufficiently generous to pay the price continuously which is strictly necessary if this knowledge and love are not to shrink but to grow. We indeed get to know realities, in proportion as we become worthy to know them,—in proportion as we become less self-occupied, less self-centred, more outward-moving, less obstinate and insistent, more gladly lost in the crowd, more rich in giving all we have, and especially all we are, our very selves. And we get to know that we really know these realities, by finding our knowledge (dim, difficult, non-transferable though it be) approving itself to us as fruitful; because it leads us to further knowledge of the realities thus known, or of other realities even when these lie apparently quite far away; and all this, in a thoroughly living and practical, in a concrete, not abstract, not foretellable, in a quite inexhaustible way.

Thus we find, through actual experience and through the similar experiences of our fellow-men, that the right and proper test for the adequacy of abstractions and of spatial, numerical, mechanical relations is, indeed, clearness and ready transferableness; but that the appropriate test for the truth concerning existences and realities is vividness (richness) and fruitfulness. The affirmations which concern abstractions and relations may be ever so empty and merely conditional; if they are clear and readily transferable, they are appropriate and adequate. The affirmations which concern existences and realities may be ever so dim and difficult to transmit; if they are rich and fruitful, they are appropriate and true. Thus in neither set of affirmations do we assent without evidence and proof; but in each set we only require *the kind* of evidence and proof natural to this particular set. And our exactingness can increase, ought indeed to increase, with the increase in the importance of the affirmations put forward within either set. But in the mathematical abstract set, I will require more and more clearness and ready transferableness, the wider and the more universal is the claim of a particular proposition; whereas in the existential concrete set I will require, in proportion to the importance of the existence affirmed, more and more richness and fruitfulness (I mean fruitfulness also in fields and levels other than those of the particular reality affirmed).

Of course, whether or no the affirmations of religion are

thus, not indeed clear, but vivid (rich), and, not indeed readily transferable, but deeply and widely fruitful, is here in no way or degree prejudged. We are only busy, so far, with our method and our standard,—not with the answer we shall get, but with the question we have a right to ask. And though even with this method and standard—with these by themselves—we may be unable to acquire religion, we most certainly will never gain religion without them, and still less in opposition to them. Without the acceptance of such a temper of mind, or at least without striving after, or some wish for, such a disposition, it is worse than waste of time to enter upon the questions of fact; worse than simple waste,—because we are then certain to come away from such a study more rebellious and empty, or more despairing and bitter, or considerably more sceptical, than we came or could come to it.

50. CHRISTIANITY AND SUFFERING

CHRISTIANITY, then, has, from the first, immensely deepened and widened, it has further revealed, not the "explanation" —which never existed for us men,—but the fact, the reality, the awful potency and baffling mystery of sorrow, pain, sin, things which abide with man across the ages. And Christianity has, from the first, immensely increased the capacity, the wondrous secret and force which issues in a practical, living, loving transcendence, utilisation, transformation of sorrow and pain, and even of sin. It is the literal fact, as demonstrable as anything that has happened or will happen to our human race can ever be, that Christianity, after some two centuries of the most terrific opposition, conquered—that it conquered in an utterly fair fight—a fight fair as regards the Christian success,—the philosophy of Greece and the power of Rome; indeed that it even conquered Gnosticism, that subtle New Paganism of the thousand elusive hues and forms, that Protean error so very dear to all over-ripe, *blasé* civilisations. It is the simple fact that Christianity conquered; and it is equally the simple fact that it did so, above all because of what it actually achieved with regard to suffering.

For Christianity, without ever a hesitation, from the first and everywhere, refused to hold, or even to tolerate, either the one or the other of the two only attempts at self-persuasion which, then as now, possess souls that suffer whilst they have not yet found the deepest. Christianity refused all Epicureanism,—since man cannot find his deepest by fleeing from pain and suffering, and by seeking pleasure and pleasures, however dainty and refined. And it refused all Stoicism,—since pain, suffering, evil are not fancies and prejudices, but real, very real; and since man's greatest action and disposition is not welf-sufficingness or aloofness, but self-donation and love. Christianity refused these theories, not by means of another theory of its own, but simply by exhibiting a Life and lives —the Life of the Crucified, and lives which continually re-live, in their endless various lesser degrees and ways, such a combination of gain in giving and of joy in suffering. Christianity thus gave to souls the faith and strength to grasp life's nettle. It raised them, in their deepest dispositions and innermost will, above the pitiful oscillations and artificialities of even the greatest of the Pagans in this central matter,— between eluding, ignoring pain and suffering, and, animal-like, seeking life in its fleeting, momentary pleasures; or trying the nobler yet impossible course,—the making out that physical, mental, moral pain and evil are nothing real, and the suppressing of emotion, sympathy and pity as things unworthy of the adult soul. Christianity did neither. It pointed to Jesus with the terror of death upon Him in Gethsemane; with a cry of desolation upon the Cross on Calvary; it allowed the soul, it encouraged the soul to sob itself out. It not only taught men frankly to face and to recognise physical and mental pain, death, and all other, especially all moral evils and sufferings as very real; it actually showed men the presence and gravity of a host of pains, evils and miseries which they had, up to then, quite ignored or at least greatly minimised. And yet, with all this—in spite of all such material for despair the final note of Christianity was and is still, one of trust, of love, of transcendent joy. It is no accident, but of the very essence of the mystery and of the power of faith, it springs from the reality of God and of His action within men's souls, that, as the nobly joyous last chapters of Isaiah (Chap. xl. to the end) contain also those wondrous utterances of the man of sorrows, so also the serenity of the Mount of the Beatitudes leads, in the Gospels, to the darkness of Calvary.

Pray believe me here: it is to Christianity that we owe our deepest insight into the wondrously wide and varied range throughout the world, as we know it, of pain, suffering, evil; just as to Christianity we owe the richest enforcement of the fact that, in spite of all this, God *is*, and that He is good and loving. And this enforcement Christianity achieves, at its best, by actually inspiring soul after soul, to believe, to love, to live this wondrous faith.

Hence all attempts to teach Christianity anything on this, central matter of pain and suffering would be, very literally, to "teach one's grandmother to suck eggs." For the very existence of the problem—I mean man's courage to face it, together with sensitiveness as to its appalling range and its baffling mystery—we owe, not to philosophy nor to science, still less to their own untutored hearts, but to religion—above all to the Jewish and Christian religion.

And note, please, that the alternative is not between "this or that non-religious view, denial, or scepticism which *does* explain suffering and evil," and "religious faith, especially Christianity, which *does not* explain them." No: this is a purely imaginary alternative: for there is no unbelief as there is no faith, there is no science as there is no popular tradition, which does or can explain these things. The real alternative is: "irreligion, which still oscillates between Epicureanism and Stoicism, systems which remain variously unreal and un-human with regard to suffering, and which know only how to evade or to travesty pain and to deny sin," and "religion, which fully fronts, indeed extends and deepens indefinitely our sense of, suffering and sin, and which, nevertheless, alone surmounts and utilises them." Thus once again, not clearness, not any ready transferableness, but efficacious power and integrating comprehensiveness appear as the true, decisive tests.

You feel—this is your keenest, yet also your most fruitful suffering—that what has happened is cruel, cruel; is what yourself, you, imperfect as you are, would have given your life to prevent. How, then, you wistfully ask, can you possibly love and trust such a power, if it exist at all,—a power, which in this case, shows itself so deaf to the most elementary and legitimate, to the most sacred of your longings and your prayers? You possessed the darling, and you loved and served it with all you were; who possesses and tends it now?

How I understand! how keen, how cutting is this pang!

And I look around me, and again I see a similar bewildering contrast repeated upon an immense scale. I remember, in our own day, the earthquake at Messina, with its thousands of cases of seemingly quite undeserved, quite unmitigated anguish, when our own admittedly most imperfect, badly bungling humanity and governments appeared, as so many small dwarfs of pity, alone pitiful, against this awful background of grim havoc and blind fury and cruelty. And, of course, we could all of us add case upon case from history and from our own experience of souls.

But please note well. Where does the keenness of this our scandal come from? Why do we, in all such cases, suffer such feelings of shock and outrage? What makes us, in the midst of it all, persist in believing, indeed persist in acting (with great cost) on the belief, that love and devotedness are utterly the greatest things we know, and deserve the sacrifice of all our earthly gifts, of our very life? Whence comes all this?— The case is, I think, quite parallel with that as to trust in reality generally. Why is it, as to such trust and such reality, that even the most hardened of the sceptics continue to trouble themselves and to trouble us all, if not as to truth, at least as to truthfulness? Why is untruthfulness so very odious? Untruthfulness is certainly most convenient. Why indeed does every at all sane mind find it so intolerable to hold itself to be completely shut up within its own impressions, to admit that these impressions are nothing but illusions, or, at least, are utterly worthless as indications of realities other than its own? Whence springs the suffering—the most keen suffering —of the thought of being thus shut up, if we *are*, in fact, thus shut up within our own purely subjective impressions and fancies? The answer, surely, is that we thus suffer because, in fact, we are *not* thus shut up, because we *do* communicate with realities other than ourselves, and hence that these realities so impress and affect us that only by a painful effort can we, violently and artificially, treat those realities as mere fanciful projections of our own.

Similarly, if there is no source and standard of love, of pity, of giving, of self-donation,—a source and standard abiding, ultimate, distinct from, deeper than ourselves, a source Itself loving, Itself a Lover, and which, somehow profoundly penetrative of ourselves, keeps us poor things, rich with at least this sense of our poverty and with this our inability to abandon love (that very costly thing) as a chimera or a mere fleeting vibration of our nerves: if there is not such a more than human (deeper and higher than human) source and standard, then the real, actual situation becomes wholly rootless and unreasonable, precisely in what it has of admittedly greatest, of most precious and most significant.

Thus, both in the matter of Truth and Reality and in the matter of Love and a Lover, we suffer, when scepticism assails us, because we are *not* simply shut up within our own fancies, because (mysteriously yet most actually) we are penetrated and moved by God, the Ultimate Reality and Truth, the Ultimate Lover and Goodness. We are moved by Him Who *is*, Who is before ever we were, Who is with us from the beginning of our existence, Who is always the first in operation whenever there is interaction between Him and us. Because He *is*, we have our unconquerable sense of Reality; because He is Love and Lover, we cannot let love go. And it is He Who made the mother's heart; it is, not simply her love, but, in the first instance, His love, with just some drops of it fallen into the mother's heart, which produce the standard within her which cries out against all that is, or even looks like, blindness and cruel fate.

For remember, please, it is not Judaism, not Christianity, not any kind of Theism that bids us, or even allows us, to hold and to accept as good in themselves the several painful or cruel or wrong things that happen in this our complicated, difficult life. None of these convictions worship Nature, or the World-as-a-whole; they all, on the contrary, find much that is wrong in Nature as we know it, and in the World-as-a whole as we actually find it. All such believers worship and adore not Nature but God—the love and the action of God within and from behind the world, but not as though this love and action were everywhere equally evident, not as though they directly willed, directly chose, all things that happen and as they happen. On the contrary: these great religions leave such a pure optimism to absolute Idealist philosophers, and to rhapsodising pantheists and poets; and these religions believe such views, wheresoever they are taken as ultimate, to be either shallow and unreal, or sorry travesties of the facts.

If, then, I be asked to whom I confide those I love when, after much utterly ineffectual-seeming devotion of my heart, I have seen them suffer fearfully and disappear from my own care and longing, I answer that I confide them to that Reality and Love, to that Real Lover, whose reality and lovingness and penetration of my heart alone make possible and actual my own poor persistent love. Thus my very bitterness and despair over the apparent insult flung at my love by the world as I know it, turns out to be but one more effect of the reality and operativeness of God, and one more reason (again not clear, not readily transferable, but rich and fruitful) for believing and trusting in Him, in Love, the Lover.

51. THE ESCHATOLOGY OF THE GOSPEL

No doctrine of the Divinity of Christ, no affirmation, even of just simply the normality of the mind of Jesus, are other than out of touch with all the real possibilities of the question, if they do not first recognise that a real Incarnation of God in man can only mean Incarnation in some particular human nature. Man in general is only an idea, it is not a fact, a reality; and God, the supremely factual, utterly real, the creator of the essential facts in man, did not, in the Incarnation, reverse either His own, God's nature, or the reflex of it, the nature of Man. The Incarnation could not, even by Himself, be made other than the entering into, and possession of, a human mind and will endowed with special racial dispositions and particular racial categories of thought. Assuredly this mind and will would be filled and moved by the deepest religious and moral truth and insight; and would be preserved from all essential error concerning the direct objects of the divine indwelling and condescension. Yet this truth and insight would of necessity show, to minds and hearts of other races and times, imaginative and emotional peculiarities—certain omissions, combinations, stresses, outlines, colourings, characteristic of the race and time of the Revealer. Otherwise, the Revealer would begin His career by being simply unintelligible to His first hearers, and even, in the long run, to the large majority of mankind; and He would, in Himself, not be normally, characteristically, man. Now it was most appropriate that the Incarnation, for purposes of religion, should take place in Jewish human nature, since the Jewish people had, already for some thirteen centuries, furnished forth amongst mankind the purest light and strongest leading in religion. Thus, however, the Revealer could not but imagine, think, feel and will the deepest truths and facts of His mission with Jewish categories, images, emotions. Such a characteristically Jewish category—although, in a lesser degree, it is common to antiquity generally—permeates the Bible from cover to cover, in so far as its writers

were Semites in blood and breeding. Everywhere the Divine
action is, as such, conceived to be instantaneous. Thus the
twenty-four hours of each of the six Days of Creation (in
Genesis i.) were very probably conceived by the narrator
as almost entirely composed of pauses between the creative
acts, these acts themselves being instantaneous. Even St.
Teresa could still, in 1562 A.D., consider the suddenness of a
vision to be one of the two decisive tests of its divine origin.
If then Jesus held that the world's present order would be
terminated by an act of God, He could not image and pro-
pound this act other than as sudden and rapid. We shall
find later on far more ultimate reasons for this category of
suddenness; yet the reason now given appears true and
operative so far as it goes.

Nowhere, however, does Jesus presuppose or teach a corresponding suddenness of change in man's dispositions or
actions, either as everywhere actually operative or even as
normally desirable. Hence, as Canon Scott Holland, in his
profound *Real Problem of Eschatology*, very acutely observes,
the nearness and suddenness of Christ's Second Coming does
not weaken but heightens the call to persistent self-purification
and uninterrupted service of others. A proximate sharp
testing awaits His hearers; but it will be a testing of, at best,
an entire long life of persistent faithfulness. And nowhere
does Jesus condemn the essential things, conditions and duties
of this life, as intrinsically evil; His own thought and practice
imply and show respect for the human body, reverence for
the ties of family and of country, even when these are tran-
scended in a complete, heroic self-abnegation. Even the
military career He nowhere condemns—centurions are left
by Him as centurions, He even praises them as such with
emphasis. And He possesses the leisureliness of mind necessary
for the full perception of the beauties or peculiarities of flower
and tree; bird, sheep and fox; sky, field and lake; of sower,
vintner, fisherman and shepherd, mason and housewife; and
He disports Himself with children. Immensely earnest and
inclusive of the most heroic asceticism as is His life, He can
yet be accused of being a wine-bibber, a friend of publicans

and sinners. All this tender leisure, observation, forthcoming friendliness—all this genial occupation with the present little things and little friends of God—all this only required the predominant intensity of expectation and detachment, characteristic of the second period of the earthly life of Jesus, to become less central in men's minds and to show itself as constituting, in the permanent scheme, but one of the two great movements of the uniquely wide, deep, various outlook and will of Jesus. The special characteristics of the first stage of the earthly life of Jesus thus come to their full development, in His closest followers, alongside of, alternately with, penetrated by, the special characteristics of the second stage. Thus could Dante find—surely, most rightly—in the Poverello of Assisi—so supremely detached, so expansively attached, so heroic without rigorism, so loving without softness—perhaps the nearest reproduction of the divine paradox of the life of Jesus Himself. On this point also we shall find a still deeper root in the teaching of Jesus, as expressive of the very soul of religion.

More and more, after the death of Jesus, did the preaching of the Kingdom, indeed all direct thought of the Kingdom, wane, and did the Church take the place of the Kingdom. This change was, in its essence, simply inevitable, right and beneficent; indeed the conception and the functioning of a Church most justly claim deep implications, nay, definite institutions, in the teaching and acts of Jesus Himself. Mr. Clutton Brock, in his *What is the Kingdom of Heaven*, 1918, very emphatically condemns those who hold that Jesus ever taught or implied a proximate cosmic cataclysm—He really taught and implied only the transfiguring power, given to the pure of heart, to see God here and now, and to see all this Here and Now as, in its essence, already the Kingdom of God. But then Mr. Brock finds himself most instructively baffled—he admits himself deeply surprised—by the fact that (although this purely interior and mystical act and attitude is really all that Jesus meant by the Kingdom) the Kingdom of God, thus incapable of coming into collision with any of the great public and world facts and forces, should have so rapidly lost its central position in the Christian teaching. In reality, the Kingdom, with its categories of intense proximity, suddenness and cataclysm, soon ceased to be central, even in the minds of Christians, for the simple reason that the given visible world persisted in lasting; that the vehemence of this group of teachings could not be maintained for long, if the gentler characteristics of the other group of teaching—equally the utterance of Jesus Himself—were to have their full realisation: and that Jesus Himself had given unequivocal indications as to how he would envisage, how He would organise, permanent Christian institutions, did the permanence of the world require —as, in fact, it was now requiring—a corresponding permanence of the Christian organisation. The acute polemic of Jesus against at least the school of Shammai amongst the Pharisees; His attitude as critic and new legislator even as regards the Law itself; and, perhaps above all, His death at the instigation of the Sanhedrin, the great official Churchmen's council of His time and country, readily obscure the nevertheless very certain facts of Jesus's organic conception of all society, civil and religious, and of His actual organising of His apostles and followers. All souls are, indeed, to Jesus, equal in a true sense—they all spring from the one God; compared with God all their differences are as nothing; and merely earthly differences do not count as ultimate differences at all. Yet this equality is not interchangeableness, nor a simply individualist, nor again a socialist, equalisation. It is an equality derived from God and operating within humanity at large as this is organised in the family and the religious community. It is an equality rich, elastic, manifold, thorough differentiation into various kinds and degrees of interdependence and mutual service. The very images dearest to Jesus —the Father and his children, the Master and his servants, the Shepherd and his sheep, the King and his subjects—show this plainly, as a quite unchanging characteristic of all His outlook. And Jesus spontaneously acts upon this fundamental conviction when He comes to require a little band of preachers and teachers. As He Himself alone had received the Messianic power and call from the one God, His Father, so He, in turn, selects twelve representatives, endowing them with intrinsic authority and power; and He places one of them at their head with quite unique gifts and duties. The institution remains small in Jesus's lifetime, not because Jesus objects to a large institution, a Church, or because this small institution is, in any essential point, different from the Church. The institution remains small simply and solely because of the Proximate Expectation: and, with the fading away of the proximity, the Preaching Band automatically becomes the Church. For already in the Preaching Band there is mission, subordination, unitary headship—the genuine religious movement from the One to the Few and thus to the Many; and from above downwards. The noblest title ever taken by the Popes—the title by which the great ones amongst them stand confirmed, and by which the bad ones amongst them stand condemned—Servant of the Servants of God—is thus in very truth the, varyingly extensive but everywhere real, call and duty of us all. And surely, in spite of the many difficulties, dangers and abuses brought into the world by neglectful or insufficiently Christian Churchmen: the Church, at its best and greatest, has, as a sheer matter of fact, grandly, indeed uniquely, proved this her capacity for preserving and perpetuating the spirit and power of Jesus Christ.

52. CRITICAL METHOD AND FAITH

And what about the entire critical method which, now for five generations, has been applied by great scholars to delimit, to fathom, to analyse the figure, the doctrine, the spirit of the historic Jesus, and this, often with the assumption, or even the proclamation, that thus only, but that thus really, can we gain the unadulterated Jesus, as He actually breathed well-nigh two thousand years ago? If we take the method thus as by itself productive of such a result, we are, very certainly, the victims of perhaps the most plausible instance of a very natural and widespread illusion. Professor James Ward and

Dr. Pringle Pattison have, each from a somewhat different starting-point, admirably brought out the fact I am thinking of. Dr. Ward compares the two chief methods of Psychology —the Genetic and the Analytic, and shows how doubtless the perfect knowledge of anything would be a knowledge of that thing at each of its stages of growth and becoming, rather than an analysis of the same thing at its fullest expansion, yet that, as a matter of fact, the analytic method alone is really completely at our service. And Dr. Pattison demonstrates the special danger inherent in the Genetic Method, even where we can most fully apply it. Let us take the embryology of man. Here the future human being—in strictness the human being, as he really exists from conception onwards— is (for all appearances) first a shapeless material substance, next a plant-like organism, then a mollusc-like, fish-like, bird-like being; only later on a mammal-like, monkey-like creature, and last of all a clearly human baby. Only God Himself can directly see a human being in those earlier forms; so that if we *will* treat each of these stages as self-explanatory, as what it appears to us apart from what we know will follow, man *is* a monkey, a fish, a plant, a shapeless material substance—the lowest designation is indeed the most scientific. This method alone is quite clear; but then, it is also quite inadequate. Human Marriage, under this treatment, becomes a mere pairing of two animals or plants; the State, a mere herding of wild animals, or the cruel invention of cannibal cave-dwellers. The God of the Jews becomes the mutterings and tremblings of a volcano in the peninsula of Sinai; indeed one specially "thorough" sage of this school discovers that religion began with, hence that it *is*, the scratching by a cow of an itch upon her back.

It cannot, on the other hand, be denied that the study of Origins properly conducted—that is, conducted with a continuous sense of the reality investigated as it gradually reveals itself in its ever fuller development—does very genuinely deepen, purify and vivify our appreciation of the full reality. For only such study can make us enter (never quite fully, yet with an otherwise unattainable poignancy) into the homely environment, the difficulty and loneliness, the sweat, tears and blood, the obscurities, inhibitions, defeats and difficult conquests, above all into the varying appearances and applications, of the self-identical reality thus studied. The very inevitableness, for an at all human life and teaching, to lose, in course of time, some of the pristine instant attractiveness of its precise pictures and emotions, is thus brought out at its fullest. Yet even this result is attained only by a combination of the analytic method, which moves back from the life of Jesus as still actually lived in Christ's mystical body, the Church, and of the genetic method, which starts from the earliest evidence of the earliest stages of Jesus Christ's life on earth and then on across the centuries. If we were restricted to one method only, the analytic method ought to be preferred, as giving us far more life and reality, indeed as, taken singly, alone capable of furnishing us with genuine life at all. Yet we can, fortunately, work by both ways simultaneously—we can move from the Christ of the Church, of our prayers, communions and inner life, back to the Jesus of the earliest documents; and, from this Jesus forwards to the Christ. This double movement will, if worked devotedly and wisely, really deepen our sense of the worlds of beauty, truth and goodness, of ideal help, of ideal reality, of divine facts, offered to us in the Church, in Jesus Christ, in God.

·   ·   ·   ·   ·   ·

53. HELL AND HEAVEN

As to Hell. It will be well for us, as concerns the question quite generally, to realise with fullness and vividness how inadequate is the prevalent easy-going, slipshod thinking, feeling and living with regard to our free will and responsibility, our moral weakness and the reality of sin. Only those profoundly awake to, and earnest about, these great facts have any right to be counted as opinions in the question of Abiding Consequences. And again it will be useful for us clearly to note how pantheistic is the general outlook of the more notable deniers

Y

of this Abidingness. It was, of course, inevitable that a John Scotus Erigena, for whom God was the sole substance and man's sin a mere nonentity, should have refused to deduce any unending effects from the behaviour of men. It was equally inevitable that such a violently naturalistic pantheist as Giordano Bruno should ceaselessly revile every notion of accountability and of sin—still more so, then, of Heaven and Hell. It was similarly inevitable that Spinoza's pantheistic system should, as such, have left no logical room or justification for that great soul's intuitions concerning the costliness, the rarity, the priceless worth of the true, ethical and spiritual life; hence that even Spinoza's influence should be deadly to any belief in any objective personal survival and any other-world Heaven or Hell. And it was inevitable again that Schleiermacher, so predominantly æsthetic and pantheistic, should have laboured hard to eliminate all belief in the abidingness of evil—evil being too little real for him at all times for this thin and shadowy thing to be likely, in his opinion, to last throughout all time. We will not, then, follow in the wake of such men. But if we walk, instead, in the foot-steps of definite and sensitive Theists we shall find that the doctrine of Abiding Consequences can, at the least, not be treated lightly—the possibility of its substantial truth will persistently demand a serious, pensive consideration.

It is true that by any and every acceptance of this doctrine, we allow that God's will or God's power does not, or cannot, effect, within the realm of human souls, its own entire triumph —a triumph which evidently consists in the subjectively free and objectively right self-determination of all awakened human souls. And we cannot escape this difficulty by holding such partial failure to spring directly from any libertarian scheme as such. For St. Augustine teaches admirably that "it is a great liberty to be able not to sin; it is the greatest liberty to be unable to sin"—a doctrine which must be true, unless God is not free. Thus we can only say that even the possibility of sin arises, not from the freedom of the will as such, but, on the contrary, from the imperfection of the freedom; and that there are doubtless reasons, connected with the power of God or with His knowledge (concerning what will, upon the whole, produce a maximum of a certain kind of spiritual happiness), why He chose, or permitted, the existing scheme of imperfect liberty amongst human souls. After all, it is not as though man could possess his *special* pathos, power, patience and peace without this, his actual, imperfection of liberty: these things, assuredly, all stand and fall together. And thus we can boldly affirm that man would, indeed, be a higher creature were Hell impossible for him; he would be something further, but he would also, throughout, be something different—man would no more be man.

And as to the essentials of Hell, I like to remember what a cultivated, experienced Roman Catholic cleric insisted upon to me, namely, the importance of the distinction between the essence of the doctrine of Hell and the various images and interpretations given to this essence: that the essence lies assuredly, above all, in the unendingness. Hence even the most terrible of the descriptions in Dante's *Inferno* could be held literally, and yet, if the sufferings there described were considered eventually to cease altogether, Hell would thereby be denied in its very root. And contrariwise, a man might be at a loss to find any really appropriate definitions, or more than popular images, for the sufferings of Hell; he might even fail to reach a clear belief in more than an unending, though not necessarily very active, disharmony and unappeased longing in the Lost; and yet he would still be holding the essence of the faith in Hell.

And as regards Hell in view of men's ignorances, errors, denials in matters of religion, there is a quaternity of most certain facts and principles which we ought never to forget. Men are as genuinely responsible, they can as really sin gravely and can as truly end with Hell, by their deliberate thinkings as by their deliberate feelings, willings, or visible acts. The deepest of all sins are precisely sins of thought, self-idolisation and arrogant revolt against the truth as perceived by the soul in its depths. Men can, however, in countless degrees and ways, be excusably ignorant, or invincibly prejudiced, concerning various facts of religion and certain

laws of the spiritual life; this, however, far more easily and
more permanently with respect to the historical facts and the
contingent institutions, such even as Jesus Christ and the
Catholic Church, than with regard to the metaphysical, non-
contingent fact and presence of God. It is well known that
the Roman Catholic Church itself is clearly on the side of
such breadth as regards Christ and the Church, and appears
strict only as concerns God. Men can, however, be without
any gift or training for the correct analysis or theory of their
own actual deepest convictions, even as to their faith in God.
Hence it matters not so much what a man thinks he thinks,
as what he thinks in actual reality. And men, especially men
of this very numerous unanalytic, untheoretic kind, can
claim much patience in such times of transition seemingly
in everything, as have been the last hundred and fifty years
in our Western Europe. Such persons are greatly over-
impressed as to the range and depth of our real discoveries
and final revolutions, and are thus bewildered as to the
ultimate facts and laws of the spiritual life, facts and laws
which persist substantially as they were.

Certain great New Testament texts appear conjointly to
cover all these four contentions. To men in general, and on all
subjects, Christ declares that "out of the heart proceed evil
thoughts," alongside of acts as heinous as murders, adulteries,
blasphemies; and again that "every idle word that men shall
speak"—assuredly, then, also every idle thought that men
shall think—they shall give account thereof at the Judgment
(St. Matt. xv. 19; xii. 36). To the (doubtless many) men who
are not aware that they are actually serving Christ in their
heroic service of their suffering fellow-creatures, to men, then,
who presumably do not at all know the historic Jesus or who
do not perceive Him to be the Christ, Christ the King says
at the Judgment, "Come, ye blessed of my Father, inherit
the Kingdom prepared for you from the foundation of the
world. Inasmuch as ye have done these things unto the least
of these my brethren, ye have done it unto me" (St. Matt.
xxv. 34-40). As to the governors, priests, soldiers, who have
actually crucified Him, Christ prays upon His cross, "Father,

forgive them, for they know not what they do" (St. Luke xxiii. 34). And as to the sceptical, superstitious and restlessly curious men of letters—men so vague and doubtful as to the nature of God Himself, as to have erected an altar inscribed "To the Unknown God"—St. Paul declares: "Whom ye ignorantly worship, Him declare I unto you" (Acts xvii. 23).

And as to Heaven. A good and simple, yet somewhat dry and conventional Roman Catholic priest, a worker for many years among souls, told me one day, in a South of England town, of the sudden revelation of heights and depths of holiness that had just enveloped and enlarged his head and heart. He had been called, a few nights before, to a small pot-house in the outskirts of this largely fashionable town. And there, in a dreary little garret, lay, stricken down with sudden double pneumonia, an Irish young woman, twenty-eight years of age, doomed to die within an hour or two. A large fringe covered her forehead, and all the other externals were those of an average barmaid who had, at a public bar, served half-tipsy, coarsely-joking men, for some ten years or more. And she was still full of physical energy—of the physical craving for physical existence. Yet, as soon as she began to pour out her last and general confession, my informant felt, so he told me, a lively impulse to arise and to cast himself on the ground before her. For there, in her intention, lay one of the simple, strong, sweet saints of God at his feet. She told how deeply she desired to become as pure as possible for this grand grace, this glorious privilege, so full of peace, of now abandoning her still young, vividly pulsing life, of placing it utterly within the hands of the God, of the Christ whom she loved so much, and who loved her so much more; that this great gift, she humbly felt, would bring the grace of its full acceptance with it, and might help her to aid, with God and Christ, the souls she loved so truly, the souls He loved so far more deeply than ever she herself could love them. And she died soon after in a perfect rapture of joy—in a joy overflowing, utterly sweetening all the mighty bitter floods of her pain. Now *that* is Supernatural.

54. CHRISTIAN IDEA OF IMMORTALITY

It is most understandable, yet none the less regrettable for us who approach the After Life problems from within religion and for religion, that two attitudes and activities of mind, as to these very problems, frequently attract—distract—the soul whilst still religiously unsettled, and (I believe in practically all cases) gravely arrest or deflect its still dim and groping religious insight. The first of these attitudes concerns the content of the Future Life; the second concerns the evidences of a Future Life. By the first attitude, the Future Life is desired and conceived as simply a prolongation of this our earthly life, less its pain and (usually) its grossness. In this way of course, and only in this way, can we men fully picture a Future Life at all—it thus is just merely a continuation of this life, with all within it that is attractive to our average tastes in our average moments. And by the second attitude we seek the evidence for the reality of this continuance in intimations which are somehow to be gained from the very persons, thus still thoroughly their old selves, who are now living in the Beyond. And these two attitudes usually go together.

It is certainly, at first sight, very remarkable that the fantastic abnormality of the form and method, which characterises all animistic and spiritualist practices, should habitually yield so less than a normal, so shrunken, banal, and boring a content. Yet such a method cannot fail to reach no farther than this very little distance.

The simple fact, assuredly, is that the soul, *qua* religious, has no interest in just simple unending existence, of no matter what kind or of a merely natural kind—an existence with God at most as the dim background to a vivid experience of its own unending natural existence. The specifically religious desire of Immortality begins, not with Immortality, but with God; it rests upon God; and it ends in God. The religious soul does not seek, find, or assume its own immortality, and thereupon seek, find, or assume God. But it seeks, finds, experiences, and loves God; and because of God, and of this, its very real though still very imperfect, intercourse with God—because of these experiences which lie right within the noblest joys, fears, hopes, necessities, certainties which emerge within any and every field of its life here below—it finds, rather than seeks, Immortality of a certain kind. The very slow but solidly sure, the very sober but severely spiritual, growth of the belief in Immortality amongst the Jews, a belief fully endorsed and greatly developed by our Lord, was entirely thus—not from Immortality of no matter what kind to God, but from God to a special kind of Immortality. Especially does Christ always keep God and the Kingdom of God central, as the beginning and end of all, and the Immortality peripheral, as but the extension and full establishment of the soul's supernatural union with, and of its supernatural activity towards, God and man.

And let us carefully note: such a method does not leave us empty of any vivid and experienced content for our conception of the Future Life. Quite the contrary: for no experiences are so real, none, in a way, are so well understood by the experiencing soul, as are its supernatural experiences. By supernatural we here mean nothing preternatural, nothing even essentially miraculous, nothing that men, who are at all complete according to man's supernatural call and awakeness, cannot, or do not, experience. We mean, on the contrary, acts, experiences, necessities which, though distinct, not only from all evil but also from all simply natural goodness, are nevertheless acts, experiences, necessities found scattered about amongst the specific qualities and ends of nature. And these acts, experiences, necessities are such that men at large, in their nobler and noblest moments, cannot help saluting and revering them. And, again, this Supernaturalness does not concern Goodness alone, but also Truth and Beauty. God is the Fountain and the Fullness, the Origin and the End, the ultimate Measure of every kind and degree, as much of Beauty and of Truth as of Goodness. Hence wheresoever there are acts, experiences, necessities of sheer self-surrender, in the deepest search and work within the visible and temporal,

the contingent and relative, to the Invisible, the Eternal, and
the Unconditional: wheresoever such self-surrender is from
those temporalities, apprehended as such, to these Eternities,
accepted, adored as such: there is the Supernatural. Walter
Bagehot, in his great study of Bishop Butler, finds two kinds
of religion—that which looks out upon the world, especially
the starlit heavens, and finds there God in their beauty; and
that which looks within upon the human soul itself, especially
the conscience, and finds here God in its sublimity; Bagehot
calls the former Natural, the latter Supernatural. But I plead
here for a conviction which finds the Natural (including a
certain Natural Religion) in the looking within, and in the
acceptance of, conscience, as well as in the looking outwards,
and in the belief in beauty; and which, again, finds the Supernatural—Supernatural Religion—within both these same
movements and materials. So long as either movements and
conviction is primarily busy with the beauty, the truth or the
goodness simply in their particular forms, and only vaguely
or derivatively assumes or implies their unconditional claim
upon the soul, you have Nature. So soon as either movement
and conviction attains to a central occupation with the
Abidingness, the Non-contingency, of the Beauty, the Truth
or the Goodness thus partially revealed and to a recognition
of their right to the unlimited service of the observer, you
have Supernature.

We have thus to discriminate, not simply between Evil and
Good, but also between Good and Good—between Natural
Good and Supernatural Good. Both these Goods come from
God; both are operative—in different proportions and in
greatly different degrees and ways—in all normal, adult and
awake human beings; and each, as we shall see, variously
requires the other, and variously participates in Heaven itself.

The morality of honest barter, of moderate living; the
requirements of the counting-house, the law-courts, the
State; Confucius, Bentham: such moralities, institutions,
persons, in their general and positive trend and in their
prevalent acceptance, are assuredly good and necessary, but
they are natural. Such moralities, institutions, persons, we

may wish to last for ever; but they do not, of themselves, suggest or require the heightened consciousness, the closer and closest intercourse with God, the reaching, in Him, of the ultimate, living Beauty, Truth and Goodness, which the religious soul seeks when it seeks Immortal Life. And let us note—it is not the absence of any explicitly religious reference that stamps these "natural" things and persons as only naturally good. The reference, in such persons, if not to God or to a God, then at least to their consciences, is fairly constant; yet we cannot well count all that is thus referred as supernatural. And the reference in Judaism and Unitarianism to God is continual, and undoubtedly constitutes even the average of these positions as, at the least, Natural Religions. Yet it can fairly be maintained that the reference is here largely dry and distant, and is there to God rather as the supreme rule and reward of average earthly honesty, decency and justice, than as the deepest meaning and the final assuagement of the soul's thirst for more and other than these things.

For assuredly there are certain other acts, dispositions, strivings, of individual souls, and there are certain other ideals and best achievements of certain institutions, which essentially transcend the character, standard and instruments of the Naturally Good. The deepest of the Jewish Psalms, the Seer whose vision of the Suffering Servant of Jehovah is incorporated in the Book of Isaiah, the serenely self-oblivious prayer of Stephen, the deacon, for his enemies whilst they stone him to death; above all, Christ's entire life and work, crowned by the forgiveness of His crucifiers even as He hangs upon the Cross, are the great and the greatest, the most fully explicit, instances of the Supernaturally Good. But indeed, off and on, here and there, sooner or later, we can find, within the larger human groups and during the longer human periods, some lives, some acts, not all different to those acts and lives—at least some touches, some desires for some such lives and some such acts. And if such acts or desires never and nowhere occurred within an entire race of men or within an entire age of the world, then that race and that age would, already by this alone, stand revealed as less

than what man actually is—a being natural in his constitution
yet variously solicited and sustained by supernatural influences, requirements, helps and aims. The Christian Church,
at all times in its indestructible ideal, and indeed always in
its fullest and fairest fruits, has been and abides the special
training ground, home, and inspirer of this supernatural
spirit. Our Lord's Beatitudes are its classical expression, and
the Feast of All Saints is the perennially touching commemor-
ation of its countless manifestations in every age, clime, race,
and religious environment.

Now the specifically religious desire for Immortality is a
desire, not only for the continuance of such supernatural acts
and dispositions, and for the continuance of the soul, in so far
as thus acting and disposed, but for the final establishment of
the soul in a world of powers, acts and persons truly adequate
to such supernaturalness. Here below, this our visible world
of time and space suffices for the naturally good acts and the
naturally good soul. Heaven is not a necessary environment
for not cheating in the sale of peas or potatoes, for not smash-
ing street lamps, for not telling calumnies against one's wife
or brother. But only Heaven furnishes the adequate environment for the elevation and expansion of spirit of a Damian,
when he, here below, devoted himself to sure leprosy for the
sake of his outcast fellow-creatures; of a Joan of Arc, when,
in the France of her day, she reaped her short earthly success
and her swiftly following witch's death; or of the average
trooper on the *Birkenhead* going down, without moving, at
attention, with the women and children being saved alive
before his eyes in those boats where he was deliberately
refusing to take a place at the cost of others, many of whom
had no special claim upon himself. Indeed all of us have
ourselves witnessed, or have learnt from eye-witnesses, deeds
or dispositions of a similar quality. Humanity will never,
universally or permanently, treat such acts as folly, or indeed
as anything less than the very flower of life. Yet to claim that
the Trades Union, or a Political or Social Party, or the State,
should or could, or ever wisely will, require such things, or
directly work for them, is assuredly quixotic. Such a demand

or hope can only lead to a dangerous Utopia, followed by a not less dangerous reaction. Thus such heroic goodness points to a Beyond, as indeed does all philosophical research, all scientific work, all artistic effort—whensoever these endeavours penetrate deeper than a certain superficial and conventional level. All such heroic, self-oblivious search and reception of Truth and Beauty, as possessing the right to such self-surrender, appear as special divine gifts rather than as mere human efforts, as glimpses of realities which, for their adequate environment and apprehension, require, not this world and this life, but another life and another world.

55. NATURE AND SUPERNATURE

WE have so far spoken as though Heaven and Hell were the sole, not only ultimate, but also immediate, alternatives for every man moved by, and called to, Supernature; and, still more, we have let it appear as though the call of the human race in general to such Supernature involved, of necessity, the call of every individual belonging to that race, to this same Supernature. We must now make some important distinctions in both these positions—for we cannot, if we do hold a Heaven and a Hell in the full sense of the terms, escape, I am confident, from acceptance of some kind of Purgatory, and of some kind of Limbo.

As concerns the supernaturally awakened souls, we cannot, surely, conceive the majority of these to be, when they die, immediately fit for Heaven, even if they be not really fit for Hell. Yet we are often reminded of certain spiritual facts which seem to rule out any intermediate state. Thus we are told that it is not Christian, nor even deeply religious in general, to think of man as ever truly owing his salvation to his own merits; he can, in strictness, owe such salvation only to the generosity and gift of God—indeed the very power to merit at all is a pure grace of God—as pure as is man's creation. Conformably with this it is insisted that the commencement, the continuation, the crowning of any soul's supernatural life, is through and through rendered possible only by God and His grace; and that it never becomes actual without the active aid of the same God and grace. Thus all supernaturally awakened souls, however free from sin, whether original or actual, we may suppose them, attain (at least on one ground entirely common to them all—their original nothingness) to Heaven through God's gift and mercy. To this is added the further contention that this gift and mercy is specially abundant in the case of those supernaturally awakened souls which die with sinful or imperfect habits and attachments still clinging to them, and which, nevertheless, attain to Heaven. And it is then asked, if all this be really so, what need there is of an Intermediate State at all.

The answer surely is that we who are still on this side of the veil, have direct and real knowledge of the manner in which God's grace and mercy operate, even though in this life only; and that, in this life, these gifts usually obey certain general laws of their own. We are able roughly to follow some of the main outlines of these orderings by God Himself of God's own generosities and gifts. We see how, in this our earthly time at least, every impure thought, untrue word or cruel act, every cowardly shrinking from the usually costly docility to our own best insight and special grace, relax or stain, or harden or deflect, our own inclinations, habits and acts, even more certainly than they similarly affect our influences and achievements in the world at large. We note how even sincere, and fairly deep, repentance for any one evil action, no more removes all such inward effects of this action than it removes all the outward effects of the same action. Thus I regret certain acts of gambling, I even cease to gamble; but this does not, of necessity, eradicate certain inclinations to gamble fully willed by me before and half willed by me still; it does not eliminate the entire gambling habit, any more than it restores to my bank, or to my creditor friends, the moneys I have gambled away from them. My repentance, at any degree of depth, will be a grace of God through Christ to me; yet this repentance and grace, unless it be of the deepest kind—an act of Pure Love as it was with the Good Thief on Calvary on Good Friday—will still leave me with variously imperfect habits and inclinations. These habits and inclinations, again, will be rectified within me, by the grace of God and Christ, but this grace will, in most cases, work slowly within innumerable new acts of mine, acts contrary in character to those old habits, and within a long self-discipline which now, step by step, retraces the previous long self-dissipation of the soul. Purgatory is thus, so far at least, a sheer fact for the soul in its relation to God during this life. But it is not reasonable to assume a radical change or supersession of so fundamental a spiritual law at the death of the body, except under the constraint of some very definite and unanswerable reason. Such a reason is not forthcoming. And hence I can find no serious ground to deny the reality of a similar Purgatory for the same soul in face of the same God in the other life. And if Purgatory exists also in the Beyond, then most of the supernaturally called souls will presumably go, at death, not to Hell, nor, in the first instance, to Heaven, but, first of all, to Purgatory.

As concerns mankind at large, we have certain general facts of human existence and of life in general, and certain ordinary teachings of theologians, which appear to indicate that many, possibly most, individual human souls do not attain to the supernatural call, choice, and consequences—that Heaven or Hell can be as little their actual final end, as Purgatory can be their immediate destination. Three large considerations seem to show that this is actually the case in the realm of human souls; that it is in full parallel with other ranges and stages of observable life; and that it is in no wise cruel or unjust.

This position appears to state an actual fact. For the majority of human beings (if we take the life of the soul to begin at the moment of the conception of the corresponding body) die before they attain the age of reason. If we take seriously even the fundamental lines, the general trend, of the Christian outlook, we must reject all reincarnation schemes; and we must require, as the ordinary prerequisite for the supernatural call of any individual soul, the mental and volitional awakeness of this soul. True, the doctrine and practice of Infant Baptism raise a difficulty here. But Infant Baptism admittedly reaches only a small minority of the cases in question, if the human soul is infused into its corresponding body at the moment of this body's conception; and if, of the human beings who attain to birth at all, much the greater number of those dying in infancy die without Baptism. And again, Baptism is held to extend to the infant the spiritual life of the Christian Church at large, and this spiritual life in the Church at large is, at the time of the baptism of the spiritually slumbering infant, possessed and practised by souls mentally and volitionally awake. And finally, the effects of such Baptism, if the infant dies in infancy, are different in degree from the effects of this same Baptism, if this baptised soul attains to maturity. Theologians have, since many a day, admitted that unbaptised infants live in the Beyond a life of natural happiness—a sort of prolongation of the happiness of children here below, less their physical sufferings, and less any supernatural experiences which may be traceable in most of them from about seven years of age onwards. Thus souls that depart this life as infants, though they be unbaptised, do not go to Hell. But souls that pass into the Beyond as infants, if they be baptised, attain indeed to Heaven, yet to a far lesser degree of the supernatural beatitude than do souls which have struggled long and much in and for the supernatural life here below, and which have died substantially fit for Heaven at last, even though they be in need of a long Purgatory first.

Some such position is also alone parallel to the facts observable in all the other ranges and levels of life known to us in any detail. Thus all wheat-seeds, all lily bulbs, all acorns contain the elementary materials and structures of richly fruitful wheat-plants, exquisitely tinted blossoms, and broad-spreading oak trees; their respective species are intended to reach, and actually do reach, in some fortunate representatives, this consummation: yet of these individual seeds, bulbs, acorns, not one in a hundred, or even less, attains to this full end of its species. So again with insects, fishes, birds, mammals: the proportion of individuals that actually attain to the full development, ideally intended for each and all, is astonishingly small. Thus, from the smallest moss or lichen up to man, we find everywhere, even though in a lesser and lesser degree, the distinction between the carefulness as to the type and species, and the apparently careless profusion as to the individual incorporations of the type. And hence life, in its manifold degrees and kinds, witnesses distinctly against any belief that mankind, and mankind alone within the world of creatures well known to us, reaches, in every individual man, the fullness of its natural and supernatural call.

And finally, the position here defended cannot justly be charged with imputing cruelty or injustice to God. For the souls that attain only to natural felicity have, *ex hypothesi,* never known the solicitations of the supernatural; all their actual, or even latent individual consciousness and needs are fulfilled within their own special kind and degree—a thing thoroughly possible, if, as we have already contended, Nature and Supernature are not one and the same call and condition, but two. Thus these souls are not the less fully happy because other human souls hunger and thirst after a higher and deeper, a different life; or because these other souls are satiated with a correspondingly different happiness. A man with much salt in his mouth requires much more drink to slake his thirst than does the man who has never tasted salt; the thirst of the man untouched by salt is slaked by a small glassful of water, the thirst of the man aroused by salt is not appeased by less liquid than a bucketful. And if we take the difference between the two classes of souls objectively, we find that the two calls and ends are largely balanced by the fact that the supernatural call and end usually involves spiritual struggles, sacrifices, dangers, profound alternatives, whilst the natural call and end is always devoid of all supernatural pains and perils.

56. THE ALTERNATIVE OF THE SUPERNATURALLY AWAKENED SOUL

WE stand now before the problem of Heaven and Hell properly so called, the final supernatural alternatives of the supernaturally awakened soul. Yet, here again, we must first clear away three very prevalent objections and misapprehensions. Let us move from the more general to the more particular difficulties.

First and foremost, then, we have to confront the opinion, increasingly prevalent in Western Europe since the beginning of the eighteenth century, one which now pervades fairly all the non-religious, and even much of the religious, thought of our day—that the conception of Heaven is, in substance, beautiful, or at least true, or at the very least harmless; but that any and every conception of Hell is essentially hideous, or at all events unreasonable, or at the very least most dangerous and noxious. Thus serious scholars attempt to prove that our Lord's utterances as to Hell are all due to misconceptions of His disciples, or even to amplifications by writers who had not heard His words; or, again, that these utterances, if really proceeding from our Lord Himself, only continue, without any special verification or emphasis, certain already prevalent opinions—that they have no organic connection with the roots of His revelation and message. Thus, too, otherwise helpful religious philosophers reduce Hell to a long Purgatory, or simply to a rhetorical or emotional expression (perceived or not perceived by our Lord Himself to be only such) for a correct and indeed noble sense of the intrinsic difference between right and wrong and of the correspondingly intrinsic differences between the respective consequences of right and of wrong—differences which are really outside of time and space, but which can only be described, at all vividly, in temporal and spatial pictures. The net result of all such teachings (quite apart from the still more prevalent and insidious Pantheistic tendencies of our time) is at the least to emphasise the conviction of Mother Julian of Norwich

that "all will be well," whilst the teaching of Christ and of
His Church will nevertheless turn out to have been true; or,
more boldly, to welcome back, as alone satisfactory, the
notions, not of Origen himself, but of some Origenists, as to
the eventual Restitution of All Things—of all souls; or, again,
quite generally, to treat as a barbarous, impertinent irruption
into our superior insight and humanity, not only the applications and details, but the very substance, of the convictions
of Tertullian, St. Augustine and Dante. What can we adduce
against such a denial?

We must first of all remember our discrimination—that the
question concerning the final destination of man, as such, is
not identical with the question concerning the final condition
of particular human beings. Hence it is quite beside the mark
to bring up the cases of little children, of idiots, of pure
savages. We must also not forget that there need be no real
question of Hell even for the majority of the supernaturally
awakened souls, if there actually exists a state and process
of purgation in the Beyond, as there undoubtedly exists such
a state and process here. Yet these provisos do not eliminate
the real possibility of Hell, as the general rule, wheresoever
is a real possibility of Heaven; they leave Heaven and Hell
as a generally inter-related couple.

We must next try vividly to realise the fact that it is not Hell
which is so much more difficult to believe in than is Heaven;
but that it is the entire specifically spiritual conception of
man, of his deepest self, which is difficult, as contrasted with
the naturalistic view of these same things. The purely naturalistic view of man conceives him as a mere superior animal,
which projects its own largely fantastic wishes on to the void
or the unknown, and which then fishes them back as objective
realities distinct from itself their true creator. And this view
is the more plausible, the more quickly statable, the more
vividly picturable, the alone readily transmittable, view.
But then, the view has all these qualities, precisely because
it stops short at the surface-impressions of things, and remains
utterly inadequate to all the deeper and deepest implications,
requirements and ends of knowledge in general, and of art,

z

ethics, philosophy and religion in particular. Yet as soon as we hold the difference between various kinds of human acts and dispositions to be always potentially, and often actually, of essential, of ultimate, of more than simply social, simply human importance, we are insisting upon values and realities that essentially transcend space and even time. Every at all noble, every even tolerably adequate, outlook always possesses some such more than merely empirical, simply contingent, or purely material and mechanical character. Plato, the Stoics, Plotinus possess this outlook, although in very different degrees; it ruled the Western world, during the Christian Middle Ages; and, after the largely negative rationality of most of the Renaissance, it gave its note of pathetic distinction and splendour to the great spirit of Spinoza, gravely cramped by Pantheism though it was in its speculation. In Kant it again reappears in a more theistic setting, and with the deep perception of that deep fact—radical evil—of man's frequent declaring, willing and doing what he well knows to be false and bad, but pleasant; in Schopenhauer it relieves the general pessimistic oppression with glimpses of a Beauty abiding and all-sustaining. And now, in these our times, we are again coming, in different lands and from different experiences and starting-points, to schemes really adequate, indeed deeply friendly, to this Transcendence present in all our nobler aspirations, acts and ends. Thus every profound search after, or belief in, the fundamental truth or essential beauty or satisfying goodness of anything—when we press it duly home and sincerely and delicately analyse it—overflows the ordinary, superficially obvious, requirements of man's knowledge, action, life. In each case we get a scheme that looks too big and too ambitious for us little men, and that involves alternatives too wide and deep for the average moments of the average mortal.

We have then, for our purpose, only to ask whether the alternatives—Heaven, Hell—are like or are unlike these ultimate implications of man's deepest needs and aspirations, elevations and falls. And the answer will assuredly be: "They are not unlike, but like."

57. OUR LORD'S MOMENTOUS TEACHING

AND we must finally consider the character of our Lord's outlook as a whole. As to this point, we not only find certain texts in the Synoptic Gospels which directly teach Hell and which put it in simple parallel with Heaven; but (an even more conclusive fact) we can clearly trace, throughout our Lord's teachings, the keen conviction, and the austere inculcation of the conviction, that the spiritual life is a great, all-important alternative and choice—a choice once for all, with consequences final and immense. The entire *texture* and implications of Jesus's outlook require such choice within this one earthly life on the part of supernaturally awakened souls, and such abidingness of the results of this their choice. "What does it profit a man if he gain the whole world and suffer the loss of his own soul?"—is but an example of what runs (as implication, allusion, pathos, entreaty, menace) throughout the whole of our Lord's teaching in proportion as, especially in its second stage, this teaching is continuously busy with man's supernatural call and the strenuous conditions and severe consequences of this call.

Only two serious objections can, I believe, be raised against this contention that our Lord Himself unequivocally taught the doctrine of fundamental alternatives and abiding consequences. The one objection is derived from an analysis and grouping of the Synoptic texts, the other is drawn from the doctrine of St. Paul.

As to the Synoptists, such serious scholars as the late Dr. H. J. Holtzmann and many others distinguish between a series of very simple sayings and parables, which reproduce our Lord's direct teachings, and the great or complicated pictures and similes, which are so many developments, by the primitive Christian community and writers, of certain elements or adumbrations of our Lord's own doctrine. And only in these latter pictures—such as Christ the King separating the sheep from the goats at the Last Judgment (St. Matt. xxv. 31–46)—do these scholars find any direct parallel

contrast between the saved and the lost, and any explicit
insistence upon the abidingness of the condition of the lost
as balancing the abidingness of the condition of the saved.
Nevertheless, even the passages thus still accepted as fully
primitive are, I submit, quite sufficient for our purpose;
since, interpreted otherwise than as involving the conviction
of abiding consequences, these sayings, so assuredly strenuous
and austere, lose all their specific point and poignancy. Thus
we are still told of "the Father which seeth in secret, who
shall reward openly"—who will forgive, or who will not
forgive, men's trespasses against Himself, according as men
forgive, or do not forgive, their fellow-men's trespasses against
themselves (St. Matt. vi. 4, 6, 18; vi. 14, 15). We are still
warned: "Fear not them which kill the body, but are not able
to kill the soul; but rather fear him which is able to destroy
both soul and body in hell" (St. Matt. x. 20). We still hear the
solemn woes pronounced against the unbelieving cities—of
the great straits that await them at the Day of Judgment
(St. Matt. xi. 21–4; xxiii. 37, 38). Jesus still insists that He
has come to divide a man from his father, and a daughter
from her mother, and that only "he that loseth his life for
my sake shall find it" (St. Matt. xi. 35–9); and, again, that
at the Day of Judgment, "two shall be in the field" or
"grinding at the mill"—"one shall be taken and the other
left" (St. Matt. xxv. 40, 41). He still exhorts us to cut off hand
or foot, or to pluck out an eye, rather than be cast with both
our hands or feet or eyes into Hell (St. Mark ix. 43–8). He
still proclaims that "he that is not with me is against me"
(St. Matt. xii. 30); and He still declares that there exists a
sin against the Spirit of God which cannot be forgiven (St.
Luke xii. 10 and the parallels). And we have still the parables
of the Two Houses built respectively on the rock and on the
sand, and resulting respectively in persistent safety and in
utter ruin; of the Unjust Steward; of the Talents; of the
Men at the Door asking admittance, when it is too late, from
the master of the house (St. Luke xiii. 24–30); and of the
Wise and Foolish Virgins. All these parables teach the
same lesson and possess the same implications. And indeed

Hell and its endlessness appear, explicitly and repeatedly, in these parables, as they also do in the corresponding series of sayings.

58. ASCETICISM AND MYSTICISM

THERE is, first, the (generally severe) Asceticism which is ever connected with at least some one phase, an early one, of every genuine Mystic's history, yet which does not differ essentially from the direct training in self-conquest to which practically all pre-Protestant, and most of the old Protestant, earnest Christians considered themselves obliged.

Now it is deeply interesting to note how marked has been, off and on throughout the last century and now again quite recently, the renewal of comprehension and respect for the general principle of Asceticism, in quarters certainly free from all preliminary bias in favour of Mediaeval Christianity. Schopenhauer wrote in 1843: "Not only the religions of the East but also genuine Christianity shows, throughout its systems, that fundamental characteristic of Asceticism which my philosophy elucidates. . . . Precisely in its doctrines of renunciation, self-denial, complete chastity, in a word, of general mortification of the will, lie the deepest truth, the high value, the sublime character of Christianity. It thus belongs to the old, true and lofty ideal of mankind, in opposition to the false, shallow and ruinous optimism of Greek Paganism, Judaism and Islam." "Protestantism, by eliminating Asceticism and its central point, the meritoriousness of celibacy, has, by this alone, already abandoned the innermost kernel of Christianity. . . . For Christianity is the doctrine of the deep guilt of the human race . . . and of the heart's thirst after redemption from it, a redemption which can be acquired only through the abnegation of self,—that is, through a complete conversion of human nature."—And the optimistically tempered American Unitarian, the deeply versed Psychologist, Prof. William James, tells us in 1902: "In its spiritual meaning, Asceticism stands for nothing less than for the essence of the twice-born philosophy." "The metaphysical mystery, that he who feeds on death, that feeds on men, possesses life supereminently, and meets best the secret demands of the Universe, is the truth of which asceticism has been the faithful champion. The folly of the cross, so inexplicable by the intellect, has, yet, its indestructible, vital meaning. . . . Naturalistic optimism is mere syllabub and sponge-cake in comparison."

Indeed, the only thing at all special to mysticism, in its attitude towards this general principle and practice of asceticism, is that it ever practises asceticism as a means towards, or at least as the make-weight and safeguard of, Contemplation, which latter is as essentially synthetic, and, in so far, peaceful and delightful, as the former is analytic, polemical and painful; whereas non-mystical souls will practise asceticism directly with a view to greater aloofness from sin, and greater readiness and strength to perform the various calls of duty. And hence, if we but grant the legitimacy of the general principle of ordinary asceticism, we shall find the mystical form of this asceticism to be the more easily comprehensible variety of that principle. For the mystic's practice, as concerns this point, is more varied and inclusive than that of others, since he does not even tend to make the whole of his inner life into a system of checks and of tension. The expansive, reconciling movement operates in him most strongly also, and, where of the right kind, this expansive movement helps, even more than the restrictive one, to purify, humble and deepen his heart and soul.

There is, however, a second, essentially different source and kind of suffering in some sorts and degrees of mysticism, and indeed in other *attraits* of the spiritual life, which is deeply interesting, because based upon a profound metaphysical apprehension. Although, at bottom, the opposite extreme to Pantheism, it readily expresses itself, for reasons that will presently appear, in terms that have a curiously pantheistic colour.

St. John of the Cross writes in 1578: "It is a principle of philosophy, that all means must . . . have a certain resemblance to the end, such as shall be sufficient for the object in view. If therefore the understanding is to be united to God, . . . it must make use of those means which can effect that union, that is, means which are most like unto God. . . . But there is no essential likeness or communion between creatures and Him, the distance between His divine nature and their nature is infinite. No creature therefore . . . nothing that the imagination may conceive or the understanding comprehend . . . in this life . . . can be a proximate means of union with God," for "it is all most unlike God, and most disproportionate to Him." "The understanding . . . must be pure and empty of all sensible objects, all clear intellectual perceptions, resting on faith: for faith is the sole proximate and proportionate means of the soul's union with God."

Now it is certain, as we have already found, that the awakened human soul ever possesses a dim but real experience of the Infinite, and that, in proportion as it is called to the Mystical Way, this sense will be deepened into various degrees of the Prayer of Quiet and of Union, and that here, more plainly than elsewhere, will appear the universal necessity of the soul's own response, by acts and the habit of Faith, to all and every experience which otherwise remains but so much unused material for the soul's advance. And it is equally certain that St. John of the Cross is one of the greatest of such contemplatives, and that neither his intuition and actual practice, nor even his sayings (so long as any one saying belonging to one trend is set off against another belonging to the other trend) contravene the Christian and Catholic positions.—Yet it cannot be denied that, were we to press his "negative way" into becoming the only one; and especially were we to take, without discount, such a virtual repudiation, as is furnished by any insistence upon the above words, of any essential, objective difference in value between our various apprehensions of Him and approaches to Him: the whole system and *rationale* of External, Sacramental and Historical Religion, indeed of the Incarnation, in any degree and form, would have to go, as so many stumbling-blocks to the soul's advance. For the whole principle of all such Religion implies the profound importance of the Here and the Now, the Contingent and the Finite, and of the Immanence of God, in various degrees and ways, within them.

Indications of this incompatibility, as little systematically realised here as in the Areopagite, are afforded by various remarks of his, belonging in reality to another trend. Thus, immediately before his denial of any essential likeness or communion between any creature and God, he says: "It is true that all creatures bear a certain relation to God and are tokens of His Being, some more, some less, according to the greater perfection of their nature." And of Our Lord's sacred Humanity he says: "What a perfect living image was Our Saviour upon earth: yet those who had no faith, though they were constantly about Him, and saw His wonderful works, were not benefited by His presence." But even here the immense importance, indeed downright necessity for Faith, of such external and historical stimuli, objects and materials, —in the latter instance all this at its very deepest,—remains unemphasised, through his engrossment in the necessity of Faith for the fructification of all these things.

In other places this Faith appears as though working so outside of all things imageable, as to have to turn rapidly away from all picturings, as, at best, only momentary starting-points for the advanced soul. "Let the faithful soul take care that, whilst contemplating an image, the senses be not absorbed in it, whether it be material or in the imagination, and whether the devotion it excites be spiritual or sensible. Let him . . . venerate the image as the Church commands and lift up his mind at once from the material image to those whom it represents. He who shall do this, will never be deluded." Here, again, along the line of argument absorbing the saint in this book, there is no fully logical ground left for the Incarnational, Historical, Sacramental scheme of the Infinite immanent in the finite, and of spirit stimulated in contact with matter, with everywhere the need of the condescensions of God and of our ascensions by means of careful attention to them.

Soren Kierkegaard, that deep solitary Dane, with so much about him like to Pascal the Frenchman, and Hurrell Froude the Englishman, and who, though Lutheran in all his bringing up, was so deeply attracted by Catholic Asceticism, has, in recent times (he died in 1855), pushed the doctrine of the qualitative, absolute difference between God and all that we ourselves can think, feel, will or be, to lengths beyond even the transcendental element,—we must admit this to be the greatly preponderant one,—in the great Spaniard's formal teaching. And it is especially in this non-Mystical Ascetic that we get an impressive picture of the peculiar kind of suffering and asceticism, which results from such a conviction to a profoundly sensitive, absorbedly religious soul; and here too we can, I think, discover the precise excess and onesidedness involved in this whole tendency. Professor Hoffding, in his most interesting monograph on his friend, tells us how "for Kierkegaard, . . . the will gets monopolised by religious Ethics from the very first; there is no time for Contemplation or Mysticism." "To tear the will away," Kierkegaard himself says, "from all finite aims and conditions . . . requires a painful effort and this effort's ceaseless repetition. And if, in addition to this, the soul has, in spite of all its striving, to be as though it simply were not, it becomes clear that the religious life signifies a dedication to suffering and to self-destruction. What wonder, then, that, for the Jew, death was the price of seeing God; or that, for the Gentile, the soul's entering into closer relations with the Deity meant the beginning of madness?" For "the soul's relation to God is a relation to a Being absolutely different from Man, who cannot confront him as his Superlative or Ideal, and who, nevertheless, is to rule in his inmost soul. Hence a necessary division, ever productive of new pains, is operative within man, as long as he perseveres in this spiritual endeavour. . . . A finite being, he is to live in the Infinite and Absolute: he is there like a fish upon dry land."

Now Prof. Hoffding applies a double, most cogent criticism to this position.—The one is religious, and has already been quoted. "A God Who is not Ideal and Pattern is no God.

Hence the contention that the Nature of the Godhead is, of necessity, qualitatively different from that of Man, has ever occasioned ethical and religious misgivings."—And the other is psychological. "Tension can indeed be necessary for the truth and the force of life. But tension, taken by itself, cannot furnish the true measure of life. For the general nature of consciousness is a synthesis, a comprehensive unity: not only contrast, but also concentration, must make itself felt, as long as the life of consciousness endures."

It is deeply interesting to note how Catherine, and at bottom St. John of the Cross and the Exclusive Mystics generally, escape, through their practice and in some of their most emphatic teachings, from Kierkegaard's excess, no doubt in part precisely because they *are* Mystics, since the exclusive Mystic's contemplative habit is, at bottom, a synthetic one. Yet we should realise the deep truth which underlies the very exaggerations of this onesidedly analytic and ascetical view. For if God is the deepest ideal, the ultimate driving force and the true congenital element and environment of Man, such as Man cannot but secretly wish to will deliberately, and which, at his best, Man truly wills to hold and serve: yet God remains ever simply incompatible with that part of each man's condition and volition which does not correspond to the best and deepest which that Man himself sees or could see to be the better, *hic et nunc*; and, again, He is ever, even as compared with any man's potential best, infinitely more and nobler, and, though here not in simple contradiction, yet at a degree of perfection which enables Him, the Supreme Spirit, to penetrate, as Immanent Sustainer or Stimulator, and to confront, as Transcendent Ideal and End, the little human spirit, so great in precisely this its keen sense of experienced contrast.

Catherine exhibits well this double relation, of true contradiction, and of contrast, both based upon a certain genuine affinity between the human soul and God. On one side of herself she is indeed a veritable fish out of water; but, on the other side of her, she is a fish happily disporting itself in its very element, in the boundless ocean of God. On the one side, snapping after air, in that seemingly over-rarefied atmosphere in which the animal man, the mere selfish individual, cannot live; on the other side, expanding her soul's lungs and drinking in light, life and love, in that same truly rich atmosphere, which, Itself Spirit, feeds and sustains her growing spiritual personality. And the *Dialogo*, in spite of its frequently painful abstractness and empty unity, has, upon the whole, a profound hold upon this great doctrine.

Yet it is in Catherine's own culminating intuition,—of the soul's free choice of Purgatory, as a joyful relief from the piercing pain of what otherwise would last for ever,—the vividly perceived contrast between God's purity and her soul's impurity, that we get, in the closest combination, indeed mutual causation, this double sense of Man's nearness to and distance from, of his likeness and unlikeness to God. For only if man is, in the deepest instincts of his soul, truly related to God, and is capable of feeling (indeed he ever actually, though mostly dimly, experiences) God's presence and this, man's own, in great part but potential, affinity to Him: can suffering be conceived to arise from the keen realisation of the contrast between God and man's own actual condition at any one moment; and can any expectation, indeed a swift vivid instinct, arise within man's soul that the painful, directly contradictory, discrepancy can and will, gradually though never simply automatically, be removed. And though, even eventually, the creature cannot, doubtless, ever become simply God, yet it can attain, in an indefinitely higher degree, to that affinity and union of will with God, which, in its highest reaches and moments, it already now substantially possesses; and hence to that full creaturely self-constitution and joy in which, utterly trusting, giving itself to, and willing God, it will, through and in Him, form an abidingly specific, unique constituent and link of His invisible kingdom of souls, on and on.

But there is a third attitude, peculiar (because of its preponderance) to the Mystics as such, an attitude in a manner intermediate between that of ordinary asceticism, and that of the suffering just described. The implications and effects of, and the correctives for, this third attitude will occupy us up to the end of this book. I refer to the careful turning-away from all Multiplicity and Contingency, from the Visible and Successive, from all that does or can distract and dissipate, which is so essential and prevailing a feature in all Mysticism, which indeed, in Exclusive Mysticism, is frankly made into the one sole movement towards, and measure of, the soul's perfection.

It is true that to this tendency, when and in so far as it has come so deeply to permeate the habits of a soul as to form a kind of second nature, the name Asceticism cannot, in strictness, be any more applied; since now the pain will lie, not in this turning away from all that dust and friction, but, on the contrary, in any forcing of the soul back into that turmoil. And doubtless many, perhaps most, souls with a pronouncedly mystical *attrait*, are particularly sensitive to all, even partial and momentary, conflict. Yet we can nevertheless appropriately discuss the matter under the general heading of asceticism, since, as a rule, much practice and sacrifice go to build up this habit; since, in every case, this abstractive habit shares with ordinary asceticism a pronounced hostility to many influences and forces ever actually operative within and around the undisciplined natural man; and since, above all, the very complements and correctives for this abstractiveness will have to come from a further, deeper and wider asceticism, to be described presently.

As to ordinary asceticism and this abstractiveness, the former fights the world and the self directly, and then only in so far as they are discovered to be positively evil or definitely to hinder positive good; it is directly attracted by the clash and friction involved in such fighting; and it has no special desire for even a transitory intense unification of the soul's life: whereas the abstractiveness turns away from, and rises above, the world and the phenomenal self; their very existence, their contingency, the struggles alive within them, and their (as it seems) inevitably disturbing effect upon the soul, are all felt as purely dissatisfying; and an innermost longing for a perfect and continuous unification and overflowing harmony of its inner life here possesses the spirit.

Now we have just seen how a movement of integration, of synthesising all the soul's piecemeal, inter-jostling acquisitions, of restful healing of its wounds and rents, of sinking back (from the glare and glitter of clear, and then ever fragmentary perception, and from the hurry, strain and rapidly ensuing distraction involved in all lengthy external action) into a peaceful, dim rumination and unification, is absolutely necessary, though in very various degrees and forms, for all in any way complete and mature souls.—And we have, farther back, realised that a certain, obscure but profoundly powerful, direct instinct and impression of God in the soul is doubtless at work here, and, indeed, throughout all the deeper and nobler movements of our wondrously various inner life. But what concerns us here, is the question whether the *complete* action of the soul (if man would grow in accordance with his ineradicable nature, environment, and specific grace and call) does not as truly involve a corresponding counter-movement to this intensely unitive and intuitive movement which, with most men, and in most moments of even the minority of men, forms but an indirectly willed condition and spontaneous background of the soul.

We have been finding, further, that all the contingencies, multiplicities and mediations which, one and all, tend to appear to the Mystic as so many resistances and distractions, can roughly be grouped under two ultimate heads. These intruders are fellow-souls, or groups of fellow-souls,—some social organism, the Family, Society, the State, the Church— who provoke, in numberless degrees and ways, individual affection, devotion, distraction, jealousy, as from person towards person. Or else the intruders are Things and Mechanical Laws, and these usually leave the Mystic indifferent or irritate or distract him; but they can become for him great opportunities of rest, and occasions for self-discipline.

Yet this distinction between Persons and Things (although vital for the true apprehension of all deeper, above all of the deepest Reality, and for the delicate discrimination between what are but the means and what are the ends in a truly spiritual life) does not prevent various gradations within, and continuous interaction between, each of these two great groups. For in proportion as, in the Personal group, the Individual appears as but parcel and expression of one of the social organisms, does the impression of determinist Law, of an impersonal Thing or blind Force, begin to mix with, and gradually to prevail over, that of Personality. And in proportion as, in the Impersonal group, Science comes to include all careful and methodical study, according to the most appropriate methods, of any and every kind of truth and reality; and as it moves away from the conceptions of purely quantitative matter, and of the merely numerically different, entirely interchangeable, physical happenings (all so many mere automatic illustrations of mechanical Law), on, through the lowly organisms of plant-life, and the ever higher interiority and richer consciousness of animal life, up to Man, with his ever qualitative Mind, and his ever non-interchangeable, ever "effortful," achievements and elaborations of types of beauty, truth and goodness in Human History,—does Science itself come back, in its very method and subject-matter, ever more nearly, to the great personal starting-point, standard and ultimate motive of all our specifically human activity and worth.

Indeed, the two great continuous facts of man's life, first that he thinks, feels, wills and acts, in and with the help or hindrance of that profoundly material Thing, his physical body, and on occasion of, with regard to, the materials furnished by the stimulations and impressions of his senses; and again, that these latter awaken within him those, in themselves, highly abstract and Thing-like categories of his mind which penetrate and give form to these materials; are enough to show how close is the pressure, and how continuous the effect, of Things upon the slow upbuilding of Personality.

Fair approximations to these two kinds of Things, with their quite irreplaceable specific functions within the economy of the human mental life,—the intensely concrete and particular sense - impressions, and the intensely abstract and general mental categories,—reappear within the economy of characteristic religion, in its Sacraments and its Doctrine.

And conversely, there exists, *in rerum naturâ*, no Science worth having which is not, ultimately, the resultant of, and which does not require and call forth, on and on, certain special qualities, and combinations of qualities, of the truly ethical, spiritual, Personality. Courage, patience, perseverance, candour, simplicity, self-oblivion, continuous generosity towards others and willing correction of even one's own most cherished views,—these things and their like are not the quantitative determinations of Matter, but the qualitative characteristics of Mind.

59. THE NEED OF CATHOLICISM TO-DAY

THERE can, to-day less than ever, be any question of abandoning this magnificent sense of the Transcendent and Infinite and of the Immanent and Redemptive Light, Life, Love, God; of levelling down to sheer naturalism—that dreary impossibility, or even simply to the once-born stage of religion. We must have the Real God, and we must have the Real Christ, the Real Church. We require, then, not Agnosticism, not non-religious Ethic, not even Unitarianism, not Quakerism. We must have Catholicism, God in man, and man conscious of sin and sorrow; nature in grace, and grace in nature; the Infinite and Spaceless in Time and Space; spirit in the body —the body, the stimulator and spring-board, the material and training ground, of spirit. And whatever may be the obscurities, complications, difficulties of the enterprise, we simply must persist in it—we must strive to awaken and utilise every stage and range of genuine life, with its special characteristics, in its right place and degree, for the calling into full action of all the rest. But such an insistent, pertinacious *organic* trend is Catholicism.

And next, this Catholicism, with a most delicate, difficult alertness and selflessness, will have to be truly *incarnational*— that is, it will have to recognise, respect, love and protect continually, not only the less full and less articulate stages of grace, in the other religions and in all they possess of what is true, but it will have to recognise, respect, love and protect also the non-religious levels and complexes of life, as also coming from God, as occasions, materials, stimulations, necessary for us men towards the development of our complete humanity, and especially also of our religion. There must at no time be any question of eliminating or weakening the transcendental, other-world, God-ward, recollective movement; it, on the contrary, will have, as keenly and penetratingly as ever, to be the great sheet-anchor of our souls and the great root of the self-identity of the Catholic religion and of its world-conquering peace. We shall only, in our other movement—in the out-going, the world-ward, the incarnational movement, have, far more keenly than men were able to realise in the past, to be attentive, active, observant, hospitable, there also—not merely with the sense of doing good, or with the wish directly to find or to introduce religious facts and categories, but especially with the conviction that these various stages and ranges, each and all, come from God, possess their own immanent laws and conditions of existence and growth, and deserve our love and service in this their nature and development. We shall feel sure that they will, in the long run, benefit (often in the most unexpected but most real ways) regions of life apparently far apart from them, and especially will aid religion, the deepest life of all. And in so doing we shall be Catholic, that is rich—more rich, in the world-ward movement, than men could be in the past: what a gain for mankind and for Catholicism!

And lastly, our Catholicism will, owing to this its greater awakeness, this its increased delicacy and sensitiveness of interior organisation and incarnationalism, acquire a great increase in the probing character of the Cross, of purification, of tension, contradiction, suspense,—since these will now be found more fully also in precisely what it loves most—in the evidences and symmetry of theology, and in the ready and assured application of religion itself. For not only has the religious man now, in one of his two necessary movements of soul, to be, and to keep himself, awake to ranges and complexes of life and reality dominated by laws and affinities other than those obtaining in religion. But, if he is not a Pietist but a Catholic, he will have to continue to utilise, to appeal to, strictly to require, history, philosophy, sociology, art for religion itself: yet he will have, in appealing to them, and in so far as he thus appeals, to abide, not by the tests of religion, still less by any impatience of his own, but simply by the proofs special to these several complexes of reality and knowledge.

Let us vividly realise that, although Catholicism has held and taught a considerable number of religious truths as so many factual happenings, yet that it has ever so taught them —thus, as factual happenings,—not on the ground of intuition but of historical evidence—i.e. it has, for its historical element, always appealed to historical documents. And indeed an abiding nucleus of factual happenings is essential to Catholicism, as Christian, as incarnational. But Catholicism—its essence which we are here studying—is directly bound up only with the persistent existence of some such nucleus, and with the persistent openness of the historical appeal and the real cogency of the historical proofs; whereas Catholicism in its essence is only indirectly, only conditionally, bound up with the factual character of all and every truth long held to be not only a spiritual truth but also a factual happening. And though the great central figure—Our Lord—and the main outlines of His life and teaching, death and apparitions, require, for the integrity of Catholicism, to be not only spiritual truths but factual happenings, it does not follow that the same is necessarily the case with every truth and doctrine concerning Him. Certainly the Descent into Hell is now conceived, by all educated Christians, in spite of their continuous acceptance of its truth and importance,—it stands in the Apostles' Creed,—not in the directly, simply factual way in which it was understood in early times. As I take the relations between the Visible and the Invisible Church, so also do I take the relations between the Factual and the Doctrinal to be neither relations of sheer co-extension nor, still less, relations of even possible sheer antagonism or sheer

2 A

mutual exclusion. On the contrary: *some*, a very real, an operative, relation exists between the Visible and the Invisible Church, and between the Factual and the Doctrinal. And indeed we know that actual life persists in furnishing us with the basis for such a double conviction;—that is, we know that *some* amount of Visible Organisation and of Factual Happening remains, and persists in connection with Invisible Reality in both cases, beyond reasonable challenge to this hour. Above all, we know that God exists and that He will continue to operate within those other complexes—history, philosophy, art, as well as within the deepest of all complexes, religion.

It is God we believe in, it is God we trust. Without His reality, and without faith in His reality, the world around us and within us is confusion and dismay. But God *is*—the all-pervading sustainer, the initiator of all light and life and love. And Catholicism apprehends, lives, and loves Him thus— universal, but in different stages and degrees; simple, but in overflowing richness; and the Supreme Reality, but self-limited and divinely respectful of the liberty given by Himself even when and where such liberty is used against Him. God slowly levels upwards, and Catholicism affirms, loves, encourages these various levels and their slow purification and elevation by and towards God, their one origin and universal home.

60. THE NECESSITY OF THE CHURCH

If we take the substitutes offered to mankind for a Church in the order of their increasing extension and subtlety, we shall move through the following five positions. (In actual life the substitutes generally consist more or less of mixtures effected between some two or three of these five theoretically possible pure positions.)

There is first the substitution which will doubtless always commend itself to the half-educated man: the Individual. Religion, where such a man is at all religiously alive, is most rightly felt to be the deepest of man's experiences. But if so, what more natural, what more unanswerable conclusion can be drawn from this, readily argues this same man, than that religion, the deepest experience, is also of necessity the most private, the most entirely private, hence again the most incommunicable—the most individual—the most exclusively individual—of all things? Besides, does not everyone know himself best? Such a man, did he know Kant, would agree with Kant when this philosopher warns us that all attempts to influence or to mould the opinions of other men in such deepest matters are always only so much harmful interference and impertinent tyranny. The later Middle Age was already largely penetrated by this spirit. Thus the English Franciscan William of Ockham, whom Luther regarded as his "dear Master," teaches at times and generally implies that a holy individual soul can, at need, of itself alone fill the place of the Church.

Then there is another, a wider outlook, that of the Waldensians and the Quakers. Here the Family in great part supplants the Church.

Next we get a position more comprehensive still, yet one, for the most part, harsher than the second—the Sect. Montanus and that genius, his fiery follower Tertullian, are good examples of this position.

And then the substitution widens out, yet also thins down, into that of the German theologian Richard Rothe, who would deliberately oust the Church in favour of the State— doubtless a great simplification, if only it prove possible and fruitful.

And finally there is the subtlest of all the substitutions, one now again very alluring to not a few fine minds—that of Philosophy. So with the Stoics and Neoplatonists of old; so with Hume, in so far as he retained any religion at all; so with the Hegelians of more or less the left, as now with Dr. Bradley and Professor Bernard Bosanquet in England, and, with little or no religious sense remaining, in Benedetto Croce in Italy. Most of the followers of M. Bergson appear to be in a similar case. All these philosophical groups have some good to say of Religion—even of Institutional Religion;

but a Church is here essentially a condescension to the multitude, a largely childish symbol and *Kindergarten* for what Philosophy alone holds and teaches with a virile adequacy.

The elements of truth variously present in these five substitutions—of the Individual, the Family, the Sect, the State, Philosophy—will appear later on. Our immediate further task concerns the direct incentives for seeking after substitutes of any kind.

We shall never reach fairness towards these processes of substitution unless we begin with the conviction that it is impossible (in view of history at large and of the history of these substitutions in particular) to put down these processes, simply and generally, to the sheer perversity of human nature. Such perversity is, indeed, very certainly more or less at work here also, yet demonstrably, upon the whole, only as a preparatory, or intensifying cause. This is certain of two facts which are simply undeniable. No institution in human history has reaped a more enthusiastic devotion and a more boundless gratitude than the Church—and this for something like a thousand years and amidst large masses first of Graeco-Roman, and then of Teutonic peoples, indeed also amongst the Celts and the Slavs. And again, these enthusiastic admirers were, by natural disposition, no better than are their descendants, nor have these descendants acquired a congenital taint unpossessed by those predecessors. Hence it is logically impossible to quote the past enthusiasm as a sure proof of the Church's goodness, and, at the same time, to take the later and present suspicion and hostility as simply evidence of men's badness. Men have remained throughout substantially the same, so that, if they weigh much as witnesses when they admire, they cannot weigh nothing as witnesses when they oppose.

The chief real causes or occasions of such frequent attempts to evade the Church, or to supersede it by means of this or that substitute, are, I think, four. I take them in the order of their growing penetration.

The Church, as a Visible Institution, is, has to be, administered by human beings. And the majority of human beings are but average mortals who inevitably tend to work the Church, to develop the Church, with insufficient balance, in a spirit of acute rivalry or of worldly ambition, or at least in a *simpliste*, short-cut manner. Yet thus to work or to develop the Church, in its multiform inevitable relations with the other God-intended activities and God-given institutions of mankind, spells, of necessity, more or less dangerous friction and ominous repression. And indeed such complications can spring in part from Churchmen truly great in other ways. Striking examples of this are the claims of not a few of the Popes of the later Middle Age and of the Renaissance. The Papacy had rendered priceless services to mankind by achieving the autonomy of the Church in face of the State—of the Church as the organ essentially of Supernature, in face of the State as the organism essentially of Nature. And again the Papacy has been from the first, and will doubtless remain to the last, the divinely intended and divinely blessed instrument and incorporation of the Visible Unity of the Church —of the Church, as essentially but one. Yet after that great, abidingly precious victory, a certain obscuration of this permanent function could not but follow when certain Popes came, in their turn, to forget, at least in practice, the specific rights and legitimate autonomy of the State. Another striking instance of a similar oblivion is the Galileo case, where the sense has not yet sufficiently awakened or is in abeyance that Science also possesses its own specific duties, rights and powers.

Again, the Church, as a Visible Institution worked and developed, in its average manifestations, largely by distinctly average men, tends to ignore, or at least to grudge and to minimise, the degrees and kinds of truth and goodness always more or less present in such other religious bodies as may possess a long duration and ethical seriousness. A remarkable example of this is furnished even by such a God-inspired genius as St. Paul, when in his systematising and speculative mood. For when in that mood the entire Old Testament Cultus can appear, to this vehement convert to the New Revelation, as exclusively a means for bringing home to its devotees a sense of their sinfulness and of the radical inability of the Jewish

Church to bring any strength whatsoever to the avoidance of the sins thus discovered.

Once more, the Church, as a Visible Institution worked and developed by average men, after conquering and winning the world "not by killing but by dying," came, some half a century after its external triumph under Constantine, to killing—to allowing, indeed to encouraging and blessing her lay children to kill in their turn, in and for matters of religious belief. The use of force in religion is, indeed, deeply embedded in the Old Testament — King Josiah's great, profoundly important and very fruitful reform was demonstrably full of it. And many of the Psalms breathe this same spirit, which indeed still appears plainly in parts of our Christian Book of Revelation.

And finally, the Church as a Visible Institution worked by average men, has shown, ever since the advent of Historical Criticism, little comprehension of, and at times an acute hostility to, disinterested scholarship, with its serious investigation and candid enunciation of the successive stages, the human occasions and the surface motives traceable in the history of the Bible and of the Church. This average attitude, on the contrary, requires a sheer identity of the successive forms, a strict sameness in even the subsidiary movements of the religious spirit. We thus find the condemnation of Richard Simon in the Roman Catholic Church, and of Bishop Colenso in the Anglican, and of William Robertson Smith and Charles Briggs in the Presbyterian Bodies.

These four checks and oppressions, especially where they appear more or less in combination, readily explain a large part of men's alienation from Institutional Christianity, even where there is not the still more decisive incentive of a decided Immanentism or even of bad living or of sheer perversity.

Nevertheless there lies ready for the docile mind the most varied, unforced, largely indirect and unexpected, cumulative and hence very powerful, evidence for the abiding need of the Church. If we are only sufficiently patient to persist in openness of mind towards the rich lessons, past and present, of the spiritual life, we shall find this evidence for the Church to be more extensive and deeper than are the evidences against it, and indeed to be alone fully germane to the issue in question.

There is, then, first, the presumption furnished by the other levels and ranges of the multiform life of man. Thus Art, we cannot deny, is developed in and through Academies, Schools, Traditions. True, artistic genius is something more and other than is such training or than all that such training can give of itself. Yet even genius cannot dispense with at least the more indirect forms and effects of such training, if this genius is to achieve its own full power and effect. So too with Science. Science assuredly does not grow solely by means of Schools, Traditions, the succession of teachers; yet it does, upon the whole, require such an environment and discipline. The same holds good of Philosophy, in its own manner and degree. And Ethics, to be rich and robust, requires the Family, the Guild, the State, not only as the ends of Ethics but also as its disporting ground and means. And similarly with Religion. Such maxims and habits of soul as "To be alone with the Alone" and "God is a Spirit, and they that would serve Him must serve Him in Spirit and in Truth" spring from many centuries of social philosophy and social religion. The facts of man's essentially mixed condition of sense and spirit, and of his essential sociality, will always, in the long run, refute and supplant, for the masses of men, every purely individualist or purely spiritual religion or attempt at such a religion. But body and society combined spell (if thus admitted on principle as essential factors of religion) nothing less than the Visible Church.

There is, next, the actual history of Religion itself. All the great religious personalities whose antecedents, doings and effects we can trace at all securely and at all fully, sprang from religious institutions, and either deliberately continued the extant institution or founded another institution, or at the least, very soon influenced history in such an institutional direction. This is the case with Gautama, the Buddha, in the full sense of the deliberate foundation of an Order and a Church. Still more is it so (as here springing from a long development of a religious society and a common worship, and as leading on to a great reinforcement of this social, common cultus) with the Jewish Prophets. We can here follow the interconnection of the Social and the Individual from Elijah onwards, ever more clearly, to Jeremiah with King Josiah's centralisation of the Hebrew worship and his organisation of a definite Church; and then, on again to Ezechiel, duly followed by the elaborate ecclesiasticism of the Priestly Code. So too with St. John the Baptist, who, all single and original as he appears, has, in reality, a long tradition and a rich social training behind him and around him. And especially is it so with St. Paul and with the great author of the Fourth Gospel. St. Paul deliberately organises the Christian Church, liberated by him from all subjection to the Jewish Church; and the Fourth Gospel presupposes throughout this Church character of Christianity.

Indeed also with Jesus Himself, as He appears in the Synoptic Gospels, we find such a social, institutional religion, if we but vividly bear in mind three very pregnant facts. The expectation of His Proximate Second Coming is a fact, at least it was a certainty for the first hearers and first recorders of the words of Jesus; and this fact has to be remembered, not simply as concerns this or that subject-matter of the recorded saying and doings of Jesus, but as it concerns them all. There is no sense in using this fact, as is now not rarely done, in explanation of the small or no place occupied in the sayings of Jesus by the Family, Labour, the State, Art, Philosophy, or rather of His (practically complete) abstraction from these great duties, problems, difficulties of manifold yet closely inter-connected human life; and not to allow for the same fact in the question of the sayings of Jesus concerning the Church. Again, if the precise term "Church" was, apparently, never uttered by the earthly Jesus, the thing itself is, in its essence, already truly present in the most undeniable of His own words, acts and organisings. For the parables which have for background or for centre the family or a kingdom, an owner of a house or a vineyard, or the parables which turn on the qualities of salt and of leaven: they all imply a social religious organism, a hierarchy of super-ordination and of sub-ordination as well as of co-ordination. And all this appears as one side of the rich living paradox which, on the other side, bids us one and all to be but the lowly servants of each other. And the actions of Jesus entirely bear out this social, organic, graduated—this Church conception of religion. These acts move, emphatically, not up from the many to the few, and on from the few to the One; nor, again, do they proceed down as a light of grace vouchsafed by God, independently of all other souls, to each soul direct, so that the economy of salvation would consist in so many parallel lines of approach, each free from all contact or crossing by the others. No: the movement here is down from the One invisible God, through the one visible, audible, tangible Jesus, on to the twelve visible men formed into a single College by Jesus Himself, and sent out by Him to preach, to heal, to forgive sins, with solemn warnings as to the guilt of those who may refuse to hear them. And this visible College is given a visible Head by the visible Jesus Himself, and Jesus deliberately changes the name of this His chief representative to the significant appellation "Rock," in return for the recognition, by Simon alone amongst the Twelve Apostles, of Jesus as the Messiah. And finally, if the Church exists, in such sayings and doings as were indisputably spoken or enacted by the earthly Jesus Himself, only in fact and in rudiment, this same Church appears, very certainly, also in name and in all its essential lineaments, well within the New Testament, indeed throughout a full two-thirds of its contents. Thus St. Paul busily organises the Church and yet simultaneously apprehends the Church as the very Body of Christ, and insists solemnly upon the two great central Sacraments, Baptism and the Holy Eucharist. We have the Johannine Gospel, penetrated from first to last with the conception of the Beloved Community and with these two great Sacraments, here the subject-matter of two solemn discourses. And indeed these Sacraments are here summed up symbolically in the Water and the Blood which flow from the pierced side of Jesus upon the Cross; and the Church is similarly symbolised by the Seamless Coat left by Jesus, the new High Priest, to mankind

—for the reality so adumbrated is to be thus indivisible except by the sins and schisms of men. Indeed, the waiting of the Beloved Disciple to let Peter pass into the empty sepulchre before himself, although he, and not Peter, had first reached the entrance, appears to be one more instance of the sense of order, of the Church and of its invisible Oneness which, indeed, penetrates the entire work. And finally the Synoptic Gospels, in their apparently later constituents, sum up for us majestically these developments. Matthew gives us the two great passages—of the Church now solemnly proclaimed by name and to be built upon the Rock, Cephas, Peter; and of the sublime commission of the Risen Christ to the Apostles, sending them out into all the world and promising to be with them to the end. And Luke gives us the prophecy of Jesus to the disciples that Satan would attempt to sift them as wheat; but that He, Christ, had prayed—not for them all, but for Simon Peter, him alone, that his faith should never fail, and that he, Simon Peter, after his conversion (not from infidelity but cowardice) was to confirm them.

Our Lord died upon the Cross in A.D. 30. The two great primitive collections of His sayings and doings, the Gospel according to St. Mark and the *Logia*, no doubt existed in written form already in the middle sixties. St. Paul's great Epistles cannot be more recent than A.D. 52–9. The Gospels of Matthew and of Luke (minus some later additions) belong probably, the first to A.D. 70–5, and the second to A.D. 78–85. The Fourth Gospel cannot be more recent than A.D. 110, and may well go back as far as A.D. 95. And already in A.D. 93–7 we have the First Epistle of St. Clement Bishop of Rome, a prelude to the world-wide claim and influence of Bishop Victor of Rome in the great Paschal controversy of A.D. 190, 191. In view of such facts it is not fantastic if Wernle (*Die Synoptische Frage*, 1899, p. 192) and Heinrich J. Holtzmann (*Die Synoptiker*, Ed. 1901)—these two highly competent Protestant specialists—hold as possible that Matthew xvi. 17–19, the great "Thou art Peter" passage, already expresses the Roman claims (*Selbstbewusstsein*). In any case, nothing could well be more certain than are the earliness, the spiritual need and fruitfulness, and the prompt emphasis, of the developments of the Church and the Sacraments. History never yields mathematical demonstration even as to the brute facts—as to their happenedness; still less can history, of itself alone, penetrate to the inner meaning of these happenednesses; hence we can, if we will, stiffen and close our minds against all these developments, we can, at least, treat them as artificial accretions. But the moral certainty special to history will then raise great difficulties against us in view of the earliness of the developments concerned, and Christianity will then be forced to appear as having fraudulently, or at least quite externally, acquired the hands and the feet, the food and the heart with which it worked, moved, sustained itself, loved and struggled against an acutely hostile world and with which it eagerly and increasingly conquered that world during those early decades and the subsequent three centuries of Catacombs. One thing in any case even the simplest logic forbids us to do. We are not free—though how often this is done!—we are not free to accept certain formulations of doctrine, which appear clear and definite only in the middle and later New Testament, as accurate enunciations of the facts and beliefs implicitly present from the first; and to evade or to explain away other, parallel developments, because we do not like their content. "God so loved the world," this great passage may appeal to us more than "Thou art Peter": yet only both, and not one only, can, for a large and logical outlook, represent the genius of Christianity, comparatively late as may be both these articulations of it.

And there is finally a third group of proofs for the need of the Church—evidence, largely delicate and difficult to trace in detail, yet very real and impressively spontaneous and convergent. We here get evidence both of the impoverishment which follows upon conscious rejection of the Social, Institutional element of religion, and of the unconscious indebtedness of the individualist, to such social and institutional religion, for much of such adequacy as he may retain. And there is, contrariwise, the evidence of the heightened good which springs from deliberate persistent acceptance of the Church as such. Here we cannot do more than give some specimens from the very large mass of facts. Thus, as to the impoverishment in the lives of Churchless religionists, we can trace a certain incompleteness in a man's humility, so long as it consists of humiliation before God alone, and as it claims to derive all its religious help without any mediation of the senses and of society—purely spiritually from the Infinite Pure Spirit alone. Complete humility imperatively demands my continuous recognition of my own multiform need of my fellow-creatures, especially of those wiser and better than myself, and of my life-long need of training, discipline, incorporation; full humility requires filial obedience and docility towards men and institutions, as well as fraternal give and take, and paternal authority and superintendence. All this, as against the first of the substitutes for the Church, Individualism. The second and fourth substitutes, the Family and the State (when taken thus not in addition to, but in lieu of, the Church), tend, the first, rather to a sentimental moralism, a mutual admiration society; and the second, to a morality and inchoate religion of a natural, a Golden Rule type, as in the cases of Confucius and of Bentham. The third substitution, that of the Sect, is rather a one-sidedness than a sheer error, and will be considered later on. But the fifth, the last substitution, that of Philosophy, is probably, for men of education, the most inflating error amongst all these substitutions. There can be no doubt that where such patronage of the toiling moiling Church folk by "superior" philosophical insight does not induce pride and complacency, this can only spring from certain rare qualities in the character concerned. In any case such a soul lacks the very definite training in the *creaturely* mind, so richly furnished by Church appurtenance.

61. THE PURIFICATION OF SCIENTIFIC DISCIPLINE

THE conception of nature of the ancient Greek Physicists, and indeed that of Aristotle, required to be profoundly dehumanised, de-sentimentalised: a rigorous mathematical determinism and soulless mechanism became the right and necessary ideal of Physical Science. But, long before the elaboration of this Concept of the oathless Thing and of its blind Force, our Lord had by His Life and Teaching, brought to man, with abidingly unforgettable, divine depth and vividness, the sense of Spirit and Personality, with its liberty and interiority, its far-looking wisdom and its regenerating, creative power of love. And for some thirteen centuries after this supreme spiritual revelation and discovery, that old anthropomorphic and anthropocentric conception of the Physical Universe continued, wellnigh unchanged, even among the earlier and middle schoolmen, and was readily harmonised with that Spiritual world. Yet they were harmonised, upon the whole, by a juxtaposition which, in proportion as the conception of nature became Determinist and Mechanical, has turned out more and more untenable; and which, like all simple juxtapositions, could not, as such, have any spiritually educative force. But Spiritual Reality has now,—for those who have become thoroughly awake to the great changes operated for good and all, in man's conception of the Physical Universe during now three centuries, —to be found under, behind, across these Physical Phenomena and Laws which both check and beckon on the mind and soul of man, in quest of their ultimate mainstay and motivation.

And let us note how much some such discipline and asceticism is required by the whole Christian temper and tradition, and the weakening of some older forms of it.

During the first three generations Christians were profoundly sobered by the keen expectation of Our Lord's Second Coming, and of the end of the entire earthly order of things, to which all their natural affections spontaneously clung: and again, up to wellnigh the Crusading age, this poignant and yet exultant expectation seized upon the hearts of Christians. And then, especially from St. Augustine's teaching onwards, an all-pervading, frequently very severe conviction as to the profound effects of original sin, a pessimistic turning away from the future of this sub-lunar world as leading up to the great Apostacy, and a concentration upon man's pre-historic beginnings, as incomparably eclipsing all that mankind would ever achieve here below, came and largely took the place as the sobering, detaching element in Christianity, of the vivid expectation of the Parousia which had characterised the earlier Christian times.

Clearly, the Parousia and the Original Sin conception have ceased to exercise their old, poignantly detaching power upon us. Yet we much require some such special channel and instrument for the preservation and acquisition of the absolutely essential temper of Detachment and Other-Worldliness. I think that this instrument and channel of purification and detachment—if we have that thirst for the More and the Other than all things visible can give to our souls (a thirst which the religious sense alone can supply and without which we are religiously but half-awake)—is offered to us now by Science, in the sense and for the reasons already described.

. . . . . .

And thus we come back to the old, sublime wisdom of St. John of the Cross, in all that it has of continuous thirst after the soul's purification and expansion, and of a longing to lose itself, its every pettiness and egoistic separateness, in an abstract, universal, quasi-impersonal disposition and reality, such as God here seems to require and to offer as the means to Himself. . . . And we are thus, perhaps, in an even closer touch with Catherine's central idea,—the soul's voluntary plunge into a painful yet joyous purgation, into a state, and as it were an element, which purges away (since the soul itself freely accepts the process,) all that deflects, stints or weakens the realisation of the soul's deepest longings,— the hard self-centredness, petty self-mirrorings, and jealous claimfulness above all.

62. SUFFERING AND GOD

THE conviction of the Otherness of God is, in the long run, as essential to full, powerful religion as any and all conviction of the Likeness of God. Belief in Suffering in God is generally commended to us as necessary if we are really to feel God like unto us, if for our feeling He is truly to be our Father, indeed more or less our elder Brother. For not only our average toil and doing, but especially our highest ethical and spiritual achievements, appear to be essentially bound up with Suffering—Suffering heroically borne or heroically overcome, yet still Suffering. Is God, then, to be so different from man as to be less than man? God is Love, is He not? Is His Love, then, to be but nominal? At least, to be less costly, hence less heroic, hence again less sublimely good, than is our own? "He who did most, shall bear most": would not God thus alone be a worthy leader? Heroism would thus be overflowingly in God and be but poorly imitated by us mortals even at our best. Browning has, of course, magnificently presented the case for this view. And, indeed, this view cannot be all false if the Christian doctrine of the Incarnation be true, which insists upon genuine, indeed immense, Suffering within one of the two natures of the one Person, Christ, Himself the fullest revelation of God vouchsafed to man.

Nevertheless I find it impossible to believe, I will not say in the falsehood, but even in any permanent unattractiveness, of the doctrine that there is no Suffering in God, as such. Sympathy, yes, indeed, overflowing Sympathy—a Sympathy which we cannot succeed in picturing vividly without drawing upon our own experiences of ourselves, where sympathy and suffering are so closely intertwined; but no Suffering in God; and Suffering, indeed overflowing suffering in Christ, but as Man, not as God. Surely, poets, even the deepest poets, require not seldom some discounting of their more enthusiastic views, by philosophers and theologians; the correction of Browning here suggested would be a relatively small one.

With the two admissions—proclamations—of Sympathy in God and Suffering in Christ, we can, and I suggest we should, retain ample food for the other, I submit still more fundamental, need and implication of the deepest religious thought and religious emotion, of Pure Joy, which would continue to attach to God as such.

And, finally, religion itself requires the Transcendence of God in a form and a degree which exclude Suffering in Him. I have purposely in this paper concentrated upon Suffering and Sympathy, and Suffering and Sin—upon the intimations of the religious sense that God is Joy, and upon the needs of this same sense that God be Joy. But I believe that, if fully pressed, this outlook involves, philosophically speaking, the following conception of the Absolute and of the relation between the Absolute and God, Metaphysics and Religion. I believe, then, that religion, at its deepest and in the long run, is not and never will be satisfied short of pressing on to, short of intimations from, the really Ultimate. It will persist as a conviction in the real, present existence of the Absolute, intimating this Its existence in the necessary implications of our thought, emotions and action, and in our most incurable dissatisfactions in Æsthetics, Ethics, Metaphysics. This Absolute is felt, is indirectly experienced, as still the centre, so to speak the core, of God. But there are two conditions attaching to this Absolute as soon as ever It acts outwards, so to speak. It cannot violate either Its own Nature within Itself, or the traces of this Its Nature within anything. It creates or initiates. Such incapacities are not Imperfect Liberty, no limitation, in the true sense of the term, at all. Aquinas, who teaches this point with emphasis, declares that it is more proper to speak of things that cannot be done, than of God as incapable of doing certain things. And, then, there *is* a limitation, which, in its degree, is a genuine limitation—a limitation which inevitably accompanies God's creative activity, and which, as such, is willed by Himself in His creative volitions. He has directly willed Creation, and has deliberately accepted such degree and kind of Self-limitation as this Creation involves.)

(But—and here is the special implication of the outlook commended—the religious sense, at its deepest and in the long run, will not, must not, be restricted to the Self-limited Creative God, or (worse still) to the persuasion that the whole of the Absolute—that God in and for Himself—has been and is absorbed in God as Creator. The religious sense, on the contrary, must be allowed to press on to, to be moved and fully satisfied only by, the Ultimate, the Absolute. This Absolute, however, is not conceived, or indirectly experienced by, such religion, Plotinus-like, as without interiority— without richness or articulation, as above all Beauty, Truth and Goodness; but as overflowing with a life articulated within Itself—a life which, indeed, freely willed Creation, a Creation whose joy indeed adds to Its Joy, yet which in Itself, apart from such Creation, is full of Joy. Thus religion would neither be a translation, by the religious sense, of the Ultimate facts of reality, these being furnished by Monistic Metaphysics —a sentimental Father-God taking the place of the real, utterly impersonal, so to say, also inwardly Absolute; nor even would Religion, though objectively true within its proper range—the Creative God—persistently ignore the Absolute. But Religion would essentially be busy with both—it would press on, through the Creative God, to the Absolute—to God within Himself, and would, within both ranges, bring real facts to our knowledge, facts none the less real and knowledge none the less certain because neither religion itself, nor, indeed, philosophy working upon these intimations, succeeds in bringing them to scientific clearness and complete interconnection.)

The thirst of religion is, at bottom, a metaphysical thirst, and the intimations of religion are, ultimately, metaphysical intimations. Here it is where such minds as that of the Dean of Carlisle are so disappointing, when they attempt to describe and to analyse religion: the pressure, the passion of the religious sense in its metaphysical quality, is to such minds a sheer puzzle and acute annoyance.

2 B

Let me then conclude with a statement, as inclusive, precise and yet short as I can make it, with regard to the problem of Suffering and God; I will, however, now include certain preliminary points and certain applications which have not been discussed, but which, I trust, will approve themselves through their close appropriateness to the entire outlook.

A man never knows, or is even dimly aware of, himself alone; his consciousness of self is always with, and on occasion of, the consciousness of something other than himself. But any and all knowledge, or any rational awareness possessed by man, not only involves certain direct experiences, but also certain "ideas" as Kant calls them—certain convictions which are not directly experienced, yet which are rendered actual by the experience, and are absolutely necessary to the experience as a rational and informative event. We experience things as contingent, as partial, as successive, as causes, as effects—especially as contingent. Yes: but we do so experience them, because the things directly experienced wake up in us the "ideas" of the Absolute, the Whole, the Simultaneous, the Uncaused, the Uneffected. Now Kant, in his richest and most constructive vein, teaches that not only what we directly experience corresponds to extant realities, but that also such "ideas" as are simply necessary to render possible such experience correspond to extant realities; that we can and should be certain also, and especially, of the latter kind of reality. Now the ethically and religiously awake and observant spirit is full, not only of direct moral and religious experiences, but also of "ideas" or convictions which awake on occasion of these experiences, and which alone make them possible in the form in which we experience them. Here also, and here especially, what is directly experienced as contingent, partial, successive, as caused or effected, and further as imperfect, as unsatisfying, is so experienced because of the "ideas" or apprehensions which awake simultaneously of the Absolute, the All-Inclusive, the Simultaneous, the Perfect, the Utterly Satisfying. And it is thus that, as against the foreground of our little frail and mixed love and joy and delectation, our small beginnings towards the fullness of spiritual being, there contrast, and by their contrast light up and give their poignant meaning to, this littleness, frailty and mixedness of our love, joy and delectation, Perfect Love, Unmixed Joy, Entire Delectation. It is quite plain and entirely certain that were man a purely changeful, transitory, contingent, rootless and accidental being, he could never know he was such, still less could he suffer, as he most certainly does suffer, from the very thought that he possibly may be only such. The Contrasting Other is real and certain—more real, richer far in reality, and quite as certain as the contingents felt to be such, since it is that Contrasting Other which gives them, for our mind and feeling, that pathetic and utterly unsatisfying character of contingency.

Now God is that Perfect Love, Unmixed Joy, Entire Delectation. He is all this, not as a bundle of separate qualities, however consummate each quality may be, but as a living, spiritual, Personalist Reality, Who Himself is all this overflowingly. I believe this to be a true account of the fundamental religious experience and apprehension. But if so, we will not admit the presence of any Evil, be it Sin or even only Sorrow, be they actual or even only potential, in Him Who thus dwarfs for us all our little human goodness and earthly joy by His utter Sanctity and sheer Beatitude. And all this Goodness and Joy God does not become, does not acquire: He simply *is* it. We will be watchful against the blurring over of the contrast between our self, as experienced by us, and other, contingent things, always experienced by us at the time: those things and we are not identical, never were and never will be. How much more, then, will we be on our guard against any real blurring of the contrast between God and ourselves. His Otherness is as essential a part of the facts and of the power of religion as His Likeness can ever be. True, God is full of loving care for us, His creatures; He knows us each and singly in all our particularity, and can and does help us to become more like unto Himself. But this Sympathy is not Suffering; and, again, we never will, indeed never can, become really identical with Him. He has allowed real, direct Suffering to come as close to Him, in the humanity of Christ, as, in the nature of things, Suffering could come. Let us be wise and sober, and rest satisfied with that deep Sympathy in God and this deep Suffering in Christ. Let us be satisfied, not only because this, and not more than this, appears indeed to be the truth, but because we thus keep secure the only quite wholesome, the only sufficiently deep, outlook for our own utilisation—the outlook for which the Ultimate Intention, as indeed already the First Cause of all things, is not Sin or Suffering or Want, but Delectation, Joy and Holiness. We will admit indeed great tracts of dreariness, suffering, sin, in our human lives, possibly also more or less amongst other intelligent creatures of God; but all the more will we treasure the pure and distinct, the personalist and abounding Holiness, Joy and Delectation of God. Even if we could find no explanation whatsoever for the existence of Evil in all its degrees and kinds, this would not abolish the reality of the evidences for, our deep need of, that Absolute Goodness, Joy and Delectation which, in our experiences, reveals to us our mixed, and largely evil, and pathetically unsatisfying, existences. We will, indeed, utilise all the suffering which may come to us in atonement for Sin and for the attainment of Joy; but we will not strain the facts of life into revealing, as the cause of all suffering, the provision of occasions for heroism and heroic joy. Still less will we find the possibility of Evil to spring directly from Liberty as such. On the contrary, we will adore in God the Perfect Liberty which spontaneously and joyously always wills alone its own Perfect Nature. We will thus rest content with an outlook, obscure and fragmentary in parts, but with tracts of glorious richness, variety, drama and tension, the whole lit up, sustained and vitalised by a continuously renewed conviction of the Perfect Goodness, the Pure Joy of God.

.   .   .   .   .   .

It was a on Good Friday forenoon in Rome, I think in 1899, that I woke up with the sunshine streaming into my bedroom—I had somehow not been called by any of my people or of the domestics. Although I hurried through my toilet and through my breakfast, it was turned eleven o'clock when I reached the nearest church—all the service already over and the doors locked. I tried two other churches—the same result. Sad and lonely, empty-headed and dreary-hearted, I turned into the Villa Borghese, and there, in an ugly, newly-planted, still very shadeless tryst, with much sand about and an already baking sun, I sat down on the ground and relieved my aching back by leaning against one of the young trees. Many green lizards were soon frisking close around me—otherwise nothing living was to be seen or heard. I sat there thus—I suppose for half an hour or more—dull and dead, conscious of nothing but myself, so I felt; of that mass of failures, disappointments, pettinesses, with a dim background, though, of men at large hardly more inviting or inspiring than myself. And all this then articulated itself into special grievances and antipathies: Churchmen and Agnostics, Jews and Protestants, also such souls amongst them all as were dear to me at other times—all seemed empty, irritating, oppressive. And then—I know of no transition or connection—then—well, suddenly, ah, another, in very truth another outlook, an utterly other state wrapped me round. I felt—I seemed to see—now without any straining, without apparently any action of my own—one great, tender good-ness and heroism pass before me after the other—the souls which, in this "eternal" Rome, had meekly suffered and had manfully agonised for God; also thinkers, and men of action, seekers after God. There were Peter and Paul, Cæcilia and Agnes of the Catacombs, Rabbi Akiba dying a witness to God in the great Circus, Marcus Aurelius lonely on his throne, Plotinus uttering winged words to his students, Augustine now growing utterly weary and restless under his sins, so near to his utter renunciation of them, and so on and on, with many another figure long dear to me. And all of them were marked by Suffering—and more or less marred by Sin. But then, behind and above all these, appeared the Master of Masters, Suffering Love gently, pathetically triumphant—Jesus Christ, Our Lord, on this the day of His utter Passion. And yet, somehow, even this, especially this utter woe, this day of that woe, they seem best expressed just simply as Good—as "Good" Friday, better than in the Italian or French or German "Holy" and the like. For was it not *good*, supremely *good* for us? Wholesome, fruitful, renovating, all-transfiguring? The Suffering, even here, was certainly an evil, but then its utilisation, how good that was! And besides, here, no Sin! Somehow here the intense Suffering led on to Joy—to the infinite Good that had sprung from this infinite Sorrow. And, then, came the final state of soul and outlook: God, God in Himself. And here, in contrast with the first outlook, where fellow-creatures had appeared so largely suffering and so truly sinful, and even in contrast with the second outlook, where Jesus Christ had appeared, sinless indeed and Joy-bringing, yet also bowed down with suffering, appeared Joy, pure Joy, an Ocean of it, unplumbed, unplumbable, with not one drop of Evil within it—not one drop of Sin or Suffering or of the possibility of either. And I did not want it otherwise—far, far from it! God was too much our Friend, for us not to rejoice that He does not suffer; and this Joy of God is too much our sustenance, it too much shows us, contrastingly, our indigence, a sight of ourselves which constitutes our specific dignity, for me, for any of those great lovers of His, to wish His Joy mixed or limited or conditional. And yet this Pure Joy was utterly compassionate, utterly sympathetic; It bent down to, It entered into, the hearts of those great little ones; It was, indeed, at work all around me at that moment. What else, in the last resort, made those dear little emerald lizards so happy there, close to my feet? And then all ended with my receiving a happy impression that all the dreariness, which had preceded all this happiness, that that too, that it, especially for me just then, had already been an effect of that contrasting Joy of God, or rather of my very dim but real apprehension of that Joy.

For indeed dreary and petty, oppressive and imprisoning, is our poor little life, on its surface and apart from God and